AF766510

Wealth Accumulation and Entrepreneurship in the Ottoman Empire, 18th to 20th Centuries

This book provides a significant contribution to our understanding of the Ottoman Empire's economic history, particularly through its exploration of local entrepreneurship, which brings new perspectives to the economic dynamics of the region.

This focus adds a valuable dimension to the broader narrative of Mediterranean social and economic developments from the 18th to the 20th century. By emphasizing the role of both Muslim and non-Muslim agents, the work challenges more Eurocentric narratives that have often influenced the historiography of economic activities in this region. The inclusion of Ottoman, Turkish, and Greek sources underlines the importance of accessing voices and records that have been underutilized in previous studies. The fact that this project is a result of Greek–Turkish academic cooperation is particularly noteworthy, as it promotes a more nuanced and comprehensive view toward shared histories in order to shed light on complex historical phenomena.

This work will be of interest to scholars of Ottoman and Mediterranean history seeking to explore the nuances of economic and social change from within the Ottoman Empire. It will also appeal to a wider audience interested in the history of early entrepreneurial activities and the complex interplay between cultural and economic dynamics in historical contexts.

Maria Christina Chatziioannou is Research Director Emerita at the Institute of Historical Research/National Hellenic Research Foundation (Athens). Her interests focus on social and economic history (18th–20th centuries.)

Sophia Laiou is Associate Professor of Ottoman History at Ionian University (Corfu). Her interests focus on the social and economic history of the Ottoman Empire.

Routledge Studies in Modern History

Time and Space in the Internet Age
Stephen Kern

Communities of Resistance and Resilience in the Post-Industrial City
A Transnational Perspective from Lyon and Pittsburgh, 1980–2010
Daniel Holland

Corruption, Anti-Corruption, Vigilance, and State Building from Early to Late Modern Times
Edited by Ricard Torra-Prat, Joan Pubill-Brugués, and Arndt Brendecke

Propaganda & Power in the Age of Globalization
The Myths We Live By
Simon Sherratt

Appearance and Identity Crisis in Modern Indian History
The Third Design (1857 A.D.—2014 A.D.)
Jeevan Jyoti Chakarawarti

The Essential Speeches of the Cold War
A Primary Source Collection
Sean Brennan

Catholics and Political Violence in the Twentieth Century
A Global History
Lucia Ceci
Translated by Stuart Oglethorpe

Wealth Accumulation and Entrepreneurship in the Ottoman Empire, 18th to 20th Centuries
Edited by Maria Christina Chatziioannou and Sophia Laiou

For more information about this series, please visit: www.routledge.com/Routledge-Studies-in-Modern-History/book-series/MODHIST

Wealth Accumulation and Entrepreneurship in the Ottoman Empire, 18th to 20th Centuries

Edited by Maria Christina Chatziioannou and Sophia Laiou

Routledge
Taylor & Francis Group
NEW YORK AND LONDON

First published 2025
by Routledge
605 Third Avenue, New York, NY 10158

and by Routledge
4 Park Square, Milton Park, Abingdon, Oxon, OX14 4RN

Routledge is an imprint of the Taylor & Francis Group, an informa business

Library of Congress Cataloging-in-Publication Data
Names: Chatzēiōannou, Maria Christina, editor. | Laïou, Sophia N., 1970– editor.
Title: Wealth accumulation and entrepreneurship in the Ottoman Empire, 18th to 20th centuries / edited by Maria Christina Chatziioannou, Sophia Laiou.
Description: New York, NY : Routledge, 2025. | Series: Routledge studies in modern history | Includes bibliographical references and index.
Identifiers: LCCN 2024036679 (print) | LCCN 2024036680 (ebook) | ISBN 9781032806648 (hardback) | ISBN 9781032816593 (paperback) | ISBN 9781003500780 (ebook) | ISBN 9781040272343 (adobe pdf) | ISBN 9781040272404 (epub)
Subjects: LCSH: Turkey—Economic conditions—1288–1918. | Turkey—History—Ottoman Empire, 1288–1918. | Wealth—Turkey—History. | Entrepreneurship—Turkey—History.
Classification: LCC HC492 .W43 2025 (print) | LCC HC492 (ebook) | DDC 330.9561—dc23/eng/20240905
LC record available at https://lccn.loc.gov/2024036679
LC ebook record available at https://lccn.loc.gov/2024036680

ISBN: 978-1-032-80664-8 (hbk)
ISBN: 978-1-032-81659-3 (pbk)
ISBN: 978-1-003-50078-0 (ebk)

DOI: 10.4324/9781003500780

The Open Access version of Chapter 7 was funded by European Research Council.

For Product Safety Concerns and Information please contact our EU representative GPSR@taylorandfrancis.com. Taylor & Francis Verlag GmbH, Kaufingerstraße 24, 80331 München, Germany.

Contents

List of Figures viii
List of Tables ix

Introduction 1
MARIA CHRISTINA CHATZIIOANNOU AND SOPHIA LAIOU

PART 1
Forms of Entrepreneurship and Social Mobility 19

1 **Aspects of Capital Accumulation in Thessaloniki of the Second Half of the 18th Century: Capital Structure, Entrepreneurial Strategies, and Economic Characteristics of a Muslim Urban Elite** 21
DIMITRIS PAPASTAMATIOU

2 **Capitalist Practices of Thessalonican Greek Merchants Around the 1820s** 36
PHOKION KOTZAGEORGIS

3 **Ottoman Greek Entrepreneurs in Istanbul in the Early 1800s** 48
SOPHIA LAIOU

4 **Wealth Accumulation and Investment Methods of Sarrafs (Moneychangers) in 18th–Century Istanbul** 63
ERTAN ÜNLÜ

5 **Signs of Wealth: Emerging Consumption in Early Modern Southeastern Europe** 76
ARTEMIS YAGOU

PART 2
The 1820s: The Dawn of a New Era 89

6 **Between Private Wealth and State Revenues: Was Ali Paşa of Ioannina a Rich Man?** 91
DIMITRIS DIMITROPOULOS

7 **Janissary Inter-Provincial Economic Practices During the 1821 Greek War of Independence** 107
YANNIS SPYROPOULOS

8 **The Wealth Accumulated by Merchants in the 1820s: Levels, Gradations, and Distributions** 123
SIMOS BOZIKIS

PART 3
Tanzimat and the New Economic Horizons 141

9 **Locality and Transnational Trade: The Role of the Ottoman Greek Merchant Entrepreneur** 143
MARIA CHRISTINA CHATZIIOANNOU

10 **Businesses and Investment Strategies in the Cigarette Industry of the Eastern Mediterranean, Late 19th to Early 20th Centuries** 158
THANASIS BETAS

11 **Motifs of Primary Accumulation in the Ottoman Empire: The Bankers of Galata and the Case of Andreas Syngros** 173
DIMITRIOS STERGIOPOULOS

PART 4
Land Possession and Entrepreneurship 187

12 **Capital and Wealth in the Ottoman Balkans at the Turn of the 19th Century: Some Evidence From Salonica** 189
YÜCEL TERZIBAŞOĞLU

13 Çiftlik Holdings in Western Anatolia: The Karaosmanoğlu Family and the Baltazzi Family in the 18th–19th Centuries 202
ALP YÜCEL KAYA

14 Wealth Inequality, *Çiftliks*, and the Question of Agrarian Capitalism in Cyprus During the 1830s 218
ANTONIS HADJIKYRIACOU

15 Stephan Spartalian: An Armenian Entrepreneur in the Age of "National Economy" of the Young Turk Period 238
YAŞAR TOLGA CORA

List of Contributors *255*
Index *258*

Figures

5.1	Pesaro jugs with Greek verses exhibited at the Benaki Museum, Athens	77
5.2	A typical mid-range English watch for the Ottoman market. Pocket watch of the fighter of the Greek War of Independence, Kanellos Deligiannis (1780–1862). Dimensions: 0.7 cm, National Historical Museum, Athens	80
8.1	The sum of the eight highest funds divided in five geographical units (Peloponnese and the Aegean islands) in the 1820s	127
12.1	Comparison of income structures of Zagliver and Langaza *çiftlik*s	196
14.1	Map showing geo-located *çiftlik*s and their value	227
14.2	Map showing settlements within a 5-km range of geo-located *çiftlik*s	228
14.3	Percentage of property holders below certain values in settlements of the whole dataset and the sample	229
15.1	Stephan Spartalian as the deputy of Izmir/Smyrna 1908	241
15.2	The stock of IEDCC worth of 25 Liras, dated 1 January 1918	247

Tables

1.1 Property structure 23
1.2 The wealthy Muslim Thessalonians 24
1.3 Property structure and groups of the Muslim urban elite 26
1.4 The Muslim urban elite as lenders and debtors 27
1.5 Loans and debts of the Muslim urban elite 27
1.6 Distribution of *çiftlik* ownership per person 28
3.1 Names of the executed or fugitive Ottoman Greek merchants, bankers, and artisans, and the sum value of their confiscated properties 52
7.1 List of merchants who used the "Speranza" to ship soap to Istanbul and the amounts sent 108
7.2 İbrahim's debt to Derviş Ali 112
8.1 The funds of 138 "wealthy entities and major merchants" in the Peloponnese and the Aegean islands in the 1820s 125
8.2 The funds of 138 "wealthy entities and merchants," as a % of national accounts of the Greek state that succeeded the Ottoman Empire in the territories in question 126
8.3 Estimates of the ability of individual groups to contribute to the capital of the National Financial Bank established in 1828 by the Greek authorities: the multiple between individual contributions 131
8.4 The multiples between the property tiers, according to draft criteria on the right to vote and to be elected in the new Greek state 131
12.1 Total budget (in akçes) for 1765 191
12.2 *Çiftlik* budgets in 1765 (in akçes) 194
12.3 Comparison of income and expenditure of Zagliver and Langaza *çiftlik*s in 1765 (in akçes) 195
14.1 Quintiles of unequal distribution of properties 221
14.2 Centiles of unequal distribution of properties 221
14.3 Descriptive statistics for dataset of property holders in Cyprus (value of property in piasters) 228

14.4 Percentage of property holders below different thresholds of total value for the whole dataset and for the sample of settlements near *çiftlik*s 229
15.1 The value of vakıf lands which were converted to residential areas, and the yearly fees paid for them 244

Introduction

Maria Christina Chatziioannou and Sophia Laiou

In defining the term "wealth accumulation," here we adopt a loose meaning, one which describes wealth accumulated in the Ottoman Empire through private entrepreneurship. Merchants for the most part, but also moneylenders, "bankers" (sarrafs), and land owners, all made strategic choices in cities and ports in the broad area of the eastern Mediterranean. Non-Muslim and Muslim merchants within the Empire and beyond its borders from the 18th until the early 20th centuries are the conspicuous agents of this book. We can follow individual paths of accumulation, distribution, and display of personal wealth in many of the 15 chapters of this book. We also see that trade, money lending, and investments in urban property were materialized by Muslim and non-Muslim agents alike; Muslims invested also in land property, while business migration and shifting economic activities are more apparent in the case of the non-Muslim agents. As might be expected, hoarding is assumed in many cases: it is manifested in perilous situations and in consuming goods. This accumulated capital is invested in a range of venture enterprises.[1]

The topics here covered involve a period that is characterized by the very dawn of capitalism. Therefore, we believe that it is necessary to briefly reflect both on it as a concept and its evolution and on the historiographical approaches concerning the forms of capitalism in the Ottoman economy. The concept of capitalism has been associated in historical research, mainly after World War II, with ports and merchants. Being intermingled with the history of Europe (1500–1800), these themes were often associated with the decline of old feudal hierarchies and the emergence of new economic elites. Maurice Dobb examined the transition from feudalism to capitalism, viewing it as a clear and well-documented passage from one mode of production to another. The debate on the transition has been extremely rich, but this scholarship has left many Ottoman regions unexplored.[2] As historians, we incorporate agency and contingency in our analysis. Thus, although we take into consideration the Ottoman institutional framework in which the economic agents acted, we avoid compiling a history from the state's perspective, but rather we focus on individuals' choices and strategies. We also are in agreement on the importance of power relations in structuring economic life, in privileging certain forms of economic knowledge, and in shaping economic outcomes.[3]

DOI: 10.4324/9781003500780-1

Before continuing, we would like to stress that we contend that since capitalism was and is a global phenomenon, forms of capitalism existed in the Ottoman Empire in the 18th century onward in the sense that there were individuals in the port cities and other large urban centers or areas that invested in trade, credit, land exploitation, and tax farming with profit-making incentives, formed business partnerships, and used elaborate forms of business transactions. The non-Muslims in particular tried by and large to act as far as possible independently of the Ottoman state, concluding their businesses outside of the state control with private contracts. Nonetheless, they all acted in an officially and institutionally non-capitalist economy until the mid-19th century,[4] where they formed "little capitalist islands in a sea of non-capitalist conditions."[5] The *Oxford Handbook of Entrepreneurship* offers a vast array of theoretical views on entrepreneurship and capitalist transformation, hence the modern definition:

> Entrepreneurship is a composite act, consisting of information gathering and processing, the identification of arbitrage opportunities, risk-taking, managing upstarts and market entry, and soliciting financial backing, technological expertise, and other inputs. These activities are substantially inter-temporal in nature-time and money are invested now in hopes of returns in the distant future.[6]

If one carefully observes our agents' cases presented in the following pages, one cannot fail to realize their organized efforts for generating future profit, income, and wealth that is their entrepreneurial activity and capitalist spirit.

Since the existence of varieties of capitalism has been widely accepted, it is fruitful to scrutinize the various agents' organizational structures and strategies so as to explore continuity and change in the various entrepreneurial paths followed. The economic actors in question in this book were engaged in activities and entrepreneurial initiatives within and outside the Ottoman Empire, in diverse economic centers in Anatolia, the Eastern Mediterranean, the Black Sea, and the Adriatic ports. In this, we encourage the shift of historiographical interest to these geographical areas and away from the Middle East that has been dominant hitherto; here it was Egypt, and the Syrian and Iraqi provinces that were explored in the context of European economic and political dominance.[7] Acknowledging European economic and political penetration in the eastern Mediterranean, we focus on local agents and how they responded and adapted to that. The importance of Istanbul (Constantinople) in generating profit, income, and wealth and in providing a diffusion of economic knowledge is testified in all the relevant case studies in question. It is also evident how important was one's political status (Ottoman subject or protegé) in the process of wealth accumulation. A major desire here on our part is to trigger discussion on early forms of capitalism, as an essential concept for understanding modernity in the eastern Mediterranean, given that capitalism has been discussed as a phenomenon of global history enhanced by transnational transactions.

The history of capitalism as related to economic history and political interpretations is a combined study that often leads one to reconsider the wider problems of merchant or industrial capitalism and inequalities in world social and economic development. This historiographical agenda following Braudel's and Wallerstein's views was very much shaped after their work in the 1960s–1980s. Based on empirical research, a large literature on Venetian, Genoese, and other pre-industrial merchants formed a corpus that dealt with the historical evolution of markets, towns, and trade, mainly in the Mediterranean area. The study of merchant capitalism became the central theme in many of these works, configuring Marxist interpretations. The term "merchant entrepreneur" was first coined in juxtaposition to other types of entrepreneurs, like the industrialist, exemplifying the successive evolutionary stages of world economic development. In this context, the Marxist periodization theory was well coordinated with the Darwinian evolution stages of historical analysis. The use of merchant capitalism itself was linked with different theories of economic development and transition theories from feudalism to capitalism. Along with the development and interpretations of capitalism, a related historiography was formed, interwoven with economic development. The concept of merchant capitalism is dense in meaning and often contradictory. It has frequently been used as an analytical tool for understanding the typology of its protagonists in the development phase of capitalism, in which the merchant entrepreneur was the dominant figure in the early modern business world.[8] The examples of the F. Datini, the Bardi family, and so many others have led the vanguard in piecing together the history of European capitalism. The Ottoman economic world is full of merchants, money changers and lenders, and artisans of various ethnic and religious backgrounds that hoarded and accumulated capital from the 18th to the 20th centuries. In contrast, some scholars have tried to disengage merchant capitalism from the known economic development of the Middle East in the Ottoman period and instead used the term "modern" capitalism.[9] In this context, later scholars began to accept that there could be variations of capitalism and that there were comparative advantages to each variation.

A fundamental question regards the relations, differences, and adaptations between the so-labeled western or European capitalism, as it was developed and studied in the Netherlands, Britain, and France, and its effects in the Ottoman Empire. The historiographical challenge here is to define the adaptation of European models of economic development and the rise of capitalism regarding continuity-change and modernity. The thesis that integration and consequently the "peripheralization" of the Ottoman economy took place between the late 16th and middle 18th centuries had defined for decades discussion on the Ottoman economy, where it was known as the "incorporation into the world economy."[10] It is not by chance that the discussion involved also the "decline theory," according to which the Ottoman Empire has decayed since the late 16th century when the end of the territorial expansion of the empire resulted in economic problems, commercialization of production, and institutional corruption, all to the detriment of its subjects. The relation of the integration of the Ottoman economy into the European economy with the idea that this had already begun before the 18th century when the empire was in "decline," is apparent. In recent bibliography, both theories have been criticized; indeed in the case of the decline theory, the concept has been successfully nullified.[11] The integration theory has been criticized too, but not totally disregarded. One of the main arguments against it was that by focusing on the macroeconomic trends of the Ottoman economy, Wallerstein left out human agency and consequently presented the economic actors as passive recipients of the global capitalistic trends.[12] Another argument put the beginning of the incorporation in the second half of the 18th century and later, and certainly not earlier.[13] Less interest, however, has gone into the discussion on how the European economic penetration in the Ottoman Empire resulted in the peripheralization of its economy. As stated above, the question is not if, but when and how this happened.

In the above-analyzed historiography, the main thesis is that capitalism spread to Ottoman urban areas through Europeans and their protégés, that is the non-Muslim Ottomans who acquired the foreign protection that the capitulations offered and enjoyed tax exemptions, reduced custom dues and extraterritoriality for legal cases that did not involve an Ottoman Muslim subject or official. The bibliography for the commercial activities of the European and Ottoman protegées in the empire is large.[14] In this book, we take the discussion to the Muslim and non-Muslim merchants and entrepreneurs, who retained their subjecthood and demonstrated a capitalistic spirit through profit-seeking ventures and investments. Halil İnalcık was the first to talk of a "capitalist spirit" and "capitalistic entrepreneurs"—referring to merchants and money-changers, as according to his analysis, in the early Ottoman period, trade and money-lending were the main economic activities that could provide substantial profits. At the same time, he pointed out specific legal parameters that did not allow the Ottoman economy to follow European economic development.[15] Moreover, publications by Fleet, Boyar, Faroqhi, and Veinstein have significantly contributed to our understanding of the trade networks that connected important economic hubs inside and outside the empire, the institutional alternatives the Ottoman non-Muslims under foreign protection had, the Levantine business in Anatolia, the Greek diaspora commercial activities, and other topics. Their contributions cover a large time period, and they highlight both the traders' activities and strategies, as well as the state's priorities.[16]

We take up the thread from the abovementioned contributions and move on to discuss the period from the 18th century until the beginning of the 20th. This can be explored as a continuum of institutional reforms and economic agency, and here we put an emphasis on entrepreneurship. In this period, the Ottoman economy was marked by large-scale monetization and privatization that started in the 18th century and culminated in the long 19th century with the reforms of Tanzimat and the intended liberalization of the Ottoman economy. It is the time span that began with economic development and was succeeded by a serious recession in the end of the 18th century, which continued with ups and downs during the whole 19th century. We can highlight here the importance of the 1820s as a transitional period for the expansion of the Ottoman economy since reforms and revolutions shaped new political borders and social and economic conditions for a vast array of individuals.[17]

In this economic environment, the Ottoman entrepreneurs tried to adjust to the changing conditions and to keep their profits secure. It was not easy, considering the lack of a state protection policy that would support the Ottoman merchants vis à vis the foreign ones for a long period of time (except for the late initiative of the formation of the "Merchants of Europe"),[18] the lack of property rights on land until the 1858 Law of land, and the exposure of the entrepreneurs to the political crises or the vagaries of the high Ottoman officials; more so if the entrepreneurs were officials themselves.[19] Nonetheless, the lack of property rights did not hinder the Muslim entrepreneurs from the late 18th century onward in turning the possession of çiftliks into a capitalist enterprise with waged labor and sale of the products on the regional or international market. In this framework, tax farming became the main entrepreneurial strategy for investments in land, a fact that underlines the entwining of political power and entrepreneurship. Moreover, even though the major political event of the Greek revolution had destroyed many of the entrepreneurial networks of the Ottoman Greeks, yet when it was over, some of the same Ottoman Greek entrepreneurs still continued their business activities in an Ottoman milieu, while others were attracted by entrepreneurial opportunities found in the newly born Greek state or elsewhere.

The concept of the westernization of the Ottoman government, associated with continuity and change in modern Turkey, has been studied in all aspects of the political, social, and economic life in the Ottoman Empire from the 18th to the 20th centuries. Scholarship is rich on the subject matter, as Feroz Ahmad has pointed out, but it was a "very shallow westernization," one which persuaded only a small if important part of Turkish society to embrace western ideas.[20] Nonetheless, Ottoman reform movements have been often regarded in the past as an economic process that forced the Ottoman Empire into foreign dominion and lost its political and economic independence. In this book, new archival research brings forth agents of wealth accumulation from diverse social and religious backgrounds, who ventured enterprises in land development and the industrial sector, thus showing Ottoman responses to the changing economic conditions in the post-Tanzimat era.

This book, thus, aims to provide a complex and nuanced understanding of capital accumulation in the Ottoman Empire from the 18th to the 20th centuries. This goal is carried out by focusing on choices and strategies applied by agents of various origins, in relation to local or regional needs and traditions.[21] These agents were in contact with the international economy and they were aware of business techniques and practices, and sometimes of basic rules of economics.[22] Their varying fortunes demonstrate that wealth accumulation in the Ottoman Empire entailed also a simultaneous struggle to overcome the political and economic barriers posed by advanced capitalist economies.

The systematic study of private fortunes, family partnerships and companies, and entrepreneurial strategies requires the application of different approaches to analyze and interpret the research questions.[23] What is more, focusing on Ottoman merchants, moneylenders, sarrafs, landowners, and their multifarious economic activities may well offer examples of alternative forms of entrepreneurship to those employed by their western counterparts. In analyzing Ottoman agents, one is dealing with aspects of business organizational structure, diversification, vertical and horizontal development, personal strategies, and managerial competences. A key matter here is how to analyze and interpret the adaptations of individual choices in a changing institutional framework within or in contact with the Ottoman economy. By locating Ottoman agency in the multiple political and geopolitical contexts of the period—national, regional, and international, Mediterranean and Balkan, East and West, all the chapters here make contributions based on solid historical evidence. The authors use documentation from various unpublished and published sources in the Ottoman Turkish and Greek languages such as probate inventories, fiscal registers and property surveys, private letters and archives, memoirs, maps, and museum objects. They add thereby to our knowledge of Ottoman economy by highlighting the originality, and the often atypical character of entrepreneurship in the 18th century right up into the 20th century. The book focuses on the entrepreneurial activities of the Ottoman subjects themselves, Muslims and non-Muslims, an issue that has been somewhat passed over (due to the lack of sources) compared with the bibliography on the European economic presence in the Ottoman Empire and the economic activities of the diasporas.[24] We also highlight the change in the consumption patterns of wealthy Ottoman subjects as a sign of intended social mobility, which—especially for the pre-Tanzimat period—to a large extent negated in practice the social stratification imposed by the Ottoman political-religious attitudes that placed the non-Muslims at a lower rank in the social scale. Thus, we question the conventional "modernizing" frameworks that have characterized European and American historiographies, according to which some core economic transactions were first formed in some "leader" or "core" countries such as Britain, before being diffused to the "periphery." Inspired by the relevant studies on distinctive and different regional capitalisms,[25] it appears that the Mediterranean countries were not as economically feeble as conventional historiography has maintained and that the eastern Mediterranean economy (which we interpret in this book generously and include Anatolia) in the Ottoman period was actively engaged through human agency in the development of modern capitalism, despite the non-capitalist political economy of the Ottoman administration until the Tanzimat period.

Book Outline

The book is divided thematically and chronologically into four parts. In the first part under the title "Forms of Entrepreneurship and Social Mobility," five contributions discern the types of entrepreneurship and the economic strategies as well as the internal dynamics that enabled social mobility. In the first chapter, Dimitris Papastamatiou analyzes the Muslim entrepreneurship in Thessaloniki, the largest port city in the Ottoman Balkans, during the second half of the 18th century. His sources are the probate inventories, which enabled him to bring forward the entrepreneurial activities of 300 Ottoman Muslims of Thessaloniki, officials and non-officials, men and women. He analyzes the business profiles, investment practices, and property structure of these entrepreneurs, and he shows that money-lending and land possession were the main wealth accumulation strategies of the Muslim upper crust. These strategies were followed by trade, investments in urban and land real estate, and tax farming. Papastamatiou categorizes the capital and the economic activities according to gender and profession, and he shows that the wealthy Ottoman Muslims of Thessaloniki possessed a diversified portfolio and availed themselves of all manner of business opportunities. Despite the internal differentiations and economic discrepancies, the author demonstrates the development of multiple economic activities by the Muslims with the aim of diminishing the risk and augmenting their profits. In this way, he overturns the stereotype that Ottoman Muslims were mostly engaged in administrative–military duties.

In his contribution, Phokion Kotzageorgis deals also with Ottoman Thessaloniki, but his focus is on the Ottoman Greek merchants and entrepreneurs of the beginning of the 19th century. Kotzageorgis traces the activities of three major Christian merchants, who were implicated in the Greek revolt that erupted in the Chalkidiki region in the spring of 1821, and as a result, they had their properties confiscated by the Ottoman authorities. Through the confiscation registers (muhallefat defterleri), Kotzageorgis presents their economic profiles, the strategies for capital accumulation and investments, and he emphasizes that beyond their participation in the trade with Europe, a significant part of their entrepreneurship was moneylending. Thus, cash circulated widely, since these big merchants not only provided credit but also received it to fund their ventures. To enrich the analysis, the author includes a comparative dimension, contrasting the Thessaloniki merchants with two Greek moneylenders operating in Istanbul during the same period. This comparative approach enables a nuanced understanding of the differences between wealthy non-Muslim merchants in the imperial capital and those in the provinces.

In a similar vein, Sophia Laiou traces the entrepreneurial activities of the Ottoman Greek big merchants of Istanbul in the beginning of the 19th century. She uses the same category of sources as Kotzageorgis and through them sheds light on the entrepreneurial networks, the business portfolios and collaborations, the investment strategies, as well as the conspicuous lifestyle patterns of the wealthy major merchants and entrepreneurs. Laiou also explores the institutional framework in which these merchants acted and their willingness, or not, to use the Islamic/state institutional "tools" and policies vis à vis their communal ones. Laiou argues that the Ottoman Greeks ventured in a political and institutional environment that favored trade and entrepreneurship as long as its repercussions (the amassed wealth) did not impinge upon the established socio-political order. In this respect, the persecutions against wealthy Ottoman Greek entrepreneurs following the Greek Revolution were not only a show of state force but were designed to highlight the political and social boundaries between Ottoman Muslims and non-Muslims.

In his chapter, Ertan Ünlü reviews a specific group of Ottoman entrepreneurs, the moneychangers and "bankers" (sarrafs). The author investigates them as capitalist entrepreneurs, venturing in a political environment that did not officially adopt a capitalist mentality. He follows the career and investment practices of four prominent non-Muslim sarrafs of Istanbul in the 18th century whose activities were entwined with the state policies and the cash needs of the state elite and therefore were closely controlled. The probate inventories that register the confiscated properties show the sources of their wealth—cash lending, provision of the Sublime Porte with luxurious merchandize, trade, tax farming, and cash management—as well as their investments, above all in conspicuous mansions. Ünlü underlines the enormous size of their wealth, but also the limits imposed by the Ottoman state on their activities. In this respect, the comparison he makes with the international merchants, whose wealth accumulation strategies were not closely controlled by the state and thus were able to preserve their wealth, is telling as far as the range of sarrafs' activities is concerned.

As wealthy entrepreneurs often demonstrated their high economic status through the display of luxurious or semi-luxurious objects ("popular luxury"), Artemis Yagou's contribution deals with two kinds of such objects, ceramic wine jugs with Greek verses from Pesaro, Italy, and imported pocket watches, and their social contexts of use. She shows that the economic success of certain Ottoman Greek merchants allowed them to enjoy high living standards and adopt new consumption patterns, marked by the acquisition and use of novel and pleasurable objects as those abovementioned. The author argues that these patterns demonstrated the self-assertion of the consumers and their higher status in comparison to other Ottoman subjects. Thus, Yagou's contribution suggests a nuanced understanding of the emergence of new consumption patterns among urban and provincial wealthy Ottoman Greek merchants that reflected broader socio-cultural changes within the Ottoman Empire.

The second part of the book entitled "The 1820s: The Dawn of a New Era" comprises three chapters that all refer to economic actors that participated in multiple transactions during this transitional period. Dimitris Dimitropoulos's contribution refers to the enormous wealth amassed by the provincial governor Tepedelenli Ali Paşa, which triggered the imagination of his contemporaries as well as of the later local historians. Through the large Greek archive of Ali Paşa, the author illuminates the inner mechanisms of the vast and complicated financial network he created with members of his extended family and various collaborators in the Ottoman capital and elsewhere, which lasted until 1820, when the Ottoman state decided to eliminate him. Dimitropoulos presents the sources of wealth (tax leases, çiftliks, moneylending, participation in the provision trade), which all depended on the state offices he assumed, and thus he demonstrates the volatility of the financial strength of Ali Paşa and contextualizes the actual meaning of the wealth of a high Ottoman official.

Yannis Spyropoulos' chapter brings forward the entrepreneurial activities of the Janissaries of Crete during the Greek Revolution, just before the dissolution of the Janissary Corps by Mahmud II in 1826. From a rare example of unofficial inter-Janissary correspondence of 1825 and the documents related to the confiscation of the cargo of a ship that carried goods belonging to Cretan Muslims, again written in 1825, the author traces the commercial activities of the Janissaries of Crete. Spyropoulos provides the business profile of the most significant janissary notable families of the island, who worked mostly in soap manufacture and trade, but also in land ownership, tax farming, and credit activity. He also reveals the role of the Janissary regiments in funding the ventures and establishing the commercial networks, and he argues that war created business opportunities even for the Janissaries, who tried to continue their businesses "as usual."

The third paper of this section deals with the wealth amassed by the 138 most prominent Greek merchants, ship-owners, and notables of the Morea and the Aegean islands, as revealed in a list compiled by the revolutionary administration in 1828. Simos Bozikis identifies international and interregional trade, ship ownership, participation in tax farming, and moneylending as the main sources of wealth amassed during the Ottoman and war periods (1821–1830). He also deals with the gradation of economic power and the distance existing between the wealthy and poor Greeks on the eve of the foundation of the Greek state. The author argues that contrary to the belief that funds were scarce due to the industrial "backwardness" of the eastern Mediterranean and southern Balkans, there was no shortage of funds. Instead, investments in other sectors with higher returns were prioritized.

The third part of the book is titled "Tanzimat and the New Economic Horizons" and comprises three chapters, which refer to the economic opportunities created in the eastern Mediterranean during the gradual liberalization of the Ottoman economy in the Tanzimat era. In the first chapter, Maria Christina Chatziioannou explores the role of locality and mobility in the accumulation of capital. She follows the economic trajectories of the Melas-Vikelas and Skaramangas families whose grandfathers were established in the Ottoman capital in the late 18th century and were engaged in international trade. The trade know-how of these Ottoman Greek merchants was shaped by their experiences in an environment directly influenced by both Ottoman and European economic features. This dual exposure allowed them to navigate the complexities of international trade with a sophisticated understanding of the cultural, economic, and political contexts. Descendants of these families represented their commercial houses in different political and national environments, where they assumed the role of intermediaries between different empires (Ottoman, Russian, Habsburg, and British) and contributed to the creation of nuclei of capitalism in the eastern Mediterranean.

In his contribution, Thanasis Betas traces the investment strategies and business initiatives in the cigarette production market in the Eastern Mediterranean. He shows how the foundation of the State Tobacco Monopoly (Régie) in the Ottoman Empire in 1884 and the invention of the cigarette-rolling machine in 1885 prompted the Ottoman Greek tobacco merchants to leave the Ottoman lands and settle in Cairo, where they established their own cigarette factories and involved in the tobacco trade. Some then returned to their homeland and established there their own factories, as happened in the case of Karathanassis and his tobacco factory in the Principality of Samos. The author highlights how the economic development of the tobacco industry in the eastern Mediterranean prompted the Greek government to facilitate the establishment of such factories in Greece too.

In the last chapter of this section, Dimitrios Stergiopoulos discusses the role of merchants and bankers originating from the Ottoman Empire, such as Syngros, in navigating institutionally different environments and introducing new banking techniques in the East. The author traces Syngros' business activities in Istanbul where he moved from the Greek state in 1845 and acted as a trader and then as a successful banker until 1872. Stergiopoulos demonstrates how Syngros adapted to the business culture and practices in the Ottoman capital, cultivating relations with key state officials. He also argues that Syngros and other men of capital from the Ottoman Empire developed new banking techniques and made themselves indispensable to the Ottoman government.

In the final part, titled "Land Possession and Entrepreneurship," the focus is on the exploitation of agrarian estates and urban lands as a form of entrepreneurship. In the first paper, Yücel Terzibaşoğlu examines the business portfolio of the Numan Paşa notable family of Thessaloniki in the second half of the 18th century. His sources are the accounting books of the family, which provide the actual flow of income and expenditures for the year 1765. The author presents the investments of the family in urban property, moneylending, and agrarian estates and argues that overall it was çiftlik possession together with the share-cropping system that was the most profit-bearing capital in comparison to the others. The çiftliks were administered by the family as a single enterprise, and it was to them as well as to other villages that the majority of loans were extended. In his contribution, Terzibaşoğlu differentiates the content of the terms "capital" and "wealth" and seeks for the logic (political or economic) behind the family enterprise.

In the second chapter, Alp Yücel Kaya examines the çiftlik entrepreneurship in Western Anatolia, by following the activities of two prominent local families, the Karaosmanoğlu and Baltazzi, who were activated in the 18th and 19th centuries. Karaosmanoğlus derived from a typical ayan family of the 18th century, whose economic power was largely based on the possession of çiftliks, which was acquired through the tax-farming system. The Baltazzis of Austro-Hungarian subjecthood were more of a merchant and financier family that also invested in çiftlik possession. The author argues that entrepreneurship in the Ottoman Empire was mainly related to the tax-farming system and that the bourgeoisie created comprised bureaucrats, who depended on the central bureaucracy, and notables or parvenus, who acted on a provincial level. In both cases, they were "capitalists in the making" and the çiftlik possession or lease held a focal position in it. The author also demonstrates the importance of a good relationship with political power as a means to successful entrepreneurship.

The third chapter of the last section refers to the wealth inequality in 1830s Cyprus and highlights the role of çiftlik formation in it. Based on the data of the wealth survey of 1832/3, which he analyzes geospatially and geostatistically, Antonis Hadjikyriacou argues that the Cypriot society was polarized, with a high degree of landlessness and poverty as a result of the dominant position held by the çiftliks. The author demonstrates the role of the agrarian capitalism that is expressed in the çiftliks' possession and production as a means of further integration into the Mediterranean and world economy and also correlates the çiftliks with the unequal distribution of wealth. Hadjikyriacou argues that the integration of the island's economy into the British capitalist one, as a result of the imposition of British colonial rule, was the end of a long process that had already started in the second half of the 18th century.

The final chapter moves from the çiftlik possession to the urban land exploitation as a form of entrepreneurial investment in the beginning of the 20th century. Yaşar Tolga Cora unfolds the evolution of—the initially designated as evkaf—land property of the Armenian entrepreneur Spartalian in Istanbul into a valuable estate capable of being traded in the land market. Ultimately, these lands became the foundation for an ambitious urban development project in the 1910s. The author explores the change in the investment patterns of the Armenian commercial elite from traditional trade to urban land speculation. Cora also challenges the notion that non-Muslim entrepreneurs like Spartalian were confined to networks within their own ethno-religious communities or were primarily under the influence of European capital. Instead, he highlights the broader network in which non-Muslim entrepreneurs operated, encompassing individuals from diverse ethno-religious backgrounds and their interactions with state officials.

In short, this book discusses explicitly or implicitly the significance of entrepreneurship within the context of the multi-ethnic Ottoman Empire, emphasizing its importance for wealth and competitiveness at a private level. It suggests that entrepreneurship was present across various ethnic and religious groups within the empire, manifested in different forms and sizes. Entrepreneurship does not always align with economic innovation but involves new economic ventures through human agency. Moreover, the book highlights the spatial dynamics within the eastern Mediterranean region and suggests a broader approach to understanding firms and markets beyond purely economic perspectives. It advocates the consideration of local, regional, and international contexts to comprehensively analyze entrepreneurial activities within the Ottoman Empire. The book takes a bottom-up historical approach, aiming to document and contextualize the phenomenon of entrepreneurship in the Ottoman Empire from an agent's perspective. It challenges some mainstream versions of the Ottoman economy, acknowledging that "profit or wealth is therefore contemplated as a possible indicator of entrepreneurial performance in particular contexts."[26] By examining historical documentation, all 15 chapters seek to elucidate how individuals and groups pursued profit, revenue, and wealth within the diverse socio-economic environment of the eastern Mediterranean during the Ottoman era.

Notes

1 The majority of the chapters were presented and discussed at the Greek Economic History Association's, 4th International Conference in Economic and Social History, "Varieties of Capitalism in the Mediterranean (18th–20th c.)," Athens, September 29 to October 1, 2022. The conference was jointly organized by the Department of Political Science and History of Panteion University and the Institute of Historical Research of the National Hellenic Research Foundation. We would like to thank the scientific and organizing committee of the conference and especially Christine Agriantoni, Andreas Kakridis, Andreas Lyberatos, Leda Papastefanaki, and Socrates Petmezas, for our long-standing discussions in the Greek Economic History Association. Our special thanks go to Antonis Anastasopoulos who offered a critical view to our introduction. We thank Margarita Liagka, who helped us formulate the final version of this book. Acknowledging the collective effort with all thirteen authors in this book is vital as it demonstrates appreciation for their contributions and highlights the collaborative nature of this enterprise.

2 Maurice Dobb, *Studies in the Development of Capitalism* (New York: International Publishers/London: Routledge & Kegan Paul, 1963); Andre Gunder Frank, *Capitalism*

and Underdevelopment in Latin America (New York: Monthly Review Press, 1967); Immanuel Wallerstein, *The Modern World System,* vol. I: *Capitalist Agriculture and the Origins of the European World Economy in the 16th Century* (New York: Academic Press, 1974); Immanuel Wallerstein, *The Modern World System,* vol. II: *Mercantilism and the Consolidation of the European World Economy, 1600–1750* (New York: Academic Press, 1980); Immanuel Wallerstein, *The Modern World System,* vol. III: *The Second Era of Great Expansion and the Capitalist World Economy, 1730–1840* (New York: Academic Press, 1989); Robert Brenner, "The Origins of Capitalist Development: A Critique of Neo-Smithian Marxism," *New Left Review* 104 (1977): 25–92; Trevor H. Aston and Charles H. E. Philpin (eds.), *The Brenner Debate: Agrarian Class Structure and Economic Development in Pre-Industrial Europe* (New York: Cambridge University Press, 1985).

3 See the debate on capitalism in Beckert Sven et al., "Interchange: The History of Capitalism," *The Journal of American History* 101, no. 2 (2014): 503–36. For diverse approaches to capitalism, see Jürgen Kocka, *Capitalism: A Short History* (Princeton, NJ: Princeton University Press, 2014); Ivan T. Berend, *An Economic History of Nineteenth-Century Europe: Diversity and Industrialization* (Cambridge: Cambridge University Press, 2013); Joyce Appleby, *The Relentless Revolution: A History of Capitalism* (New York and London: W. W. Norton & Company, 2011); Peter A. Hall and David Soskice, *Varieties of Capitalism: The Institutional Foundations of Comparative Advantage* (Oxford: Oxford University Press, 2001).

4 Şevket Pamuk, "Institutional Change and Economic Development in the Middle East, 700–1800," in *The Cambridge History of Capitalism*, ed. Larry Neal and Jeffrey Williamson, vol. 1: *The Rise of Capitalism: From Ancient Origins to 1848* (Cambridge: Cambridge University Press, 2014), 193–224.

5 Kocka, *Capitalism*, 23. See also, Ibid., 168–69.

6 See Kathy Fogel et al., "Institutional Obstacles to Entrepreneurship," in *Oxford Handbook of Entrepreneurship*, ed. Marc Casson et al. (Oxford: Oxford University Press, 2006), 571.

7 Charles Issawi, *The Economic History of the Middle East 1800–1914* (Chicago: University of Chicago, 1966); Roger Owen, *The Middle East in the World Economy 1800–1914* (London and New York: Methuen, 1981).

8 Jens Beckert, *Imagined Futures: Fictional Expectations and Capitalist Dynamics* (Cambridge: Harvard University Press, 2016); Larry Neal and Jeffrey Williamson (eds.), *The Cambridge History of Capitalism* (Cambridge: Cambridge University Press, 2014).

9 As in the case of Egypt, Peter Gran, "Late Eighteenth-Early Nineteenth Century Egypt: Merchant Capitalism or Modern Capitalism?" in *The Ottoman Empire and the World Economy*, ed. Huri Islamoglu-Inan (Cambridge: Cambridge University Press, 1987), 27–30.

10 Immanuel Wallerstein, Hale Decdeli, and Reşat Kasaba, "The Incorporation of the Ottoman Empire into the World-Economy," in *The Ottoman Empire and the World Economy*, ed. Huri Islamoglu-Inan (Cambridge: Cambridge University Press, 1987), 88–97; Immanuel Wallerstein, "The Ottoman Empire and the Capitalist World-Economy: Some Questions for Research," *Review (Fernand Braudel Center)*, no. 2–3 (1979): 389–98; See also the introduction in Huri Islamoglu-Inan, ed., *The Ottoman Empire and the World Economy* (Cambridge: Cambridge University Press, 1987), 6–19; Murat Çizakça, "Incorporation of the Middle East into the European World-Economy," *Review (Fernand Braudel Center)* 8, no. 3 (1985): 353–77. On the contrary, Kasaba maintains that the incorporation of the Ottoman empire into the world economy began in the second half of the 18th century, Reşat Kasaba, *The Ottoman Empire and the World Economy: The Nineteenth Century* (New York: State University of New York, 1988), 18–35.

11 See Donald Quataert, "Ottoman History Writing and Changing Attitudes Towards the Notion of 'Decline,'" *History Compass* 1 (2003): 1–9; Linda Darling, "Another Look

at Periodization in Ottoman History," *The Turkish Studies Association Bulletin* 26, no. 2 (2002): 19–28; Cemal Kafadar, "The Question of Ottoman Decline," *Harvard Middle Eastern and Islamic Review* 4, no. 1–2 (1997–1998): 30–75; Jane Hathaway, "Problems of Periodization in Ottoman History: The Fifteenth Through the Eighteenth Centuries," *The Turkish Studies Association Bulletin* 20, no. 2 (1996): 25–31.

12 Friedrich Lenger, "Wallerstein on Early Modern Capitalism and Global Inequality: A Reevaluation," *Socio* 15 (2021): 54.

13 Nelly Hanna, *Artisan Entrepreneurs in Cairo and Early-Modern Capitalism (1600–1800)* (Syracuse and New York: Syracuse University Press, 2011), 7–9; Edhem Eldem, "Capitulations and Western Trade," in *The Cambridge History of Turkey*, ed. Suraiya Faroqhi, vol. 3 (Cambridge: Cambridge University Press, 2006), 305–6; Gran, "Late Eighteenth-Early Nineteenth Century Egypt," 35.

14 See indicatively Despina Vlami, *Merchants in the Mediterranean: Ottoman-Dutch Trade in the Eighteenth Century* (London: I. B. Tauris, 2023); Maurits Van Boogert, "Ottoman Intermediaries in the 18th Century: Analysis of a 'Dirty Trade,'" *Oriente Moderno* 93 (2013): 515–30; Maurits Van Boogert, *The Capitulations and the Ottoman Legal System: Qadis, Consuls, and Beratlis* (Leiden: Brill, 2005).

Friedrich Lenger, "Wallerstein on Early Modern Capitalism and Global Inequality Century: Analysis of a 'Dirty Trade,'" *Oriente Moderno* 93 (2013): 515–30; İsmail Hakkı Kadı, *Ottoman and Dutch Merchants in the 18th Century* (Leiden: Brill, 2012); Edhem Eldem, *French Trade in Istanbul in the 18th Century* (Leiden: Brill, 1999); Elena Frangakis-Syrett, *The Commerce of Smyrna in the Eighteenth Century (1700–1820)* (Athens: Centre for Asia Minor Studies, 1992).

15 Halil İnalcık, "Capital Formation in the Ottoman Empire," *The Journal of Economic History* 29, no. 1 (1969): 97–140.

16 Ebru Boyar and Kate Fleet, eds., "The Ottomans and Trade," *Oriente Moderno* 25, no. 86 (2006); Suraiya Faroqhi and Gilles Veinstein, eds., *Merchants in the Ottoman Empire* (Paris and Louvain: Peeters, 2008).

17 For a broad economic view of the 1820s, Şevket Pamuk, *Uneven Centuries Economic Development of Turkey Since 1820* (Princeton and Oxford: Princeton University Press, 2018), 2–18.

18 Sophia Laiou, "The Ottoman Greek 'Merchants of Europe' at the Beginning of the 19th Century," in *Festshrift in Honor of Ioannis Theocharides Studies of the Ottoman Empire and Turkey*, ed. Evangelia Balta, Georgios Salakidis, and Theoharis Stavrides, vol. II (Istanbul: The ISIS Press, 2014), 313–31.

19 Bruce Masters, *The Origins of Western Economic Dominance in the Middle East: Mercantilism and the Economy in Aleppo, 1600–1750* (New York and London: New York University Press, 1988), 5: "The merchants of the Middle East were, on the whole, very private people. This was partly a result of the social mores of Islam and partly derived from their history. The vagaries of their sometimes despotic political leadership had taught the peoples of the region the follies of conspicuous consumption, and the merchants were circumspect in making themselves known."

20 Feroz Ahmad, *The Making of Modern Turkey* (London and New York: Routledge, 1993), 23. See also Marc Aymes, Benjamin Gourisse, and Élise Massicard, eds., *Order and Compromise: Government Practices in Turkey from the Late Ottoman Empire to the Early 21st Century* (Leiden and Boston: Brill, 2015); Reşat Kasaba, ed., *The Cambridge History of Turkey,* vol. 4: *Turkey in the Modern World* (Cambridge: Cambridge University Press, 2008); Erik J. Zürcher, *Turkey: A Modern History*, 3rd ed. (London and New York: I. B. Tauris, 2004).

21 For a fruitful view to provincial elites and their role in the Ottoman Empire, Antonis Anastasopoulos, "Introduction" and Eleni Gara, "Moneylenders and Landowners: In Search of Urban Muslim Elites in the Early Modern Balkans," in *Provincial elites in the Ottoman Empire Halycon Days in Crete V: A Symposiom Held in Rethymno,*

January 10–12, 2003, ed. Antonis Anastasopoulos (Rethymnon: Crete University Press, 2005), xi–xxviii, 135–47; Michael Ursinus, "In Search of the Homo Ottomanicus: The Cases of Nicola Pop Stafanoff and Sheykh Shemsuddin from Ottoman Macedonia (ca. 1780–1840)," in *Figures anonymes, figures d'elite: Pour une anatomie de l'Homo ottomanicus*, ed. Meropi Anastassiadou and Bernard Heyberger (Istanbul: The ISIS Press, 1999), 21–34.

22 For the first political economy book which addressed both classical political economic issues and policy recommendations for the Ottoman Empire in the 1840s see Erdem Özgür and Hamdi Genç, "Sarantis Archigenes (Serandi Arsizen), Pellegrino Rossi and the Spread of the Classical Approach in the Ottoman Empire," *European Journal of the History of Economic Thought*, no. 2–3 (2014): 421–47. Also, Deniz T. Kilinçoglu, *Economics and Capitalism in the Ottoman Empire* (London and New York: Routledge, 2015), 12–41 and for the early Ottoman period, Fatih Ermiş, *A History of Ottoman Economic Thought: Development Before the Nineteenth Century* (London: Routledge, 2014).

23 Maria Christina Chatziioannou, *On Merchants' Agency and Capitalism in the Eastern Mediterranean 1774–1914* (Istanbul: The ISIS Press, 2017); Evgenia Davidova, *Balkan Transitions to Modernity and Nation-States Through the Eyes of Three Generations of Merchants (1780s–1890s)* (Leiden: Brill, 2013).

24 Όλγα Κατσιαρδή-Hering, *Η Ελληνική παροικία της Τεργέστης (1751–1830)* [The Greek Community in Trieste, 1751–1830] (Αθήνα: Εθνικό και Καποδιστριακό Πανεπιστήμιο Αθηνών, 1986); See also Despina Vlami, *Trading with the Ottomans: The Levant Company in the Middle East* (London: I. B. Tauris, 2014); Despina Vlami, *Merchants on the Mediterranean: Ottoman-Dutch Trade in the Eighteenth Century* (London: I. B. Tauris, 2023).

25 For a recent view on the Indian way to capitalism, Tirthankar Roy, *A Business History of India: Enterprise and the Emergence of Capitalism from 1700* (Cambridge: Cambridge University Press, 2018).

26 Youssef Cassis and Ioanna Pepelasis Minoglou, "Entrepreneurship in Theory and History: State of the Art and New Perspectives," in *Entrepreneurship in Theory and History: State of the Art and New Perspectives*, ed. Youssef Cassis and Ioanna Pepelasis Minoglou (New York: Palgrave, 2005), 15.

Bibliography

Ahmad, Feroz. *The Making of Modern Turkey.* London and New York: Routledge, 1993.

Anastasopoulos, Antonis. "Introduction." In *Provincial Elites in the Ottoman Empire Halycon Days in Crete V: A Symposiom Held in Rethymno, January 10–12, 2003*, edited by Antonis Anastasopoulos, xi–xxviii. Rethymnon: Crete University Press, 2005.

Appleby, Joyce. *The Relentless Revolution: A History of Capitalism.* New York and London: W. W. Norton & Company, 2011.

Aston, Trevor H., and Charles H. E. Philpin, eds. *The Brenner Debate: Agrarian Class Structure and Economic Development in Pre-industrial Europe*. New York: Cambridge University Press, 1985.

Aymes, Marc, Benjamin Gourisse, and Élise Massicard, eds. *Order and Compromise: Government Practices in Turkey from the Late Ottoman Empire to the Early 21st Century.* Leiden and Boston: Brill, 2015.

Beckert, Jens. *Imagined Futures. Fictional Expectations and Capitalist Dynamics*. Harvard: Harvard University Press, 2016.

Beckert, Sven, Augus Burgin, Peter James Hudson, Louis Hyman, Naomi Lamoreaux, Scott Marler, Stephen Mihm, Julia Ott, Philip Scranton, and Elizabeth Tandy Shermer. "Interchange: The History of Capitalism." *The Journal of American History* 101, no. 2 (2014): 503–36.

Berend, Ivan T. *An Economic History of Nineteenth-Century Europe: Diversity and Industrialization.* Cambridge: Cambridge University Press, 2013.

Boyar, Ebru, and Kate Fleet, eds. "The Ottomans and Trade." *Oriente Moderno* 25, no. 86/1 (2006).

Brenner, Robert. "The Origins of Capitalist Development: A Critique of Neo-Smithian Marxism." *New Left Review* 104 (1977): 25–92.

Cassis, Youssef, and Ioanna Minoglou Pepelasis. "Entrepreneurship in Theory and History: State of the Art and New Perspectives." In *Entrepreneurship in Theory and History: State of the Art and New Perspectives*, edited by Youssef Cassis and Ioanna Minoglou Pepelasis, 3–21. New York: Palgrave, 2005.

Chatziioannou, Maria Christina. *On Merchants' Agency and Capitalism in the Eastern Mediterranean, 1774–1914.* Istanbul: The ISIS Press, 2017.

Çizakça, Murat. "Incorporation of the Middle East into the European World Economy." *Review (Fernand Braudel Center)* 8, no. 3 (1985): 353–77.

Darling, Linda. "Another Look at Periodization in Ottoman History." *The Turkish Studies Association Bulletin* 26, no. 2 (2002): 19–28.

Davidova, Evgenia. *Balkan Transitions to Modernity and Nation-States Through the Eyes of Three Generations of Merchants (1780s–1890s).* Leiden: Brill, 2013.

Dobb, Maurice. *Studies in the Development of Capitalism.* New York: International Publishers/London: Routledge and Kegan Paul, 1963.

Eldem, Edhem. *French Trade in Istanbul in the 18th Century.* Leiden: Brill, 1999.

Eldem, Edhem. "Capitulations and Western Trade." In *The Cambridge History of Turkey*, edited by Suraiya Faroqhi, vol. 3, 283–335. Cambridge: Cambridge University Press, 2006.

Ermiş, Fatih. *A History of Ottoman Economic Thought: Development Before the Nineteenth Century.* London: Routledge, 2014.

Faroqhi, Suraiya, and Gilles Veinstein, eds. *Merchants in the Ottoman Empire.* Paris and Louvain: Peeters, 2008.

Fogel, Kathy, Ashton Hawk, Randall Morck, and Bernard Yeung. "Institutional Obstacles to Entrepreneurship." In *Oxford Handbook of Entrepreneurship*, edited by Marc Casson, Bernard Yeung, Anuradha Basu, and Nigel Wadeson, 540–79. Oxford: Oxford University Press, 2006.

Frangakis-Syrett, Elena. *The Commerce of Smyrna in the Eighteenth Century (1700–1820).* Athens: Centre for Asia Minor Studies, 1992.

Frank, Andre Gunder. *Capitalism and Underdevelopment in Latin America.* New York: Monthly Review Press, 1967.

Gara, Eleni. "Moneylenders and Landowners: In Search of Urban Muslim Elites in the Early Modern Balkans." In *Provincial Elites in the Ottoman Empire Halycon Days in Crete V: A Symposiom Held in Rethymno, January 10–12, 2003*, edited by Antonis Anastasopoulos, 135–47. Rethymno: Crete University Press, 2005.

Gran, Peter. "Late Eighteenth-Early Nineteenth Century Egypt: Merchant Capitalism or Modern Capitalism?" In *The Ottoman Empire and the World Economy*, edited by Huri Islamoglu-Inan, 27–41. Cambridge: Cambridge University Press, 1987.

Hall, Peter A., and David Soskice. *Varieties of Capitalism: The Institutional Foundations of Comparative Advantage.* Oxford: Oxford University Press, 2001.

Hanna, Nelly. *Artisan Entrepreneurs in Cairo and Early-Modern Capitalism (1600–1800).* Syracuse, NY: Syracuse University Press, 2011.

Hathaway, Jane. "Problems of Periodization in Ottoman History: The Fifteenth Through the Eighteenth Centuries." *The Turkish Studies Association Bulletin* 20, no. 2 (1996): 25–31.

İnalcık, Halil. "Capital Formation in the Ottoman Empire." *The Journal of Economic History* 29, no. 1 (1969): 97–140.

Islamoglu-Inan, Huri, ed. *The Ottoman Empire and the World Economy.* Cambridge: Cambridge University Press, 1987.

Issawi, Charles. *The Economic History of the Middle East 1800–1914.* Chicago: University of Chicago, 1966.

Kadı, İsmail Hakkı. *Ottoman and Dutch Merchants in the 18th Century.* Leiden: Brill, 2012.

Kafadar, Cemal. "The Question of Ottoman Decline." *Harvard Middle Eastern and Islamic Review* 4, no. 1–2 (1997–1998): 30–75.

Kasaba, Resat. *The Ottoman Empire and the World Economy. The Nineteenth Century.* New York: State University of New York, 1988.

Kasaba, Reşat, ed. *The Cambridge History of Turkey*, vol. 4: *Turkey in the Modern World.* Cambridge: Cambridge University Press, 2008.

Kilinçoglu, Deniz T. *Economics and Capitalism in the Ottoman Empire.* London and New York: Routledge, 2015.

Kocka, Jürgen. *Capitalism A Short History.* Princeton, NJ: Princeton University Press, 2014.

Laiou, Sophia. "The Ottoman Greek 'Merchants of Europe' at the Beginning of the 19th Century." In *Festschrift in Honor of Ioannis Theocharides, Studies on the Ottoman Empire and Turkey*, edited by Evangelia Balta, Georgios Salakidis, and Theoharis Stavrides, vol. II, 313–31. Istanbul: The ISIS Press, 2014.

Lenger, Friedrich. "Wallerstein on Early Modern Capitalism and Global Inequality: A Reevaluation." *Socio* 15 (2021): 49–70.

Masters, Bruce. *The Origins of Western Economic Dominance in the Middle East: Mercantilism and the Economy in Aleppo, 1600–1750.* New York and London: New York University Press, 1988.

Neal, Larry, and Jeffrey Williamson, eds. *The Cambridge History of Capitalism.* Cambridge: Cambridge University Press, 2014.

Owen, Roger. *The Middle East in the World Economy 1800–1914*. London and New York: Methuen, 1981.

Özgür, Erdem, and Hamdi Genç. "Sarantis Archigenes (Serandi Arsizen), Pellegrino Rossi and the Spread of the Classical Approach in the Ottoman Empire." *European Journal of the History of Economic Thought* 2, no. 3 (2014): 421–47.

Pamuk, Şevket. *The Ottoman Empire and European Capitalism, 1820–1913. Trade, Investment and Production.* Cambridge and New York: Cambridge University Press, 1987.

Pamuk, Şevket. "Institutional Change and Economic Development in the Middle East, 700–1800." In *The Cambridge History of Capitalism*, edited by Larry Neal and Jeffrey Williamson, vol. 1: *The Rise of Capitalism: From Ancient Origins to 1848*, 193–224. Cambridge: Cambridge University Press, 2014.

Pamuk, Şevket. *Uneven Centuries Economic Development of Turkey since 1820.* Princeton and Oxford: Princeton University Press, 2018.

Quataert, Donald. "Ottoman History Writing and Changing Attitudes Towards the Notion of 'Decline.'" *History Compass* 1 (2003): 1–9.

Roy, Tirthankar. *A Business History of India: Enterprise and the Emergence of Capitalism from 1700.* Cambridge: Cambridge University Press, 2018.

Ursinus, Michael. "In Search of the Homo Ottomanicus. The Cases of Nicola Pop Stafanoff and Sheykh Shemsuddin from Ottoman Macedonia (ca. 1780–1840)." In *Figures anonymes, figures d'elite: pour une anatomie de l'Homo ottomanicus*, edited by Meropi Anastassiadou and Bernard Heyberger, 21–34. Istanbul: The ISIS Press, 1999.

Van Boogert, Maurits. *The Capitulations and the Ottoman Legal System: Qadis, Consuls, and Beratlis.* Leiden: Brill, 2005.

Van Boogert, Maurits. "Ottoman Intermediaries in the 18th Century: Analysis of a 'Dirty Trade.'" *Oriente Moderno* 93 (2013): 515–30.

Vlami, Despina. *Trading with the Ottomans: The Levant Company in the Middle East.* London: I. B. Tauris, 2014.

Vlami, Despoina. *Merchants in the Mediterranean. Ottoman-Dutch Trade in the Eighteenth Century*. London: I. B. Tauris, 2023.

Wallerstein, Immanuel. *The Modern World System*, vol. I: *Capitalist Agriculture and the Origins of the European World Economy in the 16th Century.* New York: Academic Press, 1974.

Wallerstein, Immanuel. "The Ottoman Empire and the Capitalist World-Economy: Some Questions for Research." *Review (Fernand Braudel Center)* 2, no. 3 (1979): 389–98.

Wallerstein, Immanuel. *The Modern World System*, vol. II: *Mercantilism and the Consolidation of the European World Economy, 1600–1750.* New York: Academic Press, 1980.

Wallerstein, Immanuel. *The Modern World System*, vol. III: *The Second Era of Great Expansion and the Capitalist World Economy, 1730–1840.* New York: Academic Press, 1989.

Wallerstein, Immanuel, Hale Decdeli, and Reşat Kasaba. "The Incorporation of the Ottoman Empire into the World-Economy." In *The Ottoman Empire and the World Economy*, edited by Huri İslamoğlu-İnan, 88–97. Cambridge: Cambridge University Press, 1987.

Zürcher, Erik J. *Turkey: A Modern History*. 3rd ed. London and New York: I. B. Tauris, 2004.

Κατσιαρδή-Hering Όλγα. *Η Ελληνική παροικία της Τεργέστης (1751–1830).* Αθήνα: Εθνικό και Καποδιστριακό Πανεπιστήμιο Αθηνών, 1986. [Katsiardi-Hering, Olga. *The Greek Community in Trieste, 1751–1830*. Athens: National and Kapodistrian University of Athens, 1986.]

Part 1

Forms of Entrepreneurship and Social Mobility

1 Aspects of Capital Accumulation in Thessaloniki of the Second Half of the 18th Century

Capital Structure, Entrepreneurial Strategies, and Economic Characteristics of a Muslim Urban Elite

Dimitris Papastamatiou

According to the pertinent rich literature, an indispensable characteristic of the gradual integration of the Ottoman Empire into the capitalist world economy during the second half of the 18th century was the energetic presence of European merchants in the ports of the Levant and the parallel emergence of a new and particularly dynamic regional elite composed of non-Muslim Ottoman subjects, mainly Jews and Greekophone Christians, all merchants and stoke brokers. These two groups monopolized the international commerce of the Empire, thus imposing their economic predominance on the urban centers and conditioning the otherwise ineffective enmeshment of the imperial economy in the world capitalist networks. As a corollary, the Muslim elites either, at best, preserved their privileged grasp over domestic trade, the significance of which receded in both quantitative and functional terms by the end of the 18th century, or confined themselves to a position of exclusively administrative, political, and social hegemony, while abstaining from all entrepreneurial ventures. In effect, this stereotypical account depicts a two-faced social reality composed on the one hand of a risky, progressive, and adventurous Christian and Jewish society, leading the way toward capitalistic development in the Levant, and on the other hand, of an economically inert, traditionalist but politically predominant Muslim population. The only exceptions to this monolithic narrative are the provincial Muslim magnates, the so-called *ayan*s, who participated in capital accumulation through intensive plantation-like agriculture, large-scale land estate ownership, and investments in tax farming, and second, the Janissaries who engaged themselves in industry through their participation in urban guilds and industry.

This present account of the Ottoman contribution to the establishment of a world capitalistic economy is certainly more elaborate in its details and multifarious aspects than the above rough sketch, yet, at the same time, it is highly contentious and open to criticism and debate in its particularities.[1] Leaving aside controversial issues, such as the interplay between the Ottoman administrative, judicial and economic institutions and capital accumulation, or again the flexibility and adaptability of the Ottoman fiscal policies in the face of external challenges,

DOI: 10.4324/9781003500780-3

we will now focus on the underestimated role of the Muslim urban population in the effective functioning of the Ottoman economy during the 18th century.

Our research is based on the case study of Thessaloniki, a typical Ottoman metropolis and one of the most significant urban and commercial centers of the Ottoman Balkans in the 18th and early 19th centuries. Thessaloniki became one of the major gates for western economic penetration into the Ottoman hinterland during this period, thanks to the entrepreneurial activity of a vigorous community of French merchants and their local Christian and Jewish protégées. According to the aforementioned historiographical account, based on the western travelers' impressionistic narratives and the local counsels' biased reports, the Muslims of the city are invariably depicted as being exclusively members of the state administrative mechanism and for this reason economically passive agents, or, at best, preoccupied with tax farming or traditional handicraft.[2] Notwithstanding, on the basis of Ottoman documents of the time, it has already been shown that this picture is misleading and far from accurate, for middle-class as well as wealthy Muslim city residents partook in numerous ways in the local economy as merchants, ship owners, moneylenders, craftsmen, shop owners, and company shareholders.[3] Therefore, this paper attempts to delineate further the business profile and investment policies of the Muslim urban upper crust in the economic milieu of Thessaloniki in the years from 1750 to circa 1800, on the basis of serial data extracted from the local Ottoman probate inventories.

These ledgers, *tereke* or *muhallefat defterleri* in Ottoman Turkish, were issued by the local Islamic Law (*şeriat*) court. They are detailed registers of the assets of deceased persons, recording in detail, though sometimes in a cursory manner, real estates, animals, agricultural or other products, slaves, clothes, jewels, weapons, household items, along with the estimated current monetary value of each property article, the loans and debts of the deceased, the funeral and court expenses, and, finally, the apportionment of the remaining fortune according to the strict *şeriat* law stipulations. The methodological problems raised by the nature of these documents abound and set limits to the scope of historical research. Since these drawbacks have been described thoroughly by scholars in the relevant literature, their discussion will be passed over at this point. On the contrary, it is noteworthy that since wealthy and middle-class Muslim city inhabitants constituted the most frequent clientele of a *kadı*, these documents form a reliable and highly representative sample of the Muslim population recorded. The fact that high-ranking provincial officers, mostly coming from the imperial capital, and provincial magnates (*ayan*s) are absent from the inventories of Thessaloniki does not decrease the evidential value of *tereke*s.[4]

The sample used for the paper comprises 300 probate inventories issued between 1760 and 1800.[5] All estates whose estimated value exceeds 500,000 *akçe*s have been included along with a good number of others with values larger than 100,000 *akçe*s. This prerequisite is not contingent on any theoretical or quantitative definition of prosperity but constitutes a functional as well as conventional threshold of minimal capital accumulation. It seemingly sets the limit of minimum wealth at a relatively low level; nevertheless, no more than 600 deceased out of around 5,000 cases examined crossed this demarcation line. In the years 1750–1800, the average price of a house of medium size in Thessaloniki was about 50,000 *akçe*s, an indicative framework of prices and monetary values in the local setting. At any rate, this quantitative limit is meant to be utilized as a functional tool enabling us to describe an important segment of the urban elite. It does not pretend to offer definite solutions to theoretical problems concerning prosperity and poverty.

The Structure of Capital Accumulation

Despite its random character, our sample allows some reliable and meaningful conclusions.[6] Although the *kadı*s were prone to calculation mistakes, all in all, they followed a uniform general pattern as regards the order of the recorded property items. They would invariably start with the mobile property of the deceased, namely, household equipment, clothes, jewels, weapons, and books, then they recorded her/his slaves, urban and rural real estate, *çiftlik*s with their contents, animal stock, technological equipment and tools, products and other merchandise, and cash, and finally they ended with her/his tax farms, loans, and company shares. The repetitiveness of this schema for more than a century reflects both the real structure and the conceptualization of capital accumulation. In other words, this ledger order reflects entrepreneurial priorities and strategies, economic preferences, limits, and potentials, and, above all, the nature of capital itself.

Table 1.1 records the constituent parts of Muslim capital in Thessaloniki. The predominance of loans and credit is conspicuous and indicates a highly developed monetary economy and the outstanding role of Muslims in the credit networks of the city. *Çiftlik* ownership offered an alternative route to wealth accumulation, and economic as well as possibly social hegemony; the ostensibly low participation of large land estate possession in capital formation is only seemingly so, since its real contribution is around 18% of the aggregate value property if the prices of animals, equipment, and products related to them are added in. On the contrary, a relatively low contribution is made by urban real property, and extremely slight indeed is that of tax farming, slavery, and rural real estate possession. The role of cash may be linked with credit availability—this is quite evident in cases of important money lenders.

Table 1.1 Property structure.

	Amount	*%*		*Amount*	*%*
Mobile Property	32,321,707	16.16	**Animals**	8,563,838	4.28
Slaves	1,708,010	0.85	**Equipment**	1,244,427	0.62
Cash	15,160,861	7.58	**Products and Merchandise**	14,934,509	7.47
Urban Real Estate	31,327,315	15.67	**Tax Farming**	2,011,606	1.01
Rural Real Estate	1,628,598	0.81	**Loans**	78,632,515	39.33
Çiftliks	12,416,140	6.21	**Total**	199,949,526	100

Table 1.2 The wealthy Muslim Thessalonians.

	Number	*Percentage of the Sample*	*Median Property*
Askeri	140	46.66	356,598.5
Women	73	24.33	244,731
Commoners	54	18	215,274
Ulema (scholars)	33	11	378,799

Social and Titular Status, Gender, and Wealth Distribution

Most quantitative indexes pinpoint the wide range of inequality among well-off Muslims and their lack of social cohesion as a group. The property values vary from a minimum of 100,241 to a maximum of 10,426,370 *akçe*s, the mean fortune value amounts to 666,498 *akçe*s, while the corresponding median value comes to 280,096 *akçe*s. These value discrepancies portray the disparity and deep internal stratification among Muslims with capitalistic tendencies. The conclusion is corroborated by the Gini Coefficient, reaching 0.5936 for our sample, a value higher than those of the needy (0.2501) and the low middle class (0.3524) and very close to that of the total population of Thessaloniki (0.7363).[7]

The members of the military class (*askeri*) dominate the sample in their numbers, yet this is not surprising since almost 70% of Muslim Thessalonians bore some military title. Still, their social cohesion is highly questionable. In effect, they formed two distinct strata, the first comprising those with the low-rank title of *beşe*; their median property value reached only 172,139 *akçe*s. The second group consisted of the high rank *ağa*s who stood out with a median fortune of 577,923 *akçe*s. Nearly a third of all recorded well-heeled Muslims were women, while it is also noteworthy that the few members of the religious establishment recorded among the wealthy held particularly valuable fortunes.[8]

Apparently, the military profession secured more opportunities for economic distinction. This apparent reality was mitigated by the fact that the occupational group of military Thessalonians crossed vertically all social strata of the urban population, from the wealthiest to the neediest. The distinction between the 41 *beşe*s and the 99 *ağa*s delineates the internal hierarchies and the ensuing limitations to economic rise existing within the military caste.[9]

In general, the four groups of wealthy Muslims demonstrate rather similar business attitudes and economic minds. Yet, there are some variations, reflected as such in their property structure. In particular, women retained a privileged relation with mobile property, mainly clothing and jewelry, owned a good number of land estates, almost equal to that of the military men, outdid all men in slave ownership, participated at a lower intensity in credit networks, but had no access whatsoever to tax farming. Laymen Thessalonians with no military or religious title had extremely limited access to *çiftlik* possession but were those who stood out in commerce more than other Muslims. *Ulema*s were as willing as the military men to engage in both credit and *çiftlik* economy, in effect, forming along with the army men a homogeneous group of entrepreneurs with comparable economic approaches and strategies. Access to tax farming was extremely limited to all Thessalonians, apparently because *iltizam*s were shared only by *ayan*s and delegates of the imperial capital Table 1.2 shows this reality.

Money Lending

It is debatable whether credit became the driving force of the economy only in the 18th century, or whether it had been a precondition for any enterprising venture involving monetary relations and commitments from earlier times. Whatever the case, credit was an integral part of the Ottoman economy in the 18th century, a necessity intensified in Thessaloniki, a significant port, and crossroads of regional, intra-regional, or international trading exchanges. Thessalonian magnates were eager to grant loans to individuals, groups, guilds, and villages—irrespective of religious affiliation, ethnic origin, or social status. This is documented in the lists of names of thousands of persons, occupational groups, and communities crowded together in the *tereke*s as debtors of the deceased.

A total of 187 wealthy Muslims, or 62.33% of the sample, had been granted at least one loan, with the total number of recorded loans reaching 1,756 transactions. At the same time, 119 Muslims died leaving at least one loan unpaid, the aggregate number of which added up to 601 debts. Although lending and borrowing were not restricted to entrepreneurs or professionals of the urban market but involved almost everyone in a continuous pursuit and exchange of cash—even for the satisfaction of petty daily needs, the money market was controlled by the well-off military class. Women's participation in the money market was significant in terms of loan numbers but less important than that of their male counterparts as to the volume of transferred money. On the contrary, members of the religious establishment contributed the most with the large amounts they supplied to the credit networks through a small number of loans. The domination of the military in the credit networks had its reverse aspect as well. The very same entrepreneurs would take to borrowing money, apparently in pursuit of cash as well as profit through different interests between credit and debt. These risky business tactics were not followed by the more conservative women, *ulema*s, and commoners. These aspects of lending activity are corroborated by the data included in Tables 1.3 and 1.4.

Among the creditors, some stood out as archetypal lenders, a kind of early modern proto-bankers, whose aggregate capital consisted mainly of loans and money destined for credit. One example is *kethüda* Halil Ağa bin Abdurrahman, whose 36 loans recorded under his name were his only source of wealth.[10] Bosnalı Halil Ağa ibn El-Hacc Ahmed had 39 clients in his banking ventures at the time of his death. Yet, the *molla* of the *sancak* Şeyh Ahmed Efendi ibn Şeyh Hasan Efendi[11] and Rabia bint Hasan[12] were the most significant moneylenders of the city with the incredible number of 56 and 162 persons, respectively, in their banking clientele and huge fortunes at the time of their death. On the contrary, over-borrowing might lead to a sort of after-death bankruptcy—12 military men died with debts that exceeded the aggregate value of their fortune. Ahmed Bey bin Mehmed Bey

Table 1.3 Property structure and groups of the Muslim urban elite.

	Military (Askeri)		*Women*		*Commoners*		*Scholars (Ulema)*	
	Amount	*%*	*Amount*	*%*	*Amount*	*%*	*Amount*	*%*
Mobile Property	10,501,649	90.76	16416,950	41.91	1,805,171	70.77	3,597,937	12.00
Slaves	634,440	00.59	865,470	20.21	117,900	00.51	90,200	00.30
Cash	6,989,975	60.50	3288,510	80.40	3,425,671	14.75	1,456,705	40.86
Urban Real Estate	19,355,345	17.99	5761,610	14.71	3,044,720	13.11	3,165,640	10.56
Rural Real Estate	895,588	00.83	103,560	00.26	250,740	10.08	378,710	10.26
Çiftliks	6,195,470	50.76	3,396,310	80.67	272,160	10.17	2,552,200	80.51
Animals	5,232,709	40.86	918,654	20.35	646,543	20.78	1,765,932	50.89
Tools	931,318	00.87	116,910	00.30	50,610	00.22	145,589	00.49
Products	7,324,913	60.81	1,244,644	30.18	2,457,161	10.58	3,907,791	13.03
Tax farming	1,675,540	10.56	–	–	336,066	10.45	–	–
Loans	47,833,040	44.47	7,059,155	18.02	10,820,533	46.59	12,919,787	43.09
Aggregate	107,569,987	100.00	39,171,773	100.00	23,227,275	100.00	29,980,491	100.00

Table 1.4 The Muslim urban elite as lenders and debtors.

	Lenders	*Loans*	*Debtors*	*Debts*
Askeri	101	1,045	82	478
Women	31	287	14	29
Commoners	33	231	10	26
Ulema (scholars)	22	193	13	68

Table 1.5 Loans and debts of the Muslim urban elite.

	Loans to	*Median Amount*	*Loans From*	*Median Amount*
Muslims	762	12,000	435	31,800
Christians	511	3,840	28	7.073.5
Jews	81	35,280	30	19,680
Communities	357	54,300	–	–
Vakıfs	–	–	44	11,790
Monasteries	11	72,000	–	–

was an extreme case of over-indebtedness; the value of his 16 debts was 399% of the estimated value of his property.[13]

The amounts lent varied from the minimal 155 *akçe*s a Christian sugar merchant had borrowed from Reisülküttab Refik Mustafa Efendi bin Hasan Efendi to the 2,700,000 *akçe*s owned by the inhabitants of Kassandria to *kapucubaşı* Esseyyid Abdulvahib Ağa ibn Abdülbaki[14] and the 2,160,000 *akçe*s owned to Çavuşzade Ahmed Reşid Efendi by *maden kethüdası* Ali Ağa ibn Mahmud.[15]

Muslims would lend mainly to other Muslims and Christians, though their favorite clients remained communities—a practice apparently connected with taxation. On the contrary, they would borrow mainly from *vakıf* institutions and other Muslims. Jews would be involved in this interplay, as both creditors and debtors, only when there was a need for very significant amounts of money. Table 1.5 describes these transfers of money.

The amounts of cash recorded are rather limited for a monetarized economy such as that of Thessaloniki. Yet, no safe conclusions can be drawn from the quantitative data included in the inventories, since cash was easily hidden or stolen by relatives, neighbors, or servants after the death of its owner and before the property apportionment. In the same vein, equally dubious is the under-registering of foreign or gold coins. Two rare cases with coin treasures in their possession were Amina Hanım bint Elhacc Ahmed Efendi[16] and Amina bint Ağazade Mustafa Ağa[17] who owned 143 and 104 assorted gold coins, respectively.

Çiftlik Ownership

In a period characterized by the rapid *çiftlikization* of land, large estate ownership was relatively limited among local Muslims in Thessaloniki, possibly owing to the

Table 1.6 Distribution of *çiftlik* ownership per person.

Owners	*Çiftliks*
56	1
10	2
6	3
5	4
2	5

predominance of provincial *ayan*s in the field.[18] Nonetheless, our sample comprises 79 deceased, or 26.33% of wealthy local Muslims, all owners of at least one *çiftlik*. Table 1.6 delineates a reality of limited *çiftlik* possession, with most landowners having only one plot.

The small contribution made by land estates in capital formation is corroborated by the data in Table 1.1. The median value of a *çiftlik* does not exceed 48,000 *akçe*s, an amount which is hardly double the value of an orchard or almost equal to the price of a middle-size urban house. It should be noted that, perhaps due to the legal risks and ambiguities ensuing from land ownership of the *çiftlik* type, these land estates are invariably described in the ledgers as "huts of the estate" (*çiftlik damları*), leaving a lot to be surmised as for the actual content of the term *çiftlik*. Accordingly, no information is recorded for the extent of the estate or the number of its cultivators.

It can be inferred from the register order that this minimal core of a *çiftlik* was supplemented by husbandry and wheat cultivation. Husbandry was linked fundamentally to the *çiftlik* economy, yet its spread among wealthy Muslims retained a relative autonomy from land estate ownership. A total of 143 deceased, or 47.66% of our sample, were engaged in some type of husbandry. There was a great variety of animal ownership, starting from the possession of only one donkey or mule for the needs of daily move *intra* and *extra muros*, to the ownership of sizeable herds of bovines, mainly buffalos, oxen, cows, and bulls, or large flocks of sheep and goats. For instance, Hüseyin Ağa bin El-Hacc Hasan Ağa had in his two *çiftlik*s 42 different types of bovine, two donkeys, one mule, and 506 sheep,[19] while Al-Şeyyh Mustafa Efendi bin Al-Şeyyh İbrahim Efendi bred in his three *çiftlik*s 49 bovines, eight donkeys, one mule, and 237 sheep.[20] On the contrary, Ahmed Ağa bin El-Hacc Hasan owned 10 bovines, 62 sheep, 30 goats, 2 horses, and 2 mules despite the fact that he did not belong to the group of *çiftlik* owners.[21]

Big farms, industrial units, or even simple shops usually contained some kind of elementary technological equipment. In general, wealthy Thessalonians did not demonstrate any particular interest in investments in equipment or technology. Only 108 of them, that is, 36% of our sample, possessed some kind of tool set, almost invariably of low monetary value. Big farms were equipped with sets of cheap agrarian tools (*çift aleti*) each corresponding to a worker—their estimated price fluctuated between 1,000 and 1,200 *akçe*s. Even the 50 recorded carts (*araba*s and *talikas*) did not cost more than 1,400 *akçes* each, even though they were extremely necessary for agriculture.

Large land estate economy was inextricably linked with massive agricultural production. Accordingly, *terekes* record a great variety of agricultural products, at various prices, quantities, and modes of storage in the possession of the deceased *çiftlik* holders. Among these products, wheat (*hınta*), barley (*şair*), rye (*çavdar*), millet (*darı or erzen*), fodder (*alef*), sesame (*semsem*), honey (*bal*), rice (*pirinç*), beans (*bakla*), and lentils (*mercimek*) stand out by dint of their dense registration. Reliable conclusions concerning the interplay between quantities and prices are impossible to be drawn due to the random and unsystematic character of the serial data extracted.

Overwhelmingly, the entries concerning husbandry, production, and agricultural tools delineate a highly accurate description of what a *çiftlik* really was. A typical example of such a full-blown *çiftlik* is the estate of İsmail Beşe bin Mustafa at the village of Ayo Vasili, a few kilometers to the west of Thessaloniki, where he bred 80 sheep, 27 buffaloes, and four cows, while, at the time of his death, the land had produced 374 *kile* of wheat. The *çiftlik* also contained huts for the cultivators, a vineyard of three *dönüm* and 30 pear trees.

Urban and Rural Real Estate

As Table 1.3 demonstrates, urban real estate made up around 20% of the total capital. A total of 203 recorded deceased persons owned 430 different types of urban edifices. Yet, this widespread tendency was neither homogeneous nor always productive in its nature or objectives. A total of 210 of these constructions were the houses where the deceased had lived—very few owned second residential premises that might have been let out for rent. Elhacc Mehmed bin Iskender and Fatma bint Abdurrahman Ağa were two instances of this rare kind of house owner.[22]

Houses aside, 222 disparate types of occupational constructions are recorded, all reflecting aspects of urban economy and craftsmanship. Tanneries, taverns, ovens, mills, inns, warehouses, workshops of a great variety, and even some factories are recorded in the *terekes*. Sometimes, in view of the absence of any recorded relative property item, participation of the deceased in industry becomes evident only by the respective predicate before their name, as were the cases of rope-maker (*muytab*) İsmail Beşe bin Halil or *halvacı* Ömer Beşe.[23] Still, most craftsmen owned a shop related to their craft, though frequently they would hold only a share (*hisse*) of it. For example, tanners (*debbağ*) Elhacc Mustafa bin Abdullah and Kara Mehmed Beşe bin Abdurrahman owned shares of a tannery, the former a fourth and the latter half of it, both in the tanners' quarters.[24] Some others owned only a pertinent license (*gedik*) but no occupational premises—such was the case of Ali Beşe bin Ahmed owner of the license of a mill, though no mill is recorded among his assets.[25] Others had only the necessary equipment, like Ahmed Bey bin Mehmed Bey, *molla* Mustafa bin Ahmed, or even Nimatullah bint Ess Ahmed Ağa, owners of barber equipment.[26]

Thirty-one entrepreneurs demonstrate a more complex investment policy, not restricted to a unique craftsmanship but encompassing ventures in many disparate specializations. Thus, soup maker (*çorbacı*) El-Hacc Ali Ağa ibn Hüseyin Ağa owned a blacksmith's, a carpenter's, a painter's, and a tobacconist's workshop, as well as a mattress factory.[27] In the same vein, one El-Hacc Süleyman bin Abdullah had two barber's, a halva maker's, a blacksmith's, a coffee maker's, a carpenter's, and another unspecified shop, while, at the same time, he owned the third of an inn in the fish market.[28]

Still, the importance of the industrial sector for these people should not be overemphasized since only five of them were registered as being engaged only in an urban craft. On the contrary, craftsmanship or the ownership of pertinent premises was usually complementary to other activities, like credit, land ownership, and commerce.

Some constructions were more expensive, and hence their possession was limited to a few. The ownership of the 13 recorded mills was a privilege enjoyed only by 12 Muslim Thessalonians; the median price of a mill reached 84,000 *akçe*s rendering them one of the most expensive types of building to be owned. Quite restricted also was the possession of an inn—only 11 Muslims included one in their fortune. A typical example was Ahmed Ağa bin Yunus, owner of an inn at the gate of Kelemerye, at the south end of the city.

Investment in rural estates was not very popular with Muslim city dwellers. Only 84 Muslim Thessalonians, that is, 28% of our sample, owned at least one plot, either a low-value vineyard or a more expensive orchard. Only 21 orchards are registered in the 50 years under examination, with a median value of 24,000 *akçe*s. On the contrary, the median value of the 103 recorded vineyards adds up to only 3,840 *akçe*s.

Small ownership was predominant; 53, or 63.05% of rural estate owners, possessed only one vineyard. There were a few exceptions though: one Ömer Efendi ibn Mehmed had four vineyards,[29] another El-Hacc Mehmed Ağa ibn Ömer owned three vineyards,[30] and one Hüseyin Ağa bin El-Hacc Mustafa had one orchard and two vineyards.[31] Almost all plots were situated either in the villages around the city or within the city walls in designated urban zones, like the area around the gate of Vardar at the west end of the city.

Some Minor Investments: Slave Ownership and Tax Farming

Slave ownership was not popular in Thessaloniki. Only 46 wealthy Muslim Thessalonians, among whom were 21 women, invested money in slaves. Eleven of them owned two slaves, only five possessed three, and the rest had only one. For example, *çorbacı* Esseyyid Mustafa Ağa ibn Ali had two white female slaves (*cariye*) named Rukiya and Naminda, and a white slave (*gulam*) called Ali, apparently all having turned to Islam.[32] Sixty-seven slaves are recorded in our sample, namely, 56 concubines and only 11 male slaves—25 were whites and the rest black. With a median price of 24,000 *akçe*s for a slave, these small numbers delineate the insignificant role of slaves for the urban economy.

Access to tax farming remained extremely restricted to locals during the entire period examined. Only 15 military (including seven *ağa*s and five *beşe*s) and two commoners enjoyed either a whole or half a share of some tax leasing (*bedel-i iltizam*). Little can be concluded as to the nature of the leasing since neither the nature of the tax is mentioned in the register nor is it clear whether the amounts recorded correspond to the whole fiscal burden or some remainder of it. Even among those few *mültezim*s tax farming was usually limited to one revenue source. Only Esseyyid Numan Ağa ibn Esseyyid Mehmed Efendi and Kirişzade Haseki Mustafa Ağa ibn El-Hacc Ahmed rented three revenue sources and thus corresponded more to the typical tax farmer of the time.[33] One Ömer Ağa bin Abdullah was one of few genuine *mültezim* with his entire property invested in the tax farming of salt.[34] Usually, interested businessmen adopted more complex entrepreneurial projects. El-Hacc Mehmed Ağa, holder of the tax *iltizam* of the village Kara Hasan, owned also a dyer's (*boyacı*) shop in Salonica, two *çiftlik*s at the villages of Mesmer and Ucu, at the south of the city, and nine loans to compatriots of his.[35]

Commerce and Merchants

Commerce was a rather popular source of property accumulation for the wealthy. In this respect, all the aforementioned *çiftlik* owners were affiliated with the food market as they sold significant amounts of wheat. Also, since the demarcation lines between craftsmanship and commerce were vague, all the abovementioned craftsmen can be considered to a certain degree merchants, at least at the level of retail transactions. Yet, above all, wholesale commerce would bring huge profits and, thus, it attracted the attention of aspirant businessmen. Twenty-two of them can be described as full-fledged merchants.

Ahmed Ağa bin El-Hac İbrahim was a typical entrepreneur possessing at the time of his death merchandise of impressive diversity, such as metal, soap, pepper, tobacco, coffee, flax, various types of grapes, pearls, and sugar.[36] It is not stated in the register whether these products were to be exported or had been imported, though their wide variety suggests both possibilities. He was engaged in commerce with Egypt, as it can be inferred from the significant amount of 876,486 *akçe*s destined to be forwarded to Egypt by one Ali Ağa, a partner of his. He also exploited the highly profitable customs of tobacco (*gümrük-i duhan*) of Thessaloniki. Likewise, the merchant of the *bezesten* Mustafa Ağa bin Ali sold fabrics, fez, and assorted types of clothes: at the time of his demise, he was the owner of a very rich collection of them.[37] According to the data extracted from the *tereke*s, Muslim merchants focused on the commerce of fabrics and clothes,[38] grapes,[39] silk,[40] thread,[41] weapons,[42] and, above all, wheat.

Muslims did not refrain from transport enterprises and, thus, invested important amounts in transport commerce; for instance, Kurdoğlu Beşe ibn Abdülbaki owned four transport ships (*kayik*) of various sizes,[43] while Ahmed Ağa bin Abdullah bred nine quite expensive camels.[44]

The Multi-Entrepreneur Scheme

In accordance with the general model of an entrepreneur investing her/his capital, time, and energy in a multitude of projects and thus decreasing her/his operational risks as well as increasing her/his profit potential, most Muslim Thessalonians acted as really versatile multi-entrepreneurs. For example, Elhacc Mehmed Emin Ağa bin Elhacc Ebu Bekr owned five *çiftlik*s, with their equipment, 1,040 sheep and 35 buffaloes, more than 500 mulberry trees, a large wheat production, had a clientele of 32 debtors and a two-year tax farm at the significant village of Vrasta close to Kavala.[45] Likewise, El-Hacc Abdülbaki Ağa ibn Mustafa Ağa at the time of his death had a credit clientele of 24 Christians and Muslims, five *çiftlik*s, one coffeeshop, one warehouse in the central market of the city, and a flock of 347 sheep.[46]

Some Tentative Conclusions

Our brief analysis has aspired to depict the energetic participation of Muslims of Thessaloniki in the urban economy and capital formation during the second half of the 18th century. The limitations posed by the sources used are many and do not allow us to estimate the contribution of this local urban elite to the integration of the Empire into the developing world capitalism. Nevertheless, it becomes clear that Muslim city dwellers did not restrict themselves to a marginal position within the nexus of capitalistic production relations. On the contrary, they adopted a pluralistic entrepreneurial agenda and pursued economic supremacy in the urban setting by taking advantage of all possible business opportunities. They were, above all, creditors, and, with lesser intensity, *çiftlik* owners, stock breeders, craftsmen, and merchants. Of course, there existed discrepancies, social hierarchies, and economic disparity within the Muslim society, yet these tensions do not blur the general tendencies. Moreover, it is self-evident that a lot more information is required to produce a fuller account of the economic mobilization of Muslim urban residents. For example, whether the very same people extended their economic activities in other regions of the Empire, or whether social strata with similar characteristics can be traced in other Ottoman cities—all such remain research desiderata.

Archives

Historical Archive of Macedonia (HAM), Thessaloniki, Greece, Islamic Law Court of Thessaloniki vol. 99, 103, 105, 110, 112, 115, 117a, 117b, 115, 122, 124, 128, 132, 136, 139, 140, 142, 144, 147, 149, 152, 153, 156, 160, 163, 166, and 173.

Notes

1 For an extensive discussion on the assorted aspects of Ottoman economy in this historiographic vein, see Huri Islamoğlu-Inan, ed., *The Ottoman Empire and the World-Economy* (Cambridge: Cambridge University Press, 1987). For a critical approach to this paradigm, see Şevket Pamuk, "Institutional Change and the Longevity of the Ottoman

Empire, 1500–1800," *Journal of Interdisciplinary History* 35, no. 2 (Autumn 2004): 225–47; Relli Shechter, "Market Welfare in the Early-Modern Ottoman Economy—A Historiographic Overview with Many Questions," *Journal of the Economic and Social History of the Orient* 48, no. 2 (2005): 253–76.

2 For a general overview of the economy of Ottoman Thessaloniki, see Μυρσίνη Αθανασιάδου, *Εμπορικές σχέσεις Θεσσαλονίκης—Βενετίας κατά τον 18ο αιώνα* [Commercial Relations Between Thessaloniki and Venice During the 18th Century] (Κατερίνη: Μάτι, 2006); Felix Beaujour, *Tableau du commerce de la Grèce*, vol. 1 (Paris, 1800); Michael Lascaris, *Salonique à la fin du XVIIIe s.* (Athènes, 1939), 21–58; Nikos Svoronos, *Le commerce de Salonique au XVIIIe siècle* (Paris: Presses Universitaires de France, 1956).

3 Dimitris Papastamatiou, *Wealth Distribution, Social Stratification and Material Culture in an Ottoman Metropolis. Thessaloniki According to the Probate Inventories of the Muslim Court (1761–1770)* (Istanbul: The ISIS Press, 2017); Dimitris Papastamatiou and Phokion Kotzageorgis, "Wealth Accumulation in an Urban Context: The Profile of the Muslim Rich of Salonica in the 18th Century," *Turkish Historical Review* 5 (2014): 165–99.

4 For a synopsis of the discussion on methodological complexities set by *tereke*s and a full bibliography on them, see Papastamatiou, *Wealth Distribution*, 51–68.

5 For the needs of this paper, volumes 99, 103, 105, 110, 112, 115, 117a, 117b, 115, 122, 124, 128, 132, 136, 139–40, 142, 144, 147, 149, 152–53, 156, 160, 163, 166, and 173 have been used. The archive of the Islamic Law Court of Thessaloniki is kept at the Historical Archive of Macedonia in Thessaloniki, Greece. Thence, for the references to the material studied, we will use the abbreviation HAM, standing for the Historical Archive of Macedonia, followed by the number of the volume, the number of the page and a letter denoting the place of the *tereke* on the page. All monetary values recorded in the *tereke*s of Thessaloniki are in *akçe*s.

6 It should be noted that the aggregate values of the fortunes used for our analysis are not those recorded (almost unfailingly erroneously) by the *kadı* but have been calculated on the basis of the sum of the values of the property constituent parts.

7 The first value refers to the period 1750–1800, while the last three ones only to the decade 1760–1770.

8 Twenty-four were *efendi*s four *çelebi*s, two *molla*s, one *derviş,* and two *hoca*s.

9 Moreover, two *odabaşı*s, one *alemdar,* one *paşa,* and four *bey*s are turning up in the pages of *tereke*s.

10 HAM 99/310b-312, dated July 25, 1762 (3 Muharrem 1176).

11 HAM 163/98–101, dated August 4, 1794 (7 Ramazan 1208).

12 HAM 103/149b–155, dated February 16, 1763 (2 Şaban 1176).

13 HAM 110/137–140, dated August 4, 1766 (27 Safer 1180).

14 HAM 140/216–218, dated August 17, 1781 (26 Şaban 1195).

15 HAM 140/167–169, dated July 9, 1781 (17 Receb 1195).

16 HAM 99/163–164, dated May 9, 1762 (15 Şevval 1175).

17 HAM 99/191–194, dated May 25, 1762 (2 Zil-kade 1175).

18 From the extensive literature on *çiftlik* economy, the most pertinent to our case study are: Irfan Kokdas, "Money, Peasant Mobility, Çiftliks, and Local Politics in Salonika: 1740–1820," *Comparative Studies of South Asia, Africa and the Middle East* 31, no. 1 (2014): 135–46; Sophia Laiou, "Some Considerations Regarding *Çiftlik* Formation in Western Thessaly, Sixteenth-Nineteenth Centuries," in *The Ottoman Empire, the Balkans, the Greek Lands: Toward a Social and Economic History. Studies in Honor of John C. Alexander*, ed. Elias Kolovos et al. (Istanbul: Gorgias Press, 2007), 255–78; Bruce McGowan, *Economic Life in Ottoman Europe: Taxation, Trade and the Struggle for Land, 1600–1800* (Cambridge: Cambridge University Press, 1981), 46–60; and Dimitris Papastamatiou, "The Structure, the Content and the Development of Large

Estates in the Environs of Salonica During the Period 1697–1770," in *Festschrift in Honor of Ioannis P. Theocharides: Studies on the Ottoman Empire and Turkey*, ed. Evangelia Balta, Georgios Salakidis, and Theoharis Stavrides (Istanbul: The ISIS Press, 2014), 375–402.

19 HAM 99/324–325, dated August 10, 1762 (19 Muharrem 1176).

20 HAM 117b/35–36, dated December 4, 1769 (5 Şaban 1183).

21 HAM 117b/6b–8, dated May 4, 1769 (27 Zil-hicce 1182).

22 HAM 99/183, 117b/36–37, respectively. The median price of a house was 52,200 *akçes*.

23 HAM 112/18 and 110/131–132, respectively.

24 HAM 99/208–209 and 117a/6b.

25 HAM 115/41b–42, dated February 26, 1768 (7 Şevval 1181). It is noteworthy that the median value of a license, namely, 24,000 *akçes*, was higher than that of a typical shop, which reached 18,300 *akçes*.

26 HAM 110/137–40, 115/63b–64, and 99/43–45, respectively.

27 HAM 152/13–15 and 103/113–15.

28 HAM 103/113–15, dated December 6, 1762 (19 Cemaziye-ul-evvel 1176).

29 HAM 160/22c–23, dated August 28, 1791 (28 Zil-hicce 1205).

30 HAM 166/44, dated January 15, 1796 (5 Receb 1210).

31 HAM 117b/68–69, dated February 23, 1770 (27 Şevval 1183).

32 HAM 139/17–18, dated November 3, 1780 (6 Zil-kade 1194).

33 HAM 152/49b–50 and 149/50–52, respectively.

34 HAM 105/65a, dated August 4, 1765 (16 Safer 1179).

35 HAM 117b/61–62, dated February 20, 1770 (24 Şevval 1183).

36 HAM 99/235–37, dated June 27, 1762 (5 Zil-hicce 1175).

37 HAM 103/125–27, dated December 27, 1762 (10 Cemaziye-ul-ahir 1176).

38 For other examples, see HAM 99/21–22, 99/273–74, and 103/113–15.

39 For example, see HAM 117b/6b–8.

40 For examples, see HAM 99/75, 99/183, 99/290b–91.

41 For examples, see HAM 99/295a, 99/325–26.

42 For examples, see HAM 110/134–37 and 112/53.

43 HAM 149/116, dated December 20, 1785 (17 Safer 1200).

44 HAM 105/64b-65, dated July 20, 1765 (1 Safer 1179). Each camel cost 5,430 *akçes*.

45 HAM 110/77–82, dated April 12, 1766 (2 Zil-kade 1179).

46 HAM 149/70–71, dated August 1, 1785 (25 Ramazan 1199).

Bibliography

Beaujour, Felix. *Tableau du commerce de la Grèce*, vol. 1. Paris, 1800.

Islamoğlu-Inan, Huri, ed. *The Ottoman Empire and the World-Economy*. Cambridge: Cambridge University Press, 1987.

Kokdas, Irfan. "Money, Peasant Mobility, Çiftliks, and Local Politics in Salonika: 1740–1820." *Comparative Studies of South Asia, Africa and the Middle East* 31, no. 1 (2014): 135–46.

Laiou, Sophia. "Some Considerations Regarding Çiftlik Formation in Western Thessaly, Sixteenth-Nineteenth Centuries." In *The Ottoman Empire, the Balkans, the Greek Lands: Toward a Social and Economic History. Studies in Honor of John C. Alexander*, edited by Elias Kolovos, Phokion Kotzageorgis, Sophia Laiou, and Marinos Sariyannis, 255–78. Istanbul: Gorgias Press, 2007.

Lascaris, Michael. *Salonique à la fin du XVIIIe s*. Athènes: Flamma Press, 1939.

McGowan, Bruce. *Economic Life in Ottoman Europe: Taxation, Trade and the Struggle for Land, 1600–1800*. Cambridge: Cambridge University Press, 1981.

Pamuk, Şevket. "Institutional Change and the Longevity of the Ottoman Empire, 1500–1800." *Journal of Interdisciplinary History* 35, no. 2 (Autumn 2004): 225–47.

Papastamatiou, Dimitris. "The Structure, the Content and the Development of Large Estates in the Environs of Salonica During the Period 1697–1770." In *Festschrift in Honor of Ioannis P. Theocharides. Studies on the Ottoman Empire and Turkey*, edited by Evangelia Balta, Georgios Salakidis, and Theoharis Stavrides, 375–402. Istanbul: The ISIS Press, 2014.

Papastamatiou, Dimitris. *Wealth Distribution, Social Stratification and Material Culture in an Ottoman Metropolis. Thessaloniki According to the Probate Inventories of the Muslim Court (1761–1770)*. Istanbul: The ISIS Press, 2017.

Papastamatiou, Dimitris, and Phokion Kotzageorgis. "Wealth Accumulation in an Urban Context. The Profile of the Muslim Rich of Salonica in the 18th Century." *Turkish Historical Review* 5 (2014): 165–99.

Shechter, Relli. "Market Welfare in the Early-Modern Ottoman Economy—A Historiographic Overview with Many Questions." *Journal of the Economic and Social History of the Orient* 48, no. 2 (2005): 253–76.

Svoronos, Nikos. *Le commerce de Salonique au XVIIIe siècle*. Paris: Presses Universitaires de France, 1956.

Αθανασιάδου, Μυρσίνη. *Εμπορικές σχέσεις Θεσσαλονίκης—Βενετίας κατά τον 18ο αιώνα*. Κατερίνη: Μάτι, 2006. [Athanasiadou, Myrsini. *Commercial Relations Between Thessaloniki and Venice During the 18th Century*. Katerini: Mati, 2006.]

2 Capitalist Practices of Thessalonican Greek Merchants Around the 1820s

Phokion Kotzageorgis

Recent scholarship distances itself from older views on capitalism's development.[1] According to the new approach, capitalist forms in the economy have been observed as early as the Middle Ages in the Middle East, where, due to long-distance trade, the circulation of money had increased and new forms of money transactions and contracts between merchants had developed. From there, capitalist practices passed to Italian cities of the Renaissance and spilled over into Western Europe. No longer is a Eurocentric approach adopted, according to which the capitalist model—as it developed in Western Europe in the 19th century—was imposed on the rest of the world, while the economy of non-European regions was based on non-capitalist forms of market organization. Today, those various capitalist practices that had developed during the Early Modern period in different regions outside Europe are considered early stages of capitalism. In other words, capitalist forms of economy can be found in regions such as India, South Asia, and the Ottoman Empire long before the Western model of industrial capitalism was imposed in the 19th century. This fresh approach offers great flexibility to scholars to better understand the forms developed in the economy of these regions.[2]

According to this theoretical framework, the Ottoman Empire did not develop capitalist aspects in its economy only after the mid-19th century, when it came into direct contact with the industrial capitalism of the West, but as early as in the 17th century. The case of Egypt is typical of how an Ottoman province developed capitalist forms of market organization based on its previous historical experience and without the mediation of European countries. Commercialization is the key notion to the understanding of capitalist relations.[3] The Ottoman provinces experienced European capitalism at different stages. Thus, the Balkans were among the first to experience European forms of capitalist economic activity.[4]

Within this framework, the present paper looks to identify ways of accumulating wealth practiced in a capitalist economic environment, such as the Ottoman one in the early 19th century. The selection of Thessaloniki as a case study constitutes a good example to study these ways because this Balkan metropolis was an international port and it was located in a region that experienced the integration of its economy into the global capitalist system before the middle of the 19th century.[5]

Thessaloniki was the biggest port in the Ottoman Balkans and indeed one of the largest in the Empire during the 18th century. The establishment of the French

DOI: 10.4324/9781003500780-4

consulate in 1686 was extremely important for the economic growth of the city and the international profile of its port. Eighteenth-century international trade in Thessaloniki was monopolized by French and other European (English, Dutch, Venetian, and Danish) merchants. The last quarter of the 18th century and the beginning of the 19th century was the period when international trade in the city reached its apex. It was in that specific period of 50 years before the Greek uprising of 1821 (ca. 1770–ca. 1820) that one observes, for the first time, the presence of a handful of wealthy Ottoman Greek merchants in the city.[6]

The Christians of the city, mainly Greeks, for centuries were behind the Muslim and Jewish inhabitants in both demographic strength and economic dynamism. Since there are no extant Greek sources (or they are of a scanty and fragmentary nature), we must rely on European and Ottoman sources to delineate the economic strength and capital formation of city's Christians. European sources, mainly French, have been adequately studied and have contributed to the topic, whereas the Ottoman sources have not.[7] In this chapter, I use Ottoman probate inventories as a source for collecting information about the economic profile of these merchants. Due to the Greek rebellion in the Halkidiki region and as a measure of retaliation and punishment, the Ottoman authorities of the city arrested some wealthy Christian merchants on charges of collaboration with the rebels. They confiscated their property and some of them were executed, while others succeeded in escaping to Western Europe. Basing my research on the lists of the confiscated fortunes of three well-to-do persons, I will try to shed light on the dynamics of the Christian merchants of the city and therefore present the economic profile of those capitalist entrepreneurs. According to French consular reports, in 1812–1813, there were five big Greek commercial houses in Thessaloniki: those of Kaftantzioglou, Spandoni, Kyriakou (Tzanoglou), Paiko, and Rogkoti.[8] The heads of two of them will be discussed here, giving an idea of the wealth spectrum of the group. Furthermore, I will suggest that the three merchants represented different stages in the process of the rising of Christian merchants in the Empire as regards the profile and the form of capital accumulation. Through the analysis, the extreme wealth of an Ottoman merchant in the provinces in the age of intensive capitalist practices in the empire's economy becomes plain.

The first merchant was Christos Menexes, son of Yorgos,[9] who came from the mountainous area of Agrapha in Central Greece. His profession was as a perfumer (Ott. *attar*), but according to his probate inventory, where we find quantities of tobacco among the assets, he might be involved in tobacco commerce as well. There is no other documentation regarding his commercial activity, except from the Ottoman register compiled just after Menexes's execution due to his involvement in the Greek revolt of 1821.[10] In the register, it is mentioned that he belonged to the group of the "merchants of Europe" (*Avrupa tüccarları*)[11] from 1818, according to his diploma (*berat*), which was copied in the judicial registers of the city.[12] Although not all nor even many of the non-Muslim merchants became "merchants of Europe," if someone joined the group, especially in the provinces, it meant that he was one of the wealthy men of the region. As the term implied, these merchants were involved in the international trade of the Ottoman Empire with Europe, having developed a quite extensive trade network. Therefore, Menexes was from the well-known wealthy non-Muslim merchants of the city.

According to the probate inventory compiled after Menexes's execution, the Greek merchant possessed in 1821: 62 items of houseware, valued at 768 (773 in the inventory) piasters (kuruş);[13] 18 items of silverware (*edevat-i sim*) valued at 224 piasters; 21 items of house furniture (*mefruşat*) valued at 917 piasters; 120 items of professional use, found in his warehouse, valued at 3,834 piasters; 22 real-estate properties (stores, houses, warehouses), where Menexes had a part or full ownership, valued at 55,750 piasters; and 18 loans which Menexes has given to Salonicans and four more loans to people in other places (*diyar-i ahar*), valued at 14,054 piasters. The abovementioned fortune of Menexes totaled 77,304 piasters. To this amount, must be added another 47,422 piasters, coming from 24 outstanding debts to him. Thus, the total fortune of Menexes amounted to 124,726 piasters. On the contrary, Menexes owed 120,568 piasters to 34 creditors.

From the above data, it results that Menexes's wealth came mainly (44.7%) from his possession in shared or full ownership of immovable property in the city (eight warehouses, 12 stores, and two houses), while a similar percentage (38%) came from un-settled debts. In contrast, only 11.3% came from his credit activity. However, if we add the category of un-settled debts to Menexes, we will conclude that his fortune was almost equally divided between credit and real estate, whereas household goods and merchandises constituted a small percentage (ca. 5%).

As for his credit circle, Menexes lent to Christians (40.9%), Jews (18.2%), and Muslims (13.6%), whereas those who still were in debt to him were only Muslims (59.1%) and Christians (45.8%). On the contrary, Menexes borrowed money from Muslims (31.3%) and Christian men (28.1%) and women (25%). Europeans were creditors and debtors of Menexes at approximately the same percentage rates (13.6% and 9.4%, respectively). As regards the amounts, Muslims borrowed the highest amounts (40.2% of the total), followed by Christians (24.5%), Jews (15%), and Europeans (9.6%); a Christian village borrowed money representing 10.7% of the total amount. On the contrary, Christians were the main creditors of Menexes (56.8%), followed by Muslims (20.5%) and Christian women (11.5%). Finally, as regards those with un-settled debts, Christians took the lion's share with 90.1% of the total amount, most of which money came from a Christian named Dimitraki (33,648 piasters). Thus, Menexes's clientele was mostly Muslims and Christians, the former being more consistent with their loan obligations than the latter.

The second merchant we are dealing with was Christodoulos Balanos, son of Panagiotis, a native from Serres. He was a "merchant of Europe" as well from 1818,[14] and the head of one of the five biggest Greek commercial houses of the city according to French sources, because he married the daughter of the powerful merchant Yakoumi Paikos, Anna. His economic activity was based on cotton, taking advantage of his birthplace, and having a developed commercial network with Serres.[15] This Macedonian town was one of the hubs of cotton production in the Balkans.[16] Moreover, judging from the merchandise recorded in his Ottoman probate inventory, Balanos was active in the tobacco and fur trades as well. He retained credit relations with his compatriot, the then-deputy governor of Thessaloniki, Yusuf Bey.[17] In Balanos's case, as that of Menexes's, the quantitative data for his fortune come from the Ottoman register compiled after his execution by the Ottoman authorities in 1821, because he was accused of helping the Greek rebels in the Halkidiki peninsula.[18]

According to the probate inventory, Balanos possessed at the time of his execution: 224 entries of household items or merchandise, valued at 71,355 piasters (54,744 in the register); 4 houses with full or partial ownership, valued at 16,000 piasters (26,000 in defter); 95 loans valued at 660,927 (667,124 in defter) piasters; and 78 un-settled loans valued at 156,853 (201,213 in the register) piasters. Therefore, Balanos's fortune totaled 905,135 piasters (949,082 in the register). From this amount 429,304 (434,557 in the register) piasters must be deducted Balanos's debts to 68 persons. From the above data, it is clear that Balanos's wealth came in most part from credit activity (almost three-quarters of his total wealth), whereas his household and professional items lagged a long way behind, and the real estate property accounted for less than 3% of the total. We do not know if the credit activity was related only to his profession or whether he was a well-known "bankroller" in the city's society, although not officially a *sarraf* (moneylender). His clientele came from the entire spectrum of the city's society: Muslims (36.8%), Christians (25.3%), Jews (16.8%), Europeans (14.7%), village communities (4.2%), and monasteries (2.1%). As regards those with un-settled loans, these were mainly Christians (41%), Muslims (21.8%), and village communities (15.4%), with all the other categories represented in the list too, albeit in low percentages: Christian women (2.6%), Jews (7.7%), Europeans (5.1%), monasteries (3.8%), and an Armenian (1.3%). As for his debts, Balanos owed money to Christians (33.8%), Muslims (20.5%), Jews (17.6%), Europeans (10.3%), and monasteries (2.9%).

Balanos's fortune was seven times as great as Menexes's one. It is interesting to note that the former's investment was not directed toward real estate, unlike Menexes's. He had a much wider circle of creditors and borrowers, some of whom originated from his birthplace Serres. His source of borrowing came mainly from Christians, although he borrowed equally from Jews—mainly *sarrafs*, Muslims, and Europeans. In the last group, are all the consuls of foreign countries in the city. Balanos lent also to people living in other places since one-fifth (without Serres) and one-third (including Serres) account for his debtors outside Thessaloniki. It is worth mentioning that the biggest debtor to Balanos was Yusuf Muhlis Paşa from Serres, son of the powerful local magnate Ismail Bey, who after the beginning of the Greek Revolution was appointed governor of Patras in Peloponnese. His debt to Balanos totaled 519,401 piasters. Because of this sum, the money owed by Muslims to Balanos represents almost three-quarters of the total credits. As for his lenders, Balanos did not owe a high sum of money to any particular person. It seems that the Jewish moneylenders were the most important sources to the Greek merchant. In contrast, Muslims did not lend much money to Balanos. As to the bad borrowers, almost half of them came from among the Christian community and one-fifth among the Muslims, but of the actual sums recorded as outstanding debts, a quarter came from village communities.

A last remark concerns the Europeans (*Efrenciyan*). Under this heading, in the Ottoman register, were comprised, besides Europeans living in the city, Ottoman subjects, mainly Greeks, who either were living in Europe or had the status of *protégés* of a European country. Thus, Balanos, and to a lesser extent Menexes, had developed business relations with Greek merchants of the diaspora, maybe as a member of their vast trade network. Balanos's case represents the type of a very rich Christian, who had accumulated a large capital. This he had not invested in household goods, merchandise, and real estate, but rather it was credit activity that was the most lucrative sector for capital formation. He was, in fact, an entrepreneur.

Although Manolakis Tzanoglou (in Greek sources known as Manolakis Kyriakoú) was the head of one of the five richest merchant families in the city, his case was exceptional, mainly because of his career.[19] To begin with, Manolakis was a native of Thessaloniki, and his father, Tzanis, was a prominent merchant as well. The founder of the family commercial house seems to be his grandfather, Kyriakos, about whom nothing is known. Manolakis went a step further than being a "merchant of Europe": he was appointed as vice-consul of Denmark in the city. The study of the Ottoman court registers of Thessaloniki has not revealed yet Manolakis's investiture diploma (*berat*), but according to European sources, before 1816 Manolakis had succeeded in being a *protegé* of Austria, and after 1816 in becoming Denmark's vice-consul. Manolakis was executed, without a clear reason, in May of 1822, in the context of the uprising of the small Macedonian town of Naoussa (Ott. Ağustos). Officially, he was accused by the Ottoman authorities, that although he was of *reaya* status (i.e., an Ottoman subject), he was behaving like a European. He married a woman from Europe, possibly from France, and after the Ottoman authorities had arrested him, his wife, together with his brother-in-law managed to escape abroad, probably to Marseilles, taking with them maybe most of their valuable items.

After his execution, the Ottoman authorities could not open his warehouses and his house to find Manolakis's moveable property. Thus, in the Ottoman court registers, no inventory of moveable property has survived, unlike the other two abovementioned merchants. The only material that the Ottoman authorities found inside his house was several certificates (*temessüks*) of loan contracts. In some entries of the registers, the Ottoman court recorded real estate properties of the executed or fugitive Christians, which passed to the Ottoman state's ownership. The latter tried to sell or rent them. Among these assets, there are some of Manolakis's family.

Taking into consideration the abovementioned limitations as regards the total fortune of Manolakis, the amount of his assets, found by the Ottoman authorities, reached 706,324 piasters.[20] From this, only 4.5% represented one manor house (*konak*), half of another house, and some unspecified warehouses sold in auction by the Ottoman state. The sum of 483,890 comprised loans Manolakis gave to various persons and/or communities. Certainly, we miss numerous pieces of the puzzle of Manolakis's fortune. However, we can roughly estimate his credit clientele. Manolakis lent mainly to Muslims and to village communities. In terms of both the number and the amount of loans, the Muslims constituted almost half of the total (47.1%; median: 4,238 piasters), while the villages were almost 40% (37.2%;

median: 5,523). The rest went to Christians with an interesting detail. Almost all loans given to Christians by Manolakis went to captains, who, according to an entry in another register, originated from the islands of Hydra, Spetses, and Psara, and who had visited Thessaloniki before the War of Greek Independence and traded there; or they brought bills of exchange from their islands.[21] Furthermore, Manolakis lent to the other two abovementioned merchants as well. In their probate inventory, it is recorded that he lent Menexes 2,440 piasters and Balanos 11,000. In both entries, Manolakis was recorded as the consul of Denmark (*Danimarka balyozı*).

Of the village communities, most of them were in Halkidiki peninsula and belonged to the group of mining villages (*maden kuraları*). According to a reference from the French archives, Manolakis was a client of the city's deputy governor Yusuf Bey, who was pre-purchasing huge quantities of charcoal and salt from villages which then he sold on at extremely high prices.[22] Maybe Manolakis was a partner of Yusuf in this business, and this fact explains the debts of the mining villages to Manolakis himself.

From a list of confiscated houses of fugitive Christians, we find that, besides the aforementioned real estate property, to Manolakis's family (his wife and his mother) there belonged four warehouses, one house, which was rented to the French consul, and a ruined warehouse.[23]

As for his debts, no register has survived. We can make a rough idea from the cases brought before the Ottoman court by the creditors of Manolakis after his execution, who claimed their money back. From the abovementioned sum of 706,323 piasters, 172,126 were sent to three Muslims, who might be Manolakis's creditors. From other entries of the Ottoman court registers, we find that Manolakis owed 82,000 piasters to a Jewish merchant, and 100,900 piasters to two Christian "merchants of Europe," namely, George Harissis and Spandonis. Though we cannot draw any conclusions for his full credit activity from just these entries, we can have an idea of the range of amounts that Manolakis was able to move.

Another interesting aspect of Manolakis's fortune was the possession of a farm (*çiftlik*) in the village Sarica (today Valtohori, 30 km West of Thessaloniki). The çiftlik could not be sold in auction by the Ottoman state, but it was rented out for 34,000 piasters per year.[24]

Manolakis represented the type of rich merchant, who had obtained European privileges and acquired the office of vice-consul of a European country. Although we are not well-informed about his economic activities, it seems that Manolakis was intensively involved in credit activity, although he was not officially a moneylender. It is noteworthy that he was never mentioned in the Ottoman sources as a moneylender (*sarraf*), but only as a merchant (*tacir, bazirgan*). Landholding was not a common practice at all for non-Muslims and Manolakis's farm was a sign of his extreme economic power.

The three provincial merchants represented two stages of development undergone by Ottoman Christian merchants at the turn of the 18th to 19th century, which existed simultaneously.[25] The first one is where the merchant developed a network of clients in his professional persona and then expanded his business from the regional level to the interregional and finally to the international, taking the title of "merchant of Europe." The basis of his capital remained his professional possessions with all the necessary equipment (warehouses, tools, merchandises, etc.). The second stage is when the merchant succeeded in being appointed in an official position as a European *protégé*, aspiring to evade the restrictions imposed by his *reaya*-status. Real estate property, although related to his profession and being mainly warehouses and stores, was yet a primary sector of economic activity and a manifestation of his wealth as well. However, credit was the field where such merchants were active and accumulated enormous capital. Their clientele was not restricted to their colleagues, but it was extended to all strata of the local society and beyond them since the clients could have their headquarters in Europe. Even if their connection with Europe concerned mainly Greek merchants living there, the credit relations between these merchants showed an extroversion. Although the debtors might be the buyers of merchandise, it seems highly probable that these merchants functioned as unofficial moneylenders for everyone in the city who needed cash. This is not strange at all, since rich Muslims in Thessaloniki of the 18th century were active in credit loans as well.[26] The need for cash in the city and the countryside was urgent, not least for paying the tax obligations. Therefore, money lending was a profitable field for everyone who wanted to accumulate capital.

For comparative reasons, I will mention two other cases, from the same period, of Ottoman subjects who accumulated large capital. The first concerns two Greek moneylenders of Istanbul, whose fortunes were confiscated due to their participation in the Greek Revolution, namely, Dimitrakis from Morea and Kostakis son of Scarlatos from Istanbul.[27] The loans given by the former were at the same level as that of Balanos, while those of the latter were similar to Menexes's.[28] Therefore, the two Salonican merchants, in fact, had a comparable economic profile with the moneylenders of Istanbul in terms of ways of accumulating wealth. The main and important difference, especially as concerns Dimitrakis' fortune, was his close relations with high-ranking Ottoman officials and the Palace, obviously because his entrepreneurial activities were developed in the Ottoman capital and his occupation required such connections to be successful.[29]

The fortune of a medium-level Muslim notable in Northwest Anatolia (Ott. Edremit, today Burhaniye, Turkey), named Müridzade Hacı Mehmed Ağa from 1823 gives another aspect of capital formation in the Ottoman Empire.[30] His fortune was made through three channels: moneylending, grain cultivation, and olive oil commerce. The accumulated assets were at the level of Balanos's (some 700,000 piasters). Unlike the Greek moneylenders of Istanbul, the Muslim notable in the province had a more sophisticated and diversified fortune, which comprised landholding (400 hectares of fields, 19,000 olive trees), while even his credit activity came in significant part (a quarter) from tax collection.[31] This is the crucial difference between a Muslim and a non-Muslim well-to-do in that period: the former accumulated bigger fortunes, using political networking and landholding as a source of capital; the latter had to depend almost exclusively on credit activity and on the trade network developed with the West.

Perhaps more interesting than contrasting Muslim and non-Muslim rich men, it is the comparison between center and provinces. My feeling is that a Christian rich person in a provincial city presented the same profile as one in the Ottoman capital, without differentiation in terms of the size of fortunes. They differed mainly in the nature of their clientele, the wealthy of Istanbul being more involved in high-ranking official circles and the Palace. At any rate, since the boundaries between a merchant and a moneylender were blurred, for a Christian, his initial occupation was not so important for accumulating money because the credit activity was extended to a wider circle than his colleagues and embraced all the society's strata. The ultimate in this picture was observed in Manolakis's case: he was able to possess land, to enjoy the office of vice-consul of a foreign country in the city, and maybe to be involved in tax farming through the connections developed with the Ottoman governor of the city. Ultimately, the difference between a Christian wealthy person in the capital and another in a provincial city was a matter of scale and not of content. Namely, the methods of accumulating wealth were the same. The people that formed the rich person's network were different though: in the Ottoman capital, one could extend business activity to the members of the high-ranking officials or even to the Palace.

It has been argued that within the framework of merchant capitalism, merchants have capital as their basic feature. They invest it for future profits, accepting risk and uncertainty. Credit is a way of multiplying capital. Empires made it easier for private traders by providing them with the appropriate institutional framework for entrepreneurial activity.[32] From the aforementioned analysis, it follows that the three Thessalonican merchants are typical examples of capitalists with a strong entrepreneurial nature. For them, credit was of primary importance in accumulating wealth, but they did not invest it in other enterprises to increase their profits. Their commercial activity was the base for capital accumulation, but credit gave them greater financial standing and social visibility. The state provided the appropriate institutional framework ("merchants of Europe") to protect them from European competition. However, it was also relentless when a merchant sought protection elsewhere, as the case of Manolakis Tzanoglou proves.

Archives

Historical Archive of Macedonia, Thessaloniki, Greece, Islamic Law Court of Thessaloniki vol. 203, 206, 209, 210, 213, 214, 216, 218, 219, 222

Başbakanlık Osmanlı Arşivi (BOA), Istanbul, Turkey

DBM.MHF.d.13339

C.ML. 147/6242

Notes

1 I thank my colleague, Assoc. Prof. Sophia Laiou, for her comments on this paper.

2 Nelly Hanna, *Artisan Entrepreneurs in Cairo and Early-Modern Capitalism (1600–1800)* (Syracuse and New York: Syracuse University Press, 2011), Chapter 1. More briefly in: Nelly Hanna, "Artisans, Guilds, and Capitalist Development in Cairo, 1600–1800," in *Capitalisms: Towards a Global History*, ed. Kaveh Yazdani and Dilip M. Menon (Oxford: Oxford University Press, 2020), 326–28; Eren Duzgun, "Property,

Geopolitics, and Eurocentrism: The 'Great Divergence' and the Ottoman Empire," *Review of Radical Political Economics* 50, no. 1 (2018): 26–27. More generally see: Andre G. Frank, "The World Economic System in Asia Before European Hegemony," *Historian* 56, no. 2 (1993): 276.

3 Hanna, *Artisan Entrepreneurs*.

4 Hanna, *Artisan Entrepreneurs*, 25.

5 Reşat Kasaba, *The Ottoman Empire and the World Economy: The Nineteenth Century* (New York: SUNY Press, 1988), 6.

6 For the trade of Thessaloniki during the 18th century, the standard work is still: Nikos Svoronos, *Le commerce de Salonique au XVIIIe siècle* (Paris: Presses Universitaires de France, 1956).

7 For the 18th century, the Ottoman sources, mainly from the local Ottoman archive, have been used in publications of E. Ginio, D. Papastamatiou, and I. Kokdas, while for the 19th century, the books of V. Dimitriadis and M. Anastassiadou have been based on the Ottoman sources from the same archive. See, for example, Eyal Ginio, "When Coffee Brought About Wealth and Prestige: The Impact of Egyptian Trade on Salonica," *Oriente Moderno* 25, no. 1 (2006): 93–107; Irfan Kokdas, "When the Countryside Is Free: Urban Politics, Local Autonomy and the Changing Social Structure in Ottoman Salonika, 1740–1820" (PhD diss., Binghamton University, 2013); Dimitris Papastamatiou, *Wealth Distribution, Social Stratification and Material Culture in an Ottoman Metropolis: Thessaloniki According to the Probate Inventories of the Muslim Court (1761–1770)* (Istanbul: The ISIS Press, 2017); Meropi Anastassiadou, *Salonique, 1830–1912: Une ville ottoman à l'âge des Réformes* (Leiden: Brill, 1997); Βασίλης Δημητριάδης, *Η Θεσσαλονίκη της παρακμής. Η ελληνική κοινότητα της Θεσσαλονίκης κατά τη δεκαετία του 1830 με βάση ένα οθωμανικό κατάστιχο απογραφής του πληθυσμού* [Thessaloniki of the Decline: The Greek Community of Thessaloniki During 1830's According to an Ottoman Population Survey] (Ηράκλειο: Πανεπιστημιακές Εκδόσεις, 1997).

8 Ευάγγελος Χεκίμογλου, *Η ιστορία της επιχειρηματικότητας στη Θεσσαλονίκη*, vol. II/1: *Η οθωμανική περίοδος* [The History of the Entrepreneurship in Thessaloniki, vol. II/1: The Ottoman Period] (Θεσσαλονίκη: Πολιτιστική Εταιρεία Επιχειρηματιών Βορείου Ελλάδος, 2004), 185.

9 For him, see the concise information in: Χεκίμογλου, *Η ιστορία*, 183–85.

10 The register is copied in: Historical Archive of Macedonia (HAM), Islamic Law Court of Thessaloniki, vol. 206, 110–15 [hereafter: HAM 206, 110–15], dated 25 Muharrem 1237/October 22, 1821. The register can be found also in the Başbakanlık Osmanlı Arşivi [hereafter: BOA], DBM.MHF.d.13339. It has been partly translated in Greek in: Ιωάννης Κ. Βασδραβέλλης, *Οι Μακεδόνες εις τους υπέρ της ανεξαρτησίας αγώνας 1796–1832* [The Macedonians in the Struggle for the Independence, 1796–1832], 2nd ed. (Θεσσαλονίκη: Εταιρεία Μακεδονικών Σπουδών, 1950), 216–17. See also: Φωκίων Κοτζαγεώργης, "Ρωμιοί εκτελεσθέντες και φυγάδες στη Θεσσαλονίκη του 1821 [Executed and Fugitive Rums in Thessaloniki of 1821]," *Μεσαιωνικά και Νεοελληνικά* 14 (2021): 166–67.

11 This group was formed by Sultan Selim III in 1802 to stop the trend of non-Muslim Ottoman merchants, who sought and got European protection and then became the "protégés" (Ott. *mustamin* or *beratlı*) of European countries (Sophia Laiou, "The Ottoman Greek 'Merchants of Europe' at the Beginning of the 19th Century," in *Festschrift in Honor of Ioannis P. Theocharides. Studies on the Ottoman Empire and Turkey*, ed. Evangelia Balta, Georgios Salakidis, and Theoharis Stavrides, vol. II (Istanbul: The ISIS Press, 2014), 315.

12 The *berat* is found in: HAM, 203, 58 (I Ramazan 1233/July 5–14, 1818). It was preceded by a *ferman* to the judge of Thessaloniki regarding this topic.

13 For comparative reasons, I notice that in Thessaloniki of 1820, according to the official market prices (*narh*) the daily wage of a mason (skilled worker) was 65 *paras* (or 1.6 piaster) and 1.3 kg milk cost 14 *paras* (or 0.35 piaster) (HAM, 206, 1).

14 HAM, 203, 137 (I Şaban 1233/June 6–15, 1818).

15 For Christodoulos Balanos see: Χεκίμογλου, *Η ιστορία*, 185–87.

16 Bruce McGowan, "The Age of the Ayans, 1699–1812," in *An Economic and Social History of the Ottoman Empire, 1300–1914*, ed. Halil İnalcık and Donald Quataert (Cambridge: Cambridge University Press, 1994), 687, 738.

17 A dozen entries in Balanos's probate inventory is found regarding loans that were given by Balanos to Yusuf Pasha from Serres, to his relatives or members of his retinue.

18 The register, surviving in a bad situation, is copied in: HAM, 206, 118–31 (25 Muharrem 1237/October 22, 1821), while another register records the jewelry of Balanos (HAM, 209, 5–14). Both were translated partially in Greek in: Βασδραβέλλης, *Οι Μακεδόνες*, 218–21, 237–38. See also: Κοτζαγεώργης, "Ρωμιοί εκτελεσθέντες," 167–68. For the problems arisen from the management of the arrears of Balanos's debts, see: Δημήτρης Παπασταματίου, Φωκίων Κοτζαγεώργης, *Στις παρυφές της Επανάστασης. Μια νέα προσέγγιση του αγώνα στην Χαλκιδική με βάση οθωμανικό τεκμηριακό υλικό* [On the Fringes of the Revolution: A New Approach to the Struggle in Halkidiki According to Ottoman Archival Material] (Αθήνα: Εκδόσεις ΕΑΠ, 2021), 97–98.

19 For this person, see Χεκίμογλου, *Η ιστορία*, 171–173; Κοτζαγεώργης, "Ρωμιοί εκτελεσθέντες," 171–75, where references to the Ottoman sources in HAM and BOA about Manolakis.

20 The registers contain entries of Manolakis's borrowers are as follows: HAM, 210, 15–16 (10 Şaban 1238/April 22, 1823); 214, 6 (6 Rebiyülahır 1240/November 28, 1824); 218, 59/2 (19 Ramazan 1242/April 16, 1827); 219, 22/2 (3 Zilhicce 1243/June 16, 1828); and 222, 95/1 (21 Şevval 1244/April 26, 1829). See also: BOA, C.ML. 147/6242 (5 Zilkade 1237/July 24, 1822). For Manolakis's fortune see also: Παπασταματίου, Κοτζαγεώργης, *Στις παρυφές*, 92–93, 222–23, where the debtors of Manolakis, and 99–101, where the management problems regarding his loans that had arisen after his death.

21 HAM, 213, 84. See Greek translation in: Βασδραβέλλης, *Οι Μακεδόνες*, 311–12.

22 Χεκίμογλου, *Η ιστορία*, 173.

23 HAM, 214, 8 (n.d.); 216, 35/1 (Cemaziyülahır 1241/January 11 to February 8, 1826); 222, 70 (27 Şaban 1244/March 4, 1829).

24 HAM, 213, 69 (15 Şevval 1239/June 13, 1824).

25 Obviously, there were cases of merchants who passed from the first to the second stage, like Manolakis.

26 Phokion Kotzageorgis and Dimitris Papastamatiou, "Wealth Accumulation in an Urban Context: The Profile of the Muslim Rich of Thessaloniki in the Eighteenth Century on the Basis of Probate Inventories," *Turkish Historical Review* 5 (2014): 171–78, 190.

27 Σοφία Λαΐου, "Οθωμανοί Έλληνες σαράφηδες στην Κωνσταντινούπολη του 1821 [Greek Ottoman "Bankers' (Sarrafs) Moneychangers in Istanbul of 1821]," *Μεσαιωνικά και Νέα Ελληνικά* 14 (2021): 217–38.

28 Namely, Dimitrakis lent loans of an amount of 796,915.5 piasters (Λαΐου, "Οθωμανοί Έλληνες," 227), while Balanos 817, 780 piasters. On the contrary, Kostakis, at the time of his death, had lent 110,405 piasters (Λαΐου, "Οθωμανοί Έλληνες," 232), while Menexes stood at 61,479 piasters.

29 Λαΐου, "Οθωμανοί Έλληνες," 229–30.

30 Suraiya Faroqhi, "Wealth and Power in the Land of Olives: Economic and Political Activities of Müridzade Hacı Mehmed Agha, Notable of Edremit," in *Making a Living in the Ottoman Lands, 1480–1820*, ed. Suraiya Faroqhi (Istanbul: The Isis Press, 1995), 297–317.

31 Suraiya Faroqhi, "Wealth and Power in the Land of Olives: Economic and Political Activities of Müridzade Hacı Mehmed Agha, Notable of Edremit," in *Making a Living in the Ottoman Lands, 1480–1820*, ed. Suraiya Faroqhi (Istanbul: The Isis Press, 1995), 313 and table 2.

32 Maria Christina Chatziioannou, "Introduction," in *On Merchants' Agency and Capitalism in the Eastern Mediterranean, 1774–1914*, ed. Maria Christina Chatziioannou (Istanbul: The ISIS Press, 2017), 22.

Bibliography

Anastassiadou, Meropi. *Salonique, 1830–1912. Une ville ottoman à l'âge des Réformes.* Leiden: Brill, 1997.

Chatziioannou, Maria Christina. *On Merchants' Agency and Capitalism in the Eastern Mediterranean, 1774–1914.* Istanbul: The ISIS Press, 2017.

Duzgun, Eren. "Property, Geopolitics, and Eurocentrism: The 'Great Divergence' and the Ottoman Empire." *Review of Radical Political Economics* 50, no. 1 (2018): 24–43.

Faroqhi, Suraiya. "Wealth and Power in the Land of Olives: Economic and Political Activities of Müridzade Hacı Mehmed Agha, Notable of Edremit." In *Making a Living in the Ottoman Lands, 1480–1820*, edited by Suraiya Faroqhi, 297–317. Istanbul: The ISIS Press, 1995.

Frank, Andre G. "The World Economic System in Asia Before European Hegemony." *Historian* 56, no. 2 (1993): 259–76.

Ginio, Eyal. "When Coffee Brought About Wealth and Prestige: The Impact of Egyptian Trade on Salonica." *Oriente Moderno* 25, no. 1 (2006): 93–107.

Hanna, Nelly. *Artisan Entrepreneurs in Cairo and Early-Modern Capitalism (1600–1800).* Syracuse, NY: Syracuse University Press, 2011.

Hanna, Nelly. "Artisans, Guilds, and Capitalist Development in Cairo, 1600–1800." In *Capitalisms. Towards a Global History*, edited by Kaveh Yazdani and Dilip M. Menon, 327–48. Oxford: Oxford University Press, 2020.

Kasaba, Reşat. *The Ottoman Empire and the World Economy. The Nineteenth Century.* New York: SUNY Press, 1988.

Kokdas, Irfan. "When the Countryside Is Free: Urban Politics, Local Autonomy and the Changing Social Structure in Ottoman Salonika, 1740–1820." PhD diss., Binghamton University, 2013.

Kotzageorgis, Phokion, and Dimitris Papastamatiou. "Wealth Accumulation in an Urban Context. The Profile of the Muslim Rich of Thessaloniki in the Eighteenth Century on the Basis of Probate Inventories." *Turkish Historical Review* 5 (2014): 165–99.

Laiou, Sophia. "The Ottoman Greek 'Merchants of Europe' at the Beginning of the 19th Century." In *Festschrift in Honor of Ioannis P. Theocharides. Studies on the Ottoman Empire and Turkey*, edited by Evangelia Balta, Georgios Salakidis, and Theoharis Stavrides, vol. II, 313–31. Istanbul: The ISIS Press, 2014.

McGowan, Bruce. "The Age of the Ayans, 1699–1812." In *An Economic and Social History of the Ottoman Empire, 1300–1914*, edited by Halil İnalcık and Donald Quataert, 724–42. Cambridge: Cambridge University Press, 1994.

Papastamatiou, Dimitris. *Wealth Distribution, Social Stratification and Material Culture in an Ottoman Metropolis. Thessaloniki According to the Probate Inventories of the Muslim Court (1761–1770).* Istanbul: The ISIS Press, 2017.

Svoronos, Nikos. *Le commerce de Salonique au XVIIIe siècle.* Paris: Presses Universitaires de France, 1956.

Βασδραβέλλης, Ιωάννης Κ. *Οι Μακεδόνες εις τους υπέρ της ανεξαρτησίας αγώνας 1796–1832.* 2nd ed. Θεσσαλονίκη: Εταιρεία Μακεδονικών Σπουδών, 1950. [Vasdravellis, Ioannis K. *The Macedonians in the Struggles for Their Independence, 1796–1832.* 2nd ed. Thessaloniki: Society for Macedonian Studies, 1950.]

Δημητριάδης, Βασίλης. *Η Θεσσαλονίκη της παρακμής. Η ελληνική κοινότητα της Θεσσαλονίκης κατά τη δεκαετία του 1830 με βάση ένα οθωμανικό κατάστιχο απογραφής του πληθυσμού.* Ηράκλειο: Πανεπιστημιακές Εκδόσεις Κρήτης, 1997. [Demetriades, Vassilis. *Thessaloniki of the Decline: The Greek Community of Thessaloniki During*

1830's According to an Ottoman Register of Population Census. Herakleion: Crete University Press, 1997.]

Κοτζαγεώργης, Φωκίων. "Ρωμιοί εκτελεσθέντες και φυγάδες στη Θεσσαλονίκη του 1821." *Μεσαιωνικά και Νεοελληνικά* 14 (2021): 163–87. [Kotzageorgis, Phokion. "Greek Ottomans Executed and Fugitives in Salonica in 1821." *Medievalia et Neohellenica* 14 (2021): 163–87.]

Λαΐου, Σοφία. "Οθωμανοί Έλληνες σαράφηδες στην Κωνσταντινούπολη του 1821." *Μεσαιωνικά και Νέα Ελληνικά* 14 (2021): 217–38. [Laiou, Sophia. "Ottoman Greek Sarrafs in Istanbul in 1821." *Medievalia et Neohellenica* 14 (2021): 217–38.]

Παπασταματίου, Δημήτρης, Κοτζαγεώργης, Φωκίων. *Στις παρυφές της Επανάστασης. Μια νέα προσέγγιση του αγώνα στην Χαλκιδική με βάση οθωμανικό τεκμηριακό υλικό*. Αθήνα: Εκδόσεις ΕΑΠ, 2021. [Papastamatiou, Dimitris, and Phokion Kotzageorgis. *On the Fringes of the Revolution: A New Approach to the Struggle in Halkidiki According to Ottoman Archival Material*. Athens: Hellenic Open University, 2021.]

Χεκίμογλου, Ευάγγελος. *Η ιστορία της επιχειρηματικότητας στη Θεσσαλονίκη*, vol. II/1: *Η οθωμανική περίοδος*. Θεσσαλονίκη: Πολιτιστική Εταιρεία Επιχειρηματιών Βορείου Ελλάδος, 2004. [Hekimoglou, Evanghelos. *The History of the Entrepreneurship in Thessaloniki,* vol. II/1: *The Ottoman Period.* Thessaloniki: Cultural Society of Entrepreneurs of Northern Greece, 2004.]

3 Ottoman Greek Entrepreneurs in Istanbul in the Early 1800s

Sophia Laiou

The Ottoman Trade, 1750s–1820s

The Ottoman economy in the 18th century passed through two different stages: from the economic development which lasted until the 1760s, induced by the absence of an internal political crisis after 1730 and the non-involvement in a military adventure in Europe (although the empire conducted wars in the East), to the recession that began during the war with Russia (1768–1774) and worsened in the following decades.[1] Nonetheless, the economic problems did not result in the decline of trade and consumption did not recede, especially in Istanbul and other large Ottoman cities.[2] Although the domestic and Eastern trade cannot be assessed, it is certain that, in the period under study, they both continued or even increased.[3] From the mid-18th century, trade with the West also grew.[4] The pattern of exchange between the Ottoman Empire and its Western trade partners consisted of the export of raw materials (cotton, wool, foodstuff, etc.) and the import of manufactured or semi-manufactured (textiles, metals, tools, paper), colonial (coffee, sugar), and luxurious or semi-luxurious goods (watches, furniture, glassware, porcelain cups, etc.).[5] The European merchants took advantage of the favorable status in the trade activity provided to them by the capitulations (*ahdnames*), which, although at first were intended to provide legal coverage to the non-Muslim foreigners who traded in the Ottoman territories, in the first decades of the 19th century became a tool for European economic and political control in the Eastern Mediterranean.[6] Moreover, the trade concessions encouraged the Ottoman Christian traders to avail themselves of the increased foreign competition and assume the role of the intermediary and broker with the European merchants. Those Ottoman Christians who had the economic means to acquire (buy) the "foreign protection" and become "*beratlı*," could trade under the same privileged conditions as their European counterparts.[7] The global rise of the price of grain along with the opening of the Black Sea to foreign navigation in 1783, combined with the rise of consumption in the large Ottoman cities, further encouraged the Ottoman Christians to become involved even more in the external trade with the West, either as Ottoman subjects or as *beratlıs*.[8] The Ottoman government, for its part, being influenced by the empire's military defeats since 1774, felt at the very least uncomfortable with the emerging European political and economic control of the Eastern Mediterranean, ever more

DOI: 10.4324/9781003500780-5

apparent through the foreign protection system. The Ottoman state responded by initiating in 1802 and applying in 1806 the system of the "Merchants of Europe," which provided the Ottoman Christians with the same trade privileges available under the capitulations. The government sought to control as many areas as possible in the external trade with Europe and so reimpose political and social control over its subjects.[9]

The abovementioned developments are usually analyzed on macro-economic terms, representing a stage of the gradual incorporation of the Ottoman economy into the global one, during which the Ottoman economy assumed a peripheral role in the global division of labor.[10] The incorporation theory views the economic development from the state's point of view. However, regardless of when and where the incorporation took place, the increase in trade multiplied the opportunities for enrichment for anyone who could invest in it or participate as an intermediary. Trade also created a number of other jobs to do with the transfer or the processing of commodities, enlarging thus the range of people who could benefit from the process. In this respect, a focus on human agency may reveal the internal economic and social dynamics in the Ottoman port cities, which participated in the external trade. I believe that the "long" 18th century witnessed not only some sort of diffusion of power from the center to the provinces through the Muslim and Christian notables but also a diffusion of wealth through tax farming and trade. In this chapter, I intend to discuss the activities of the wealthy Ottoman Greek[11] traders and entrepreneurs of Istanbul in the beginning of the 19th century and describe the sources of their wealth, their entrepreneurial strategies, and the institutional environment in which they traded. Before referring to the traders themselves, a discussion is necessary of the economic environment of the Ottoman capital in the 18th century.

The Ottoman Greek economic agency

Istanbul was not only the capital of an empire but also the main import port and consuming center.[12] The Ottoman capital faced various challenges throughout the 18th and the beginning of the 19th centuries of which probably the most significant was the population increase caused by the continuous arrivals of immigrants.[13] The nutritional and material needs of more than 400,000 inhabitants by the end of the 18th century,[14] permanent or not, as well as those of the Palace were covered by the numerous workshops and shops, and through the imports from the Ottoman provinces and abroad. In the ports of Istanbul proper and Galata, ships from the Ottoman ports, Egypt, the European ports, and the Black Sea were arriving on a daily basis. The same is true for the caravans carrying goods from the Balkans, Anatolia, and the East.

The Ottoman Greeks constituted the second population group after the Muslims in Istanbul. This estimation, however, due to the lack of population surveys in the 18th century, is based only on travelers' reports or information provided by contemporary Ottoman writers.[15] As a rough idea, in a survey of the adult men in Istanbul in 1826–1827, the Greeks amounted to 20,000, Muslims 45,000 and the Armenians 30,000.[16] In the 18th century, the Greeks mostly lived across the Golden Horn and the sea of Marmara, in Galata and Tatavla, as well as in the villages on the Bosporus. Some participated in the wholesale and Black Sea trade and had their businesses in the *hans* of Istanbul proper and Galata.[17] In an interesting French report regarding the trade conditions in Istanbul in the middle of the 18th century, the Greeks are described either as merchants or as members of the Phanariote circle. The French writer underlined the formers' involvement in cloth and textile trade and in the trade of Russian furs and skins and added that some of the Ottoman Greeks were bankers (*sarrafs*).[18] As far as the Greek sources are concerned, a few and occasional references in the Greek chronicles of the 18th century mention the big merchants ("πραγματευτές"), who supplied the sultanic harem and high Ottoman officials with luxurious items, on the occasion of their being executed and their property confiscated.[19] Thus, the Greek sources refer to the rare cases of merchants who had a business cooperation with the Sublime Porte, and not to the majority who participated in the Ottoman import trade and/or the capitals' retail trade. In this respect, apart from the rare information found in European sources,[20] for the Ottoman Greek traders, we possess no other concrete evidence regarding their activities, collaborations, and social status outside of the Ottoman sources. Despite the patchiness and fiscalist nature of most of the latter[21] and often the need to read between the lines or "look for a needle in the haystack," the Ottoman sources remain basically the only ones to elucidate the economic activities of the Greek merchants and entrepreneurs of the Ottoman capital.

The confiscated properties in 1821

Based on the above, I explore the economic activities of the Ottoman Greek big merchants and entrepreneurs of Istanbul, who often appear in the Ottoman sources as "*bazirgân*." The term denoted the substantial merchants: those who habitually endeavored in external and interregional trade, and often did not have a permanent basis (as opposed to the regular merchants, "*tüccar*"), but who yet possessed enough capital to invest in various enterprises.[22] Some also practiced other entrepreneurial activities such as banking (*sarraflık*) and, after 1806, participated in the group of the "Merchants of Europe" (*Avrupa Tüccarı*).

The chapter uses the confiscation registers (*muhallefat defterleri*). This kind of register was compiled by the Ottoman government whenever the property of an Ottoman official or subject was confiscated as punishment for an offense. In the spring of 1821, when the Greek war of independence broke out, the Ottoman state executed a number of Ottoman Greeks, who permanently resided or worked in the Ottoman capital, and confiscated their movable and immovable properties on the accusation of taking part in the rebellion against the Ottoman empire. It did the same with the properties of the Ottoman Greeks who managed to flee from the capital. Various registers were therefore compiled for the confiscated properties. In one of them, written on 15 October 1821 (18 Muharrem 1237),[23] the confiscated properties of 80 executed or fugitive Ottoman Greeks are included, consisting of houses, plots, warehouses, workshops, and shops with their possessions. Out of the 80, 36 people of different economic status were involved in the urban economy and the rest belonged mostly to the Phanariote elite (including the female relatives), and its retinue. Of the 36, 15 belonged to the group of "Merchants of Europe," two were *sarrafs*, five were guild members and four of them participated in textile manufacture and trade (*çuhacı, şalcı*), one was the "kalfa of merchants" ("*tüccar kalfası*") and two were greengrocers. For the rest, there is no professional identity given, but they are described as relatives of specific members of the list, as partners (Lukaki, partner of the big merchant Dimitri Skina), or—simply—as non-Muslims (*zimmis*). Considering that the properties were registered to be sold "to anyone who wanted to from the Muslims and the groups ('taifes') of the Armenians and Jews,"[24] the estimated value was included. Although this register does not include all the wealthy Ottoman Greek merchants and entrepreneurs in Istanbul at the specific period, it does provide a clear picture of the economic strength and also stratification within the Greek community, and the sources of wealth.

The value of the confiscated property of the 36 Ottoman Greeks amounted to 936, 955 piasters (kuruş) and corresponded to 60.2% of the total value of the properties included in the register.[25] The majority consisted of waterside residences in the villages of Bosporus and the quarter of Fener, houses, rooms (*oda*) in the *hans* and shops together with their possessions, tools and equipment (*gedik*),[26] as well as merchandize (*mülk*), and a few plots of land, including two land estates (*çiftliks*) in the nearby judicial districts (*kazas*).

In Table 3.1, which shows the classification of the properties based on their sum value, the large economic differentiation is apparent. The first ten Ottoman Greeks possessed 71% (670,725) of the confiscated property of the 36, consisting not only of houses but also of rooms (*oda*) in the commercial buildings, warehouses, and shops. They were merchants involved in the trade with Europe (Merchants of Europe) (including the cloth dealer), a *sarraf,* and a son of *sarraf*; even among them, big differences are detectable. Although the specific register does not include the loans and debts, another one includes this information for several executed or fugitive Ottoman Greeks in 1821.[27] Thus, we find that the wealthiest Ottoman Greek according to the confiscation register, Dimitri son of Apostolo papa, lent 69 people 934,736 piasters—an impressive sum of money that was provided over a long period of time. Most of the borrowers were Christian merchants from various Ottoman cities (Thessaloniki, Serres, Smyrna, etc.) and to a lesser degree Muslim members of the guild of tobacco pipe manufacturers (*çubukçu*) in the Ottoman capital.[28] It also appears that Dimitri participated in maritime trade by lending money to captains-cum-merchants. For instance, he lent captain Yanopoulo, under Russian protection, 31,442 piasters for "his share for the ship's papers and fare."[29] A part of his profits was invested in large, built (*kârgir*) "*konak*" in Tepebaşı quarter whose value was estimated to 71,000 piasters. In front of it, there were also a built house of 30,000 piasters and a newly built, unfinished "*konak*" of 25,000 piasters.[30] The recitation of the houses shows the gradual enrichment of their owner, who from a house moved to a *konak*, even as he started to build a new one.

Table 3.1 Names of the executed or fugitive Ottoman Greek merchants, bankers, and artisans, and the sum value of their confiscated properties.

Name	*Identity*	*Value in Piasters*
Dimitri son of Apostolo papa	AT*	146,000
Dimitri Skina	AT	121,675
Mavromati	AT	62,000
Dimitri Ralli	AT	60,000
Dimitraki Moralı	*sarraf*	58,750
Cira Antoni	Cloth dealer (*çuhacı*)	57,800
Komiano	Merchants' *kalfa*	50,250
Alexopoulo	AT	48,150
Bese Yorgi or Christopoulo	AT	35,100
Strati	Son of Skarlato *sarraf*	33,000
Yorgi Samata	AT	31,000
Mela Yorgi	AT	21,750
Kostaki	Son of Kotsin (Kotsinoğlu), AT	19,800
Savva	greengrocer	18,250
Anagnostis	AT, shawl trader (*şalcı*)	18,100
Douma		17,500
Mihail Silaver?	AT	16,850
Yanko son of Zarifi	AT	14,100
Tsorbatzioglu Asterio		13,700
Kyriaki	AT	12,000
Spyro son of Thanasis	AT	11,105
Haci Vasili	Member of the guild of the *sarrafs*	11,000
Oskoli	Fur merchant	10,000
no name	Member of the guild of silk manufacturers	8,000
Tabakopoulo	AT	7,800
Yorgo	Guild member	5,000
Lukaki	Partner of Dimitri Skina	5,000
Nikolaki	Son-of-law of Dimitri son of Apostolo papa	4,600
Yanni Kyriako	Relative of Bese Yorgi	4,000
Dimitri	Son-of-law of Dimitraki Moralı	3,500
Dimitraki	Son of Tzalik	3,000
Haci Apostolo	Member of the guild of tobacco sellers	2,500
Uzun Hristo	Greengrocer	2,350
Stefanos	Son of Antoni *çuhacı*	2,025
Tzortzi	Son of Pouli	800
Kostaki	Son of Skarlato *sarraf*	500

*AT: Avrupa Tüccarı, Merchants of Europe. Source: BOA, DBŞM.MHF.d. 1338.

It is also worth mentioning the case of Dimitri Skina, who appears as the second wealthiest Ottoman Greek. Most probably, he was related to the Phanariote family of Skina, coming from Thessaly and settled in the Ottoman capital in the beginning of the 18th century.[31] Dimitri Skina son of Dimos from Volos joined the group of the Merchants of Europe in 1806; until 1808, he was one of the two representatives of the group in the Sublime Porte, a position that shows his higher status among his colleagues. In 1802, he imported from Trieste cloth, household items, and metals, but under the Austrian protection.[32] Thus, by the beginning of the 19th century, Dimitri Skina was already a successful merchant, capable of acquiring the foreign protection, which he abandoned in 1806 when he embraced the state policy and became a "Merchant of Europe."[33] It is also interesting that apart from the cloth shop, Skina possessed the *gedik* of four "rooms" in the Valide *han*, and that, in two of them, there was also merchandize. The value of the "rooms" ranged between 2,525 and 10,500 piasters;[34] although there is no information as to their content, one can surmise that they could be used for storing imported commodities and/or they were workshops for processing the latter. The sale of imported goods to guild members for processing and the commissioning of certain products or even the participation in the guild (e.g., the guild of cloth dealers) must have been common practice, although the Ottoman sources are usually silent.[35] In this respect, Skinas must have acted both as a big merchant and the owner of workshops, who was involved in the production process.

The merchants listed above traded mostly luxurious and semi-luxurious textiles, aiming to meet the needs of the non-Muslim and Muslim elite of Istanbul. The registration of the confiscated commodities found in the "room" of the Merchant of Europe, Mavromati in the Valide *han* helps us to understand the range of commodities he and his colleagues traded: English wool, silk, and cotton (printed or not) textiles, belts made in Chios (*Sakızkârı kuşak*), furs and fur caps, fringes, etc., all valued 17,500 piasters.[36] However, the textile trade was not the main staple, since often merchants adjusted their orders according to the local demand, and, thus, they imported metals, nails, paper, skins, plates, and glassware or sold local products such as pipes, etc.[37] Some possessed warehouses such as the wealthy Merchants of Europe, Dimitri Ralli and Alexopoulo, who both owned such in the Havyar *Han* in Galata. Ralli possessed two warehouses, valued at 20,000 piasters, and Alexopoulos one, valued at 11,000 piasters.[38] As mentioned above, Galata was the destination port for the commodities arriving from Europe and the Black Sea. It seems that both merchants were involved in the import wholesale trade from these areas. For instance, we know that in 1802 Alexopoulos imported from Russia large quantities of iron (32,184 kantars) and caviar (35 barrels), but this time as a Russian "*beratlı*" ("Mosko").[39] It is noteworthy that both merchants owned expensive stone houses in the same area of Tatavla and both managed to save themselves from the persecutions in 1821 by fleeing the Ottoman capital.[40]

Firms, partnerships and credit

The establishment of trade firms was a standard procedure that helped to raise capital and reduce the business risk. The practice was followed not only by those involved in large enterprises but also by merchants who participated in small or modest ones.[41] The importers based in Istanbul were business partners with those who dispatched the commodities from the Ottoman provinces or abroad. In this framework, business association meant the participation in a commercial house with branches in the ports and cities from where commodities were imported, and whose members very often belonged to the same (extended) family or had a common origin.[42] On the contrary, merchants and artisans who were not involved in the import trade formed simple partnerships which did not result in establishing a commercial house. An example of such a partnership is the one formed between Dimitraki son of Tzalik (see Table 3.1), who was executed in March, and the son of Zafir (Zafiroğlu).[43] Dimitraki was a shawl merchant, as was his father, Tzalik,[44] and together with his partner owned a "room" in the Çuhacı *han*. The Ottoman authorities seized the commodities found in it and interrogated ("istintak olundığı vechehle") Zafiroğlu, presumably for hidden cash and assets. In the register compiled by the authorities, it is stated that the estimated value of the "things" ("eşya"), shawls, and other commodities was 200,000 piasters.[45] Together with the loans provided by the partners (320,920 piasters) and a small sum of money found in the "room" (5,349.5 piasters), the total sum amounted to 526,274.5 piasters. The debts owed by them (333,850 piasters) together with their invested capital (sermaye) amounted to 445,137 piasters. Thus, the net profit, including each partner's share, was 81,137.5 piasters. Dimitraki owned 33.3% and Zafiroğlu 66.6% of the firm: it may be assumed that Dimitraki provided—along with the cash—the space, the work and probably part of the clientele inherited by his father, and Zafiroğlu the largest part of the capital for the purchase of the textiles.[46] In light of the aforementioned, the partnership was based on a contract, most probably written in Greek, and their shares were unequal. This kind of partnership must have been quite common in the early 1800s.

Although the Islamic law provided a solid legal framework for the establishment of the commercial firms,[47] the non-Muslim Ottoman merchants and artisans had also the possibility of establishing them on the basis of a private—that is, unofficial—agreement, according to Byzantine and customary law.[48] In the Ottoman capital, the presence of the Patriarchal court and Synod provided a significant alternative venue for the Orthodox partners who wanted to establish or dissolve a business partnership.[49] If the Ottoman-Greek partners had foreign protection, they were subject to the foreign law, unless they wished to have recourse to the Ottoman court of law.[50] In light of the aforementioned, the possibility of having access to a system different from the state-official legal one by which to establish a commercial firm provided the Ottoman Orthodox merchants flexibility, which the Ottoman Muslims did not have. On the other hand, this does not mean that non-Muslim Ottomans did not make recourse to the Ottoman courts for business matters. In fact, they did, either to solve disputes regarding the payment of shares between partners or to dissolve partnerships and declare the repayment of all debts. Pending new evidence, however, there were not among them those who participated in big, international commercial firms.

The institutional framework is an important factor in economic development. In this respect, there has been much talk about the impediments raised by the specific stipulations of the Islamic law regarding commercial firms: they did not have a legal personhood, the firms were established for one trade mission only, and in case of death, it was not possible for one member to inherit the whole or the largest part of a commercial firm.[51] With the exception of the length of a commercial firm, which could be extended,[52] the other two stipulations were inflexible because they were part of the Islamic law. Nonetheless, the ease of finding or dissolving a commercial firm with an oral agreement may have enabled merchants and artisans to overcome these problems.[53]

The funding of the economic activities required access to credit networks. Here, Islamic law did not impose any impediments since the well-known prohibition of interest was silently overlooked or circumvented through legal devices.[54] Apart from the *sarrafs*, who financed the financial enterprises of the Ottoman officials and entrepreneurs, interest-bearing loans and bills of exchange were standard means of cash circulation among merchants and artisans. The analysis of the list of debtors and creditors of various entrepreneurs reveals their financial networks and contacts and their possible investments in other enterprises. For instance, the aforementioned Dimitri son of Apostolo papa financed mostly Ottoman Christian merchants in Istanbul and other Ottoman cities and, to a lesser degree, guilds and Ottoman Muslims. Although there is no reference to the interest, it is certain that all the sums included it, or the latter would be paid separately under a private agreement.

Conclusions

In light of the aforementioned, several remarks can be made. First, some of the Ottoman Greek big merchants and entrepreneurs were involved only in the textile trade. However, specialization was not always the norm and merchants adapted their activities according to the local demands. Notably, this conclusion is based not only on the aforementioned confiscation registers but also on the Istanbul customs registers of the late 18th and beginning of the 19th century, where the same merchants imported textiles together with metals or glassware.

Second, these people invested in various commercial and/or maritime enterprises mainly through loan-giving and thus diversified their portfolios to multiply the possible sources of income and at the same time minimize the business risk. The continuous cash circulation through moneylending, the investments in various enterprises and the diversification of the business portfolio, the taking advantage of the opportunities of the legal pluralism as foreign subjects and later of the benefits they enjoyed as Merchants of Europe were the main strategies employed by the Ottoman Greek merchants and entrepreneurs. Indeed, certain Ottoman Greek entrepreneurs managed to accumulate considerable wealth, and it is not a surprise that the wealthier were "Merchants of Europe," that is they participated in the foreign trade.

Third, the commercial and entrepreneurial activity took place in a political and economic environment which encouraged long-distance trade and the import of a large variety of qualified and cheap products, especially into the Ottoman capital where the consumption needs of the Palace, the elites, and the increasing population were demanding. In fact, as Genç showed, what characterized the Ottoman commercial policy was the priority placed on providing for the needs of the consumers in general, by letting the imports enter free, contrary to the occasional state interventions in exports. The principle of "provizionism" was accompanied by the policy of revenue increase (fiscalism) and the need to maintain the social and economic balance ("traditionalism").[55] Of the three principles, Genç considered the first one as the most important.[56]Although aspects of Genç's theory have been criticized,[57] there is no objection raised to the importance of provisionism, at least for Istanbul and other large cities. The Ottoman state let the international trade run free, anticipating a rise in the customs-generated income and intervening only in case of a declaration of war. It is evident that the emphasis was on the consumer and not the merchant or artisan. By the same token, the state was not interested in ensuring any reciprocity for the Ottoman traders, who were active in the economically powerful foreign states that enjoyed capitulations (namely, France, Britain, and the Dutch). It intervened only when the traders themselves asked for the Ottoman state's intervention.[58]

In this respect, the Ottoman Greek traders who participated in the external trade and did not have any business relation with the state itself or its officials[59] were free to act, as long as they paid their duties, did not profiteer, and their activities did not threaten the traditional political and social hierarchy. This kind of indifference under certain circumstances could become a favorable one.[60] The emphasis, however, on the maintenance of the socio-political order, meaning the allegiance of the Ottoman Greeks to the Ottoman political domination and the acknowledgment of the Ottoman Muslims' superiority, could set political impediments to their economic activities, as it did not allow their access to political power if and when they wished so, and, above all, it increased the insecurity. The persecutions against the wealthy Ottoman Greek entrepreneurs of Istanbul that followed the eruption of the Greek revolution were intended to underline the social and political boundaries between Ottoman Muslims and non-Muslims.

Archives

Başbakanlık Osmanlı Arşivi (BOA), Istanbul, Turkey
D.BŞM.MHF.d 1338, 13342, 13612
Y.B.4.119
D.BŞM.d.07038
Tarih-i Lütfi [Lütfi's History], I. Istanbul: Ottoman Printing House, 1874.

Notes

1 Mehmet Genç, "L' Économie Ottomane et la guerre au XVIIIe siècle," *Turcica* 27 (1995): 177–96; Şevket Pamuk, "The Ottoman Empire in the Eighteenth Century," *Itinerario* 24, no. 3–4 (2000): 111–12.

2 Suraiya Faroqhi, "Research on the History of the Ottoman Consumption: A Preliminary Exploration of Sources and Models," in *Consumption Studies and the History of the Ottoman Empire, 1550–1922*, ed. Donald Quataert (New York: State University of New York Press, 2000), 24.

3 Edhem Eldem, "Capitulations and the Western Trade," in *The Cambridge History of Turkey*, ed. Suraiya Faroqhi, vol. 3 (Cambridge: Cambridge University Press, 2006), 285–86.
4 Mehmet Genç, "A Study of the Feasibility of Using Eighteenth-Century Ottoman Financial Records as an Indicator of Economic Activity," in *The Ottoman Empire and the World Economy*, ed. Huri İslamoğlu-İnan (Cambridge: Cambridge University Press, 1987), 358–59.
5 Bruce McGowan, "The Age of the Ayans-Trade," in *An Economic and Social History of the Ottoman Empire*, ed. Halil İnalcık and Donald Quataert, vol. II (Cambridge: Cambridge University Press, 1994), 725.
6 Eldem, "Capitulations and the Western Trade," 294; Reşat Kasaba, *The Ottoman Empire and the World Economy: The Nineteenth Century* (New York: Suny Press, 1988), 32–4.
7 Cihan Artunç, "The Price of Legal Institutions: The Beratlı Merchants in the Eighteenth-Century Ottoman Empire," *The Journal of Economic History* 75, no. 3 (2015): 720–48.
8 Kasaba, *The Ottoman Empire and the World Economy*, 18.
9 Sophia Laiou, "The Ottoman Greek "Merchants of Europe' at the Beginning of the 19th Century," in *Festshrift in Honor of Ioannis Theocharides Studies of the Ottoman Empire and Turkey*, ed. Evangelia Balta, Georgios Salakidis, and Theoharis Stavrides, vol. II (Istanbul: The ISIS Press, 2014), 313–31; Bruce Masters, "The Sultan's Entrepreneurs: The Avrupa tüccaris and the Hayriye tüccaris in Syria," *International Journal of Middle East Studies* 24, no. 4 (1992): 579–97.
10 Immanuel Wallerstein, Hale Decdeli, and Reşat Kasaba, "The Incorporation of the Ottoman Empire into the World-Economy," in *The Ottoman Empire and the World-Economy*, ed. Huri İslamoğlu-İnan (Cambridge: Cambridge University Press, 1987), 88–100; Murat Çizakça, "Incorporation of the Middle East into the European World Economy," *Review* 8, no. 3 (1985): 353–78. The latter argues that the incorporation began in the second half of the 16th century, that there was a recovery of the Ottoman economy in the late 17th and 18th century, and that the process was completed in the 19th century (Ibid., 371–374). The incorporation theory was recently criticized—at least for the 18th century—not as to the actual fact of the integration, but as to its long-term results for the Ottoman economy, namely the peripheralization, Nelly Hanna, *Artisan Entrepreneurs in Cairo and Early Modern Capitalism (1600–1800)* (Syracuse and New York: Syracuse University Press, 2011), 7; Eldem, "Capitulations and the Western Trade," 305–6.
11 By Ottoman Greeks, I mean the Greek-speaking Orthodox subjects.
12 Edhem Eldem, *French Trade in Istanbul in the 18th Century* (Leiden: Brill, 1999), 23–25; Edhem Eldem, "From Imperial to Peripheralized Capital," in *The Ottoman City Between East and West*, ed. Edhem Eldem et al. (Cambridge: Cambridge University Press, 1999), 162–63.
13 Betül Başaran and Cengiz Kırlı, "Some Observations on Istanbul's Artisans During the Reign of Selim III (1789–1807)," in *Bread from the Lion's Mouth: Artisans Struggling for a Livelihood in Ottoman Cities*, ed. Suraiya Faroqhi (New York and Oxford: Berghahn Books, 2015), 259–77.
14 According to William Eton, by the end of the 18th century the population was 426,000 of whom the permanent inhabitants were around 300,000. William Eton, *A Survey of the Turkish Empire* (London: Printed for T. Cadell, Jun. and W. Davies, 1798), 282.
15 Alexandros Gika, of Phanariot origin, estimated that among "the Greeks, Armenians and Jews . . . the Greeks are the most numerous," Elias Habesci, *The Present State of the Ottoman Empire* (London: K Baldwin, 1784), 364. The same opinion is expressed by the traveler James Dallaway, *Constantinople Ancient and Modern with Excursions to the Shores and Islands of the Archipelago and to the Troad* (London: T. Bensley, T. Cadell, Junr. & W. Davies, 1797), 15–16. The Armenian İnciciyan, who was born in Istanbul, reported that there were approximately 100,000 Christians, including "Rum" and Armenians, Ğugas İnciciyan, *XVIII aslında İstanbul* [Istanbul in the 18th Century], 2nd ed. (Istanbul: Baha Matbaası, 1976), 19.

16 *Tarih-i Lütfi* [Lütfi's History], vol. I (Istanbul: Ottoman Printing House, 1874), 279. The survey took place after the massacres and executions of Ottoman Greeks in 1821 due to the Greek rebellion.
17 Sophia Laiou, "The Ottoman State and the Black Sea Trade, End of the Eighteenth-Beginning of the Nineteenth Century," in *Istanbul and the Black Sea Coast*, ed. Edhem Eldem and Sophia Laiou (Istanbul: The ISIS Press, 2018), 21–26.
18 The report is published by Eldem, "From Imperial to Peripheralized Capital," 158–60, who described it as "a treatise on 'commercial anthropology' (160).
19 Αθανάσιος Κομνηνός Υψηλάντης, *Τα μετά την Άλωσιν*, ed. Αρχιμανδρίτης Γερμανός Αφθονίδου Σιναΐτου (Κωνσταντινούπολη, 1870); Καισάριου Δαπόντε Σκοπελίτου, "Κατάλογος Ιστορικός [Historical Catalogue]," *Μεσαιωνική Βιβλιοθήκη Κ. Σαθά*, vol. 3 (Βενετία, 1872); Σέργιου Μακραίου, "Υπομνήματα εκκλησιαστικής ιστορίας (1750–1800) [Memoranda of Ecclesiastic History]," *Μεσαιωνική Βιβλιοθήκη Κ. Σαθά*, vol. 3 (Βενετία, 1872). They all refer to Dimitri Skanavi from the island of Chios (see also the paper of Ertan Ünlü in this volume).
20 See Eldem, *French Trade*, passim.
21 Eldem, "Capitulations and Western Trade," 287–89, where he compares the European and Ottoman sources for the trade activities.
22 Halil İnalcık, "Capital Formation in the Ottoman Empire," *The Journal of Economic History* 29, no. 1 (1969): 98.
23 BOA, D.BŞM.MHF d.1338.
24 ". . . ehl-i İslâm ve Ermeni ve Yahud taifelerinden her kim talib olur ise füruht olunmak içün," BOA, D.BŞM.MHF d.1338, 2.
25 The total value amounted to 1,556,695 piasters.
26 In the 18th century, "*gedik*" meant the license to practice a trade and also the tools, equipment, the raw materials in a workshop; see Suraiya Faroqhi, *Artisans of Empire: Crafts and Craftspeople Under the Ottomans* (London: Bloomsbury Publishing, 2012), 119.
27 BOA, Y.B.4.119.
28 The same Dimitris son of Apostolos papa was registered as fugitive in a similar register compiled by the Ottoman authorities in Thessaloniki. There he appears as the lender of 50,207 piasters, which the state endeavored to claim it from the borrowers; see Φωκίων Κοτζαγεώργης, "Ρωμιοί εκτελεσθέντες και φυγάδες στη Θεσσαλονίκη του 1821 [Executed and Fugitive Rums in Thessaloniki of 1821]," *Μεσαιωνικά και Νεοελληνικά* 14 (2021): 177.
29 BOA, Y.B.4.119, 138: "Rusya tüccarından kapudan Yorği Yanopulo tacirin gemi sened ve navlosundan hissesi ğuruş 31,442."
30 BOA, D.BŞM.MHF d.1338, 19. Dimitris also possessed a smaller seaside house in Büyükdere of 20,000 piasters value. Ibid., 3.
31 Eugéne Rizo-Rangabé, *Livre d'or de la noblesse phanariote en Grèce, en Roumanie, en Russie, en Turquie* (Athenes: S. C. Vlastos, 1892), 123–24.
32 D.BŞM.d.7038, 2, 9, 10.
33 His relation to the Phanariote family of Skina may have influenced his decision.
34 BOA, D.BŞM.MHF.d.13338, 26. They were all sold to the Commodities Customs' Supervisor (Emtıa Gümrük Emini) Seyyid Ahmed Ağa.
35 Peter Gran has referred to the "managerial and administrative function in relation to guild labour and day labour" of the Egyptian merchants in the late 18th century; see Peter Gran, "Late Eighteenth-Early Nineteenth Century Egypt: Merchant Capitalism or Modern Capitalism?" in *The Ottoman Empire and the World Economy*, ed. Huri Islamoglu-Inan (Cambridge: Cambridge University Press, 1987), 28, 30–1. For the putting-out system, see also Eugenia Davidova, *Balkan Transitions to Modernity and Nation-States* (Leiden and Boston: Brill, 2013), 23–9; Amanda Philipps, *Sea Change: Ottoman Textiles Between the Mediterranean and the Indian Ocean* (Oakland: University of California Press, 2021), 135, 137. Dimitris Skanavis from Chios was a member

(or even the head?) of the cloth-dealers guild and at the same time he was characterized as big merchant (*bazirgân*) and *sarraf.*

36 BOA, D.BŞM.MHF.d.13342, 5–6. There were also items such as a silver candlestick, pipes, a silver spoon and a fork, which could have been used by the merchant himself. Notably, the estimated value of his household possessions, found in the house in Fener, was 5,000 piasters. Ibid., 4–5.

37 For example, in the room of the Merchant of Europe Kostaki Kotsinoğlu in the *han* of Astarcılar, were found several types of textiles together with three pipes with mouth-pieces made from amber (*kehribar ağızlıklı çibuk*), 30 white plates, and one prayer beads (*tesbih*), BOA, D.BŞM.MHF.d.13342, 10.

38 BOA, D.BŞM.MHF.d.13338, 25.

39 BOA, D.BŞM.d.07038, 14.

40 BOA, D.BŞM.MHF.d.13338, 19,20. Alexopoulos' house was valued at 37,150 and Dimitri Rallis' at 40,000 piasters.

41 According to Yi, partnership "was quite common among the guildsmen" of the 17th century Istanbul, see Eunjeong Yi, *Guild Dynamics in Seventeenth-Century Istanbul* (Leiden and Boston: Brill, 2004), 98.

42 See Despoina Vlami and Ikaros Mandouvalos, "Entrepreneurial Forms and Processes Inside a Multiethnic Precapitalist Environment: Greek and British Enterprises in the Levant (1740s–1820s)," *Business History* 55, no. 1 (2013): 98–118; Maria Christina Chatziioannou, "Creating the Pre-Industrial Ottoman-Greek Merchant: Sources, Methods and Interpretation," in *On Merchants' Agency and Capitalism in the Eastern Mediterranean 1774–1914* (Istanbul: The ISIS Press, 2017), 37–8.

43 BOA, DBŞM.MHF.d. 13612. It consists of only one page. Mihail D. Sturdza, *Grandes Familles de Grèce d'Albanie et de Cosntantinople*, 2nd ed. (Paris, 1999), 152, mentions the four Zamfiropoulo or Zafiropoulo brothers from Jannena who settled in Istanbul in the late 18th century and became traders.

44 The profession of Tzalik is mentioned in the confiscation register, DBŞM.MHF.d. 1338, 2, where the name of Nikolaki "son of the shawl trader Tzalik" is also included (Şalcı Calik oğlu olub Boğdan voyvodası yanında olan Nikolaki'nin . . ."). In contemporary Greek sources that cite the names of the Greeks who were executed, Dimitraki is characterized as merchant ("πραγματευτής"), whom the Ottomans accused of wanting to become the Chief Admiral, see Unknown Author, "Χειρόγραφο του 1821 έτους [Manuscript of the Year 1821]," *Πανδώρα* (1864): 200. The accusation was based on the plan of the secret association Philiki Etaireia, which apparently was made known to the Ottoman authorities, to establish the Greek power in the Ottoman capital in 1821. Regardless of the plan, however, the fact that Dimitraki's brother, Nikolakis, was "close to the voyvoda of Moldavia" made Dimitraki guilty of interfering in the Greek revolution.

45 All the belongings and commodities together with the cash found in the room were transferred to the imperial treasury, BOA, DBŞM.MHF.d. 13612, 2.

46 Dimitraki had invested 31.287 and his share from the profits ("faizinden hissesi") according to the contract ("ber müceb-i mukavele") amounted to 27,046.7 piasters. Zafiroğlu's capital was 80,000 piasters and his share 54,090.13 piasters.

47 Murat Çizakça, *A Comparative Evolution of Business Partnerships* (Leiden: Brill, 1996), 3–9.

48 Γεώργιος Ροδολάκης, "Εμπορικές εταιρείες στην Ύδρα 1792–1820 [Commercial Companies in Hydra 1792–1820]," *Επετηρίς του Κέντρου Ερεύνης της Ιστορίας του Ελληνικού Δικαίου* 27–28 (1980–1981): 679. Customary law was a combination of the Byzantine law and the established commercial practices in the Eastern Mediterranean in the medieval and modern period; see Ροδολάκης, "Εμπορικές Εταιρείες," 685. The French Commercial Code of 1807 must have affected the establishment of the commercial firms by the Ottoman Greeks. Ibid.

49 For the expansion of the ecclesiastic judicial authority to the civil-law cases in the second half of the 18th century, see Eugenia Kermeli, "The Right to Choice: Ottoman Justice vis-à-vis Ecclesiastical and Communal Justice in the Balkans Seventeenth-Nineteenth Centuries," in *Studies in Islamic Law: A Festschrift for Colin Imber*, ed. Andreas Christmann and Robert Gleave (Oxford: Oxford University Press, 2007), 182.
50 Maurits Van Boogert, *The Capitulations and the Ottoman Legal System* (Leiden: Brill, 2005), 34–42.
51 Timur Kuran, *The Long Divergence: How Islamic Law Held Back the Middle East* (Princeton, NJ: Princeton University Press, 2011), 61, 64, 66; Artunç, "The Price of Legal Institutions," 737–38.
52 See Çizakça, *A Comparative Evolution*, 79, 81, where he cites examples of partnerships established under Islamic law that lasted for several years.
53 Yi, *Guild Dynamics*, 95; Kuran, *The Long Divergence*, 281.
54 Pamuk, "The Ottoman Empire," 106.
55 Mehmet Genç, *Osmanlı İmparatorluğu'nda Devlet ve Ekonomi* [State and Economy in the Ottoman Empire] (Istanbul: Ötüken Neşriyat, 2000), 41–63.
56 Mehmet Genç, *Osmanlı İmparatorluğu'nda Devlet ve Ekonomi* [State and Economy in the Ottoman Empire] (Istanbul: Ötüken Neşriyat, 2000), 76.
57 Eldem, "From Imperial to Peripheralized Capital," 141; Hanna, *Artisan Entrepreneurs*, 10.
58 İsmail Hakkı Kadı, *Ottoman and Dutch Merchants in the 18th Century* (Leiden: Brill, 2012), 20–21, 168, 295–98. On the contrary, the capitulations provided to the subjects of the Kingdom of the Two Sicilies (1740), of Denmark (1757), Prussia (1761), and Russia (1783) included articles concerning the reciprocity; see Mehmet Demiryürek, "The Legal Foundations of the Commercial Relations Between The Ottomans and Neapolitans," *Bilig* 69 (2014): 61.
59 In these cases, the chances for wealth accumulation were better, but the post-mortem confiscation of the property was very probable following an accusation or the fact that the merchants got rich through the state's offices or needs. See Fatma Möge Göçek, *Rise of the Bourgoisie, Demise of the Empire: Ottoman Westernization and Social Change* (New York and Oxford: Oxford University Press, 1996), 92.
60 "They (merchants) certainly could not declare " 'l'état c'est moi' but they could plausibly claim, during the best of times, 'l'état n'est pas contre moi,'" Şevket Pamuk, *Uneven Centuries: The Economic Development of Turkey Since 1820* (Princeton, NJ and Oxford: Princeton University Press, 2018), 76.

Bibliography

Artunç, Cihan. "The Price of Legal Institutions: The Beratlı Merchants in the Eighteenth-Century Ottoman Empire." *The Journal of Economic History* 75, no. 3 (2015): 720–48.

Başaran, Betül, and Cengiz Kırlı. "Some Observations on Istanbul's Artisans During the Reign of Selim III (1789–1807)." In *Bread from the Lion's Mouth. Artisans Struggling for a Livelihood in Ottoman Cities*, edited by Suraiya Faroqhi, 259–77. New York and Oxford: Berghahn Books, 2015.

Chatziioannou, Maria Christina. *On Merchants' Agency and Capitalism in the Eastern Mediterranean 1774–1914*. Istanbul: The ISIS Press, 2017.

Çizakça, Murat. "Incorporation of the Middle East into the European World Economy." *Review* 8, no. 3 (1985): 353–78.

Çizakça, Murat. *A Comparative Evolution of Business Partnerships*. Leiden: Brill, 1996.

Dallaway, James. *Constantinople Ancient and Modern with Excursions to the Shores and Islands of the Archipelago and to the Troad.* London: T. Bensley, T. Cadell, Junr. & W. Davies, 1797.

Davidova, Eugenia. *Balkan Transitions to Modernity and Nation-States*. Leiden and Boston: Brill, 2013.

Demiryürek, Mehmet. "The Legal Foundations of the Commercial Relations between the Ottomans and Neapolitans." *Bilig* 69 (2014): 53–74.

Eldem, Edhem. *French Trade in Istanbul in the 18th Century*. Leiden: Brill, 1999a.

Eldem, Edhem. "From Imperial to Peripheralized Capital." In *The Ottoman City between East and West*, edited by Edhem Eldem, Daniel Goffman, and Bruce Alan Masters, 135–206. Cambridge: Cambridge University Press, 1999b.

Eldem, Edhem. "Capitulations and the Western Trade." In *The Cambridge History of Turkey*, edited by Suraiya Faroqhi, vol. 3, 283–335. Cambridge: Cambridge University Press, 2006.

Eton, William. *A Survey of the Turkish Empire*. London: Printed for T. Cadell, jun. and W. Davies, 1798.

Faroqhi, Suraiya. "Research on the History of the Ottoman Consumption: A Preliminary Exploration of Sources and Models." In *Consumption Studies and the History of the Ottoman Empire, 1550–1922*, edited by Quataert Donald, 15–44. New York: State University of New York Press, 2000.

Faroqhi, Suraiya. *Artisans of Empire. Crafts and Craftspeople under the Ottomans*. London: Bloomsbury Publishing, 2012.

Genç, Mehmet. "A Study of the Feasibility of Using Eighteenth-Century Ottoman Financial Records as an Indicator of Economic Activity." In *The Ottoman Empire and the World Economy*, edited by Huri İslamoğlu-İnan, 345–73. Cambridge: Cambridge University Press, 1987.

Genç, Mehmet. "L' Économie Ottomane et la guerre au XVIIIe siècle." *Turcica* 27 (1995): 177–96.

Genç, Mehmet. *Osmanlı İmparatorluğu'nda Devlet ve Ekonomi [State and Economy in the Ottoman Empire]*. Istanbul: Ötüken Neşriyat, 2000.

Göçek, Fatma Möge. *Rise of the Bourgoisie, Demise of the Empire: Ottoman Westernization and Social Change*. New York and Oxford: Oxford University Press, 1996.

Gran, Peter. "Late Eighteenth-Early Nineteenth Century Egypt: Merchant Capitalism or Modern Capitalism?" In *The Ottoman Empire and the World Economy*, edited by Huri Islamoglu-Inan, 27–41. Cambridge: Cambridge University Press, 1987.

Habesci, Elias. *The Present State of the Ottoman Empire*. London: K Baldwin, 1784.

Hanna, Nelly. *Artisan Entrepreneurs in Cairo and Early Modern Capitalism (1600–1800)*. Syracuse, NY: Syracuse University Press, 2011.

İnalcık, Halil. "Capital Formation in the Ottoman Empire." *The Journal of Economic History* 29, no. 1 (1969): 97–140.

İnciciyan, Ğugas. *XVIII aslında İstanbul [Istanbul in the 18th Century]*. 2nd ed. Istanbul: Baha Matbaası, 1976.

Kadı, İsmail Hakkı. *Ottoman and Dutch Merchants in the 18th Century*. Leiden: Brill, 2012.

Kasaba, Reşat. *The Ottoman Empire and the World Economy. The Nineteenth Century*. New York: Suny Press, 1988.

Kermeli, Eugenia. "The Right to Choice: Ottoman Justice vis-à-vis Ecclesiastical and Communal Justice in the Balkans Seventeenth–Nineteenth Centuries." In *Studies in Islamic Law: A Festschrift for Colin Imber*, edited by Andreas Christmann and Robert Gleave, 165–211. Oxford: Oxford University Press, 2007.

Kuran, Timur. *The Long Divergence. How Islamic Law Held Back the Middle East*. Princeton, NJ: Princeton University Press, 2011.

Laiou, Sophia. "The Ottoman Greek 'Merchants of Europe' at the Beginning of the 19th Century." In *Festschrift in Honor of Ioannis Theocharides Studies of the Ottoman Empire and Turkey*, edited by Evangelia Balta, Georgios Salakidis, and Theoharis Stavrides, vol. II, 313–31. Istanbul: The ISIS Press, 2014.

Laiou, Sophia. "The Ottoman State and the Black Sea Trade, End of the Eighteenth-Beginning of the Nineteenth Century." In *Istanbul and the Black Sea Coast*, edited by Edhem Eldem and Sophia Laiou, 15–26. Istanbul: The ISIS Press, 2018.

Masters, Bruce. "The Sultan's Entrepreneurs: The Avrupa tüccaris and the Hayriye tüccaris in Syria." *International Journal of Middle East Studies* 24, no. 4 (1992): 579–97.

McGowan, Bruce. "The Age of the Ayans-Trade." In *An Economic and Social History of the Ottoman Empire*, edited by Halil İnalcık and Donald Quataert, vol. II, 724–42 Cambridge: Cambridge University Press, 1994.

Pamuk, Şevket. "The Ottoman Empire in the Eighteenth Century." *Itinerario* 24, no. 3–4 (2000): 111–12.

Pamuk, Şevket. *Uneven Centuries. The Economic Development of Turkey since 1820.* Princeton and Oxford: Princeton University Press, 2018.

Philipps, Amanda. *Sea Change: Ottoman Textiles Between the Mediterranean and the Indian Ocean.* Oakland: University of California Press, 2021.

Rizo-Rangabé, Eugéne. *Livre d'or de la noblesse phanariote en Grèce, en Roumanie, en Russie, en Turquie*. Athenes: S. C. Vlastos, 1892.

Sturdza, Mihail D. *Grandes Familles de Grèce d'Albanie et de Cosntantinople*. 2nd ed. Paris: chez l'auteur, 1999.

Van Boogert, Maurits. *The Capitulations and the Ottoman Legal System*. Leiden: Brill, 2005.

Vlami, Despoina, and Ikaros Mandouvalos. "Entrepreneurial Forms and Processes Inside a Multiethnic Precapitalist Environment: Greek and British Enterprises in the Levant (1740s–1820s)." *Business History* 55, no. 1 (2013): 98–118.

Wallerstein, Immanuel, Hale Decdeli, and Reşat Kasaba. "The Incorporation of the Ottoman Empire into the World-Economy." In *The Ottoman Empire and the World-Economy*, edited by Huri İslamoğlu-İnan, 88–100. Cambridge: Cambridge University Press, 1987.

Yi, Eunjeong. *Guild Dynamics in Seventeenth-Century Istanbul.* Leiden and Boston: Brill, 2004.

Αγνώστου συγγραφέα. "Χειρόγραφο του 1821 έτους." *Πανδώρα* (1864): 200. [Unkown Author. "Manuscript of the Year 1821." *Pandora* (1864): 200.]

Δαπόντε, Καισάριου Σκοπελίτου. "Κατάλογος Ιστορικός." *Μεσαιωνική Βιβλιοθήκη Κ. Σαθά*, vol. 3. Βενετία, 1872. [Daponte, Kaisariou Skopelitou. "Historical Catalogue." In *Medieval Library of K. Satha*, vol. 3. Venice, 1872.]

Κομνηνός Υψηλάντης, Αθανάσιος. *Τα μετά την Άλωσιν*, edited by Αρχιμανδρίτης Γερμανός Αφθονίδου Σιναΐτου. Κωνσταντινούπολη, 1870. [Komninos Ypsilantis, Athanasios. *After the Conquest*, edited by Archbishop Germanos Afthonidou Sinaitou. Istanbul, 1870.]

Κοτζαγεώργης, Φωκίων. "Ρωμιοί εκτελεσθέντες και φυγάδες στη Θεσσαλονίκη του 1821." *Μεσαιωνικά και Νεοελληνικά* 14 (2021): 163–87. [Kotzageorgis, Phokion. "Greek Ottomans Executed and Fugitives in Salonica in 1821." *Medievalia et Neohellenica* 14 (2021): 163–87.]

Μακραίου, Σέργιου. "Υπομνήματα εκκλησιαστικής ιστορίας (1750–1800)." Μεσαιωνική Βιβλιοθήκη Κ. Σαθά, vol. 3. Βενετία, 1872. [Makraiou, Sergiou. "Memoranda of Ecclesiastic History." In *Medieval Library of K. Satha*, vol. 3. Venice, 1872.]

Ροδολάκης, Γεώργιος. "Εμπορικές εταιρείες στην Ύδρα 1792–1820." *Επετηρίς του Κέντρου Ερεύνης της Ιστορίας του Ελληνικού Δικαίου* 27–28 (1980–1981): 673–98. [Rodolakis, Georgios. "Commercial Companies in Hydra 1792–1820." *Yearbook of Research Centre for the History of Greek Law* 27–28 (1980–1981): 673–98.]

4 Wealth Accumulation and Investment Methods of Sarrafs (Moneychangers) in 18th–Century Istanbul

Ertan Ünlü

Introduction

The Ottoman political economy of the early modern period, characterized by the principles of provisionism, fiscalism, and traditionalism, did not have a capitalist mentality aimed at the accumulation of unlimited capital. Therefore, a bourgeois class like that in Western Europe did not emerge in the Ottoman Empire until the mid-19th century. The control that the Ottoman Empire exercised over the production and distribution systems through mechanisms such as hisba and confiscation played a role in this. This pragmatically flexible control was also selectively applied to the commercial and financial sectors, which were significant investment areas for capital formation. The reason for the exercise of the control was that the sectors concerned were regarded as a kind of public service for the purpose of funding public finances. In this respect, it was difficult, if not impossible, to raise significant capital in the early modern Ottoman world: the state had somehow confiscated this capital through its interventions. However, despite these interventions merchants and sarrafs (moneychangers) were the only capitalist entrepreneurs in the early modern Ottoman economic order, the so-called proto-bourgeoisie.[1]

This paper focuses on the sarrafs, one species of capitalist entrepreneurs in the Ottoman world, and discusses their method of wealth acquisition and investment. The aim is to understand how sarrafs became rich and what investment instruments they used to maintain their wealth. The focus is on the 18th century, a period of both continuity and transformation for the Ottoman Empire. This was a period of growth that offered significant economic opportunities and was the golden age of the Ottoman sarrafs.

It is not possible here to discuss in detail the full range of methods of wealth acquisition and investment for all the sarrafs active in the Ottoman world during the relevant period. Accordingly, some selected examples are used. The İstanbul sarrafs,[2] who occupied an important place within the larger group, are at the center of the study. Four high-ranking sarrafs who were executed at different times, whose property was confiscated, and who collaborated with state institutions and ruling elites were chosen as examples. They are Yakub (d. 1752), sarraf of the chief harem eunuch Morean Beşir Ağa, Bedros (d. 1786), sarraf of the imperial mint, Dimitri of Chios (d. 1788), sarraf of the elder Esma Sultan, and Artin (d. 1790),

DOI: 10.4324/9781003500780-6

an Egyptian-Armenian sarraf. Although studies of these sarrafs exist in the literature,[3] their methods of wealth acquisition and investment have not been compared. This chapter examines their manner of wealth acquisition and investment methods, comparing them for their similarities or differences.

A Brief Look at the Ottoman Sarrafs

It is not clear when sarrafs became visible as professionals in the Ottoman world. Sarrafs are mentioned in Ottoman sources from the 15th century onward. In addition to the Ottoman currency, the fact that many types of coinage with different names and denominations were in circulation contributed to their emergence. The exchange of money was the main function of the sarrafs. However, this function, an important source of income for them, was not their only activity. They enjoyed two separate but related functions, public and private. These included the transfer and storage of money, mediation in the purchase and sale of real estate, the financing of statesmen as well as various institutions such as mines, customs, the mint, and so on, and the financing of the treasury through short-term loans.[4]

The sarrafs, who became indispensable agents for various segments of the state and society, were generally of Greek, Jewish, and Armenian origin. Levantine groups were also interested in the exchange of money. Muslims were included but were less active than the others. It should also be noted that the balance between these groups changed from time to time, depending on political and economic conditions.[5]

Not all sarrafs in the Ottoman Empire had the same status. They were divided into two categories, "reputable" and "ordinary," according to their capital. Ordinary sarrafs had little capital, but, after they became rich and gained a reputation, they entered the more prestigious category thanks to the certificates they obtained. Reputable sarrafs, on the contrary, were treasury sarrafs and had a larger capital. These are the ones indicated when we talk about the sarrafs of the empire. Treasury sarrafs, also known as big merchants or bazirgans, had the right to engage in tax farming.[6]

It is not known whether sarrafs were subject to such a distinction in the early period of the Ottoman Empire. It is clear, however, that they must have had considerable capital to be able to work with the state. After all, as capitalist entrepreneurs, they were the exception in an economic system based on limiting capital accumulation. It is therefore possible that such a distinction was made indirectly by the empire. Although other financial intermediaries existed in the Ottoman Empire—consisting of various individuals and institutions from which individuals could borrow, not everyone with capital could work as a sarraf of whatever rank. A person's identification as a sarraf in the Ottoman Empire depended on the approval of the sultan.[7]

In this, the sarrafs organized their activities as a group of artisans within the framework of the gedik method.[8] Their activities were also supported by the state. The sarrafs, as one of the most important actors in the Ottoman Empire, were in a sense like a privileged subject of the sultan. Shaping the financial structure of the empire, they were active both in İstanbul and in the provinces. In this way, they created a financial network that extended from the center to the countryside. The functioning of the imperial monetary circulation also depended on the sarrafs. This situation continued until the development of modern banking.[9]

Here it should be noted that the activities of sarrafs in the Ottoman Empire changed over time, depending on circumstances. From the mid-16th century onward, the growing need for cash in the empire and the corresponding spread of tax farming (iltizam) were the main factors behind the rapid rise of the sarrafs. By the end of the 17th century, mukataas were granted to tax farmers for life as malikâne, making the sarrafs an indispensable player in the economic structure of the empire. At the same time, the sarrafs organized themselves into a guild (1691).[10]

It is thus undeniable that the sarrafs played an important role in the financial and economic structure of the Ottoman Empire. Although the state protected the sarrafs, confiscations, imprisonments, and executions, considered the normal consequences of the turmoil in Ottoman political life, haunted them. Even so, all these risks, indicators of state interventionism, could not shake their position in the imperial scene. As a result, the sarrafs were gradually transformed from traditional money and credit businessmen into a financial bourgeoisie that established international connections.[11]

Four Sarrafs, Partners in Destiny, on the Road to Wealth

Yakub, the sarraf of Beşir Ağa, Bedros, the sarraf of the imperial mint, Dimitri, the sarraf of Esma Sultan, and Artin, the Egyptian-Armenian sarraf, were four partners in destiny: they lived in the Ottoman Empire in the 18th century. They practiced the same profession in İstanbul, the capital of the Ottoman Empire, a place that offered important economic opportunities to its inhabitants. They paid the price of working with the state with their lives in their accumulation of wealth.

Yakub, son of Hovanes, came to İstanbul from Eğin about 60 years before his death and was of Armenian origin. He had a brother named Agob and was married to Anna.[12]

Bedros's father's name, as a Greekified Armenian, was Kiryako. Bedros, who was married to Maryore, had two daughters named Varvara and Karinko and three sons named Dimitraki, Yorgaki, and İstavraki. His brother-in-law Yorgaki and his father-in-law Luka were other members of the family recorded in the sources.[13]

Dimitri, who was of Greek origin, settled in the capital of the empire as a member of the Skanavi family, who were involved in the silk trade in Chios. His father was Hacı Konstantin, and his mother was Zanilo. He had two brothers, Tzani and Nikola. In turn, Dimitri had six sisters. Dimitri had two marriages; one of his wives' name was İzmiragda. Dimitri had four daughters and four sons, one of whom was an orphan. His daughters were Adri, Erkiri, Tarsınca, and Lukraşani. His sons were Nikolaki, Yorgaki, Kostaki, and Tzani. His sons-in-law were Nikola İskeleci, Yakomu, and İstamadi. They were also merchants. Dimitri also had a grandchild named Tarsınca in the records.[14]

Artin, who immigrated to İstanbul from Egypt, was also Armenian. His father was Kogas. Artin, who was married to Karlı, also had a daughter named Azaduhi.[15]

Apart from Artin, who lived in Langa Yenikapısı, the other three sarrafs lived on the shores of the Golden Horn and the Bosporus. Yakub settled in a big house in Beşiktaş, which was divided into two parts and had different structures. A large house in Fenerkapısı and the waterfront villa in Büyükdere were other places where he lived. Bedros also lived in a house with running water and a barn, in Fener. He also had a villa in Tarabya. In addition, there were other buildings such as cellars, storehouses, pools, and so on inside the villa grounds. He also had a church built in the garden of this villa. So, like Yakub, his life as a sarraf went beyond the limits set by the state.

Dimitri also settled in Fener. His house here was in two parts and had a supply of water inside. The beach house in Kuruçeşme was Dimitri's other daily residence. Dimitri, who lived in Chios and İstanbul, was not afraid to show off his wealth. The money and property he donated reflected this. Indeed, he was a sarraf who had a say in his own society. It should be noted here that Yakub and Bedros were not in any way inferior to Dimitri.[16]

Yakub, one of the sarrafs described in the sources with adjectives such as bazirgan and hodja had been trained as an apprentice. After working for a few years with his compatriot Harutyun Amira, who had brought him from Eğin, he opened his own sarraf shop in Vezir Han. In his career as a sarraf after working first for another powerful sarraf, his rise came about after he married Treasurer Süleyman Ağa's sister, Anna. It was Süleyman Ağa who introduced him to Beşir Ağa. While this brought Yakub to the pinnacle of his economic and political power, it also led him to his own downfall. The hubris that Beşir Ağa exhibited because of his influence over Sultan Mahmud I spread to those around him. Yakub too was no less infected than his master Beşir Ağa. Therefore, with the execution of Beşir Ağa (11 July 1752), Yakub also met the same end (20 July 1752).[17]

Like Yakub, Bedros was an apprenticed sarraf; his master was İstefan. The person who changed the destiny of Bedros, whose shop and office were in Büyük Yeni Han, was Sıdkı Mustafa Efendi. During Mustafa Efendi's term as mint minister (1760–1763), Bedros was appointed sarraf of the mint as a partner of his master İstefan. This position, a turning point in Bedros' career, also brought about his end. Bedros was executed on 19 April 1786, accused of corruption at the mint and treason against the state. The chronicles of the time though tell a different story. According to them, Bedros, who had ties with Halil Hamid Paşa (d. 1785), opposed Nikola Mavroyani, who had grown up under the protection of the Algerian Gazi Hasan Paşa (d. 1790), in his efforts to become the Wallachian voivode. Mavroyani took his revenge by having Bedros killed. The murder of Bedros was therefore a part of the conflicts between the factions of Hasan Paşa and Halil Hamid Paşa.[18]

Dimitri of Chios was a resident of Küçük Yeni Han. He practiced his profession as a sarraf in two adjoining rooms. Esma Sultan also contributed to his rise. However, with the death of Esma Sultan on 13 August 1788, Dimitri's fate changed. Like Bedros, Dimitri was accused of treason and corruption and was executed on 16 August 1788. His brother Tzani also met the same end on 30 September/1 October 1788.[19]

It is not clear when and how Artin, who later came to İstanbul and practiced as a sarraf in his room in Yeni Han, began this profession. However, he was mentioned in the sources as an Egyptian sarraf during the Egyptian governorships of Raif İsmail Paşa (31 August 1778 to 8 July 1779/13 October 1779 to 1 October 1780). Artin continued in this role during the Egyptian governorships of Silahdar Mehmed Paşa (10 June 1783 to 27 December 1784) and Hacı İsmail Paşa (13 January 1789 to 22 March 1791). However, he did not survive the period of Hacı İsmail Paşa. He was executed on 31 July 1790, on the grounds that he was involved in the rebellion of İbrahim Bey and Murad Bey, two of the Mamluk lords of Egypt.[20]

Wealth Levels of Sarrafs

Before considering the wealth levels of the four sarrafs, it should be noted that the available data are limited to the confiscated assets of the sarrafs. The picture that emerges should therefore be seen in the context of the unique structure of the probate records.

Sarraf Yakub's assets were confiscated together with those of Beşir Ağa and Süleyman Ağa. It is therefore not possible to separate their individual holdings completely.[21] However, it is possible to say something about sarraf Yakub's wealth by looking at the archive documents. The amount that sarraf Yakub received from his colleagues in the form of loans was 297,554 piasters (kuruş). He also had 466,022 piasters from government officials and various merchants. In addition, the value of Yakub's rooms in the Vezir Han and his house in Fener, as well as the cash and gold held with sarraf Bedros in the Keresteci Han and Nikoğos in the Kürkçüler Han, respectively, amounted to 234,787.5 piasters. To this, was added the sum of 78,460 piasters belonging to his brother Agob. Around 34,295 piasters were obtained from Yakub's possessions, which were sold by the imperial treasury on several different days. In addition, the amount raised for some of the properties sold was 19,725 piasters. This amount, some 1,130,844 piasters, reveals by itself the extent of Yakub's wealth as a sarraf. But this is just the tip of the iceberg. It is possible that Yakub's wealth was much greater than this figure.[22] However, debts of unknown amounts were also part of Yakub's financial position. It is important to remember that calculations can change.[23]

Bedros' wealth rivaled that of Yakub. While 99,940 piasters came from the sale of his properties, 39,582.22 piasters came from the sale of his possessions. In addition, Bedros had received 1,041,234 piasters from government officials and merchants. In total, his wealth amounted to 1,180,757.22 piasters. After deducting debts of 977,853.5 piasters, there remained a considerable amount of 202,903.72 piasters.[24]

Dimitri's wealth reached a total value of 2,622,645 piasters. This considerable sum corresponded to about one-third of the empire's entire fixed budget income of 8,973,500 piasters in 1788. Of this amount, 2,300,921 piasters came from debts to be collected. A further 200,845 piasters came from the sale of properties and 120,879 piasters from the sale of goods. After deducting debts of 1,034,585 piasters, 1,588,060 piasters remained.[25]

It is difficult to estimate the total wealth of the Egyptian sarraf Artin. His house and his room in the han were left to his family. On the contrary, it turned out that Artin had received 110,311.5 piasters from various people. This figure alone proves that he was no ordinary sarraf. Moreover, Artin paid out about 500,000 piasters when İsmail Paşa was appointed governor of Egypt. Therefore, it is certain that Artin was one of the most important sarrafs of the empire.[26]

Their Wealth-Gaining Processes

As we mentioned above, sarraf Yakub was trained as an apprentice and opened his own sarraf shop in Vezir Han with his brother Agob. Here, Yakub dealt with ordinary business such as money exchanging, which was an important source of income for sarrafs in the early days. However, with the sarraf of Beşir Ağa, the situation began to change, as they worked as a money company. Yakub's accounts receivable with and without promissory notes from sarrafs, government officials, merchants, and so on, as well as his cash and gold in hand, reflected this.

Yakub, having made the most of his opportunity to become wealthy, was not content to be a mere sarraf. He also supplied the palace with precious stones, jewelry, watches, clothes, and so on. He was involved in international trade networks and had connections with many French, British, and Dutch merchants. Yakub also played a role in tax farming, which was an indispensable part of the sarraf's activities in the Ottoman world in the 18th century. In fact, no tax farming or office sale could take place during this period without passing through the control of his master, Beşir Ağa. Inevitably, he became a part of the channel through which money and wealth flowed.[27]

Bedros, one of the sarrafs of the Büyük Yeni Han, began his career with his master İstefan. He then became his master's partner and sarraf of the mint. This important role was the turning point in Bedros' rise to wealth. The sarraf of the mint not only carried out all the monetary transactions of the minister of the mint but also financed the mines, mukataas, farms, and so on operated by the mint, as well as dealing with some other expenses.[28] Being the sarraf of the mint was not Bedros' only duty in this institution. With the status of a silversmith's lieutenant, he also purchased silver for the mint. In the later stages of his career, he became foreman of the mint with a daily wage of 60 coins.

In addition to his career at the mint, which was an important source of income and opportunity for him, Bedros also worked as a sarraf at the tobacco customs office. He was also one of the most experienced silversmiths in İstanbul, together with his partner İstefan. Bedros also had a capital partnership with sarraf Abraham and his brother-in-law Yorgaki. His sons İstavraki, Dimitraki, and Yorgaki were also partners with their father. Bedros' wife and daughters also contributed to the family in the form of debts and claims. In that sense, it was a family business. As a sarraf with such a diversified portfolio, Bedros' clients included high-ranking statesmen such as pashas, voivodes, sarrafs, merchants, and so on, as well as people from various levels of the bureaucracy and society. Their debts ranged from 40 to 200,000 piasters. But Bedros did not only grant loans. He also received money from various people, either in trust or as a loan, to finance himself. Thus, we can say that Bedros was managing money with interest. The amount of 9,400 piasters he received in trust from Osman Ağa and the 5,970 piasters he received from Mehmed Ağa should be considered in this context. Changing money was not the only source of income on his way to wealth. He was also an entrepreneur with a broad commercial outlook. The fact that he had two ships trading in grain on the Danube, in the names of his sons Dimitraki and Yorgaki, was evidence of this. As a merchant, Bedros was also a sarraf, involved in international networks. His relationship with Kanorta, the Prussian interpreter, is noteworthy in this respect. In addition, Bedros, through his deputy Yanaki, made bricks and sold them in the brick kilns of Hasköy. He also had shares in bakeries in Arnavutköy and Emirgan. Further, he acted as the tax farmer of the Tahyanos and Celebkeşan-ı Yenişehir mukataas, which he owned with his brother-in-law and partner, sarraf Yorgaki. As a sarraf, he also benefited from tax farming.[29]

Dimitri of Chios began his career as a member of a wealthy merchant family interested in the silk trade. Esma Sultan, however, had a hand in his rise. Esma Sultan, who had great influence as the sister of Abdülhamid I (1774–1789), made Dimitri known in İstanbul circles. Dimitri, careful to take the right steps on the road to wealth, thus created a wide portfolio of clients belonging to different layers of society, including Esma Sultan, Beyhan Sultan, Emine Sultan, Raif İsmail Paşa, Melek Mehmed Paşa, Cihanzade Hüseyin Bey, the Hatmanzades, and the executive elites at various levels. Dimitri also managed money with interest. He also received money for himself in cash from various people and sarrafs. An indication of this was that Karaosman Ağa's wife, Hatice Hatun, received 10 piasters every three months from the property of two orphans, in return for the 1,430 piasters she gave to Dimitri. The sarrafs Artin and Kifork and the people working for Dimitri who demanded money from the loan agreement are other examples of this situation.

But these were not Dimitri's only interests. Dimitri was also a multi-talented entrepreneur. The broadcloth (çuha) craft he made in Sandal Bedesten was one indication of this. To increase his capital and reduce his risks, Dimitri also engaged in various businesses such as jewelry making, running grocery stores, alongside butchery and bakery businesses, tailoring, and management in the sherbet business.

Dimitri, who led an active commercial life, also played a role in tax farming as a financier. This included claims on and debts to tax collectors and tax farmers. Dimitri also supplied the palace with various items. Here, he worked with many partners who were related to him, many of whom were involved in trade. It is therefore certain that Dimitri ran a large family business, consisting of his wife İzmaragda and his brothers, brothers-in-law, sons, daughters, grandchildren, and nephews. The fact that his nephew Konstantin and his son-in-law Nikola could claim capital as company property is a sign of this. Dimitri, with his wide commercial network through the partnerships he had established, was also active in international trade. The debt–credit relationship between Baydaroğlu İlyas Anton, chief interpreter to the British consul in Aleppo, and Abbuşoğlu İbrahim, the deputy to the British court in Baghdad, is indicative of this.[30]

The Egyptian-Armenian sarraf Artin, who worked as a sarraf in Yeni Han, also had a unique client portfolio. Artin worked not only with the Egyptian governors and their men but also with other ruling elites at various levels of the bureaucracy, as well as with ordinary individuals. But, with a few exceptions, the loans he granted were generally small amounts. In addition to the loans that were part of the sarraf's routine, Artin was also interested in trade. He had claims on Bekir Ağa for goods and on Ebubekir Bey for horses. Artin was also granted privileges by the Egyptian governors to collect taxes, such as the Bender-i Dimyat cizye (capitation tax) and lordship (ağalık) and the Bender-i İskenderiye lordship. Thus, on his way to wealth, he also engaged in tax farming.[31]

Investment Channels of Sarrafs

In the literature, it is emphasized that the investment by the sarrafs in their assets was in two main economic areas: mobile assets and real estate.[32] This is also clearly visible in the wealth components of our sample of sarrafs. It is here apposite to take a closer look at their investment channels.

For Yakub Hovanesyan, the sarraf of Beşir Ağa, it is fitting to mention his two large houses in Beşiktaş and Fenerkapısı, as well as his waterfront villa in Büyükdere. Although these houses were places he used in his daily life, they were ultimately an investment tool. The sale of the house in Beşiktaş to the sarraf Bedros for 12,000 piasters illustrates this.

Moreover, Yakub's property investments were not limited to these. In addition to his room and gedik in the Vezir Han, he also owned the gedik of four rooms in the same han. His holdings in real estate extended further still: half of a sarraf shop in Mahmutpaşa and half of a house and a cellar in Galata; three acres of land in Çatalservi, a barn in Fenerkapısı, three bay boathouses in Galata, and three houses with a rental income of 59.5 piasters, the so-called Armenian rooms, 29-room Yahudhane in Sinan Paşa district in Beşiktaş. In short, Yakub was a serious property investor, in terms of both using his wealth and increasing it.

On the contrary, as a sarraf, Yakub also invested in mobile assets to build his wealth. Cash was extremely important to a sarraf. As noted above, this aspect is evidenced by the amount of promissory and non-promissory notes held against colleagues and others in his client portfolio through credit relationships. In addition to Yakub's rooms in the Vezir Han and his house in Fener, the money and gold held in the Keresteci Han with the sarraf Bedros and with Nikos in the Kürkçüler Han were also added to this. Yakub, as Eldem points out, resembled a walking wallet. Nor were his investments limited to cash and gold. There were many valuable items in his homes and workplaces that could be instantly converted into cash, such as fabrics, watches, furniture, furs, and so on.[33]

Bedros, the mint sarraf, also showed similar tendencies to Yakub in terms of wealth accumulation. He also transferred a considerable part of his wealth into real estate. In addition to the house in Fener where he lived with his family and the villa on the waterfront in Tarabya, these properties included the sarraf's shop and rooms in Valide and Yeni Han. There were also the houses of his son Dimitraki and his daughter Varvara in Yeniköy, and the house and land of his other son Yorgaki in Fener. But this was just a drop in the ocean. Eventually, Bedros acquired other rent-generating properties, some of which he bought and some of which he acquired in exchange for receivables. These properties, which also show his multifaceted portfolio and interests, consist of houses, ranges, vineyards, plots of land, shops, and premises such as grocery stores, butchers, bakers, hairdressers, greengrocers, and so on. The property in Sivriada, two ships on the Danube, and a han in İzmir were among them. The value of these properties, some of which were sold, ranged from 40 to 10,000 piasters.

Bedros' investments in mobile assets as a sarraf were also remarkable. His loans and the capital reserves of his partners come first. The 5,875 piasters in cash and 845 pieces of gold found in his shop and room in Yeni Han and his houses in Fener and Tarabya were also significant. This is in addition to other items that could be converted into cash.[34]

Dimitri had also invested in property to capitalize on his wealth. Apart from Mudanya, his properties were concentrated in İstanbul and Chios. While a significant proportion of these belong to Dimitri, almost half of them belong to his wife Izmaragda. Here, the house in Fener and the beach house in Kuruçeşme should have pride of place. But Dimitri also had houses in Arnavutköy and on the island of Burgaz. Other properties, scattered in places such as Karaköy, Galata, and Büyükdere, were also added to these everyday dwellings. These properties included households and farms used for commercial or rental purposes, plots of land, vineyards, orchards and gardens, rooms and shops of bakers, tailors, grocery stores, etc. In addition to these properties, some of which he sold, there were the shops and rooms of sarraf and chukka in Yeni Han and Sandal Bedesten.

Dimitri also had many properties in Chios, such as tower houses, vineyards, fields, and silk cellars. He acquired his property in Mudanya, consisting of a bakery, a shop, and an olive grove, in exchange for a debt of 12,000 piasters.

Again, as required by his office as sarraf, Dimitri kept a significant portion of his wealth in mobile assets. In total, 3,992 piasters in cash and 868 gold coins from İstanbul and Egypt were confiscated from the shops and rooms in Küçük Yeni Han. Other jewelled and non-jewelled objects, fabrics, furs, carpets, and so on were also found in the rooms and shops, as well as in other areas of his daily life.[35]

Artin, the Egyptian sarraf, was different from the others in terms of investment. Apart from his house and the sarraf's shop, no other property was discovered. He did not have many possessions there. In this sense, Artin was more modest than his colleagues on the shores of the Bosporus and the Golden Horn.

On the contrary, it is also possible that Artin, who financed the Egyptian governors, preferred more in the way of cash capital, as seen above. Debt–credit relations generally consisted of sums given by way of trust and bonds.[36]

Conclusion

Yakub, the sarraf of Beşir Ağa, Bedros, the sarraf of the imperial mint, Dimitri of Chios, the sarraf of Esma Sultan, and Artin, the Egyptian sarraf, were four sarrafs who were fully part of the Ottoman world of the 18th century and who paid the price of cooperation with the state with their lives. Such people acted out their lives on the imperial stage, rising and falling on the wheel of fortune. Although the reasons for their deaths were different, traces of the Ottoman Empire's interventionist perspective, which it applied with pragmatic selectivity in the acquisition of capital, can be detected in all their life stories. After their deaths, their property was confiscated by the state.

In this respect, it is clear that the sarrafs concerned were not as fortunate as the great international merchants, both Muslim and non-Muslim, such as Ismail Abu Taqiyya.[37] These last had more freedom to acquire capital and were able to preserve their wealth better.[38] The main reason for this disparity is that the sarrafs, unlike international merchants, were more closely linked to the state in their business dealings, and they also lived in the ruling center of the empire. As a result, they could not escape state control as easily as others did.

Despite this vulnerability, the four sarrafs who worked with state institutions and their ruling elites acquired disproportionate wealth, reflected in their lives. In the end, their wealth was considerable, although there were yet differences between them. In this sense, they were like the sarrafs of the treasury, and different from the ordinary sarrafs of the empire. For their wealth was many times greater than that of the others.

It should be stressed that their profession played a crucial role in their acquisition of these considerable assets, which amounted to millions of piasters. These sarrafs built up a cosmopolitan client portfolio by working with high-ranking elites and state institutions. They also fulfilled the requirements of being a sarraf, such as providing funds, managing money with interest, and establishing capital partnerships. However, being a sarraf was far from the only source of their wealth. They maximized the last by being enterprising and relying on various avenues such as trade and tax farming. Therefore, their characterization of capitalist entrepreneurs in the early modern Ottoman economic order is a very appropriate definition. It is likely not correct to say that this definition covers all the sarrafs operating in the 18th-century Ottoman world, though other sarrafs doubtless showed similar tendencies on their way to wealth.

Finally, the methods of assessing the wealth of each sarraf are more or less the same. They preferred to invest in more mobile assets as a prerequisite for becoming a sarraf. Credit claims, cash, and gold found in their homes and han rooms, and other valuables are all indicators of this. It should be noted too that the items in their homes that could be immediately converted into cash were a part of their daily lives.

If we exclude Artin, the property investments of the others were also dazzling. All in all, buying of real estate beyond their day-to-day living needs was a paramount investment.

Archives

Başbakanlık Osmanlı Arşivi (BOA), Istanbul, Turkey
AE.SMHD.I. 158/11904
C.ML. 665/27227
D.BŞM.d. 3206

D.BŞM.MHF. 41/39, 41/40, 41/41, 41/43, 41/44, 41/46, 41/66, 42/30
D.BŞM.MHF.d. 12598, 12601, 12602, 12605, 12658, 13698
D.BŞM.ZMT.d. 13801, 13805, 13807, 13813
KK.d. 2447
MAD.d. 10354
TSMA.d. 10460, 2217
TSMA.e. 710/3

Notes

1 Halil İnalcık, "Capital Formation in the Ottoman Empire," *The Journal of Economic History* 29, no. 1 (1969): 97–140; Mehmet Genç, *Osmanlı İmparatorluğunda Devlet ve Ekonomi* [State and Economy in the Ottoman Empire] (Ankara: Ötüken Neşriyat, 2012), 45–88; Erol Özvar, "Servet ve Güvenlik Arasında Osmanlı Sultanı [Ottoman Sultan Between Security and Wealth]," *Türklük Araştırmaları* 13 (2003): 47–60; Şevket Pamuk, *Osmanlı İmparatorluğu'nda Paranın Tarihi* [A Monetary History of the Ottoman Empire] (İstanbul: İş Bankası Kültür Yayınları, 2012), 10–21; Murat Çizakça, "Osmanlı Devleti ve Ekonomik Hayat: Vergilendirme, Kamu Finansmanı ve Ticaret Kontrolleri [The Ottoman Government and Economic Life: Taxation, Public Finance and Trade Controls]," in *Türkiye Tarihi Bir Dünya Gücü Olarak Osmanlı İmparatorluğu 1453–1603*, ed. Suraiya Faroqhi and Kate Fleet, vol. 2 (İstanbul: Kitap Yayınevi, 2016), 303–44.

2 For a few studies on Sarrafs and İstanbul's Sarrafs, see Yavuz Cezar, "The Role of the Sarrafs in the Ottoman Finance and Economy in the Eighteenth and Nineteenth Centuries," in *Frontiers of the Ottoman Studies*, ed. Colin Imber, Rhodes Murphey, and Keiko Kiyotaki, vol. I (London: I. B. Tauris, 2005), 61–76; Ömerül Faruk Bölükbaşı, "İstanbul Sarrafları (1691–1835) [İstanbul's Moneychangers (1691–1835)]," *Türk Kültürü İncelemeleri* 30 (2014): 19–96.

3 Ertan Ünlü, *18. Yüzyılın İkinci Yarısında Osmanlı'da Sarraflar ve İlişki Ağları* [Moneychangers and Relationship Networks in the Ottoman Empire During the Second Half of the 18th Century]; Ertan Ünlü, "18. Yüzyılda Osmanlı Eliti Bir Darphane Sarrafının Muhallefatı: Bedros Nam-ı Diğer Petraki [The Heritage of an Ottoman Elite and Mint Sarraf in the 18th Century: Bedros, also Known as Petraki]," *OTAM (Journal of the Center for Ottoman Studies Ankara University)* 43 (January 2018): 281–318; Ertan Ünlü, "18. Yüzyılda Sarraf Katlleri: "Devlet Malına Halel' in mi, Hizipleşmenin mi Kurbanları? [Sarraf Executions in the 18th Century: Were They the Victims of 'Harming Government Property' or 'Factionalism'?]," *Osmanlı Araştırmaları* 52 (September 2018): 99–133; Ertan Ünlü, "Mısır Sarrafı Artin (?-1790) [Artin the Egyptian Sarraf (?-1790)]," in *Sosyal & Beşeri Bilimler Alanında Akademik Çalışmalar*, ed. Sema Sağlık-Uğur İnan, vol. 1 (Ankara: Gece Kitaplığı, 2023), 203–17; Edhem Eldem, "İstanbul: İmparatorluk Payitahtından Periferileşmiş Bir Başkente [Istanbul: From Imperial to Peripheralized Capital]," in *Doğu ile Batı Arasında Osmanlı Kenti Halep, İzmir ve İstanbul*, ed. Edhem Eldem, Daniel Goffman, and Bruce Masters (İstanbul: Tarih Vakfı Yurt Yayınları, 2012), 165–247; Σοφία Λαΐου, "Εμπόριο και πίστη στην Κωνσταντινούπολη του 18ου αιώνα: η περίπτωση του Χιώτη Δημήτρη Σκαναβή [Trade and Credit in 18th Century Constantinople: The Case of Dimitris Scanavis of Chios]," *Τα Ιστορικά* 64 (2016): 83–100; Onnik Jamgoçyan, *Osmanlı İmparatorluğu'nda Sarraflık, Rumlar, Museviler, Frenkler, Ermeniler* [Moneychangers in the Ottoman Empire, Grecs, Jews, Franks, Armenians] (İstanbul: Yapı Kredi Yayınları, 2017), 44–50.

4 Ünlü, *Yüzyılın İkinci*, 45–46.

5 Ünlü, *Yüzyılın İkinci*, 46–50.

6 Ünlü, *Yüzyılın İkinci*, 50–51.

7 Ünlü, *Yüzyılın İkinci*, 51–52.

8 Gedik is defined as the right to practice a particular profession and the tools necessary for the practice of a profession. This is also the case for İstanbul sarrafs. For more information on this subject, see Bölükbaşı, "İstanbul Sarrafları," 28–31.
9 Ünlü, *Yüzyılın İkinci*, 52–55.
10 Ünlü, *Yüzyılın İkinci*, 55–56.
11 Ünlü, *Yüzyılın İkinci*, 56–57.
12 Eldem, "İstanbul," 200–9; Jamgoçyan, *Osmanlı İmparatorluğu'nda Sarraflık*, 44–50.
13 Ünlü, *Yüzyılın İkinci*, 67–69.
14 Ünlü, *Yüzyılın İkinci*, 103–5.
15 Ünlü, "Mısır Sarrafı Artin," 206.
16 Ünlü, *Yüzyılın İkinci*, 91–97, 128–38; Eldem, "İstanbul," 200–9; Jamgoçyan, *Osmanlı İmparatorluğu'nda Sarraflık*, 44–50.
17 Eldem, "İstanbul," 200–9; Jamgoçyan, *Osmanlı İmparatorluğu'nda Sarraflık*, 44–50.
18 Ünlü, *Yüzyılın İkinci*, 70–84.
19 Ünlü, *Yüzyılın İkinci*, 109–17.
20 Ünlü, "Mısır Sarrafı Artin," 203–17.
21 The amount of cash confiscated from these three men was around 4,000,000 piasters. 300,000 piasters was obtained from the sale of property and slaves. See Eldem, "İstanbul," 200–9.
22 Yakub's confiscated wealth was more than 60 million piasters. See Jamgoçyan, *Osmanlı İmparatorluğu'nda Sarraflık*, 44–50.
23 AE.SMHD.I. 158/11904; C.ML. 665/27227; D.BŞM.d. 3206; D.BŞM.MHF.d. 12598, 12601, 12602, 12605, 12658, 13698; D.BŞM.MHF. 41/39, 41/40, 41/41, 41/43, 41/44, 41/46, 41/66, 42/30; D.BŞM.ZMT.d. 13801, 13805, 13807, 13813; KK.d. 2447; MAD.d. 10354, pp. 421–58; TSMA.d. 10460, 2217; TSMA.e. 710/3.
24 Ünlü, *Yüzyılın İkinci*, 84–88.
25 Ünlü, *Yüzyılın İkinci*, 117–24.
26 Ünlü, "Mısır Sarrafı Artin," 203–17.
27 D.BŞM.ZMT.d. 13813; MAD.d. 10354, pp. 421–58; Eldem, "İstanbul," 200–9; Jamgoçyan, *Osmanlı İmparatorluğu'nda Sarraflık*, 44–50.
28 For extensive information on the mint and mint sarrafs, see Ömerül Faruk Bölükbaşı, *18. Yüzyılın İkinci Yarısında Darbhâne-i Âmire* [The Imperial Mint in the Second Half of the 18th Century] (İstanbul: İstanbul Bilgi Üniversitesi Yayınları, 2013).
29 Ünlü, *Yüzyılın İkinci*, 88–91, 150–67.
30 Ünlü, *Yüzyılın İkinci*, 124–28, 167–90.
31 Ünlü, "Mısır Sarrafı Artin," 203–17.
32 Metin Ziya Köse, *Galata'da Sarraf İşletmeleri (1691–1733), İşletme Yönetimi, Sermaye ve Yatırım* [Sarraf Enterprises in Galata (1691–1733), Business Management, Capital and Investment] (İstanbul: Kriter Publishing House, 2021), 126.
33 MAD.d. 10354, 421–58; Eldem, "İstanbul," 200–9; Jamgoçyan, *Osmanlı İmparatorluğu'nda Sarraflık*, 44–50.
34 Ünlü, "18. Yüzyılda Osmanlı Eliti"; Ünlü, *Yüzyılın İkinci*, 97–102.
35 Ünlü, *Yüzyılın İkinci*, 138–44.
36 Ünlü, "Mısır Sarrafı Artin," 203–17.
37 Nelly Hanna, *Osmanlı Kahire'sinde Tüccar Olmak* [To Be a Merchant in Ottoman Kairo in 1600: The Life and Times of Isma'il Abu Taqiyya] (İstanbul: Küre Yayınları, 2006).
38 For information on the greater freedom for international merchants regarding profit limits, see İnalcık, "Capital formation," 97–140; Çizakça, "Osmanlı Devleti," 341–2.

Bibliography

Bölükbaşı, Ömerül Faruk. *18. Yüzyılın İkinci Yarısında Darbhâne-i Âmire [The Imperial Mint in the Second Half of the 18th Century]*. İstanbul: İstanbul Bilgi Üniversitesi Yayınları, 2013.

Bölükbaşı, Ömerül Faruk. "İstanbul Sarrafları (1691–1835) [İstanbul's Moneychangers (1691–1835)]." *Türk Kültürü İncelemeleri [Turkish Culture Studies]* 30 (2014): 19–96.

Cezar, Yavuz. "The Role of the Sarrafs in the Ottoman Finance and Economy in the Eighteenth and Nineteenth Centuries." In *Frontiers of the Ottoman Studies*, edited by Colin Imber, Rhodes Murphey, and Keiko Kiyotaki, vol. I, 61–76. London: I. B. Tauris, 2005.

Çizakça, Murat. "Osmanlı Devleti ve Ekonomik Hayat: Vergilendirme, Kamu Finansmanı ve Ticaret Kontrolleri [The Ottoman State and Economic Life: Taxation, Public Finance and Trade Controls]." In *Türkiye Tarihi Bir Dünya Gücü Olarak Osmanlı İmparatorluğu 1453–1603 [The History of Turkey: The Ottoman Empire as a World Power, 1453–1603]*, edited by Suraiya Faroqhi and Kate Fleet, vol. 2, 303–44. İstanbul: Kitap Yayınevi, 2016.

Eldem, Edhem. "İstanbul: İmparatorluk Payitahtından Periferileşmiş Bir Başkente [Istanbul: from Imperial to Peripheralized Capital]." In *Doğu ile Batı Arasında Osmanlı Kenti Halep, İzmir ve İstanbul [Ottoman Cities Between East and West, Aleppo, Izmir, and Istanbul]*, edited by Edhem Eldem, Daniel Goffman, and Bruce Masters, 165–247. İstanbul: Tarih Vakfı Yurt Yayınları, 2012.

Genç, Mehmet. *Osmanlı İmparatorluğunda Devlet ve Ekonomi [State and Economy in the Ottoman Empire]*. Ankara: Ötüken Neşriyat, 2012.

Hanna, Nelly. *Osmanlı Kahire'sinde Tüccar Olmak [To Be a Merchant in Ottoman Kairo in 1600: The Life and Times of Isma'il Abu Taqiyya]*. İstanbul: Küre Yayınları, 2006.

İnalcık, Halil. "Capital Formation in the Ottoman Empire." *The Journal of Economic History* 29, no. 1 (1969): 97–140.

Jamgocyan, Onnik. *Osmanlı İmparatorluğu'nda Sarraflık, Rumlar, Museviler, Frenkler, Ermeniler [Moneychangers in the Ottoman Empire, Grecs, Jews, Franks, Armenians]*. İstanbul: Yapı Kredi Yayınları, 2016.

Köse, Metin Ziya. *Galata'da Sarraf İşletmeleri (1691–1733), İşletme Yönetimi, Sermaye ve Yatırım [Moneychangers Enterprises in Galata (1691–1733), Business Management, Capital and Investment]*. İstanbul: Kriter Publishing House, 2021.

Özvar, Erol. "Servet ve Güvenlik Arasında Osmanlı Sultanı [Ottoman Sultan Between Security and Wealth]." *Türklük Araştırmaları [Turkish Studies]* 13 (2003): 47–60.

Pamuk, Şevket. *Osmanlı İmparatorluğu'nda Paranın Tarihi [A Monetary History of the Ottoman Empire]*. İstanbul: İş Bankası Kültür Yayınları, 2012.

Ünlü, Ertan. "18. Yüzyılda Osmanlı Eliti Bir Darphane Sarrafının Muhallefatı: Bedros Nam-ı Diğer Petraki [The Heritage of an Ottoman Elite and Mint Moneychanger in the 18th Century: Bedros, also Known as Petraki]." *OTAM (Ankara Üniversitesi Osmanlı Tarihi Araştırma Ve Uygulama Merkezi Dergisi [Journal of the Center for Ottoman Studies Ankara University])* 43 (January 2018): 281–317.

Ünlü, Ertan. "18. Yüzyılda Sarraf Katlleri: 'Devlet Malına Halel' in mi, Hizipleşmenin mi Kurbanları? [Moneychangers' Executions in the 18th Century: Were They the Victims of 'Harming Government Property' or 'Factionalism'?]." *Osmanlı Araştırmaları [Ottoman Studies]* 52 (September 2018): 99–133.

Ünlü, Ertan. "Mısır Sarrafı Artin (?-1790) [Artin the Egyptian Moneychanger (?-1790)]." In *Sosyal & Beşeri Bilimler Alanında Akademik Çalışmalar [Academic Studies in Social Sciences & Humanities]*, edited by Sema Sağlık-Uğur İnan, vol. 1, 203–17. Ankara: Gece Kitaplığı, 2023.

Ünlü, Ertan. *18. Yüzyılın İkinci Yarısında Osmanlı'da Sarraflar ve İlişki Ağları [Moneychangers and Relationship Networks in the Ottoman Empire During the Second Half of the 18th Century]*. İstanbul: Timaş Akademi Kitaplığı, 2024.

Λαΐου, Σοφία. "Εμπόριο και πίστη στην Κωνσταντινούπολη του 18ου αιώνα: η περίπτωση του Χιώτη Δημήτρη Σκαναβή." *Τα Ιστορικά* 64 (2016): 83–100. [Laiou, Sophia. "Trade and Credit in 18th Century Constantinople: The Case of Dimitris Scanavis of Chios." *Ta Istorika* 64 (2016): 83–100.]

5 Signs of Wealth

Emerging Consumption in Early Modern Southeastern Europe

Artemis Yagou

Introduction

Historians have been paying increasing attention to the phenomena of wealth accumulation and capitalist development that took place in the Ottoman Empire between the 18th and early 20th centuries, the publication of this volume being a reflection of this interest. Specific political and economic developments during the late eighteenth and early nineteenth centuries are of great significance to historians of Greece in particular. In that period, the Russo-Ottoman treaty of Küçük Kaynarca in 1774, the opening of the Black Sea to foreign navigation in 1783, and later the Napoleonic Wars (1803–1815) all helped to create a favorable framework for Ottoman Greek merchants and facilitated their economic expansion. Greek traders were instrumental in the growth of mercantile activities between the Eastern Mediterranean and Western Europe and played an important intermediary role between European powers and the Ottoman world.[1] Although in the past such mediation activities have been treated by Greek historiography as signs of dependence and underdevelopment, in light of new research,[2] we view them as successful acts within a transregional brokerage system and as steps toward an advantageous incorporation into the wider system of division of labor.

The expansion beyond local trade and the penetration into lucrative export markets led to substantial financial prosperity and wealth accumulation among certain segments of the Greek Orthodox populations of the Empire. This situation clashed with the inescapable fact that these groups were second-class citizens in the Empire and suffered many kinds of discrimination.[3] Nevertheless, the financial success of Greek merchants allowed them to enjoy high living standards and adopt new consumption patterns. Their financially improved status was materialized in daily life through the acquisition and enjoyment of novel products, primarily—but not exclusively—imported from Western Europe.

In this context, this chapter focuses on the circulation of objects and on new consumption trends in early modern southeastern Europe, with emphasis on the Greek populations. The approach followed is embedded in the object-based research discourse, which employs artifacts as primary sources and is complemented by textual and iconographic sources.[4] Doing history through objects, mostly from museum collections, promotes an experiential understanding and enables an effective

DOI: 10.4324/9781003500780-7

linkage of the material and technical with economic, social, aesthetic, and other factors.[5] When examined methodically and thoroughly, objects tend to surprise us with their complexity; they also resist easy interpretation. The more objects are examined, the more different aspects are being discovered, exposing "patterns, relationships, and complexities that would otherwise remain hidden."[6] In this vein, the chapter deals with emerging consumption trends, manifested through the acquisition and use of novel and pleasurable objects. These expressed on a material level the rise of new mentalities, as will be shown by the examples of two object types.

Wine Jugs: Not Just for Drinking

The first group of objects under discussion are the ceramic wine jugs manufactured in Pesaro, Italy, by the firm of Casali and Callegari and its successors during the last decades of the 18th century and in the beginning of the 19th century (Figure 5.1).[7] These ceramic jugs follow a pre-existing and quite common formal typology, with a characteristic trefoil spout, and bear painted decoration with multicolored floral, animal, or abstract themes.

What is special about them is that they are inscribed with verses written in Greek, of a mostly satirical or didactic content related to wine drinking, entertainment, and well-being. The verses express the difficulties of life but also convey a sense of humor and the joy of togetherness.[8] The jugs were intended for, and

Figure 5.1 Pesaro jugs with Greek verses exhibited at the Benaki Museum, Athens. Photo by author. Used with permission.

sometimes directly commissioned by Greek buyers from the region of Epirus, today in northwestern Greece. Epirus boasted centers of commerce, wealth, and education of an emerging middle class, such as Ioannina and Kalarrytes. The economic power of this rising Greek bourgeoisie was coupled with flourishing education, European cultural orientation, and the shaping of a distinct identity.[9] By acquiring and using customized products, as these jugs were, owners were expressing their individual identity. The use of these artifacts was embedded within the communal, for drinking feasts and other group rituals, as well as for decoration of the home interior.

Especially when displayed in large numbers, the jugs were manifestations of personal financial success and heightened social status. Despite the modest nature and fragility of these objects, the large number of surviving items suggests that they resulted from quantity production. Compared with more exclusive, luxury products of Venetian or Bohemian glassmaking or French porcelain, which were also imported to southeastern Europe around the same time, these ceramic artifacts stand out as exemplary items of large-scale production intended for broader social groups.

As such, they express new mentalities, above all the emergence of consumer desire by individuals outside highly privileged elites. The individuals who bought or even directly commissioned these customized products, most likely Greek merchants, do not appear as passive subjects, but as knowledgeable, confident, and proactive consumers who wished to assert themselves. Despite the severe limitations they would experience as Christian subjects of the Ottoman Empire, they were keen to generate expressions of self-affirmation and to leave a personal imprint on their environment. Furthermore, these mundane, everyday objects may be seen as having subtle political connotations. Although the messages inscribed on them refer to wine drinking and life's struggles and are not directly political, at the same time they express confidence and represent a new awareness. Arguably, there is a clear affinity with everyday consumer objects from other cultural contexts during the same time period, carrying political messages.[10] The jugs therefore operate not only as functional vessels but also as powerful statements in three-dimensional form.[11]

Given the aforementioned properties, the jugs can be discussed on the basis of the classification model formulated by historian Giorgio Riello.[12] Following this model, I argue that the jugs under discussion are examples of "popular luxury":

> Bought for their appeal and innovation, these items entailed a certain degree of skill, but not necessarily extensive financial investment in fixed capital for their manufacture. Most such objects could be purchased ready-made, although they could be customized. . . . Their main difference compared to "undifferentiated" products is that they were market-oriented ready-made products, conscious of the variations and vagaries of fashion, conspicuous consumption, and consumer whimsy.[13]

This definition, to which the Pesaro jugs conform, essentially describes a material culture of "new luxuries" differentiated from the sumptuous, inaccessible "old luxuries." The opulence of the latter was substituted by less durable materials that were cheaper and more accessible. What distinguishes the everyday products that become the "new luxuries" is the design in an increasing range of different styles, colors, and formats; variety and customization became more and more significant. It was not the absolute value or high quality of these goods that made them precious, but their symbolic role.[14] The relevant phenomena have been studied extensively in relation to the western and northern parts of Europe.[15] As the example of the Pesaro jugs shows, comparable phenomena were also present in early modern southeastern Europe, although they remain so far under-researched.[16]

Watches: More Than Machines

The discussion may be extended to products incorporating new technologies, in particular pocket watches, mostly based on the verge escapement mechanism, which were imported from Europe, especially from England, France, and Switzerland (Figure 5.2). During the long 18th century, English and continental firms produced large numbers of these products for the large and highly lucrative markets of the Ottoman Empire. The most special feature of these watches was their distinctive numbering style; in other words, the use on the dial of "Ottoman-era numerals" used with the Arabic script predominant at the time in the Ottoman Empire. The numerals mark the hours from 1 to 12 and the minutes from 5 to 60. Although these numerals are used with the Arabic script, it would be confusing to call them "Arabic," as we use that designation nowadays for the numbers used with the Latin alphabet.[17]

The production of European clocks and watches for the Ottoman markets was not a new phenomenon. Elaborate and extremely precious watches made in Western Europe had been used as diplomatic gifts for the Sultan and high-ranking officials already since the 16th century. Gradually, a "mass" market of more accessible watches was developed during the 18th century by European watchmakers keen to exploit the markets of the Ottoman Empire. Mid- to low-price watches were shipped to Mediterranean ports like Smyrna and Thessaloniki and from there distributed widely.[18] These watches, both technical novelties and fashionable accessories, were highly popular among the middle and low strata of the local multi-ethnic and multi-confessional populations. Although there is so far no systematic study of the buyers and users of these artifacts, research on wills and probate inventories suggests that they were owned and much appreciated by the Greek populations.[19] The timekeeping function was significant primarily for Muslims, who needed to know the time of the daily prayers. More generally, watches embodied a delicate and complex relationship between utility and prestige.[20]

The symbolic properties of these artifacts were intertwined with their design, which underpinned diversification and personalization. Personal expression was materialized above all through the design of the cases in which the watch was kept. Typically, the watch mechanism, the so-called movement, was enclosed in cases made of silver, tortoise shell, and other materials; sometimes, there were three or more cases, hence the term "onion watches." These containers not only provided vital protection to the mechanism but, through their rich decoration, were

Figure 5.2 A typical mid-range English watch for the Ottoman market. Pocket watch of the fighter of the Greek War of Independence, Kanellos Deligiannis (1780–1862). Dimensions: 0.7 cm. National Historical Museum (Athens, Greece), Id. No. 4974. Used with permission.

also vehicles for the expression of identity. Floral motifs such as tulips and abstract rococo patterns were popular among the Ottomans. It was common for the cases to be made locally and to be combined with imported watch mechanisms. Thus, it was possible to offer customized, personalized designs to clients, according to their own taste. Additionally, personalization was made feasible through various decorative attachments, such as the "chatelaine," namely, a chain for suspending a watch or piece of jewelry on one's garments, one or more winding keys, seals, or other trinkets. Chains and accessories sometimes came with the watch, but often they were commissioned and added locally, in a style suiting the taste and status of the buyer. It appears that the importance of these watches lay more in their symbolic rather than their functional properties.[21]

The possession, consumption, and display of novel technical artifacts were means by which people distinguished themselves from each other and expressed themselves. A mannequin from the Benaki Museum in Athens depicts how a man would proudly wear and show off his watch, as an accessory to his garments. Such phenomena of conspicuous consumption have been studied extensively in relation to the western and northern parts of Europe; they were also manifested in early modern southeastern Europe but have received less attention so far. The popularity of such items went hand in hand with the rise of the individual and the growing significance of pleasurable consumption. Indeed, these watches were at the same time technical novelties, investment items, and fashionable accessories. Like the Pesaro jugs, they can also be classified as examples of popular luxury, following the aforementioned definition by Riello.[22] At a time of increasing mobility in work or leisure, a portable technical object was a sign of innovation and distinction embedded in new forms of socialization through product use in the public sphere. What mattered most in these situations was embracing change, pursuing novelty, actively seeking diversity and fun, and experiencing sensual gratification.[23] These phenomena were present or emerging among the Ottoman populations, as they were among the European ones, reflecting the internal dynamics of societies in flux and constituting "common threads in the worldwide experience."[24]

The market for these watches was complex and highly competitive. Hallmarks stamped on the watch cases provided information important for quality control. These hallmarks would indicate the specific properties of the materials used (especially silver), the place and date of manufacture, the name of the maker, as well as other information related to import or repair status. Another way to establish the watch's identity was by engraving the maker's name and the serial number on the watch's mechanism. The quality of the engraving of hallmarks and serial numbers, occasional misspellings, and other details are vital in helping us assess whether a watch is original or a fake; which leads to the matter of forgeries.

The success and good reputation of English makers led to the production and distribution of forgeries—practiced mainly, but not exclusively, by Continental, especially Swiss, makers. These manufacturers took advantage of the growth of the luxury trade and the high demand for English watches for the Eastern markets and specialized in making cheaper watches for those markets. Continental forgeries were usually of poor quality and easily detected, as forgers were careless about fine detail and more concerned with acquiring quick money.[25] Fake English watches often had the names of their makers falsely signed or misspelled; the information etched on surviving watches can therefore be misleading. Additionally, the abuse of hallmarks intensifies the problems of identification and provenance. Continental copiers or fakers would import empty English hallmarked silver cases and fit them to their own, usually cheaper mechanisms, making identification even more difficult. Furthermore, sometimes London manufacturers themselves illicitly imported Swiss movements, cases, and even complete watches, to be sold very profitably under their own names as London-made products.[26] Therefore, the history and practice of watch forgery have many aspects, which make the distinction between "genuine" and "fake" a highly contested matter. At the same time, it is important to stress that the end users of these products were most likely unaware of or indifferent to the distinction between "genuine" and "fake." The watches were precious to their owners anyway, as they enabled them to self-fashion themselves and to show off in the public space, thus actively participating in new forms of socialization.[27]

Conclusion: The Extra Dimension

The two examples presented, jugs and watches, were, respectively, low-tech and high-tech by the standards of the time. Though quite different, they share certain properties that allow us to classify both as popular luxury. They reveal the growing significance of pleasurable consumption of various novel artifacts, especially imported ones, in southeastern Europe during the long 18th century. Studying these and similar object groups enables us to better understand the distribution and use of products in a geographical area and a time period that remain so far insufficiently studied from the perspective of consumers and users. Consumer culture, a global phenomenon with many facets, was unfolding in the Ottoman Empire like in other parts of the world. Local societies were open to the world, willing to embrace novelty in different forms and engage in new practices in which personal choice and identity were very important.

The close study of these objects and their contexts of use suggests that users were assertive figures, making their own consumption choices and expressing themselves through a variety of objects employed in a range of new practices. In these processes, the role of customization and personalization through different design options was crucial. The performative potential inherent in the use of novel objects in both private and public spaces was also highly significant. Through the adaptive appropriation and use of novel artifacts, individuals forged new identities. Future research of a comparative and interdisciplinary nature may further illuminate the changing manifestations of consumption processes and shed more light on the development of consumer society in early modern southeastern Europe. The ways in which emerging forms of luxury were interwoven with new mentalities deserve special attention.

Certain segments of the Greek populations, in particular, enjoying comfortable living standards during the pre-revolutionary period, used and cherished artifacts like the aforementioned examples. Nevertheless, these people remained subjects of an authoritarian master and were deprived of basic rights. Arguably, the consumption of beautiful and innovative objects opened up new horizons for them and enabled them to imagine a better life. The Greek war of independence that followed was the beginning of turning this fantasy into reality.

Notes

1 Traian Stoianovich, *Between East and West: The Balkan and Mediterranean Worlds*, vol. 4: *Material Culture and Mentalités: Land, Sea and Destiny* (New Rochelle, NY: Aristide D. Caratzas, 1995); Sophia Laiou, "The Ottoman Greek "Merchants of Europe' at the Beginning of the 19th Century," in *Festschrift in Honor of Ioannis Theocharides: Studies on the Ottoman Empire and Turkey*, ed. Evangelia Balta, Georgios Salakidis, and Theoharis Stavrides, vol. II (Istanbul: The ISIS Press, 2014); Δημήτρης Παπασταματίου, Φωκίων Κοτζαγεώργης, *Ιστορία του Νέου Ελληνισμού κατά τη Διάρκεια της Οθωμανικής Πολιτικής Κυριαρχίας* [History of the New Hellenism During the Ottoman Political Domination] (Αθήνα: Σύνδεσμος Ελληνικών Ακαδημαϊκών Βιβλιοθηκών, 2015).

2 Simon Schaffer, Lissa Roberts, Raj Kapil, and James Delbourgo eds., *The Brokered World: Go-betweens and Global Intelligence 1770–1820* (Sagamore Beach, MA: Watson Publishing International, 2009).

3 Karen Barkey, *Empire of Difference: The Ottomans in Comparative Perspective* (Cambridge: Cambridge University Press, 2008), especially 109–53; Edhem Eldem, "Greece and the Greeks in Ottoman History and Turkish Historiography," *The Historical Revue/ La Revue Historique* 6 (2009): 27–40; Edhem Eldem, "Plurality, Cosmopolitanism, and Integration: The Dangers of Comparing the Incomparable," in *The Economics of Urban Diversity: The Ruhr Area and Istanbul*, ed. Darja Reuschke, Monika Salzbrunn, and Korina Schönhärl (New York: Palgrave Macmillan, 2013), 47–62; Hasan Çolak, "The Nature and Limits of Toleration in the Early Modern Ottoman Empire," *Groniek Historisch Tijdschrift* 217 (2017): 377–88.

4 E. McClung Fleming, "Artifact Study: A Proposed Model," *Winterthur Portfolio* 9 (1974): 153–73; Laurel Thatcher Ulrich et al., *Tangible Things: Making History Through Objects* (Oxford: Oxford University Press, 2005); Neil MacGregor, *A History of the World in 100 Objects* (London: Penguin, 2012); Daniel Miller, "Consumption," in *Handbook of Material Culture*, ed. Christopher Tilley et al. (London: Sage, 2013), 341–54; Karen Harvey, ed., *History and Material Culture: A Student's Guide to Approaching Alternative Sources* (New York and London: Routledge, 2018); Anne Gerritsen and Giorgio Riello, eds., *Writing Material Culture History* (London: Bloomsbury Academic, 2021).

5 Sophia Handaka, "The Objectification of History and the Historicizing of Objects: Understanding Neo-Hellenic Secular Art and Material Culture," in *The Greek World Under Ottoman and Western Domination: 15th–19th Centuries*, ed. Paschalis Kitromilides and Dimitris Arvanitakis (New York: Alexander S. Onassis Public Benefit Foundation, 2008), 93–105.

6 Ulrich et al., *Tangible Things*, 20.

7 Μιχαήλ Π. Λάμπρος, "Περί Ηπειρωτικών Ενεπίγραφων Μαστραπάδων [On Inscribed Epirote Jugs]," *Παρνασσός* 7 (1883): 269–73; Κατερίνα Κορρέ Ζωγράφου, *Τα Κεραμεικά του Ελληνικού Χώρου* [The Ceramics of Greece] (Αθήνα: Μέλισσα, 1995); Όλγα Κατσιαρδή-Hering, *Λησμονημένοι Ορίζοντες Ελλήνων Εμπόρων: Το Πανηγύρι στη Senigallia (18ος–αρχές 19ου αιώνα)* [Forgotten Horizons of Greek Merchants: The Fair at Senigallia (18th–early 19th c.] (Αθήνα: Καραβίας, 1989).

8 Βασίλης Κυριαζόπουλος, Αγγελική Χαριτωνίδου, "Ελληνικά στιχοπλάκια σε ιταλικούς μαστραπάδες [Italian Jugs with Greek Verses]," in *Πρακτικά—4ο Συμπόσιο Λαογραφίας του Βορειοελλαδικού Χώρου, Ιωάννινα 10–12 Οκτωβρίου 1979* (Θεσσαλονίκη: Ίδρυμα Μελετών Χερσονήσου του Αίμου, 1983), 83–125; Basile Kyriazopoulos and Angele Charitonidou, "Poterie de Pesaro décorée de vers en grec moderne," *Faenza* 66 (1980): 353–55.

9 Ελένη Κουρμαντζή-Παναγιωτάκου, *Η Νεοελληνική Αναγέννηση στα Γιάννενα: Από τον Πάροικο Έμπορο στον Αθανάσιο Ψαλίδα και τον Ιωάννη Βηλαρά (17ος–αρχές 19ου Αιώνα)* [The Neohellenic Renaissance at Yannena: From the Diaspora Merchant to Athanasios Psalidas and Ioannis Vilaras (17th–early 19th c.)] (Αθήνα: Gutenberg, 2007); Petros T. Pizanias, *The Making of the Modern Greeks: 1400–1820* (Newcastle: Cambridge Scholars Publishing, 2020).

10 For example, in the 1760s, English potters produced and exported for American colonial consumers brightly colored teapots with inscriptions against certain types of taxation imposed by the English rulers. Timothy H. Breen, *The Marketplace of Revolution: How Consumer Politics Shaped American Independence* (Oxford: Oxford University Press, 2005), xii–xiv. Similarly, earthenware plates with the motto "Vive la liberté" and related symbols such as flags and laurel wreaths were produced in France in the late eighteenth century, around the time of the French Revolution. Leora Auslander, "Beyond Words," *The American Historical Review* 110, no. 4 (October 2005): 1030–33.

11 Artemis Yagou, "Popular Luxury in Southeastern Europe in the Long Eighteenth Century: A Case-study of Italian Ceramics and Ottoman Greek Clients," *Journal of Early Modern History* 24, no. 4–5 (September 2020): 407–29. See also Άγγελος Δεληβοριάς, *Ο Ελληνικός Πολιτισμός της Προεπαναστατικής Ελλάδας ως Βασικός Συντελεστής του Αγώνα της Ανεξαρτησίας* [The Greek Culture of Pre-Revolutionary Greece as a Basic Factor of the Struggle for Independence] (Αθήνα: Μουσείο Μπενάκη, 2021).
12 Giorgio Riello, "Strategies and Boundaries: Subcontracting and the London Trades in the Long Eighteenth Century," *Enterprise and Society* 9, no. 2 (June 2008): 243–80.
13 Riello, "Strategies and Boundaries," 264.
14 Bruno Blondé et al., eds., *Fashioning Old and New: Changing Consumer Patterns in Western Europe (1650–1900)* (Turnhout: Brepols, 2009).
15 Peter N. Stearns, *Consumerism in World History: The Global Transformation of Desire* (London and New York: Routledge, 2001); Jan de Vries, *The Industrious Revolution: Consumer Behaviour and the Household Economy, 1650 to the Present* (Cambridge: Cambridge University Press, 2008); Frank Trentmann, *Empire of Things: How We Became a World of Consumers, from the Fifteenth Century to the Twenty-First* (London: Penguin, 2017).
16 Fatma Müge Göçek, *East Encounters West: France and the Ottoman Empire in the Eighteenth Century* (New York and Oxford: Oxford University Press, 1987); Fatma Müge Göçek, *Rise of the Bourgoisie, Demise of the Empire: Ottoman Westernization and Social Change* (New York and Oxford: Oxford University Press, 1996).
17 Otto Kurz, *European Clocks and Watches in the Near East* (London: Warburg Institute, 1975), 74. The terms "watches for the Turkish market" and "Turkish numerals" have also been used in various publications. I prefer to employ the terms "watches for the Ottoman market" and "Ottoman-era numerals" as more accurate.
18 Kurz, *European Clocks and Watches*; Ian White, *English Clocks for the Eastern Markets: English Clockmakers Trading in China and the Ottoman Empire 1580–1915* (Ticehurst: Antiquarian Horological Society, 2012).
19 Στέλιος Α. Παπαδόπουλος, Χρυσόστομος Φλωρέντης, *Κείμενα για την Τεχνική και την Τέχνη* [Texts on Technology and Art] (Αθήνα: Πολιτιστικό Ίδρυμα Ομίλου Πειραιώς, 1990).
20 Andreas Lyberatos, "Clocks, Watches and Time Perception in the Balkans: Studying a Case of Cultural Transfer," in *Encounters in Europe's Southeast: The Habsburg Empire and the Orthodox World in the Eighteenth and Nineteenth Centuries*, ed. Harald Heppner and Eva Posch (Bochum: Winkler, 2012), 231–54.
21 Rossitsa Gradeva, "On 'Frenk' Objects in Everyday Life in Ottoman Balkans: The Case of Sofia, mid-17th–mid-18th Centuries," in *Relazioni Economiche tra Europa e Mondo Islamico, secc. XIII–XVIII/ Europe's Economic Relations with the Islamic World, 13th–18th Centuries, Atti della "Trentottesima Settimana di Studi*, ed. Simonetta Cavaciocchi (Prato: Istituto Internazionale di Storia Economica F Datini-Le Monnier, 2007), 775–76.
22 Artemis Yagou, "Novel and Desirable Technology: Pocket Watches for the Ottoman Market (late 18th–mid 19th c.)," *ICON* 24 (2018–2019): 78–107; Artemis Yagou, "Mechanical and Precious: An Ottoman-Era Watch from the Deutsches Museum Collection," in *Technology, Novelty, and Luxury*, ed. Artemis Yagou, *Deutsches Museum Studies* 12 (2022): 73–92.
23 James Grehan, "Smoking and 'Early Modern' Sociability: The Great Tobacco Debate in the Ottoman Middle East (Seventeenth to Eighteenth Centuries)," *The American Historical Review* 111, no. 5 (2006): 1352–77; Shirine Hamadeh, *The City's Pleasures: Istanbul in the Eighteenth Century* (Seattle: University of Washington Press, 2007); Blondé et al., *Fashioning Old and New*.
24 Grehan, "Smoking and 'Early Modern' Sociability," 1353.
25 White, *English Clocks for the Eastern Markets*, 68.

26 Roger Smith, "The Swiss Connection: International Networks in Some Eighteenth-Century Luxury Trades," *Journal of Design History* 17, no. 2 (2004): 123–39.
27 Artemis Yagou, "Issues of Authenticity in Pocket Watches for the Ottoman Market," in *Museums—Places of Authenticity,* ed. Dominik Kimmel and Stefan Brüggerhoff (RGZM-Tagungen, Band 42) (Heidelberg: Propylaeum, 2020), 385–92.

Bibliography

Auslander, Leora. "Beyond Words." *The American Historical Review* 110, no. 4 (October 2005): 1015–45.

Barkey, Karen. *Empire of Difference: The Ottomans in Comparative Perspective*. Cambridge: Cambridge University Press, 2008.

Blondé, Bruno, Natacha Coquery, Jon Stobart, and Ilja van Damme, eds. *Fashioning Old and New: Changing Consumer Patterns in Western Europe (1650–1900).* Turnhout: Brepols, 2009.

Breen, Timothy H. *The Marketplace of Revolution: How Consumer Politics Shaped American Independence*. Oxford: Oxford University Press, 2005.

Çolak, Hasan. "The Nature and Limits of Toleration in the Early Modern Ottoman Empire." *Groniek Historisch Tijdschrift* 217 (2017): 377–88.

De Vries, Jan. *The Industrious Revolution: Consumer Behaviour and the Household Economy, 1650 to the Present.* Cambridge: Cambridge University Press, 2008.

Eldem, Edhem. "Greece and the Greeks in Ottoman History and Turkish Historiography." *The Historical Revue/La Revue Historique* 6 (2009): 27–40.

Eldem, Edhem. "Plurality, Cosmopolitanism, and Integration: The Dangers of Comparing the Incomparable." In *The Economics of Urban Diversity: The Ruhr Area and Istanbul,* edited by Darja Reuschke, Monika Salzbrunn, and Korina Schönhärl, 47–62. New York: Palgrave Macmillan, 2013.

Fleming, E. McClung. "Artifact Study: A Proposed Model." *Winterthur Portfolio* 9 (1974): 153–73.

Gerritsen, Anne, and Giorgio Riello, eds. *Writing Material Culture History.* London: Bloomsbury Academic, 2021.

Göçek, Fatma Müge. *East Encounters West: France and the Ottoman Empire in the Eighteenth Century.* New York and Oxford: Oxford University Press, 1987.

Göçek, Fatma Müge. *Rise of the Bourgoisie, Demise of the Empire: Ottoman Westernization and Social Change*. New York and Oxford: Oxford University Press, 1996.

Gradeva, Rossitsa. "On 'Frenk' Objects in Everyday Life in Ottoman Balkans: The Case of Sofia, Mid-17th- Mid-18th Centuries." In *Relazioni Economiche tra Europa e Mondo Islamico, secc. XIII-XVIII/Europe's Economic Relations with the Islamic World, 13th-18th Centuries, Atti della 'Trentottesima Settimana di Studi*, edited by Simonetta Cavaciocchi, 769–99. Prato: Istituto Internazionale di Storia Economica F Datini-Le Monnier, 2007.

Grehan, James. "Smoking and 'Early Modern' Sociability: The Great Tobacco Debate in the Ottoman Middle East (Seventeenth to Eighteenth Centuries)." *The American Historical Review* 111, no. 5 (2006): 1352–77.

Hamadeh, Shirine. *The City's Pleasures: Istanbul in the Eighteenth Century*. Seattle: University of Washington Press, 2007.

Handaka, Sophia. "The Objectification of History and the Historicizing of Objects: Understanding Neo-hellenic Secular Art and Material Culture." In *The Greek World under Ottoman and Western Domination: 15th–19th Centuries*, edited by Paschalis Kitromilides and Dimitris Arvanitakis, 93–105. New York: Alexander S. Onassis Public Benefit Foundation, 2008.

Harvey, Karen, ed. *History and Material Culture: A Student's Guide to Approaching Alternative Sources.* New York and London: Routledge, 2018.

Kurz, Otto. *European Clocks and Watches in the Near East.* London: Warburg Institute, 1975.

Kyriazopoulos, Basile, and Angele Charitonidou. "Poterie de Pesaro décorée de vers en grec moderne." *Faenza* 66 (1980): 353–55.
Laiou, Sophia. "The Ottoman Greek 'Merchants of Europe' at the Beginning of the 19th Century." In *Festschrift in Honor of Ioannis Theocharides, Studies on the Ottoman Empire and Turkey*, edited by Evangelia Balta, Georgios Salakidis, and Theoharis Stavrides, vol. II, 313–31. Istanbul: The ISIS Press, 2014.
Lyberatos, Andreas. "Clocks, Watches and Time Perception in the Balkans: Studying a Case of Cultural Transfer." In *Encounters in Europe's Southeast: The Habsburg Empire and the Orthodox World in the Eighteenth and Nineteenth Centuries*, edited by Harald Heppner and Eva Posch, 231–54. Bochum: Winkler, 2012.
MacGregor, Neil. *A History of the World in 100 Objects*. London: Penguin, 2012.
Miller, Daniel. "Consumption." In *Handbook of Material Culture*, edited by Christopher Tilley, Webb Keane, Susanne Küchler, Michael Rowlands, and Patricia Spyer, 341–54. London: Sage, 2013.
Pizanias, Petros T. *The Making of the Modern Greeks: 1400–1820*. Newcastle: Cambridge Scholars Publishing, 2020.
Riello, Giorgio. "Strategies and Boundaries: Subcontracting and the London Trades in the Long Eighteenth Century." *Enterprise and Society* 9, no. 2 (June 2008): 243–80.
Schaffer, Simon, Lissa Roberts, Raj Kapil, and James Delbourgo, eds. *The Brokered World: Go-betweens and Global Intelligence 1770–1820*. Sagamore Beach, MA: Watson Publishing International, 2009.
Smith, Roger. "The Swiss Connection: International Networks in Some Eighteenth-Century Luxury Trades." *Journal of Design History* 17, no. 2 (2004): 123–39.
Stearns, Peter N. *Consumerism in World History: The Global Transformation of Desire*. London and New York: Routledge, 2001.
Stoianovich, Traian. *Between East and West: The Balkan and Mediterranean Worlds*, vol. 4: *Material Culture and Mentalités: Land, Sea and Destiny*. New Rochelle, NY: Aristide D. Caratzas, 1995.
Trentmann, Frank. *Empire of Things: How We Became a World of Consumers, from the Fifteenth Century to the Twenty-First*. London: Penguin, 2017.
Ulrich, Laurel Thatcher, Ivan Gaskell, Sara Schechner, and Sarah Anne Carter, eds. *Tangible Things: Making History Through Objects*. Oxford: Oxford University Press, 2005.
White, Ian. *English Clocks for the Eastern Markets: English Clockmakers Trading in China and the Ottoman Empire 1580–1915*. Ticehurst: Antiquarian Horological Society, 2012.
Yagou, Artemis. "Novel and Desirable Technology: Pocket Watches for the Ottoman Market (Late 18th—Mid 19th c.)." *ICON* 24 (2018/2019): 78–107.
Yagou, Artemis. "Issues of Authenticity in Pocket Watches for the Ottoman Market." In *Museums—Places of Authenticity?*, edited by Dominik Kimmel and Stefan Brüggerhoff (RGZM—Tagungen, Band 42), 385–92. Heidelberg: Propylaeum, 2020a.
Yagou, Artemis. "Popular Luxury in Southeastern Europe in the Long Eighteenth Century: A Case-study of Italian Ceramics and Ottoman Greek Clients." *Journal of Early Modern History* 24, no. 4–5 (September 2020b): 407–29.
Yagou, Artemis. "Mechanical and Precious: An Ottoman-Era Watch from the Deutsches Museum Collection." In *Technology, Novelty, and Luxury*, edited by Artemis Yagou, vol. 12: *Deutsches Museum Studies* (2022): 73–92.
Δεληβοριάς, Άγγελος. *Ο Ελληνικός Πολιτισμός της Προεπαναστατικής Ελλάδας ως Βασικός Συντελεστής του Αγώνα της Ανεξαρτησίας*. Αθήνα: Μουσείο Μπενάκη, 2021. [Delivorrias, Angelos. *The Greek Culture of Pre-Revolutionary Greece as a Basic Factor of the Struggle for Independence*. Athens: Benaki Museum, 2021.]
Ζωγράφου, Κατερίνα Κορρέ. *Τα Κεραμεικά του Ελληνικού Χώρου*. Αθήνα: Μέλισσα, 1995. [Zografou-Korre, Katerina. *The Ceramics of Greece*. Athens: Melissa, 1995.]
Κατσιαρδή-Hering, Όλγα. *Λησμονημένοι Ορίζοντες Ελλήνων Εμπόρων: Το Πανηγύρι στη Senigallia (18ος—αρχές 19ου αιώνα)*. Αθήνα: Καραβίας, 1989. [Katsiardi-Hering, Olga.

Forgotten Horizons of Greek Merchants: The Fair at Senigallia (18th–Early 19th c.). Athens: Karavias, 1989.]

Κουρμαντζή-Παναγιωτάκου, Ελένη. *Η Νεοελληνική Αναγέννηση στα Γιάννενα: Από τον Πάροικο Έμπορο στον Αθανάσιο Ψαλίδα και τον Ιωάννη Βηλαρά (17ος-αρχές 19ου Αιώνα).* Αθήνα: Gutenberg, 2007. [Kourmantzi-Panagiotakou, Eleni. *The Neohellenic Renaissance at Yannena: From the Diaspora Merchant to Athanasios Psalidas and Ioannis Vilaras (17th–Early 19th c.).* Athens: Gutenberg, 2007.]

Κυριαζόπουλος, Βασίλης, Χαριτωνίδου, Αγγελική. "Ελληνικά στιχοπλάκια σε ιταλικούς μαστραπάδες." In *Πρακτικά—4ο Συμπόσιο Λαογραφίας του Βορειοελλαδικού Χώρου, Ιωάννινα, 10–12 Οκτωβρίου 1979*, 83–125. Θεσσαλονίκη: Ίδρυμα Μελετών Χερσονήσου του Αίμου, 1983. [Kyriazopoulos, Basile, and Angele Charitonidou. "Italian Jugs with Greek Verses." In *Proceedings—4th Symposium of Northern Greece Folklore, Ioannina, October 10–12, 1979*, 83–125. Thessaloniki: Institute for Balkan Studies, 1983.]

Λάμπρος, Μιχαήλ Π. "Περί Ηπειρωτικών Ενεπίγραφων Μαστραπάδων." *Παρνασσός* 7 (1883): 269–73. [Lambros, Michael P. "On Inscribed Epirote Jugs." *Parnassos* 7 (1883): 269–73.]

Παπαδόπουλος, Στέλιος Α., Φλωρέντης, Χρυσόστομος. *Κείμενα για την Τεχνική και την Τέχνη.* Αθήνα: Πολιτιστικό Ίδρυμα Ομίλου Πειραιώς, 1990. [Papadopoulos, Stelios A., and Chrysostomos Florentis. *Texts on Technology and Art.* Athens: The ETBA Cultural Foundation, 1990.]

Παπασταματίου Δημήτρης, Κοτζαγεώργης Φωκίων. *Ιστορία του Νέου Ελληνισμού κατά τη Διάρκεια της Οθωμανικής Πολιτικής Κυριαρχίας.* Αθήνα: Σύνδεσμος Ελληνικών Ακαδημαϊκών Βιβλιοθηκών, 2015. [Papastamatiou, Dimitris, and Phokion Kotzageorgis. *History of the New Hellenism During the Ottoman Political Domination.* Athens: Syndesmos Ellinikon Akadimaikon Vivliothikon, 2015.]

Part 2

The 1820s

The Dawn of a New Era

6 Between Private Wealth and State Revenues

Was Ali Paşa of Ioannina a Rich Man?

Dimitris Dimitropoulos

At the beginning of December 1820, the newspaper *Niles' Weekly Register* of Baltimore, USA, published the following news report:

> Trieste, Sept. 17. A Greek vessel, which arrived here yesterday from Corfu, announces that squadron of Ali Pacha had surrendered to that of the Porte on the first attack, by the treachery of the Greek crews. Two sons of Ali Pacha, who were on board, were put in irons and sent to Constantinople. Ali Pacha had been abandoned by most of his followers, and the Turks had entered Janina. It is said that he has retired with about 200 men into the castle of Janina, from which it will be difficult for him to escape. It is said that the treasures amassed in that fortress, which is very strong, amount to 23.000.000 of dollars, the fruit of his robberies and oppression during forty years. The Greeks generally rejoice at the fall of their tyrant.[1]

This was not the first time the newspaper had published news stories from the Greek territories, often peppered with inaccuracies just like this one. Fifteen months later, the newspaper published another story on the execution of Ali Paşa, including a reference to the gold he had in his possession:

> A comparatively inconsiderable quantity of treasure was found in his citadel [compared] to what was expected—it is stated that he had emptied his chests of gold into the lake and put to death those who had been employed in the service, [so] that the exact place might remain known only to himself.[2]

In November 2022, a strange news item made the rounds on the Greek media. A house in Ioannina was rendered uninhabitable due to illegal excavations conducted in a neighboring plot of land by treasure hunters looking for the treasure of Ali Paşa.[3] The story may sound bizarre, but it is actually just another addition to a long string of stories, narratives, and rumors about the famous "Ali Paşa treasure," which have been circulating for more than two centuries, starting immediately after his death.[4] The existence of this allegedly vast treasure has become firmly entrenched in the Balkan imaginary, rousing passions and raising hopes with the tantalizing promise of a unique get-rich-quick opportunity. The treasure has

DOI: 10.4324/9781003500780-9

spawned legends, triggered arguments and debates, and generated plenty of unsuccessful expeditions by treasure hunters who are convinced that it is hidden in this or that place. The literature on Ali Paşa is riddled with references to his wealth, outdone only by the intensely speculative para-literature on the subject, which is also the source of the various improbable scenarios surrounding Ali Paşa's lost treasure. Indeed, the fact that his persecutors found only meager amounts of wealth in his coffers in Ioannina has not daunted prospective treasure hunters in the least but has instead excited their imagination, since it was seen as proof that the treasure had been successfully stashed away before his death, or even that it had helped fund the Greek revolution.

The testimonies of European travelers, the accounts of his courtiers, contemporary written evidence, material remnants from his residences, and a multitude of oral traditions spreading by word of mouth compose a thick layer of information on the topic, and although these accounts might vary in provenance and credibility, Ali Paşa's mythical wealth is invariably at the center of them. The image of Ali Paşa as an avaricious usurper, an obscenely wealthy but also miserly man, has become commonplace in the sizeable and diverse literature on the ruler of the territories that today constitute Southern Albania and Western and Central Greece.[5]

But what did this wealth consist of? The seraglios, the harems, the money and jewelry, and the movable and immovable assets that were accumulated by the Vezir of Ioannina, his sons, and his grandsons at the peak of their power had captured people's imagination. Nevertheless, for all the studies in the relevant literature which blend historical evidence with unreliable, impressionistic information,[6] there are also serious works that approach the issue earnestly and systematically.[7] Ali Paşa's *çiftlik*s and various revenues have also been investigated by modern financial historians. Findings from the Ottoman records in Constantinople have allowed researchers, mainly experts in the Ottoman Empire, to locate concrete evidence on Ali's financials. These are registries compiled by the Porte's representatives after Ali's death in order to establish a clear overview of his assets and proceed with all the actions necessary for their management. Among these materials, emphasis has been put on the lists of the villages that are characterized as Ali Paşa's *çiftlik*s, based on the records compiled after his death.[8] These records show the state of his fortune in 1822 when his power had diminished substantially after he had been stripped of all offices and been in conflict with the Sultan for almost two years. Therefore, they do not accurately portray his financial situation in the heyday of his house. Even so, they are still indicative of his power and the impressive size of the region over which he held sway.

Moreover, calculating Ali Paşa's wealth in currency became an intriguing and recurring question in historiography. Using the same Ottoman sources, modern researchers have attempted to put a monetary value on Ali Paşa's fortune at the time of his death. Some estimate that it amounted to 27 million piasters (*kuruş*) and the total wealth of Ali and his sons to 43 million piasters.[9] These sums might provide a sense of scale for the capital inflows into Ali Paşa's treasury, but at the same time, I believe that they can obfuscate his fortune's true size, as they attempt to narrow it down to a simple number when his wealth was so diffuse and scattered that it is impossible to attribute a definitive value to it in currency. Besides, all available evidence is derived from fragmentary data that cannot possibly provide a complete picture of his finances, while also relying on the assumption that there is an ideal direct correlation between the power, office, and influence of Ali Paşa and his personal and familial fortune, namely, the totality of his wealth whether in coin or land. But was that actually the case?

During the late 18th and early 19th century, when Ali Paşa emerged and rose to prominence, there was a series of provincial power-holders who temporarily accumulated and consolidated significant amounts of power and wealth,[10] flourishing under the eye of the Ottoman central government, who either condoned or tolerated them. These local magnates held public office and were appointed to administrative positions in the Empire which allowed them to collect a wide array of state revenues. They ascended to dominance by utilizing their powerful extended families and passing down positions of power from one generation to the next, thus establishing a strong and influential house. They also diversified their financial activities beyond the realm of public finances.[11] In this way, they differed from the affluent, urban Ottomans of the past, whose wealth derived solely from land owning, money lending, and a web of financial activities.[12] Instead, these new influential figures combined their power with high-ranking local administrative positions.

The nature of ownership in the Ottoman world does not coincide exactly with the exclusive and exclusionary relationship between object and owner stipulated by Greco-Roman law and the ownership model of the Western European Christian world.[13] In the Ottoman reality, ownership, at least of immovable assets, constituted mostly the possession of rights, even if in practice this possession ended up resembling a Western European form of ownership. This concept of rights or, more accurately, of successive layers of rights superimposed over immovable property, had wider practical implications for the Ottoman officials, both in central government and in provincial administration, since their wealth was accumulated through a web of leasing and subcontracting revenues.

Ottoman officeholders led a life characterized by insecurity, volatility, and precariousness. Their wealth was a product of their office and their relationships with the Sultan's circle. If an officeholder fell into disfavor, his assets would be confiscated and he would be executed; in other words, officeholders lived in fear of losing not just their fortunes but their lives.[14] Though different in many other respects, precarity is the common element linking the Muslim *ayan* and the Phanariots, their Christian equivalent in Constantinople and the Danubian Principalities, whose ascent and downfall were also directly associated with the Sultan's favor which was granted on a personal basis, at least until the major crisis triggered by the Greek Revolution.[15]

Due to his meteoric rise and precipitous downfall, leading to the eventual disappearance of his house, I believe that Ali Paşa's trajectory deviates from the typical stories of other provincial powerholders. However, it is a concrete example of the direct correlation between the accumulation of power and wealth and the Sublime Porte, since most of the assets amassed by Ali, his sons, and grandsons derived from the granting of concessions by the Porte, starting with Ali's appointment to the Paşalik of Ioannina and, more importantly, his assignment to the position of Commander of the *Derbends* (*derbend nazırı*, Guardian of the Mountain Passes). Therefore, it is no surprise that his wealth evaporated after he was proscribed by the Sultan.[16]

The question then becomes: Did Ali Paşa possess any assets that did not hinge on his position in the Ottoman administrative system or was he a mere usufructuary, extracting profit from assets that were public or, at least, of unclear ownership? Let us take a closer look at some of the components of his purported fortune:

a) The building compounds he owned and resided in were directly dependent on his public office.[17] Ali Paşa's various seraglios, which were spread across the territories he controlled, were built with funds accumulated through his position or from extraordinary levies imposed on the populations under his jurisdiction.
b) Ali might have possessed considerable swaths of arable land, grazing fields, and *çiftlik* villages, but this possession did not constitute a straightforward form of total ownership. In practice, what he possessed was enhanced rights to the local production or, more generally, to the land's potential yield in revenue or produce,[18] a privilege directly associated with the appropriation powers granted to him by his office. The large number of emerging *çiftlik*s, the so-called "*çiftliki*-zation" of the land, was part of this process.[19] It was a situation that generated constant conflict and uncertain results since its outcome was dependent on how networked and powerful the implicated parties were in each case.[20]
c) The revenues pouring into his coffers came from a vast and complex network of sources. It was an enterprise of gigantic proportions, not only for its time but even by today's standards. Although it was based in Ioannina and had Constantinople as its point of reference, it was geographically diffuse both within and beyond the borders of the Paşaliks controlled by Ali and his family.[21] It was also a multifaceted operation that comprised an expansive range of enterprises.[22] Indicatively, some of them were: leasing and subleasing tax revenues, offering security and protection services, trading agricultural and livestock products (mostly acquired through the land tenure relations he had established), money-lending and usury, exploitation/confiscation of property not claimed by inheritance (known as "machloulika," from the Turkish *mahlul*, to escheat), and other complex tasks relating to tax collection, which were not strictly public, since they also affected the function of the market within the context of a centrally guided financial system. The more characteristic examples are "tzelepiko," a livestock tax paid in kind, *iştira/mubayaa*, the obligation to sell commodities at a fixed price, and "palto," a duty on tobacco.[23] Ali Paşa employed a wide array of practices to extract profits, including but not limited to, farming out the revenues from *timar* lands, awarding *malikâne* contracts to straw men or even non-existent persons, transacting directly with the representatives of Christian communities who had undertaken, sometimes at Ali's own behest, the lump-sum payment of the local taxes according to the *maktu* system, and leveraging communal and other debt with third parties, especially the craft guilds of Ioannina.[24]

d) Paying for protection or, rather, capitulating to Ali Paşa's protection racket, determined the height of the appropriated funds.[25] One of the most characteristic practices was "agaliki," the practice of extracting extra revenue from the local Christian communities that had been forced to come under Ali Paşa's patronage.[26]
e) Ali Paşa traded large quantities of products which he accumulated through farming tax revenue and imposing extractive land tenure relations on farmers. This endeavor appears to have been profitable but operated outside standard commercial practices.[27] The goods traded were mostly grains, especially wheat, but also livestock, mostly sheep and goats, which he collected and channeled to Constantinople. In fact, for more than 30 years, Ali Paşa regularly bought the tax revenues from the *mubayaa* and the "tzelepiko" of Thessaly and other regions, organizing a complex supply network that handled products, funds, and transportation. The process of appropriating these products from farmers at the low prices set by the Sublime Porte and using them to provision the capital required an extensive network of collaborators and a considerable amount of power and control but also yielded substantial profits.[28] Indicatively, in 1829, Veli Paşa mentions in an *arzuhal* addressed to his father that "tzelepiko" is "our household's primary *irat* [source of income]."[29]
f) Finally, his fortune included the cash he collected from various sources in the form of coins or jewelry which he kept in his residence, as well as the money he moved in the form of securities and bills of exchange (*poliçe*).

I believe that the workings of this complex apparatus, which allowed Ali Paşa's rule to grow in power and expand in size, are still not fully known or completely understood. It relied on the bonds of the conjugal and extended family as well as the relationships developed through kinship, rank, locality, mutuality, and vested interest. It required the integration and active participation of a multitude of people with distinct responsibilities and the establishment of a network that allowed the accumulation of huge amounts of funds as well as the distribution and diffusion of these funds through a hierarchical system across various groups of participants. Two elements necessary for such a vast network to function were faith in the ruler and trust among the participants, both of which were affirmed through traditional honor and morality codes. Indicatively, contemporary correspondence is replete with appeals to a sense of honor and integrity and threats of shame and disgrace. Besides moral obligation, the military might of a large troop of soldiers, financed by Ali himself, the use of violence, threats, and fear, as well as widespread bribery were also key components of the financial operation he had established.

Therefore, it becomes clear that Ali Paşa's vast apparatus was funded through a variety of sources. I believe that the observation of a French military official who had stayed in the area and had first-hand knowledge of the issue is particularly astute: "His revenues are very considerable, but it is impossible to estimate them [with] any degree of exactitude, because he follows no fixed rule in the repartition and collection of his imposts."[30] However, it should be noted that these considerable revenue inflows were matched by equally large outflows. A significant number of people, both within and outside Ali Paşa's ruling system, relied on it for their livelihood, whether they received a regular salary (*ulûfe*) or leased some form of revenue. It is impossible to calculate with any semblance of precision the total costs incurred by Ali Paşa's rule: compensating all the people responsible for administering, managing, and operating this complex system; maintaining armed troops in order to retain power and control; offering tributes and bribes to gain support and facilitate procedures; financing his and his household's lavish lifestyle (relatives, harem, servants, guards, seraglio maintenance); and, finally, buying the approval of the population through favorable interventions and charitable work. Indicatively, only some partial costs can be found in accounts and other accounting evidence in his archive, but as they focus on specific revenues at specific times in specific regions, they are too diffuse and scattered to paint a complete picture.[31]

Besides, despite the multitude of individual accounts about Ali Paşa's wealth, it is even difficult to calculate the height of his total profits, as they were particularly susceptible to unforeseen outside factors. One characteristic example is Ali Paşa's tenure as Commander of the *Derbend*s. We know that this position was crucial to his career,[32] mainly because it allowed him to extend his power and influence, both official and unofficial, beyond the limits of his own Paşalik, and gave him the opportunity to keep numerous armed men on his payroll, while cultivating a climate of fear which bolstered his protection racket, thus establishing a network of connections with an array of local notables and communities. It is certain that beyond these intangible benefits, this endeavor yielded actual material profit. But how high was it?

In April 1797, when Ali Paşa had already been in office for ten years, his man in Constantinople, Stefanos Misou, informed him that the vali of Rumeli was offering 100,000 piasters for the position, estimating that it would generate 200,000 piasters in earnings.[33] In February 1814, Hüseyin, Ali Paşa's agent (*kapı çuhadarı*) in Constantinople, warns him that there is talk of eliminating the position entirely and assigning the guardianship of the passes to the local Paşas. He goes on to inform him about the meetings he had in order to forestall this negative development and urges Ali Paşa to spare no expense and offer gifts to those vying for abolition in order to win their favor. He even goes as far as to suggest providing a high-level official with a monthly stipend.[34] In June of the same year, Hüseyin raised the issue again, writing that the gift (*hediye*) offered to the Sultan must be of a value corresponding to the "height of a king."[35] In January 1820, when Ali Paşa's future is starting to look dire, Hüseyin Bey, who is now stationed in Larisa, reports a conversation with Süleyman, the new Paşa of the region, who feigns unwillingness to take on the guardianship of the mountain passes even though he is told that it yields 500,000 piasters in profits.[36] By May, Ali Paşa's enemies had resolved what was described as "their greatest concern";[37] Ali had been removed from office and the new Commander of the *Derbend*s, Süleyman, was trying to negotiate the withdrawal of Ali Paşa's guards who were purposefully stalling.[38]

It becomes evident that even Ali's contemporaries provided different estimates for the profits generated by the position of Commander of the *Derbend*s. Ali Paşa managed to hold on to this office by any means necessary for more than 30 years, a testament to his power and ability. His long tenure contributed enormously to what became a fundamental element of the financial apparatus he established: a vast network of collaborators and the constant movement of large sums both in cash and securities. Managing this operation and keeping track of all the necessary figures required specialized personnel capable of understanding the details of each settlement, the pertinent deadlines, and the delicate maneuvering needed in order to charge, accept, collect, or reimburse all these sums. Ali Paşa and members of his family had representatives (*kapı çuhadarı*) stationed in Constantinople and other large cities. These agents of Ali Paşa's house were in constant communication with their lords, always ready to resolve any issues that might arise.

A letter by Hüseyin, Ali Paşa's *çuhadar* in Constantinople, dating from 1814, provides a detailed description of how these representatives worked, how tax revenues were farmed to buyers, how long these buyers had to pay the taxes, whether in installments or a lump sum, as well as the methods they used to delay payment. Speed and flexibility were required in order to maintain valuable personal connections, make necessary visits, and attend face-to-face meetings, in addition to managing an extensive network of bribery for high-ranking officials. Ali Paşa himself appears to have been in direct control of expenditures relating to gifts and tributes while also keeping close track of their effectiveness. An exchange quoted by Hüseyin is indicative. Ali claims that he does offer gifts, but he also wants them to produce results because "it's not like I have a *darphane* (mint) cutting *asper*s."[39]

The financiers (*sarraf*) who worked with Ali Paşa, especially those based in the capital of the Ottoman Empire, played an active role in managing his networks and operations.[40] The 1813–1814 register (*defter*) of Gasparis, an Armenian *sarraf* in Constantinople who collaborated with Ali, indicates the scale of the transactions being cross-referenced by these financiers. In turn, the frequency, geographical distribution, and scope of the recorded activities provide a sense of scale for the height of the funds moving through Ali Paşa's treasury. According to these expense reports, Ali Paşa spent 857,242.20 piasters in 1813 and 995,521.25 in 1814 through Gasparis alone. Of these sums, about 60% was allocated for the purchase of tax rights, yearly leases of tax revenues (*mukataa*), customs tariffs, and the subletting of rights to *timar* lands. The rest was mostly distributed among Ali's people in Constantinople in the form of monthly salaries (*aylık*) or was used to fund bribes and purchase gifts for officials. These were expenditures in expectation of profit—investments, so to speak, which had a yearly rate of return.[41] The nature of the evidence does not allow us to make assumptions about Ali's possible inflows of funds, but it does paint a picture of the financial environment in which he was operating. However, calculating his profit margins or estimating the profits of the entire Ali Paşa financial system is not possible since it would require incorporating a series of factors and economic figures that, in my opinion, cannot be accurately appraised.

Besides, the very nature of these transactions left room for huge financial discrepancies. The different ways in which these divergences were settled or resolved depended on circumstance, influence, and the transitory distribution of power among the implicated officeholders. One of the many testimonies on the economic, or rather extra-economic, environment in which Ali Paşa operated describes Ali's efforts to place one of his own people in the office of voivode in Naoussa in 1814. Ali was willing to pay a bribe of 10,000 piasters, but the official in question demanded to be paid the same amount in zecchini (Venetian gold coins). With the currency exchange rate at the time standing at about 1 zecchino to 14 piasters, Ali was being called to pay 14 times the intended amount.[42]

The existence of documents containing yearly economic data on the tax liabilities of villages and the rights owners of tax revenues indicates that Ali Paşa's financial staff, his treasurers (*defterdar*), and his treasurer-in-chief (*hazinedar*) kept accounts on the funds given and received on at least a yearly basis. Did the data in these individual registers eventually end up in the equivalent of a comprehensive spreadsheet encompassing all his inflows and outflows, a sort of balance sheet for his entire treasury? It is doubtful. In any case, no document compiling all these partial data into an overarching financial record for Ali's whole enterprise has been found.

But did the vezir of Epirus even have a central treasury? Did his sons and grandsons manage their own financials and what were the limits of their independence? It seems that Ali's apparatus was internally structured according to his own choices and decisions, similarly to how the Sultan imposed his will on his subordinates on the level of the Empire.[43] According to evidence from 1811, when Ali's power was at its peak, the vezir himself had attempted to compile a written record of the distribution of offices, duties, and roles among the members of his family while they were on a military campaign in Sofia on his orders.[44] Although Ali Paşa invokes his age to justify compiling this list, it is obvious that it is not supposed to function as a will dividing an inheritance, but as a record of the distribution of power and responsibility among the members of a family who are expected to work in tandem.

Did the revenues collected and the expenditures incurred by the members of Ali Paşa's family become integrated into a unified, consolidated financial administration under the authority of the pater familias? Did Ali himself decide which revenues he would claim from the Sublime Porte and then determine how the profits would be distributed to his relatives and courtiers? It is not entirely clear how the vezir of Ioannina handled his personal finances, but some letters addressed to him by his sons point to the existence of a common treasury. For example, when Muhtar Paşa arrived in Nafpaktos, the chief town of the Paşalik to which he was appointed, he sent a letter to his father in which he details the financial needs of his territory, informs him of current expenses and obligations, requests provisions and supplies, and states that he will soon send comprehensive accounting reports (*defter*) on all outstanding transactions.[45]

In the same vein, in December 1818, Veli Paşa was answering his father's veiled prompting to provide him with economic assistance so that he could rebuild his seraglio in Tepelenë which had been destroyed in a fire. Veli informs Ali Paşa that he would never have even considered such a course of action because "your highness is the master of everything and it is within your power to use money from the payroll of the army troops in your service for other purposes."[46] In June 1820, when Ali Paşa's conflict with the Sublime Porte was already brewing, Muhtar Paşa mentioned to his father that he had received 60,500 piasters to cover the payroll of his army troops, but that he was still waiting on another 100,000 piasters to be used as payment to the soldiers for services rendered. In fact, he reassures his father that "the money you will send me will be accounted for, you're not going to lose anything."[47]

On February 23, 1822, Ali Paşa's severed head was exhibited in the courtyard of his seraglio, placed on a tray on a marble column for everyone to see. According to an eyewitness, Robert Walsh, an Irish vicar, there was a sign with a long text (*yafta*) posted on the opposite wall, publicly explaining the reasons for his execution. It began with the following words:

> The head hear [*sic*] exposed is that of a traitor to religion, known by the name Tepedelenly Ali Pacha. It is notorious, that during thirty or forty successive years, this Tepedelenly Ali Pacha, had been loaded with favours by the Porte, which entrusted to him the government of several provinces and districts. Himself, his sons, and those connected with them, have received numerous benefits from the Sultan.[48]

I believe that Ali Paşa's *yafta* accurately represents the Ottoman reality. The three or four decades of Ali Paşa's ascent, his affluence and approval, were contingent on the power vested in him by the Sublime Porte. Losing Sultan's favor, or clashing with him in any way, led to religious stigmatization, economic collapse, and, ultimately, dishonorable death, which is exactly what happened when Ali was deposed and proscribed by the piaPorte at the beginning of 1820. Ali Paşa's wealth, just like the wealth of the other officeholders like him, known as *ayan*, hinged entirely on the power bestowed upon them. It could not exist without it. In fact, in the cases when this wealth was accumulated through entrepreneurial activities relating directly or indirectly to public finances, it was even more precarious since the Ottoman administration did not make a clear distinction between private wealth and public revenue.[49] The position of Ali Paşa and his ilk in the Ottoman system was both a privilege and a trap. Especially someone as powerful and influential as Ali Paşa was essentially protected by his office. The moment he stopped being a Paşa, he was bound to lose not just his fortune, but his life.

Archives

Αρχείο Αλή πασά Συλλογής Ι. Χώτζη, Γενναδείου Βιβλιοθήκης [Ali Paşa Archive, I. Chotzis Collection, Gennadius Library], edited by Panagiotopoulos Vasilis, in collaboration with Dimitropoulos Dimitris, Michailaris Panagiotis, vol. 1–4. Athens: Institute of Historical Research/National Hellenic Research, 2007–2009.

Notes

I would like to thank Eleni Vosinaki for the English translation of my paper.

1 *Niles' Weekly Register* 19, no. 482 (December 2, 1820): 220.

2 *Niles' Weekly Register (1814–1837)* 22, no. 558 (May 18, 1822): 180.

3 "Αναζητώντας τον χαμένο θησαυρό του Αλή πασά [Searching for Ali Paşa's Lost Treasure]," www.ertnews.gr/video/anazitontas-ton-chameno-thisayro-toy-ali-pasa/.
4 Βασίλης Παναγιωτόπουλος, "Εισαγωγή [Introduction]," in *Αρχείο Αλή πασά Συλλογής Ι. Χώτζη, Γενναδείου Βιβλιοθήκης*, ed. Βασίλης Παναγιωτόπουλος, in collaboration with Δημήτρης Δημητρόπουλος, Παναγιώτης Μιχαηλάρης, vol. 4 (Αθήνα: Ινστιτούτο Νεοελληνικών Ερευνών, Εθνικό Ίδρυμα Ερευνών, 2009), 91–97.
5 From the recent literature, see Katherine E. Fleming, *The Muslim Bonaparte: Diplomacy and Orientalism in Ali Paşa's Greece* (Princeton, NJ: Princeton University Press, 1999), 38–43.
6 Indicatively see Δημήτριος Κ. Βαρδουνιώτης, "Οι θησαυροί του Αλή πασά [The Treasures of Ali Paşa]," in *Εθνικόν Ημερολόγιον του έτους 1914* (Αθήνα, 1914), 364–68; Κώστας Καιροφύλας, "Τι απέγιναν οι θησαυροί Αλή και Βελή πασά [What Happened to the Treasures of Ali Paşa and Veli Paşa]," *Ηπειρωτική Εστία* 17 (1968): 27–32.
7 Most prominent among them is the study by André Andréades, "Ali pacha de Tébelin économiste et financier," *La Revue des Études Grecques (j.)* 25 (1912): 427–60, while Nik. Patselis has also collected some interesting data in his study Νικόλαος Πατσέλης, "Η οικονομική πολιτική και ο πλούτος του Αλή πασά των Ιωαννίνων [Economic Policy and the Wealth of Ali Paşa of Ioannina]," *Αρχείον των Οικονομικών και Κοινωνικών Επιστημών* 16 (1936): 115–47. For a synthetic critical approach on the subject, see Παναγιωτόπουλος, "Εισαγωγή," 90–112; Μαρία Κ. Ανεμοδουρά, "Πολιτικές και οικονομικές δομές στην επικράτεια του Αλή πασά Τεπεντελενλή. Από τον "Ανατολικό Δεσποτισμό' ως τη νεωτερικότητα [Political and Economic Structures in the Territories Ruled by Tepedelenli Ali Paşa: From "Oriental Despotism' to Modernism]" (PhD diss., Εθνικό και Καποδιστριακό Πανεπιστήμιο Αθηνών, 2020), 256–470.
8 Indicatively, see the studies by Hamiyet Sezer, "Tepedelenli Ali paşa'nın çiftlikleri üzerine bir araştırma," *Belleten* 62 (1998): 75–106; Hamiyet Sezer, "Tepedelenli Ali Paşa ve Ogulların Çiftlik ve Gelirlerine İlişkin Yeni Bilgi—Bulgular," *Osmanli Tarihi Araştırma ve Uygulama Merkezi Dergisi (OTAM)* 18 (2005): 333–57 (the Greek translation annotated by Eirini Kalogeropoulou can be found in Hamiyet Sezer, "Νέες πληροφορίες και ευρήματα σχετικά με τα τσιφλίκια και τα εισοδήματα του Αλή Πασά και των γιων του [New Information and Findings About the Çiftliks and Revenues of Ali Paşa and His Sons]," trans. and annot. Eirini Kalogeropoulou, *Instrumenta Studiorum Balkanica*, IHR/NHRF digital library, www.eie.gr/nhrf/institutes/inr/instr-studiorumbalk/instr-studiorumballkarticles-gr.html). See also Fatma Öncel Yusufoglu, "Agrarian Relations and Estate (Chiftlik) Agriculture in Ottoman Thessaly (c. 1770–1880)" (PhD diss., Bogazici University, 2018), 72–117, 251–68; Ανεμοδουρά, *Πολιτικές και οικονομικές δομές*, 267–328. The information from the Ottoman sources fill the list of the 930 çiftliks compiled by Christoforos Philitas, a teacher from Epirus (Σπυρίδων Π. Αραβαντινός, *Ιστορία Αλή πασά του Τεπελενλή* [The History of Tepedelenli Ali Paşa], vol. 2 (Αθήνα: Εκ του Τυπογραφείου των Καταστημάτων Σπυρίδωνος Κουσουλίνου, 1895), 601–10) and the list of *çiftlik*s belonging to Veli Paşa at *Αρχείο Αλή πασά,* 2, 544–53, doc. 1365; Ιωάννης Γιαννόπουλος, "Τα τσιφλίκια του Βελή πασά υιού του Αλή πασά [The *Çiftliks* of Veli Paşa, Son of Ali Paşa]," *Μνήμων* 2 (1972): 135–58.
9 Ahmet Uzun, "Tepedelenli Ali paşa ve mal varlığı," *Belleten* 65, no. 244 (2001): 1058–60 (the Greek translation in Ahmet Uzun, "Ο Αλή πασάς ο Τεπελενλής και η περιουσία του [Tepedelenli Ali Paşa and his Fortune]," trans. Giorgos Syrmas, *Instrumenta Studiorum Balkanica*, IHR/NHRF digital library, 30–32, www.eie.gr/nhrf/institutes/inr/instr-studiorumbalk/instr-studiorumballkarticles-gr.html).
10 Ali Yaycioglou, "Provincial Power-Holders and the Empire in the Late Ottoman World: Conflict or Partnership?" in *The Ottoman World*, ed. Christine Woodhead (New York: Routledge, 2012), 436–52.
11 Ali Yaycioglou, *Partners of the Empire: The Crisis of the Ottoman Order in the Age of Revolutions* (Stanford: Stanford University Press, 2016), 68–69, 96–98.

12 Eleni Gara, "Moneylenders and Landowners: In Search of Urban Muslim Elites in the Early Modern Balkans," in *Provincial Elites in the Ottoman Empire Halycon Days in Crete V: A Symposiom Held in Rethymno, January 10–12, 2003*, ed. Antonis Anastasopoulos (Rethymno: Crete University Press, 2005), 135–47. For an illustration of the scope and distribution of their activities, see also the well-documented case of Thessaloniki's Muslim rich in Phokion Kotzageorgis and Dimitris Papastamatiou, "Wealth Accumulation in an Urban Context: The Profile of the Muslim Rich of Thessaloniki in the Eighteenth Century on the Basis of Probate Inventories," *Turkish Historical Review* 5 (2014): 165–99.

13 For the concept of property in the Ottoman world, see Joseph Schacht, *An Introduction to Islamic Law* (Oxford: Oxford University Press, 1982), 134–43.

14 Yaycioglou, *Partners of the Empire*, 107–9.

15 On the similarities and differences between the Phanariots and the *ayan,* see Christine Philliou, *Biography of an Empire: Governing Ottomans in an Age of Revolution* (Berkeley and Los Angeles: University of California Press, 2011), 22–35.

16 Παναγιωτόπουλος, "Εισαγωγή," 4, 30–36.

17 See Mary Emily Neumeier, "The Architectural Transformation of the Ottoman Provinces Under Tepedelenli Ali Paşa, 1788–1822" (PhD diss., University of Pennsylvania, 2016), 35–95.

18 Some attempts at estimating the land tax revenues in areas controlled by Ali Paşa were made by Σπύρος Ι. Ασδραχάς, *Ελληνική κοινωνία και οικονομία, ιη΄ και ιθ΄ αιώνες* [Greek Society and Economy, 18th and 19th century] (Αθήνα: Ερμής, 1982), 79–144; Γιώργος Προγουλάκης, "Στα εδάφη του Αλή πασά: παραγωγή, γαιοπρόσοδος, κερδοφορία του χρήματος [Economy in Ali Paşa's Territories: Production, Land Revenues and Investment Profits]," *Τα Ιστορικά* 32 (2000): 73–88.

19 On the *çiftlik* formation process, see Bruce McGowan, *Economic Life in Ottoman Europe: Taxation, Trade and the Struggle for Land, 1600–1800* (Cambridge: Cambridge University Press, 1981), 135–41; Sophia Laiou, "Some Considerations Regarding Çiftlik Formation in the Western Thessaly, Sixteenth-Nineteenth Centuries," in *The Ottoman Empire, the Balkans, the Greek Lands: Toward a Social and Economic History. Studies in Honor of John C. Alexander*, ed. Elias Kolovos et al. (Istanbul: The ISIS Press, 2007), 255–77. For a critical review of the extensive literature, see Yannis Spyropoulos, Stefanos Poulios, and Antonis Anastasopoulos, "Çiftliks, Landed Elites, and Tax Allocation in Eighteenth-Century Ottoman Veroia," *European Journal of Turkish Studies* (2022), https://doi.org/10.4000/ejts.6647.

20 See relevant examples in Fatma Öncel, "Land, Tax and Power in the Ottoman Provinces: The Malikâne-Mukataa of Esma Sultan in Alasonya (c.1780–1825)," *Turkish Historical Review* 8 (2017): 63–65; Aysel Yıldız, "Politics, Economy, and *Çiftliks*: The History of Four *Çiftliks* in Larissa (Yenişehir-i Fener)," *Turkish Historical Review* 11 (2020): 57–60.

21 A research team at the University of Stanford has attempted to trace the network of Ali Paşa through his correspondence and other evidence: Ali Yaycioglu et al., "Visualizing Ali Pasha Order: Relations, Networks and Scales," Research Project Mapping Ottoman Epirus (Center for Spatial and Textual Analysis (CESTA) Stanford University in Collaboration with Institute of Historical Research/National Hellenic Research Foundation), https://mapoe.stanford.edu/projects/visualizing-ali-Paşa-order-relations-networks-and-scales.

22 For the meaning and use of the term "enterprise," see Yaycioglou, *Partners of the Empire*, 99–100.

23 The trade in mutton and goat meat, grain, and tobacco which took place through these tax obligations was considered to lie outside the regular product market, in the sense that the goods were collected at fixed prices after the announcement of a central edict. Nevertheless, due to the sheer volume of the accumulated products, regular commercial transactions were also inevitably affected.

24 Dimitris Dimitropoulos, "Aspects of the Working of the Fiscal Machinery in the Areas Ruled by Ali Paşa," in *The Ottoman Empire and the Rise of Balkan Nationalisms 1789–1832 Conflict, Transformation, Adaptation,* ed. Antonis Anastasopoulos and Elias Kolovos (Rethymno: University of Crete, 2007), 63–70; Ανεμοδουρά, *Πολιτικές και οικονομικές δομές*, 256–470.

25 This practice was common among the *ayan*. See Yūzō Nagata, "Ayan in the Anatolia and the Balkans," *Provincial Elites in the Ottoman Empire Halycon Days in Crete V: A Symposiom Held in Rethymno, January 10–12, 2003*, ed. Antonis Anastasopoulos (Rethymno: Crete University Press, 2005), 282–85.

26 For the meaning and function of "agaliki," see Δημήτρης Δημητρόπουλος, "Αγαλίκι [Agaliki]," *Τα Ιστορικά* 50 (2009): 73–82.

27 Παναγιωτόπουλος, "Εισαγωγή," 105–7.

28 Δημήτρης Δημητρόπουλος, "Αγορά, φόροι και εξαναγκασμοί: το 'τζελέπικο' στις περιοχές του Αλή πασά [Market, Taxation and Extortion: 'Tzelepiko' in the Territories Ruled by Ali Paşa]," in *Αγορές και πολιτική. Ιδιωτικά συμφέροντα και δημόσια εξουσία, 18ος–20ός αι.*, ed. Χριστίνα Αγριαντώνη, Λήδα Παπαστεφανάκη, Μαρία Χριστίνα Χατζηιωάννου (Βόλος: Πανεπιστημιακές Εκδόσεις Θεσσαλίας, 2016), 99–111.

29 *Αρχείο Αλή πασά*, 2, 259–60, doc. 1192.

30 Guillaume de Vaudoncourt, M*emoirs on the Ionian Islands, Considered in a Commercial, Political, and Military Point of View; in Which Their Advantages of Position Are Described, as Well as Their Relations with the Greek Continent, Including the Life and Character of Ali Pacha, the Present Ruler of Greece*, trans. William Walton (London: Baldwin, Cradock and Joy, 1816), 278.

31 For examples, see the accounting ledgers of Ali Paşa's harem in Tepelenë for the year 1818, *Αρχείο Αλή πασά*, 3, 25–57, doc. 1052–53.

32 On offices and rank, see Μαρία Ανεμοδουρά, "Από τον Kurt Ahmet paşa ως τον Ali paşa Tepedelenli. Η Εποπτεία (Nazırlık) των Δερβενίων της Δυτικής Ρούμελης στα τέλη του 18ου αιώνα [From Kurt Ahmet Paşa to Ali Paşa Tepedelenli. The Command (Nazırlık) of the Derbent Pass in Western Rumelia at the End of the 18th Century]," in *Μηχανισμοί ελέγχου και πειθάρχησης, 19ος-20ός αιώνας*, ed. Δημήτρης Δημητρόπουλος, Βαγγέλης Καραμανωλάκης (Αθήνα: Ινστιτούτο Ιστορικών Ερευνών/ Εθνικό Ίδρυμα Ερευνών, 2022), 13–29.

33 *Αρχείο Αλή πασά*, 1, 46–49, doc. 29.

34 *Αρχείο Αλή πασά*, 2, 420–26, doc. 712.

35 *Αρχείο Αλή πασά*, 2, 445–55, doc. 722.

36 *Αρχείο Αλή πασά*, 4, 376–79, doc. 1266.

37 *Αρχείο Αλή πασά*, 4, 393–95, doc. 1271.

38 *Αρχείο Αλή πασά*, 4, 442–48, doc. 1307.

39 *Αρχείο Αλή πασά*, 2, 403–10, doc. 705.

40 Ανεμοδουρά, *Πολιτικές και οικονομικές δομές*, 341–49.

41 Δημήτρης Δημητρόπουλος, "Ο σαράφης του Αλή πασά στην Κωνσταντινούπολη 1813–1814. Οικονομικές δοσοληψίες και συναλλαγές [Ali Pasha's Financier in Constantinople 1813–1814: Financial Transactions and Money Transfers]," in *Θεωρητικές αναζητήσεις και εμπειρικές έρευνες, Πρακτικά Διεθνούς Συνεδρίου Οικονομικής και Κοινωνικής Ιστορίας, Ρέθυμνο, December 10–13, 2008*, ed. Σωκράτης Πετμεζάς, Τζελινα Χαρλάφτη, Ανδρέας Λυμπεράτος, Κατερίνα Παπακωνσταντίνου (Αθήνα: Φιλοσοφική Σχολή, Πανεπιστήμιο Κρήτης—Αλεξάνδρεια, 2012), 210–20.

42 *Αρχείο Αλή πασά*, 2, 413–15, doc. 707. On the currency exchange rate, see Ευτυχία Λιάτα, *Φλοριά δεκατέσσερα στένουν γρόσια σαράντα. Η κυκλοφορία των νομισμάτων στον βενετοκρατούμενο και τουρκοκρατούμενο ελληνικό χώρο, 15ος–19ος αι* [Fourteen Florins Equal Forty Piasters: Coin Circulation in the Greek Territories Under Venetian and Turkish Rule, 15th–19th c.] (Αθήνα: Κέντρο Νεοελληνικών Ερευνών/Εθνικό Ίδρυμα Ερευνών, 1996), 246.

43 Παναγιωτόπουλος, "Εισαγωγή," 100.
44 *Αρχείο Αλή πασά*, 2, 209–11, doc. 571.
45 *Αρχείο Αλή πασά*, 2, 549–51, doc. 296.
46 *Αρχείο Αλή πασά*, 3, 175, doc. 1126.
47 *Αρχείο Αλή πασά*, 3, 453–54, doc. 1312.
48 An English translation of the *yafta* is published by Robert Walsh, "Appendix," in *Narrative of a Journey from Constantinople to England* (London: Frederick Westley and A.H. Davis, 1828), 391. For the Ottoman original, see Ηλίας Κολοβός, "Το κομμένο κεφάλι, ο *γιαφτάς* και οι τάφοι του Αλή Πασά [The Severed Head, the Yafta and the Tombs of Ali Paşa]," in *Ο Αλή πασάς και η εποχή του*, ed. Βασίλης Παναγιωτόπουλος, Δημήτρης Δημητρόπουλος (collective volume under publication by IHR/NHRF).
49 Yaycioglou, *Partners of the Empire*, 43–45.

Bibliography

Andréades, André. "Ali pacha de Tébelin économiste et financier." *La Revue des Études Grecques (j.)* 25 (1912): 427–60.

Dimitropoulos, Dimitris. "Aspects of the Working of the Fiscal Machinery in the Areas Ruled by Ali Paşa." In *The Ottoman Empire and the Rise of Balkan Nationalisms 1789–1832. Conflict, Transformation, Adaptation*, edited by Antonis Anastasopoulos and Elias Kolovos, 61–72. Rethymno: University of Crete, 2007.

Fleming, Katherine E. *The Muslim Bonaparte. Diplomacy and Orientalism in Ali Paşa's Greece.* Princeton, NJ: Princeton University Press, 1999.

Gara, Eleni. "Moneylenders and Landowners: In Search of Urban Muslim Elites in the Early Modern Balkans." In *Provincial Elites in the Ottoman Empire Halycon Days in Crete V: A Symposiom Held in Rethymno, January 10–12, 2003*, edited by Antonis Anastasopoulos, 135–47. Rethymno: Crete University Press, 2005.

Kotzageorgis, Phokion, and Dimitris Papastamatiou. "Wealth Accumulation in an Urban Context. The Profile of the Muslim Rich of Thessaloniki in the Eighteenth Century on the Basis of Probate Inventories." *Turkish Historical Review* 5 (2014): 165–99.

Laiou, Sophia. "Some Considerations Regarding Çiftlik Formation in the Western Thessaly, Sixteenth-Nineteenth Centuries." In *The Ottoman Empire, the Balkans, the Greek Lands: Toward a Social and Economic History. Studies in Honor of John C. Alexander*, edited by Elias Kolovos, Phokion Kotzageorgis, Sophia Laiou, and Marinos Sariyannis, 255–77. Istanbul: The ISIS Press, 2007.

McGowan, Bruce. *Economic Life in Ottoman Europe. Taxation, Trade and the Struggle for Land, 1600–1800.* Cambridge: Cambridge University Press, 1981.

Nagata, Yūzō. "Ayan in the Anatolia and the Balkans." In *Provincial Elites in the Ottoman Empire Halycon Days in Crete V: A Symposiom Held in Rethymno, January 10–12, 2003*, edited by Antonis Anastasopoulos, 269–94. Rethymno: Crete University Press, 2005.

Neumeier, Mary Emily. "The Architectural Transformation of the Ottoman Provinces Under Tepedelenli Ali Paşa, 1788–1822." PhD diss., University of Pennsylvania, 2016.

Öncel, Fatma. "Land, Tax and Power in the Ottoman Provinces: The Malikâne-Mukataa of Esma Sultan in Alasonya (c.1780–1825)." *Turkish Historical Review* 8 (2017): 54–74.

Philliou, Christine. *Biography of an Empire. Governing Ottomans in an Age of Revolution.* Berkeley and Los Angeles: University of California Press, 2011.

Schacht, Joseph. *An Introduction to Islamic Law.* Oxford: Oxford University Press, 1982.

Sezer, Hamiyet. "Tepedelenli Ali paşa'nın çiftlikleri üzerine bir araştırma [A Research on the Çiftliks of Tepedelenli Ali pasha]." *Belleten* 62 (1998): 75–106.

Sezer, Hamiyet. "Tepedelenli Ali Paşa ve Ogulların Çiftlik ve Gelirlerine Iliskin Yeni Bilgi—Bulgular [New Information and Findings About the Çiftliks and Revenues of Ali Paşa and His Sons]." *Osmanli Tarihi Araştırma ve Uygulama Merkezi Dergisi (OTAM) [Journal of Ottoman History Research and Application Centre]* 18 (2005): 333–57.

Sezer, Hamiyet. "Νέες πληροφορίες και ευρήματα σχετικά με τα τσιφλίκια και τα εισοδήματα του Αλή Πασά και των γιων του" [New Information and Findings About the Çiftliks and Revenues of Ali Paşa and his Sons], translated and annotated by Eirini Kalogeropoulou, *Instrumenta Studiorum Balkanica*. Institute of Historical Research/National Hellenic Research Foundation Digital Library. www.eie.gr/nhrf/institutes/inr/instr-studiorumbalk/instr-studiorumballkarticles-gr.html

Spyropoulos, Yannis, Stefanos Poulios, and Antonis Anastasopoulos. "Çiftliks, Landed Elites, and Tax Allocation in Eighteenth-Century Ottoman Veroia." *European Journal of Turkish Studies* [online] (2022). https://doi.org/10.4000/ejts.6647

Uzun, Ahmet. "Tepedelenli Ali paşa ve mal varlığı [Tepedelenli Ali Paşa and His Fortune]." *Belleten* 65, no. 244 (2001): 1035–78.

Uzun, Ahmet. "Ο Αλή πασάς ο Τεπελενλής και η περιουσία του [Tepedelenli Ali Paşa and his Fortune]," translated by Syrmas Giorgos, *Instrumenta Studiorum Balkanica*. Institute of Historical Research/National Hellenic Research Foundation IHR/NHRF Digital Library. www.eie.gr/nhrf/institutes/inr/instr-studiorumbalk/instr-studiorumballkarticles-gr.html

Vaudoncourt de, Guillaume. M*emoirs on the Ionian Islands, Considered in a Commercial, Political, and Military Point of View; in Which Their Advantages of Position Are Described, as Well as Their Relations with the Greek Continent, Including the Life and Character of Ali Pacha, the Present Ruler of Greece*, translated by William Walton. London: Baldwin, Cradock and Joy, 1816.

Walsh, Robert. *Narrative of a Journey from Constantinople to England.* London: Frederick Westley and A. H. Davis, 1828.

Yaycioglou, Ali. "Provincial Power-holders and the Empire in the Late Ottoman World. Conflict or Partnership?" In *The Ottoman World*, edited by Christine Woodhead, 436–52. New York: Routledge, 2012.

Yaycioglou, Ali. *Partners of the Empire: The Crisis of the Ottoman Order in the Age of Revolutions.* Stanford: Stanford University Press, 2016.

Yaycioglu, Ali, Antonis Hadjikyriacou, Erik Steiner, and Fatma Öncel. "Visualizing Ali Pasha Order: Relations, Networks and Scales." In research project *Mapping Ottoman Epirus*. Center for Spatial and Textual Analysis (CESTA) Stanford University in collaboration with Institute of Historical Research/National Hellenic Research Foundation (Athens). https://mapoe.stanford.edu/projects/visualizing-ali-Paşa-order-relations-networks-and-scales.

Yıldız, Aysel. "Politics, Economy, and Çiftliks: The History of Four Çiftliks in Larissa (Yenişehir-i Fener)." *Turkish Historical Review* 11 (2020): 28–65.

Yusufoglu, Fatma Öncel. "Agrarian Relations and Estate (Chiftlik) Agriculture in Ottoman Thessaly (c. 1770–1880)." PhD diss., Bogazici University, 2018.

Ανεμοδουρά, Μαρία Κ. "Πολιτικές και οικονομικές δομές στην επικράτεια του Αλή πασά Τεπεντελενλή. Από τον 'Ανατολικό Δεσποτισμό' ως τη νεωτερικότητα." PhD diss., Εθνικό και Καποδιστριακό Πανεπιστήμιο Αθηνών, 2020. [Anemodoura, Maria K. "Political and Economic Structures in the Territories Ruled by Tepedelenli Ali Paşa. From 'Oriental Despotism' to Modernism." PhD diss., National and Kapodistrian University of Athens, 2020.]

Ανεμοδουρά, Μαρία. "Από τον Kurt Ahmet paşa ως τον Ali paşa Tepedelenli. Η Εποπτεία (Nazırlık) των Δερβενίων της Δυτικής Ρούμελης στα τέλη του 18ου αιώνα." In *Μηχανισμοί ελέγχου και πειθάρχησης, 19ος-20ός αιώνας*, edited by Δημητρόπουλος Δημήτρης, Καραμανωλάκης Βαγγέλης, 13–29. Αθήνα: Ινστιτούτο Ιστορικών Ερευνών/Εθνικό Ίδρυμα Ερευνών, 2022. [Anemodoura, Maria. "From Kurt Ahmet Paşa to Ali Paşa Tepedelenli: The Command (Nazırlık) of the Derbent Pass in Western Rumelia at the End of the 18th Century." In *Mechanisms of Control and Discipline, 19th—20th Century*, edited by Dimitris Dimitropoulos and Vangelis Karamanolakis, 13–29. Athens: Institute of Historical Research/National Hellenic Research Foundation, 2022.]

Αραβαντινός, Σπυρίδων Π. *Ιστορία Αλή πασά του Τεπελενλή*, vol. 2. Αθήνα: Εκ του Τυπογραφείου των Καταστημάτων Σπυρίδωνος Κουσουλίνου, 1895. [Aravantinos,

Spyridon P. *The History of Tepedelenli Ali Paşa*, vol. 2. Athens: Ek tou typografeiou ton Katastimaton Spyridonos Kousoulinou, 1895.]

Ασδραχάς, Σπύρος Ι. *Ελληνική κοινωνία και οικονομία, ιη΄ και ιθ΄ αιώνες*. Αθήνα: Ερμής, 1982. [Asdrachas, Spyros I. *Greek Society and Economy, 18th and 19th Century*. Athens: Hermes, 1982.]

Βαρδουνιώτης, Δημήτριος Κ. "Οι θησαυροί του Αλή πασά." In *Εθνικόν Ημερολόγιον του έτους 1914*, 364–68. Αθήνα: Εστία, 1914. [Vardouniotis, Dimitrios K. "The Treasures of Ali Paşa." In *National Diary of the Year 1914*, 364–68. Athens: Estia, 1914.]

Γιαννόπουλος, Ιωάννης. "Τα τσιφλίκια του Βελή πασά υιού του Αλή πασά." *Μνήμων* 2 (1972): 135–58. [Giannopoulos, Ioannis. "The *Çiftliks* of Veli Paşa, Son of Ali Paşa." *Mnemon* 2 (1972): 135–58.]

Δημητρόπουλος, Δημήτρης. "Αγαλίκι." *Τα Ιστορικά* 50 (2009): 73–82. [Dimitropoulos, Dimitris. "Agaliki." *Ta Istorika* 50 (2009): 73–82.]

Δημητρόπουλος, Δημήτρης. "Αγορά, φόροι και εξαναγκασμοί: το τζελέπικο' στις περιοχές του Αλή πασά." In *Αγορές και πολιτική. Ιδιωτικά συμφέροντα και δημόσια εξουσία, 18ος-20ός αι.*, edited by Αγριαντώνη Χριστίνα, Παπαστεφανάκη Λήδα, Χατζηιωάννου Μαρία Χριστίνα, 99–111. Βόλος: Πανεπιστημιακές Εκδόσεις Θεσσαλίας, 2016. [Dimitropoulos, Dimitris. "Market, Taxation and Extortion: 'Tzelepiko' in the Territories Ruled by Ali Paşa." In *Markets and Politics. Private Interests and Public Power, 18th-20th c.*, edited by Christina Agriantoni, Leda Papastefanaki, and Maria Christina Chatziioannou, 99–111. Volos: University of Thessaly Press, 2016.]

Δημητρόπουλος, Δημήτρης. "Ο σαράφης του Αλή πασά στην Κωνσταντινούπολη 1813–1814. Οικονομικές δοσοληψίες και συναλλαγές." In *Θεωρητικές αναζητήσεις και εμπειρικές έρευνες*, Πρακτικά Διεθνούς Συνεδρίου Οικονομικής και Κοινωνικής Ιστορίας, Ρέθυμνο 10–13.12.2008, edited by Πετμεζάς Σωκράτης, Χαρλαύτη Τζελίνα, Λυμπεράτος Ανδρέας, Παπακωνσταντίνου Κατερίνα, 207–28. Αθήνα: Φιλοσοφική Σχολή Πανεπιστημίου Κρήτης—Αλεξάνδρεια, 2012. [Dimitropoulos, Dimitris. "Ali Paşa's Financier in Constantinople 1813–1814. Financial Transactions and Money Transfers." In *Theoretical Reflections and Experiential Research, Proceedings of the International Conference on Economic and Social History, Rethymnon, 10–13 December 2008*, edited by Sokrates Petmezas, Gelina Harlaftis, Andreas Lymperatos, and Katerina Papakonstantinou, 207–28. Athens: School of Philosophy, University of Crete—Alexandreia, 2012.]

Καιροφύλας, Κώστας. "Τι απέγιναν οι θησαυροί Αλή και Βελή πασά." *Ηπειρωτική Εστία* 17 (1968): 27–32. [Kairofylas, Kostas. "What Happened to the Treasures of Ali Paşa and Veli Paşa." *The Epirus Review* 17 (1968): 27–32.]

Κολοβός, Ηλίας. "Το κομμένο κεφάλι, ο *γιαφτάς* και οι τάφοι του Αλή Πασά." In *Ο Αλή πασάς και η εποχή του*, edited by Παναγιωτόπουλος Βασίλης, Δημητρόπουλος Δημήτρης (collective volume under publication by Ινστιτούτο Ιστορικών Ερευνών/Εθνικό Ίδρυμα Ερευνών). [Kolovos, Elias. "The Severed Head, the *Yafta* and the Tombs of Ali Paşa." In *Ali Paşa and His Time*, edited by Vasilis Panagiotopoulos and Dimitris Dimitropoulos. Collective volume under publication by Institute of Historical Research/National Hellenic Research Foundation.]

Λιάτα, Ευτυχία. *Φλοριά δεκατέσσερα στένουν γρόσια σαράντα. Η κυκλοφορία των νομισμάτων στον βενετοκρατούμενο και τουρκοκρατούμενο ελληνικό χώρο, 15ος–19ος αι.* Αθήνα: Ινστιτούτο Ιστορικών Ερευνών/Εθνικό Ίδρυμα Ερευνών, 1996. [Liata, Eftychia. *Fourteen Florins Equal Forty Piasters. Coin Circulation in the Greek Territories under Venetian and Turkish Rule, 15th–19th c.* Athens: Institute of Historical Research/National Hellenic Research, 1996.]

Παναγιωτόπουλος, Βασίλης. "Εισαγωγή." In *Αρχείο Αλή πασά Συλλογής Ι. Χώτζη, Γενναδείου Βιβλιοθήκης*, edited by Παναγιωτόπουλος Βασίλης, in collaboration with Δημητρόπουλος Δημήτρης, Μιχαηλάρης Παναγιώτης, vols. 1–4. Αθήνα: Ινστιτούτο Ιστορικών Ερευνών/Εθνικό Ίδρυμα Ερευνών, 2007–2009. [Panagiotopoulos, Vasilis. "Introduction." In *Ali Paşa Archive, I. Chotzis Collection, Gennadius Library*, edited by Vasilis Panagiotopoulos, in collaboration with Dimitris Dimitropoulos and Panagiotis Michailaris, vols. 1–4. Athens: Institute of Historical Research/National Hellenic Research, 2007–2009.]

Πατσέλης, Νικόλαος. "Η οικονομική πολιτική και ο πλούτος του Αλή πασά των Ιωαννίνων." *Αρχείον των Οικονομικών και Κοινωνικών Επιστημών* 16 (1936): 115–47. [Patselis, Nikolaos. "Economic Policy and the Wealth of Ali Paşa of Ioannina." *Economic and Social Sciences Archive* 16 (1936): 115–47.]

Προγουλάκης, Γιώργος. "Στα εδάφη του Αλή πασά: παραγωγή, γαιοπρόσοδος, κερδοφορία του χρήματος." *Τα Ιστορικά* 32 (2000): 73–88. [Progoulakis, Giorgos. "Economy in Ali Paşa's Territories: Production, Land Revenues and Investment Profits." *Ta Istorika* 32 (2000): 73–88.]

7 Janissary Inter-Provincial Economic Practices During the 1821 Greek War of Independence

Yannis Spyropoulos

To date, little attention has been paid to the fact that the Greek General State Archives' (GRGSA) Central Service in Athens holds a large number of unstudied Ottoman documents pertinent to the period of the Greek Revolution. This does not come as a surprise, since the discovery of these documents often constitutes a difficult task, given that many of them are uncatalogued or misplaced in seemingly irrelevant folders. However, these sources are worth unearthing and exploring as they often contain material that can offer us a rare insight into how Muslim individuals and officials experienced the 1821 Greek Revolution.[1] The material examined in this chapter represents one such case.

The documents examined here were discovered in the "Archive of Ministerio/Secretariat/Ministry of Justice, Capodistrian Administration" collection (fol. 60–108[2]).[3] As becomes clear from their content, they were compiled in 1825 and dispatched with the ship "Speranza" of a certain captain Antoni which departed from Kandiye (Candia or modern Herakleion in Crete), going to Istanbul. The vessel was intercepted *en route* by Greek revolutionaries who confiscated its cargo belonging to Cretan Muslims, along with any letters/documents that were found on board: this is how the sources in question ended up among the archives of the Greek government.

The "Speranza" was flying a Russian flag. This is an interesting fact considering that the boat was captured by Greek revolutionaries, especially given that the captain was of Greek origin, as can be easily deduced from the letters contained in the folder.[4] Chartering foreign ships to transport merchandise within the Ottoman Empire was a well-established practice in Crete.[5] However, the fact that local Muslims chose a boat with a Russian flag and a Greek captain to send their commodities to the capital most probably reflects their impression that such a vessel stood a better chance of passing safely through the Greek naval lines.

Indeed, Ottoman sources from the Istanbul Archives clearly show that the Greek War of Independence did considerable damage to Istanbul's maritime connections on all the major sea routes tying it to the empire's Arab provinces and Anatolian ports through the Aegean. A registration of all vessels coming to and leaving Istanbul in late 1822 to early 1823, over a total of four weeks of maritime activity,[6] shows that the most active maritime routes of the Ottoman Empire in the Mediterranean—the ones linking Istanbul vertically to Egypt through ports

DOI: 10.4324/9781003500780-10

located in Crete, Chios, and Izmir,[7] were almost completely disconnected from the empire's capital. The very few vessels traveling these routes flew European flags, indicating the complete disruption of Ottoman navigation in the region. Under these circumstances, it seems reasonable that the Muslims of Kandiye considered freighting a European ship as their best chance for their cargo to reach Istanbul.

From the confiscated documents we understand that Captain Antoni's ship was used by many members of the Cretan Muslim elite for sending to Istanbul various types of merchandise, among which were 36 bags of coins (*sürre*) in various currencies and large amounts of soap.[8] According to their agreement with the captain, the latter was to receive a payment of 7.5 piasters (*kuruş*) for every 1,000 piasters and 100 *paras* for each *kantar* (30 okes) of soap he could transfer to the Ottoman capital. The list of soap merchants who entrusted the Greek captain with transporting their merchandise is given in Table 7.1.

The provided list sheds light on the roles played by Cretan Muslim elites and the Janissaries in the trading relationship between Kandiye and Istanbul, as well as the economic effects of the Greek War of Independence on this trade dynamic. To understand these aspects fully, a brief overview of the evolution of Crete's soap production and trade is essential.

Table 7.1 List of merchants who used the "Speranza" to ship soap to Istanbul and the amounts sent.

Name	*Sacks (Çuval)*	*Chests (Sandık)*	*Okes (Kıyye)*[9]
Derviş Ali Tarakçızâde	14		875
Molla Hüseyin working for Efendakizâde	60		3,303
Hacegân Efendi	4		167
Esseyyid Mehmed Efendi	48		2,049
Şerif Ahmed Ağa	8		523
Mehmed Ağa Veznedâr	19		1,057
Defterdâr Efendi	5	5	193
Deli Ahmed Ağa Memişoğlu[10]	41		2,253
Kâtib-i Gümrük Arif Ağa	16		1,013
Salih Ağa Zalakoğlu	25		1,500
Osman Ağa Kamaryalı	25		1,393
İbrahim Efendi working for Kalupsız	25		1,389
Metropolut[11]	28	2	1,611
Mazlum Ağa Pehlivanzâde	15		943
Haseki Mustafa Ağa	33		1,792
Elhac Efendi	25		1,505
Mazlum Ağa Zenecizâde	22		1,240
Celuzâde Derviş Ağa	52		2,781
Osman Ağa Neracioğlu	10		569
Total	**459**	7	**26,156**

Source: GRGSA's Central Service, "Archive of Ministerio/Secretariat/Ministry of Justice, Capodistrian Administration," no number (digitized pictures no. 64 and 73).

During the 18th century, Crete's economic focus shifted toward olive oil production, becoming a key component of the island's external trade.[12] At the beginning of the century, French merchants dominated this market by purchasing Crete's olive oil and supplying the soap factories in France. Simultaneously, local soap factories were developed as Cretans engaged in export trade, facilitated by French merchants who established trading companies on the island, effectively serving as credit institutions in the absence of an Ottoman banking system.

As local businesses thrived and new markets expanded, Cretan producers recognized their advantage over the French capitalists, thereby attracting more French capital to the local market, while intensifying competition with European merchants.[13] However, an influx of French loans and reliance on local producers led to debt accumulation, economic recession, and bankruptcies.[14] In the time of the Seven Years' War and the French Revolution, French shipping and capital gradually left Crete, to be replaced by other merchants, many of them locals.

During this period, the influence of powerful Janissary regimental funds as credit organizations expanded on the island. Affluent Muslim families, including Janissaries, played multiple roles in olive oil production and trade. They acted as landowners, merchants, soap manufacturers, and participants in related tax farming. With rising investments, they initiated family-run businesses overseeing the entire process. Soap production in Kandiye involved small workshops initially, but larger soap factories emerged as investments grew, leading to factory consolidation and a decline in the smaller businesses.

In the second half of the 18th century, prominent soap-making families with military backgrounds emerged, acquiring wealth by controlling land holdings and tax-farming rights. Initially engaged in the olive oil trade, their descendants transitioned to soap production. Ottoman sources show that Christian soap makers disappeared over time, as military families monopolized the industry in Kandiye. By 1811, only four soap makers remained in the town, holding a production and distribution monopoly, with three of them being distinguished military figures.[15]

The dominant role of the military class in the soap trade of Kandiye becomes evident in the list of merchants found onboard the "Speranza." Although it is not easy to identify each and every one of the soap merchants in the document, whenever such an identification is possible, their connections to the Janissary Corps are evident. For instance, the biggest of all merchants seen in the list is from the Efendaki or Afendakaki Janissary family that controlled the greater part of the *nahiye* of Sitia and resided in Kandiye, where they not only owned a soap factory and significant properties but also engaged in lending money and trading various commodities, such as wheat. The court registers of Kandiye provide evidence of the family's governance in Sitia for at least three generations. The Efendakis had financial connections with the 14th and 37th *cemâ'at* Janissary regiments as well as the 30th and 18th *bölük* regiments of the same corps, they played significant roles as military leaders and negotiators during the Greek Revolution in 1821 and they appeared as representatives of the Janissaries in demands made to the government.[16]

Another notable Janissary family mentioned among the list of soap merchants trading with Istanbul is the Pehlivanoğlus. Members of the family possessed extensive land and valuable properties in Kandiye, Merambello, Temenos, Monofatsi, and Pediada. While they were involved in the production of substantial amounts of grain and engaged in the trade of various agricultural products, their primary business activity revolved around soap production and trade. They also rented *mukâta'a*s (tax farming rights) and provided moneylending services, particularly to members of guilds.[17] Veli Pehlivanoğlu, one of the family's most prominent members, was "one of the *ağa*s in the Janissary Corps" and "among the rich *mukâta'a* holders."[18] When he died in 1811, the authorities in Istanbul collaborated with the central Janissary command to confiscate his property. As is evident from a record of his estate, Veli and his three brothers ran a family business that had extensive dealings with a large part of the Janissary elite in Kandiye. The Pehlivanoğlus had high-ranking officers in the 42nd *cemâ'at* regiment, maintained close ties with the abovementioned Efendaki family, and had borrowed heavily from another Janissary regiment, the 14th *cemâ'at*.[19]

The Kalupsız family, also on the list, was one of the most powerful Janissary families in Kandiye. Sources reveal that they played a leading role in the town's army and were active in local political life.[20] The Kalupsızes had established familial connections with high-ranking officers in the 30th *bölük*, from which they borrowed substantial sums of money. They possessed property in Kandiye and engaged in business partnerships with Christians. Additionally, they owned soap factories and bakeries and were involved in money lending. Certain members of the family also held the position of *malikâne ağa*s (life-long tax farmers) in the Cretan region of Malevizi.[21]

Similarly, various other people mentioned in the list of soap merchants were connected to Janissary regiments and households through financial and familial bonds. For instance, three members of the Memişoğlu family, Rıdvan, İsmail, and İbrahim, had received several loans from the 37th and the 42nd *cemâ'at*, and the 18th *bölük* regiments in 1826,[22] Derviş Ali Tarakçızade owed 8,400 piasters to the 14th *cemâ'at* of the same corps,[23] Osman Ağa Kamaryalı had familial bonds with high ranking local Janissaries, while members of his family had received loans from the 14th *cemâ'at* of the Janissaries,[24] and Haseki Mustafa Ağa was himself a member and an officer of this last regiment.[25] This connection was crucial, as the direct or indirect relationship of the individuals in the list with the Janissaries not only gave them easier access to credit but also ensured more or less non-state intervention in their commercial activities and thus a significant increase in their profit from them.[26]

Although there is no way to gauge the impact that the Greek War of Independence had on the commercial activity of all the merchants who were engaged in the trade in soap, a list of the amounts of this product sent from Kandiye to Istanbul during the Islamic year 1234 (1818–1819) records a total of 18,686 *kantar*s or 560,580 okes sent with 34 ship freights on vessels captained exclusively by Ottomans.[27] Considering the complete disruption of Ottoman navigation in the Aegean shown above and the use of a foreign ship for the transfer of soap in this case, it would not be far-fetched to assume that the 26,156 okes sent with the "Speranza" would represent one of the very few attempts of the local elites at shipping soap to Istanbul. Given that Crete was in the late 18th and early 19th centuries the main provider of soap to the Istanbul market,[28] we can easily understand that the repercussions of the war on both the provisioning of the empire's capital and the economy of Crete must have been enormous.

The organization and maintenance of the huge trans-provincial olive oil and soap trade would not have been possible without the involvement of commercial and administrative networks beyond Crete. The primary hub for these connections was Istanbul, although other major commercial cities like Izmir also played a significant role, particularly due to the presence of a large Cretan population under the protection of the local Janissary unit.[29] In the framework of their entrepreneurial activities, the soap makers of Crete collaborated with numerous ship owners from the Aegean islands and Istanbul, as well as metropolitan guilds of grocers and soap makers who handled the sale of the quantities they produced.[30] Most importantly, the Janissary merchants of Crete used the organizational structure of their regiments as platforms on which they established their own commercial agents in Istanbul.

Indicative of this practice is yet another source which is to be found among the confiscated documents of the "Speranza," namely, a letter containing part of a commercial correspondence between Odabaşızâde Derviş Ali Efendi and Muradoğlu İbrahim, residents of Istanbul and Kandiye respectively, business partners, and members of the 14th *cemâ'at* regiment of the Janissaries.[31] The epistle, which was sent by İbrahim to Derviş Ali, was compiled in March/April 1825 (Şa'bân 1240). The letter was marked with the number 8642, equivalent to the Arabic letters "b-d-u-h," a talismanic combination used for inducing the document's safe delivery,[32] and the symbol of the 14th *cemâ'at*, that is, a tent, within which the number and first letter of the regiment is written. The unpretentious drawing of the regiment's emblem and the many spelling errors found in the text lead me to assume that it was most probably not composed by a Janissary regimental scribe (*miyâne yazıcısı*), but either by İbrahim himself or by someone in his familial/professional milieu who had some knowledge of letter writing.

İbrahim and Derviş Ali, the protagonists of the letter, were operating within the same networks as the above rich Cretan Janissary families, trading, however, in commodities other than soap and olive oil. In fact, as the letter shows, the cargo that İbrahim sent to Derviş Ali was a small one and its capture did not result in a great loss for the two partners: it only consisted of five sacks and 13 old knives. The five sacks were marked with red paint and shipped upon the request of a certain Mitafoğlu Derviş Ağa, while the knives were to be given, probably for sharpening, to a professional knife-maker in Istanbul who was also to make five new knives and send them to Crete. Given the small value of the cargo shipped, it seems that the main reason behind the letter's dispatch was not to arrange the selling and repair of the aforementioned items, but something more

Table 7.2 İbrahim's debt to Derviş Ali.

Justification	*Piasters*	*Para*
Money owed to Derviş Ali's brother	278	20
From the sale of grain	51	30
For the freighting of the ship	136	
From the sale of flour	411	19
From the sale of mackerel	300	
Expenses	*–49*	*–23*
Total	**1,128**	**6**

Source: GRGSA's Central Service, "Archive of Ministerio/Secretariat/Ministry of Justice, Capodistrian Administration," no number (digitized picture no. 87).

important, that is, to settle the payment of a debt that İbrahim owed to Derviş Ali (see Table 7.2).

From the calculations of İbrahim's debt, recorded in the letter's second page, it becomes clear that some of the main goods that the two partners imported to Crete from Istanbul were grain, flour, and fish (mackerel), although this does not mean that these were the only products they had been trading. Grain and flour were highly valued products on Crete: from the beginning of the 18th century, when the Cretan economy shifted to the production of olive oil at the expense of vine and grain crops, the local treasury faced great difficulties in collecting locally the amount of wheat needed for the in-kind payments of the numerous local military forces established on the island. As a result, the import of cereals had become an indispensable practice for the provincial administration which left plenty of space for unchecked profiteering on the side of the local elites.[33] The 1821 Revolution made things even worse by doubling the number of soldiers who had to be provisioned, while almost obliterating the local cereal production and, in turn, the in-kind revenues that resulted from it.[34] In view of this increased demand for grain on Crete,[35] it makes perfect sense that İbrahim's largest debts to Derviş Ali were related to this trade. This fact also acts as a reminder that war did not always act as an obstacle to trade, but sometimes it could also be seen by daring merchants as an opportunity for profit.

Another merchandise Derviş Ali was sending to İbrahim was mackerel (*uskumru*), probably salted (*çiroz*), as it had to endure a few days' trip. In peacetime importing fish to an island would not sound like a wise business move, yet it appears that under the prevalent war conditions, İbrahim had managed to find a niche in the market of Kandiye, selling a previously shipped batch of five barrels for 60 piasters each.

In other words, the letter offers information on two partners-in-trade who sought out market opportunities in the midst of war. To find out even more about these individuals and the ways in which their Janissary identity affected their activities, however, one has to resort to the juxtaposition of the information available in the letter with data extracted from other sources, such as payrolls and the records of the judicial court (*kadı sicilleri*) of Kandiye.

According to various official sources, the 14th *cemâ'at*, the Janissary regiment in which the two partners were registered, was one of the regiments with the steadiest presence on Crete.[36] Although Kandiye was its official basis, the 14th *cemâ'at* was also one of the regiments which, throughout the 18th century, maintained a strong representation in Istanbul, amounting to at least 125 people in 1762—the last year for which we have related data, a number which equaled roughly a quarter of its total manpower.[37] In fact, all 196 Janissary regiments had soldiers who were stationed at the empire's capital at all times and were accommodated in partial regimental structures called "half regiments" (*nısf ortalar*). These partial structures were under the command of appointed officers and, although they were considered to be "branches" of their core regimental structures (which are tagged in the sources the "whole/entire" regiment [*bütün/tam orta*]),[38] they enjoyed large administrative and financial autonomy from the latter.

It is highly probable that Derviş Ali was one of the 14th *cemâ'at*'s men permanently appointed to the capital, although it seems that members of his family, who owned estates both in Kandiye and in the close by villages,[39] were still living in Crete, some of them even visiting Istanbul from time to time before the war.[40] Kandiye's judicial records make it clear that both Derviş Ali's and İbrahim's families had strong connections to the military establishment of Crete, with many of the people who bore the same family names as them having been registered in Janissary regiments and, in one case, in the local *cebeci* (armorer) corps of Kandiye.[41] Furthermore, as I will explain, the two partners were making use of their affiliation with the 14th *cemâ'at* to fund their business, similarly to what hundreds of other individuals were doing in the same city.

In 1826, just one year after the letter was written, Mahmud II proceeded to abolish the Janissary complex. In the case of Crete, we still have the confiscation records of the waqf properties of the five regiments of Kandiye.[42] The confiscated assets—without counting their real estate and the cash of one of the regiments, which had mysteriously disappeared—amounted to an approximate 1,000,000 *piasters*, with two-thirds of the sum being in the form of loans issued to private individuals.[43] The 14th *cemâ'at*, the regiment of Derviş Ali and İbrahim, was first as regards its lending power, having upon disbandment 201 loans amounting to 242,081 piasters. Janissary loans were provided to a diverse range of individuals, including merchants, members of guilds, landowners, and tax farmers, thereby supporting a wide range of economic investments both on the island and elsewhere. These loans served as a source of financial assistance to various segments of the population, including ordinary residents in towns and villages, lower-ranking soldiers, small traders, and shopkeepers, as well as a significant portion of the island's economic, administrative, and military elite.

Among the long list of loan certificates (*temessük*) given to the regiments' debtors, we also find a loan worth 245 piasters, given by the fund of the 14th *cemâ'at* to two partners, Derviş and İbrahim.[44] Seeing the names of the letter's two protagonists among those of the aforementioned regiment's debtors does not come as a surprise: as explained above, many of the soap merchants who sent their cargo to Istanbul with the same ship as Derviş Ali and İbrahim were also receiving loans from the Janissary regiments of Kandiye. Additionally, it has to be noted that the 14th *cemâ'at* had an extended presence in different guilds and professional groups in the town.[45] In this framework, the members of the aforementioned *orta*, like Derviş Ali and İbrahim, could capitalize on their affiliation in various ways. For instance, although trading knives probably did not constitute the two merchants' main commercial activity, it seems as no coincidence that the 14th *cemâ'at* was the regiment that dominated the guild of knife-sellers of Kandiye in the early 19th century.[46] It is, thus, reasonable to assume that the two partners were making at least some profit by importing knives to the local guild which mainly consisted of their comrades-in-arms.

The aforementioned cases are not the only *kadı sicilleri* documents where we find information about the people mentioned in the letter. In an 1818 probate inventory of a certain Osman son of İbrahim—a tailor based in Kandiye—we find out that he owed 11,496 *para*s to our Derviş Odabaşıoğlu, with whom it seems that he had some kind of business collaboration. Given that Osman had among his possessions great amounts of "Istanbul fabric made of mohair" (*İslâmbol şâlîsi*), we would assume that Derviş, being a resident of Istanbul, acted as his intermediary supplier. This assumption can be further substantiated by the fact that, on the letter's front page, it is explicitly mentioned that Odabaşıoğlu was based at the Balkapanı Hanı, a marketplace infamous for its rebellious Janissary porters and well known for its fabric-trade services.[47] Last but not least, we ought to take into account the fact that the patronymic of the tailor who owed money to Odabaşıoğlu was İbrahim. Could Muradoğlu İbrahim, the sender of our letter, have been Osman's father? One can only speculate. That being said, the letter reveals that other family members of the two entrepreneurs were involved in their trade, as well: in the analysis of İbrahim's debt to Derviş Ali the former adds 278 piasters, which he owed to the latter's brother.

Conclusion

The puzzling questions concerning not only the background but also the fate of the people mentioned in the letter analyzed above are many. Did their partnership survive the long war? How did the destruction of the Janissary corps—only a year and a half after the letter was written—affect their enterprise? Did they manage to rebuild their business on different foundations or did the abolition of their regiment take their company down with it? No matter how many bewildering questions are created and the hypotheses one has to resort to in order to unearth the information hidden behind the lines of such Ottoman epistles, it is important to note that this letter is very valuable in that it constitutes one of the very few extant examples of unofficial inter-Janissary correspondence.[48] At the same time, it offers us a glimpse into the practices used by the Muslims of Cretan origins who tried to establish trade with Istanbul in the midst of war. İbrahim's business partnership with Derviş Ali was formed within the networks of a Janissary regiment with a strong presence in both Crete and Istanbul and was based on the use of every available resource offered to them by their affiliation, as they struggled to find their way through the economic opportunities/imperatives created by the circumstances brought about by the Greek War of Independence. Moreover, the letter of the two partners helps us better understand the symbolic role that the Janissary Corps played as an institution to which its members could resort to obtaining a sense of security in hard times. The emblem drawn on the letter sent by İbrahim to Derviş Ali undoubtedly stood as a reminder to anyone's eye it caught that the message contained in it ought to be delivered to its recipient, as the latter was protected by a mighty establishment. Only a year and a half before their abolition, the Janissaries appeared omnipresent, powerful, and ready to stand up for their affiliates.

On another level, the examination of the Ottoman sources contained in the GRGSA folder related to the capture and confiscation of the "Speranza"'s cargo by the Greek authorities, presents us with a rare opportunity to peek into the entrepreneurial endeavors of the Janissary networks of Crete as their members tried to keep the severely damaged commercial connection of the island with Istanbul alive. When putting the documents of the folder into their historical context, we understand that the Greek War of Independence had largely reversed the outcome of a decades-long struggle of the local Muslim elite to create a prosperous local soap industry whose export trade was unconstrained by foreign commercial navigation.

That being said, even under these harsh conditions, Janissary regimental capital seems to have remained one of the main driving forces behind the Cretan soap trade, as was also the case with other commercial enterprises connecting Kandiye to Istanbul. As can be seen, for instance, in the case of İbrahim and Derviş Ali—two Janissaries who operated a modest trans-provincial business partnership—Janissary common funds were also financing Crete's trade in grain and other commodities. Last but not least, an interesting take from this last case is that war could be seen by some Cretan merchants not only as an impediment but also as an opportunity to find new niches in the local market and to capitalize on the scarcity of staple goods created by the war on the island.

Overall, the sources analyzed here underline the importance of trade and money-lending as aspects of Ottoman Muslim entrepreneurship in the beginning of the 19th century, adding to our understanding of capital accumulation in the Ottoman Empire in the late early modern period. They also point to the existence of a wealth of relevant information waiting to be discovered: as explained in the beginning of this chapter, the GRGSA's Central Service contains a considerable number of Ottoman documents related to the 1821–1830 period which are yet to be studied. Hopefully, future research at the GRGSA will bring more information on the functioning of such entrepreneurial networks to light and will offer us a better view of how Muslims dealt with the economic challenges created by the Greek War of Independence.

Acknowledgments

Research for this chapter received funding from the European Research Council (ERC) under the European Union's Horizon 2020 research and innovation program (grant agreement No 849911).

European Research Council

Established by the European Commission

Archives

General State Archives, Greece (GRGSA)

Archive of Ministerio/Secretariat/Ministry of Justice, Capodistrian Administration, fol. 64, 67, 73, 74, 78.

Local Archive of Hydra, Notarial Code 6:27

Turkish Archive of Herakleion (TAH), Herakleion, Greece

Başbakanlık Osmanlı Arşivi (BOA), Istanbul, Turkey

A.DVN.İZN.d.920, 92, 922

C.BH.218/158, 159

HAT.650/31789 C

MAD.d.3946:527–31

DVNSMHM.d.146:22/71

İstanbul Müftülüğü Şeriyye Sicilleri Arşivi, Galata Mahkemesi, Istanbul, Turkey

Notes

1 For some such documents I have translated in another article of mine, see Γιάννης Σπυρόπουλος, "Τέσσερις μικρές ιστορίες μουσουλμάνων στο πλαίσιο του κρητικού 1821 [Four Short Stories of Muslims in the Context of the Cretan 1821]," in *Κρήτη 1821–1830: Αναγνώσεις μιας ατελέσφορης Επανάστασης*, ed. Μανόλης Βουρλιώτης, Μανόλης Δρακάκης, and Γιάννα Πατρουδάκη (Αθήνα: Μπαρτζουλιάνος, 2021), 265–82. For a catalog listing some of the Ottoman sources to be found in the GRGSA's Central Service, see Γιάννης Γκλαβίνας and Αμαλία Παππά, "Οθωμανικά και καραμανλίδικα τεκμήρια στην Κεντρική Υπηρεσία των Γενικών Αρχείων του Κράτους [Ottoman and Karamanlid Documents at the Central Service of the General State Archives]," in *Τουρκολογικά. Τιμητικός τόμος για τον Αναστάσιο Κ. Ιορδάνογλου*, ed. Γιώργος Σαλακίδης (Θεσσαλονίκη: Σταμούλης, 2012), 19–46.

2 The documents have not been numbered by the GRGSA. Thus, the numbers given here represent those of the digitized pictures of the collection found in http://arxeiomnimon.gak.gr.

3 I would like to thank Manolis Vourliotis for his help in locating the documents examined here.

4 The entire name of the captain was Antonis Kairis Astavitas (Αντώνης Καΐρης Ασταβήτας); GRGSA, Archive of Ministerio/Secretariat/Ministry of Justice, Capodistrian Administration, fol. 73, 73–74, 78.

5 Daniel Panzac, "Négociants ottomans et capitaines français: la caravane maritime en Crète au XVIIIe siècle," in *L'Empire Ottoman, la république de Turquie et la France*, ed. Hâmit Batu (Istanbul and Paris: Éditions Isis & Association pour le Développement des Études Turques, 1986), 99–118.

6 Başbakanlık Osmanlı Arşivi (BOA), A.DVN.İZN.d.920, 921, 922; C.BH.218/158, 159.

7 Daniel Panzac, "International and Domestic Maritime Trade in the Ottoman Empire During the 18th Century," in *Commerce et navigation dans l'Empire Ottoman au XVIIIe siècle* (Istanbul: The ISIS Press, 1996), 204. Also, see Edhem Eldem, "Strangers in their Own Seas? The Ottomans in the Eastern Mediterranean Basin in the Second Half of the Eighteenth Century," *Studi Settecenteschi* 29–30 (2014): 53–54; Daniel Crecelius, "Damiette and Syrian-Egyptian Trade in the Second Half of the Eighteenth Century," in *Syria and Bilad al-Sham Under Ottoman Rule: Essays in Honour of Abdul-Karim Rafeq*, ed. Peter Sluglett and Stefan Weber (Leiden and Boston: Brill, 2010), 159–60, 161; Zoe Ann Griffith, "Egyptian Ports in the Ottoman Mediterranean, 1760–1820" (PhD diss., Brown University, 2017), 172.

8 GRGSA, Archive of Ministerio/Secretariat/Ministry of Justice, Capodistrian Administration, fol. 64, 73, 78. Crete was one of the most important soap and olive oil suppliers of Istanbul. For the trade of these products, see Γιάννης Σπυρόπουλος, *Οθωμανική διοίκηση και κοινωνία στην προεπαναστατική δυτική Κρήτη: Αρχειακές Μαρτυρίες (1817–1819) [Ottoman Administration and Society in Prerevolutionary Western Crete: Archival Testimonies (1817–1819)]*, ed. Ασπασία Παπαδάκη (Ρέθυμνο: Γενικά Αρχεία του Κράτους, 2015), 83–91; Γιάννης Σπυρόπουλος, "Κοινωνική, διοικητική, οικονομική και πολιτική διάσταση του οθωμανικού στρατού: οι γενίτσαροι της Κρήτης, 1750–1826 [Social, Administrative, Economic and Political Dimensions of the Ottoman Army: The Janissaries of Crete, 1750–1826)]" (PhD diss., Πανεπιστήμιο Κρήτης, 2014), 270–81.

9 Each amount is recorded in *kantar*s and okes. To convert *kantar*s of soap into okes, I have used the 1:30 ratio given in a *ferman* from late 1820 which is to be found in Turkish Archive of Herakleion (TAH) 43:125–126. However, the sum given by the scribe is slightly lower than my calculation (876 *kantar*s and 6 okes or 26,016 okes).

10 For more details on the merchandise sent with the same ship by Deli Ahmed Ağa Memişoğlu to his partner in Istanbul, Mazlum Ağa, see GRGSA, Archive of Ministerio/Secretariat/Ministry of Justice, Capodistrian Administration, fol. 67.

11 Although I cannot be sure about the identity of this individual, the reference here might be to the Metropolitan of Crete. If this is the case, he is the only Christian featured among the otherwise Muslim merchants of the list.

12 Molly Greene, *A Shared World: Christians and Muslims in the Early Modern Mediterranean* (Princeton, NJ: Princeton University Press, 2000), 125–26, 134–40.

13 Γιολάντα Τριανταφυλλίδου-Baladié, "Οι πιστώσεις στις εμπορικές συναλλαγές στην Κρήτη τον 18° αιώνα [Credit in Commercial Transactions in Crete in the 18th Century]," in *Πεπραγμένα Ε΄ Διεθνούς Κρητολογικού Συνεδρίου*, vol. 3 (Ηράκλειο: Εταιρία Κρητικών Ιστορικών Μελετών, 1985), 222–28.

14 Γιολάντα Τριανταφυλλίδου-Baladié, *Το εμπόριο και η οικονομία της Κρήτης (1669–1795) [Trade and the Economy of Crete (1669–1795)]* (Ηράκλειο: Βικελαία Βιβλιοθήκη, 1988), 149.

15 Βασίλης Κρεμμυδάς, *Οι σαπουνοποιίες της Κρήτης στο 18ο αιώνα [The Soap Factories of Crete in the 18th Century]* (Αθήνα: τυπ. Κ. Μιχαλάς, 1974), 32, 34, 37–39, 42; Βασίλης Κρεμμυδάς, "Δρόμοι της Μεσογείου, δρόμοι της Κρήτης; ένα αδύνατο ζεύγμα: ο χαρακτήρας του εμπορίου και της βιομηχανίας, 1750–1850 [Roads of the Mediterranean, Roads of Crete; an Impossible Pairing: The Nature of Trade and Industry, 1750–1850]," in *Πεπραγμένα Θ΄ Διεθνούς Κρητολογικού Συνεδρίου,* Keynote Speech Volume (Ηράκλειο: Εταιρία Κρητικών Ιστορικών Μελετών, 2006), 125–26, 129; Guillaume-Antoine Olivier, *Travels in the Ottoman Empire, Egypt, and Persia*, vol. 2 (London: T. N. Longman and O. Rees, 1801), 248–49; TAH.3:286; 37:132; 40:64, 110; 42:142, 197–199.

16 TAH.19:281–282; 34:165–167; 39:187–188; 42:51, 161, 207; 43:132; 45:98–117; 48:60; BOA, HAT.650/31789 C; F. W. Sieber, *Ταξιδεύοντας στη νήσο Κρήτη το 1817 [Travelling on the Island of Crete in 1817]*, trans. Διόνα Μούστρη (Αθήνα: Ιστορητής, 1994), 180–82, 234; Βασίλειος Ψιλάκης, *Ιστορία της Κρήτης από της απωτάτης αρχαιότητος μέχρι των καθ' ημάς χρόνων [History of Crete from Ancient Times to the Present Day]*, vol. 3 (Χανιά: Νέα Έρευνα, 1909), 46, 76, 185–87, 201, 205, 239, 386–87, 685–87, 689; Καλλίνικος Κριτοβουλίδης, *Απομνημονεύματα του περί αυτονομίας της Ελλάδος πολέμου των Κρητών [Memoirs of the War of Cretans for the Autonomy of Greece]* (Αθήνα: Τυπογραφείο Αθήνας, 1859), 9, 42; Εμμανουήλ Αγγελάκης, "Ο γενιτσαρισμός εν Σητεία [Janissarism in Siteia]," *Κρητικαί Μελέται* 1, no. 1–2 (1933): 39–47, 91–92, 120–22, 157–59, 187–91, 216–20, 254–58; Νικόλαος Σταυρινίδης, "Το τραγούδι του Μαζλούμ Αγά ή Μπαλουξή [The Song of Mazlum Agha or Balouxis]," *Αμάλθεια* 2, no. 5 (1971): 53; Βασίλης Δημητριάδης and Διονυσία Δασκάλου, eds., *Ο Κώδικας των Θυσιών. Ονόματα και δημευμένες περιουσίες των χριστιανών αγωνιστών της ανατολικής Κρήτης κατά την Επανάσταση του 1821 [Register of Sacrifices: Names and Confiscated Properties of Christian Combatants of Eastern Crete During the Revolution of 1821]*, trans. Βασίλης Δημητριάδης, Ελένη Καραντζίκου, Πηνελόπη Φωτεινού, and Χρυσούλα Χριστοδουλάρα (Ηράκλειο: Πανεπιστημιακές Εκδόσεις Κρήτης και Βικελαία Δημοτική Βιβλιοθήκη Ηρακλείου, 2003), 363–64.

17 TAH.19:281–282; 34:165–167; 37:109, 132; 41:121.

18 TAH.40:140–141.

19 TAH.41:93; 42:56–57, 207; 45:98–117; BOA, C.ML.299/12159.

20 TAH.32:90–92, 99.

21 TAH.3:398–399; 19:281–282; 32:26; 37:108, 132; 38:86–87; 40:110; 41:14, 134–135; 43:76; 45:97–118. On another family member, see TAH.40:2.

22 TAH.45:101, 102, 109, 110, 116.

23 TAH.45:105.

24 TAH.45:53–4.

25 TAH.43:136.

26 For the importance of Janissary judicial immunity and special extradition in this process, see Σπυρόπουλος, "Οι Γενίτσαροι της Κρήτης," 232–39.

27 TAH.43:14.

28 Ayşe Nükhet Adıyeke, "XVIII. Yüzyılda İstanbul'un Zeytinyağı ve Sabun İhtiyacının Karşılanmasında Girit'in Rolü [The Role of Crete in Meeting Istanbul's Olive Oil and Soap Needs in the Eighteenth Century]," in *XV. Türk Tarih Kongresi, Ankara: 11–15 Eylül 2006. Kongreye Sunulan Bildiriler [15th Congress of Turkish History, Ankara: September 11–15, 2006. Papers Presented at the Congress]*, vol. 4, part 3 (Ankara: Türk Tarih Kurumu Basımevi, 2010), 1743–45.

29 On İzmir's role in the Cretan soap trade and other trade destinations in the Ottoman Empire, see Τριανταφυλλίδου-Baladié, *Το εμπόριο*, 99 and *passim*; Κρεμμυδάς, "Δρόμοι της Μεσογείου, δρόμοι της Κρήτης," 127. On Cretan Muslims and soldier merchants and shopkeepers in İzmir at the time under examination, see Γιάννης Σπυρόπουλος, "Διακοινοτική βία στη Σμύρνη το 1821: μια ευρύτερη οπτική των

γεγονότων [Intercommunal Violence in Smyrna in 1821: A Broader Perspective of the Events]," in *Οθωμανική Κρίση και Ελληνική Επανάσταση,* ed. Ελένη Γκαρά (Αθήνα: Εκδόσεις του 21ου, forthcoming).

30 See, for instance, TAH.37:132, 43:14, and GRGSA, Local Archive of Hydra, Notarial Code 6:27 (the contract is not numbered). I would like to thank Minas Antypas for bringing to my attention this last source, which does not mention the transfer of soap but pertains to the freighting of a Christian ship by a member of one of the most important Cretan Janissary families, the Efendakis, who are also to be found in the list presented here.

31 A transcription and analysis of the text of this letter is also to be found in my article "Yunan Bağımsızlık Savaşı Sırasında Ele Geçirilen İki Yeniçeri Mektubunun Düşündürdükleri [Reflections on Two Janissary Letters Seized During the Greek War of Independence]," in *Payitaht Yeniçerileri: Padişahın "Asi" Kulları, 1700–1826 [The Janissaries of Istanbul: The Sultan's "Rebel" Servants, 1700–1826]*, ed. Aysel Yıldız, Yannis Spyropoulos, and M. Mert Sunar (Istanbul: Kitap Yayınevi, 2022), 37–62.

32 For the use of this word, see James W. Redhouse, *A Turkish and English Lexicon: Shewing in English the Significations of the Turkish Terms* (Istanbul: A. H. Boyajian, 1890), 348. For various words and expressions which were believed to have a fortunate influence and were, thus, imprinted on letters, see Δημήτριος Γιαγτζόγλου, "Η προσωπική επιστολογραφία ως πηγή για την κοινωνική και πολιτισμική ιστορία των Οθωμανών [Personal Correspondence as a Source for the Social and Cultural History of the Ottomans]" (MA thesis, Πανεπιστήμιο Κρήτης, 2018), 84–89.

33 Σπυρόπουλος, *Οθωμανική Διοίκηση*, 74–83; Σπυρόπουλος, "Οι Γενίτσαροι της Κρήτης," 188–89, 263–70.

34 Σπυρόπουλος, "Οι Γενίτσαροι της Κρήτης," 196; Σπυρόπουλος, *Οθωμανική Διοίκηση*, 76.

35 For the shortage of Kandiye in grain, see, for instance, Şükrü *Ilıcak, ed., "Those Infidel Greeks:" The Greek War of Independence Through Ottoman Archival Documents*, vol. 1 (Leiden: Brill, 2021), 542–43, vol. 2, 1314–15.

36 Σπυρόπουλος, "Οι Γενίτσαροι της Κρήτης," 72–73.

37 BOA, MAD.d.3946:527–531.

38 For the *nısf ortaları*, see Abdulkasim Gül, "18. Yüzyılda Yeniçeri Teşkilatı [Janissary Organization in the 18th Century]" (PhD diss., Atatürk Üniversitesi, 2020), 183–84, 453, and *passim*.

39 TAH.45:128–129.

40 See, for instance, the case of a certain Süleyman Odabaşıoğlu Ağa son of Mehmed, a resident of Kandiye who died while visiting Istanbul in 1813; TAH.41:59–60. For some other Odabaşıoğlus, probably members of the same family, found in the *kadı sicilleri* of Kandiye in the early nineteenth century, see TAH.37:79; 41:115. A certain Giridî Derviş Ali was recorded in the Galata court record in October 24, 1798, however the long time separating the two documents renders it quite unlikely that he was the same person as the recipient of the letter in question; İstanbul Müftülüğü Şeriyye Sicilleri Arşivi, Galata Mahkemesi, 541:81.

41 TAH.37:79; 40:97; 41:59–60, 115; 45:102.

42 TAH.45:98–117.

43 Σπυρόπουλος, "Οι Γενίτσαροι της Κρήτης," 209–10.

44 TAH.45:104.

45 Σπυρόπουλος, "Οι Γενίτσαροι της Κρήτης," 216.

46 For some references to knife makers affiliated with the 14th *cemâ'at*, see TAH.37:136; 40:9, 24; 43:17.

47 Câbî Ömer Efendi, *Câbî Târihi [Cabi's History]*, vol. 1, 460–61, 628; Semavi Eyice, "Balkapanı Hanı [Balkapanı Inn]," in *TDV İslâm Ansiklopedisi [TDV Encyclopedia of Islam]*, vol. 5 (Istanbul: Türkiye Diyanet Vakfı, 1992), 33. Also, see BOA, DVNSMHM.d.146:22/71.

48 On this matter, see Spyropoulos, "Yunan Bağımsızlık Savaşı," 37–62.

Bibliography

Adıyeke, Ayşe Nükhet. "XVIII. Yüzyılda İstanbul'un Zeytinyağı ve Sabun İhtiyacının Karşılanmasında Girit'in Rolü [The Role of Crete in Meeting Istanbul's Olive Oil and Soap Needs in the Eighteenth Century]." In *XV. Türk Tarih Kongresi, Ankara: 11–15 Eylül 2006. Kongreye Sunulan Bildiriler [15th Congress of Turkish History, Ankara: September 11–15, 2006. Papers Presented at the Congress]*, vol. 4, part 3, 1743–45. Ankara: Türk Tarih Kurumu Basımevi, 2010.

Crecelius, Daniel. "Damiette and Syrian-Egyptian Trade in the Second Half of the Eighteenth Century." In *Syria and Bilad al-Sham under Ottoman Rule: Essays in Honour of Abdul-Karim Rafeq*, edited by Peter Sluglett and Stefan Weber, 155–75. Leiden and Boston: Brill, 2010.

Efendi, Câbî Ömer, *Câbî Târihi [Cabi's History]*, vol. 1. Ankara: Türk Tarih Kurumu Basımevi, 2003.

Eldem, Edhem. "Strangers in Their Own Seas? The Ottomans in the Eastern Mediterranean Basin in the Second Half of the Eighteenth Century." *Studi Settecenteschi* 29–30 (2014): 25–57.

Eyice, Semavi. "Balkapanı Hanı [Balkapanı Inn]." In *TDV İslâm Ansiklopedisi [TDV Encyclopedia of Islam]*, vol. 5. Istanbul: Türkiye Diyanet Vakfı, 1992.

Greene, Molly. *A Shared World: Christians and Muslims in the Early Modern Mediterranean*. Princeton, NJ: Princeton University Press, 2000.

Griffith, Zoe Ann. "Egyptian Ports in the Ottoman Mediterranean, 1760–1820." PhD diss., Brown University, 2017.

Gül, Abdulkasim. "18. Yüzyılda Yeniçeri Teşkilatı [Janissary Organization in the 18th Century]." PhD diss., Atatürk Üniversitesi, 2020.

Ilıcak, Şükrü, ed. *"Those Infidel Greeks": The Greek War of Independence Through Ottoman Archival Documents*, vol. 1. Leiden: Brill, 2021.

Olivier, Guillaume-Antoine. *Travels in the Ottoman Empire, Egypt, and Persia*, vol. 2. London: T. N. Longman and O. Rees, 1801.

Panzac, Daniel. "Négociants ottomans et capitaines français: la caravane maritime en Crète au XVIIIe siècle." In *L'Empire Ottoman, la république de Turquie et la France*, edited by Hâmit Batu, 99–118. Istanbul and Paris: Éditions Isis & Association pour le Développement des Études Turques, 1986.

Panzac, Daniel. "International and Domestic Maritime Trade in the Ottoman Empire During the 18th Century." In *Commerce et navigation dans l'Empire Ottoman au XVIIIe siècle*, 189–206. Istanbul: The ISIS Press, 1996.

Redhouse, James W. *A Turkish and English Lexicon: Shewing in English the Significations of the Turkish Terms*. Istanbul: A. H. Boyajian, 1890.

Sieber, F. W. *Ταξιδεύοντας στη νήσο Κρήτη το 1817 [Travelling on the Island of Crete in 1817]*, translated by Μούστρη Διόνα. Αθήνα: Ιστορητής, 1994.

Spyropoulos, Yannis. "Yunan Bağımsızlık Savaşı Sırasında Ele Geçirilen İki Yeniçeri Mektubunun Düşündürdükleri [Reflections on Two Janissary Letters Seized During the Greek War of Independence]." In *Payitaht Yeniçerileri: Padişahın "Asi" Kulları, 1700–1826 [The Janissaries of Istanbul: The Sultan's "Rebel" Servants, 1700–1826]*, edited by Aysel Yıldız, Yannis Spyropoulos, and M. Mert Sunar, 37–62. Istanbul: Kitap Yayınevi, 2022.

Αγγελάκης, Εμμανουήλ. "Ο γενιτσαρισμός εν Σητεία." *Κρητικαί Μελέται* 1, no. 1–2 (1933): 39–47, 91–92, 120–22, 157–59, 187–91, 216–20, 254–58. [Aggelakis, Emmanouel. "Janissarism in Siteia." *Cretan Studies* 1, no. 1–2 (1933): 39–47, 91–92, 120–22, 157–59, 187–91, 216–20, 254–58.]

Γιαγτζόγλου, Δημήτριος. "Η προσωπική επιστολογραφία ως πηγή για την κοινωνική και πολιτισμική ιστορία των Οθωμανών." MA thesis, Πανεπιστήμιο Κρήτης, 2018. [Giagtzoglou, Dimitrios. "Personal Correspondence as a Source for the Social and Cultural History of the Ottomans." MA thesis, University of Crete, 2018.]

Γκλαβίνας, Γιάννης, Παππά, Αμαλία. "Οθωμανικά και καραμανλίδικα τεκμήρια στην Κεντρική Υπηρεσία των Γενικών Αρχείων του Κράτους." In *Τουρκολογικά. Τιμητικός τόμος για τον Αναστάσιο Κ. Ιορδάνογλου*, edited by Σαλακίδης Γιώργος, 19–46. Θεσσαλονίκη: Σταμούλης, 2012. [Gklavinas, Giannis, and Amalia Pappa. "Ottoman and Karamanlid Documents at the Central Service of the General State Archives." In *Turkologica. A Volume in Honor of Anastasios K. Iordanoglou*, edited by Giorgos Salakidis, 19–46. Thessaloniki: Stamoulis, 2012.]

Δημητριάδης, Βασίλης, Δασκάλου, Διονυσία, eds. *Ο Κώδικας των Θυσιών. Ονόματα και δημευμένες περιουσίες των χριστιανών αγωνιστών της ανατολικής Κρήτης κατά την Επανάσταση του 1821*, translated by Δημητριάδης Βασίλης, Καραντζίκου Ελένη, Φωτεινού Πηνελόπη, Χριστοδουλάρα Χρυσούλα. Ηράκλειο: Πανεπιστημιακές Εκδόσεις Κρήτης και Βικελαία Δημοτική Βιβλιοθήκη Ηρακλείου, 2003. [Dimitriadis, Vasilis, and Dionysia Daskalou, eds. *Register of Sacrifices: Names and Confiscated Properties of Christian Combatants of Eastern Crete During the Revolution of 1821*, translated by Vasilis Dimitriadis, Eleni Karantzikou, Pinelopi Foteinou, and Chrysoula Christodoulara. Heraklion: Crete University Press and Vikelaia Library of Heraklion, 2003.]

Κρεμμυδάς, Βασίλης. "Δρόμοι της Μεσογείου, δρόμοι της Κρήτης; ένα αδύνατο ζεύγμα: ο χαρακτήρας του εμπορίου και της βιομηχανίας, 1750–1850." In *Πεπραγμένα Θ΄ Διεθνούς Κρητολογικού Συνεδρίου*, Keynote Speech Volume, 123–31. Ηράκλειο: Εταιρία Κρητικών Ιστορικών Μελετών, 2006. [Kremmydas, Vasilis. "Roads of the Mediterranean, Roads of Crete; an Impossible Pairing: The Nature of Trade and Industry, 1750–1850." In *Proceedings of the 9th International Congress of Cretology, Keynote Speech Volume*, 123–31. Heraklion: Society of Cretan Historical Studies, 2006.]

Κρεμμυδάς, Βασίλης. *Οι σαπουνοποιίες της Κρήτης στο 18ο αιώνα*. Αθήνα: τυπ. Κ. Μιχαλάς, 1974. [Kremmydas, Vasilis. *The Soap Factories of Crete in the 18th Century*. Athens: K. Michalas, 1974.]

Κριτοβουλίδης, Καλλίνικος. *Απομνημονεύματα του περί αυτονομίας της Ελλάδος πολέμου των Κρητών*. Αθήνα: Τυπογραφείο Αθήνας, 1859. [Kritovoulides, Kallinikos. *Memoirs of the War of Cretans for the Autonomy of Greece*. Athens: Typografio of Athens, 1859.]

Σπυρόπουλος, Γιάννης. "Διακοινοτική βία στη Σμύρνη το 1821: μια ευρύτερη οπτική των γεγονότων." In *Οθωμανική Κρίση και Ελληνική Επανάσταση*, edited by Γκαρά Ελένη. Αθήνα: Εκδόσεις του 21ου, forthcoming. [Spyropoulos, Yannis. "Intercommunal Violence in Smyrna in 1821: A Broader Perspective of the Events." In *Ottoman Crisis and the Greek Revolution*, edited by Eleni Gara. Athens: Editions of the 21st, forthcoming.]

Σπυρόπουλος, Γιάννης. "Κοινωνική, διοικητική, οικονομική και πολιτική διάσταση του οθωμανικού στρατού: οι γενίτσαροι της Κρήτης, 1750–1826." PhD diss., Πανεπιστήμιο Κρήτης, 2014. [Spyropoulos, Yannis. "Social, Administrative, Economic and Political Dimensions of the Ottoman Army: The Janissaries of Crete, 1750–1826." PhD diss., University of Crete, 2014.]

Σπυρόπουλος, Γιάννης. "Τέσσερις μικρές ιστορίες μουσουλμάνων στο πλαίσιο του κρητικού 1821." In *Κρήτη 1821–1830: Αναγνώσεις μιας ατελέσφορης Επανάστασης*, edited by Βουρλιώτης Μανόλης, Δρακάκης Μανόλης, Πατρουδάκη Γιάννα, 265–82. Αθήνα: Μπαρτζουλιάνος, 2021. [Spyropoulos, Yannis. "Four Short Stories of Muslims in the Context of the Cretan 1821." In *Crete 1821–1830: Readings of an Ineffective Revolution*, edited by Manolis Vourliotis, Manolis Drakakis, and Gianna Patroudaki, 265–82. Athens: Bartzoulianos, 2021.]

Σπυρόπουλος, Γιάννης. *Οθωμανική διοίκηση και κοινωνία στην προεπαναστατική δυτική Κρήτη: Αρχειακές Μαρτυρίες (1817–1819)*, edited by Παπαδάκη Ασπασία. Ρέθυμνο: Γενικά Αρχεία του Κράτους, 2015. [Spyropoulos, Yannis. *Ottoman Administration and Society in Prerevolutionary Western Crete: Archival Testimonies (1817–1819)*, edited by Aspasia Papadaki. Rethymnon: General State Archives, 2015.]

Σταυρινίδης, Νικόλαος. "Το τραγούδι του Μαζλούμ Αγά ή Μπαλουξή." *Αμάλθεια* 2, no. 5 (1971): 52–63. [Stavrinidis, Nikolaos. "The Song of Mazlum Agha or Balouxis." *Amaltheia* 2, no. 5 (1971): 52–63.]

Τριανταφυλλίδου-Baladié, Γιολάντα. "Οι πιστώσεις στις εμπορικές συναλλαγές στην Κρήτη τον 18° αιώνα." In *Πεπραγμένα Ε΄ Διεθνούς Κρητολογικού Συνεδρίου*, vol. 3, 222–28. Ηράκλειο: Εταιρία Κρητικών Ιστορικών Μελετών, 1985. [Triantafyllidou-Baladié, Yolanda. "Credit in Commercial Transactions in Crete in the 18th Century." In *Proceedings of the 5th International Congress of Cretology*, vol. 3, 222–28. Heraklion: Society of Cretan Historical Studies, 1985.]

Τριανταφυλλίδου-Baladié, Γιολάντα. *Το εμπόριο και η οικονομία της Κρήτης (1669–1795)*. Ηράκλειο: Βικελαία Βιβλιοθήκη, 1988. [Triantafyllidou-Baladié, Yolanda. *Trade and the Economy of Crete (1669–1795)*. Heraklion: Vikelaia Library of Heraklion, 1988.]

Ψιλάκης, Βασίλειος. *Ιστορία της Κρήτης από της απωτάτης αρχαιότητος μέχρι των καθ' ημάς χρόνων*, vol. 3. Χανιά: Νέα Έρευνα, 1909. [Psilakis, Vasileios. *History of Crete from Ancient Times to the Present Day*, vol. 3. Chania: Nea Ereuna, 1909.]

8 The Wealth Accumulated by Merchants in the 1820s

Levels, Gradations, and Distributions

Simos Bozikis

Set at a time when one sphere of dominance yields to another, my approach finds itself at a crossroads. What is the underlying justification for continuing to view matters through the Ottoman structural lens? To a degree, this approach can be validated by the fact that the immediate consequences of this transition were primarily political.[1] The Greek Revolution of 1821, also referred to as the Greek Struggle for Independence, had a profound effect on production, trade, and monetary relations, which, however, were all nonetheless constrained by the overall trends and actualities in the Eastern Mediterranean.[2] In fact, the economic power base of "the wealthy and the merchants" that we are investigating here can be traced back to the Ottoman structure. The accumulation of wealth had occurred prior to 1821, and its influences persisted, with variations, under the new conditions.

The group at hand had gained their wealth mainly through the following, often intersecting, economic activities, as well as through the adaptation of these activities to the prevailing opportunities and constraints. Wealth was engendered through trade (of goods and money) both on the mainland and specially abroad, embracing the Black Sea, the Levant, and the West. It had capitalized on the opportunities presented by the Napoleonic Wars and the internal needs that arose with the Greek Revolution (restoration of the economy in wartime, supplying the warring sides, looting and plunder, etc.).[3] It acquired further resources through borrowing in the context of trade[4] and in community affairs (covering tax obligations and pre-purchase of production)[5] and from concluding loans with the Greek revolutionary state. It continued, even after 1821, with complete control of the field of tax farming and the purchase-operation of facilities that constituted capital stock (mills in the countryside, workshops in the cities, etc.).[6]

The material I am examining does not cover the entire financial holdings of the "wealthy and the merchants" in the Peloponnese and the Aegean islands, nor, of course, does it entail the whole of this group. It concerns an aspect of the overall situation: more specifically, it deals with the amount of liquid capital available to a large number of families, as per the estimates and sources of officials of the new Greek state. I am thus reviewing the amount of funds and the number of "wealthy and the merchants," as these are derived from these official estimates; furthermore,

DOI: 10.4324/9781003500780-11

I divide them into classes/grades, so as to showcase more effectively the distribution of the accumulated wealth. I wish to determine the sizes of wealth at the base of the social pyramid, using some indicative information from Cyprus (magnitude of assets) and Crete (value of land, workshops, houses). Finally, I am offering a set of comparisons to illustrate the considerable discrepancy between the amassed funds mentioned above and the assets held by individuals in the lowest tiers of society.

Thus, by considering the importance of the numbers, including the amounts and various weightings, I am first showcasing the distribution of wealth, or more precisely, of a segment of it, in the territory which in the 1820s transitioned from the Ottoman Empire to the control of the new Greek state. Second, I have compiled a body of evidence proving the presence of available funds in this same area, thus contradicting the formerly widespread notion of "absence and scarcity" (although indeed such instances were occasionally so), to explain the development trajectory followed in the territory in question.[7]

References and Overall Figures

The main reference material of this text comes from the Ioannis Kapodistrias' Archive kept in the Archives of the Prefecture of Corfu.[8] It was taken from the voluminous "Catalogue on the Wealthy and the Merchants in the Greek Territory" (doc. no. 18) file 474, Outgoing collection.[9] It comprises a series of individual lists—Hydriots, Spetsiots, Psarians, Ermoupolitans-Syriots, and Peloponnesians—each containing two main pieces of information: persons and amounts that outline their "status," all calculated in Spanish thalers.[10] It appears that the Catalogue, in its given form, was put together in early 1828, when Governor Ioannis Kapodistrias was trying to gain insight into the funds held by the powerful people in the area. His purpose in this, among other objectives, was to secure contributions to the National Financial Bank, then in the process of being set up.[11]

In this chapter, I follow the above lists, but I would like to stress some of the constraints surrounding them. The group of Psarians consisted of people who did not live in Psara; after the "catastrophe of 1824," they had moved to Ermoupolis, Aegina, and elsewhere.[12] The lists of Hydriots and Spetsiots are seemingly separate, but, in fact, individuals of such origins can also be found on the list of Ermoupolis. Finally, the group of Ermoupolitans-Syriots embraces some other quite heterogeneous cases: local landowners and merchants, as well as shipowners and merchants from the surrounding islands (Hydra, Paros, Patmos, Kasos, Crete, and elsewhere), from the Ionian Islands, Epirus, and so on,[13] and even merchants from Chios, Mytilene, Smyrna, and Istanbul.[14]

In terms of the number of cases per group, it should be stressed that the recording is not exhaustive. It is though quite significant and representative enough to allow us to form a global picture of the accumulation of wealth at that time. In total, the Catalogue includes 255 "wealthy entities and merchants," 138 of whom have their funds listed in cash.[15] It also includes some information that allows us

Table 8.1 The Funds of 138 "wealthy entities and major merchants" in the Peloponnese and the Aegean islands in the 1820s.

Groups	*Funds (Thalers)*	*Wealthy Individuals, Including an Indication of Their Funds*	*Geometric Mean (Thalers)*	*Total of Wealthy Individuals in the Catalogue*	*Primary Capacities*[(i)]
Peloponnesians	265,000	15	14,500	77	K-M
Hydriots	1,315,000	16	38,100	35	S-M
Spetsiots	428,000	18	19,800	18	S-M
Psarians	125,000	8	14,400	30	S-M
Hydriots	710,000	81	4,900	95	E-P
Total	*2,843,000*	*138*	*8,900*	*255*	

Note: [(i)] K=*kocabaşıs*-notables until 1821, M=merchants (some with investments also in shipping, in the case of Ermoupolis), and S=shipowners-merchants (who in the case of Hydra, Spetses and Psara, occasionally carried out communal functions). Source: GSA/AC/KA/OUT., f. 474, doc. 18.

to estimate the funds for the total 255 persons (Table 8.1). More specifically, the manuscript contains:

- 15 Peloponnesians with "statuses" of 5–50 thousand thalers, and 62 other individuals or groups from the same region, without listing any amount.
- 16 Hydriots with "statuses" of 10–600 thousand thalers, in addition to 19 relevant cases without an indication of the money amounts and further information on the presence of more wealthy individuals in Hydra (in addition to the 16 Hydriots above) holding funds of 5–10 thousand thalers.[16]
- 18 Spetsiots with "statuses" of 8–60 thousand thalers, including references to a few more with funds in the amount of 5–6 thousand thalers, without specifying their number.
- 8 Psarians with "statuses" of 10–30 thousand thalers, with another 22 relevant cases without an indication of money amounts, as well as information of more wealthy individuals (in addition to the above 8) with funds in the amount of 4–6 thousand thalers.
- 81 Ermoupolitans-Syriots with "statuses" from 800 to 150 thousand thalers, and another 14 without an indication of the money amounts held.

According to this material, the subset of the "138" families and partnerships owned funds (*kapitali*) worth 2.8 million thalers [= 42 million piastres (*kuruş*), in 1828]. All "255," based on the statistical distribution, the amount range, and so on, must have been worth a total of 3.4 million thalers (= 51 million piastres, in 1828).

For brevity's sake in this presentation, let me simply state what these totals were comparable to. Given the geographical region in question, which, as already noted, was at a critical juncture in terms of political sovereignty, my benchmark will be certain accounts of the successor state in this region (Table 8.2). More explicitly

Table 8.2 The funds of 138 "wealthy entities and merchants," as a % of national accounts of the Greek state that succeeded the Ottoman Empire in the territories in question.

A. Funds of "Wealthy Individuals and Merchants" (Amounts in Million Thalers)		*B. National Accounts of the New Greek State in 1833*[(i)] *(amounts in million thalers)*		*Ratio A: B*
The subset of '138' families		III. Public expenditure	2.53	I : III = 112%
	2.84	IV. GDP at current prices	9.31	I : IV = 31%
		V. Public debt	20.19	I : V = 14%

Note: [(i)] For these figures, Σίμος Μποζίκης, *Χρήμα, χρέος, κράτος: νόμισμα, πίστη και εξουσία στην Ελλάδα, 1821–1832* (Αθήνα: Ασίνη, forthcoming). Source: GSA/AC/KA/OUT., f. 474, doc. 18.

then, the funds of these "138" subjects corresponded to 14% of the national Greek debt (internal and external)—as formed over the decade of the struggle for independence—and was equivalent to a third of the GDP, but exceeded the annual public revenue. That is, the wealth accumulated prior to this point in time was actually greater than the economic dimension of the newly established Greek state. Given the population size (753,400 people), this demonstrates the existence of groups with a much-enhanced power in the region in question, a part of which, during that particular decade, had ceased to be a territory of the Ottoman Empire.

The available material also allows us to form a rough picture of the distribution of economic power in the Peloponnese and the Aegean islands. The data reveals (a) three to four very wealthy families per province in the Peloponnese or, alternatively, to one rich family per thousand families in the general population, a reasonable proportion for a region in which the notables (proesti) played a dominant role; and (b) 5–15 very rich families per thousand, in the case of Hydriots, Spetsiots, Psarians, and Syriots, again in a reasonable proportion, given the population numbers involved in trade and that these places were shipping hotspots.[17]

The importance of these power groups is fully recognized in the relevant literature:[18] merchants and notables (who owned land) in the Peloponnese, participating in tax farming and in various commercial-financial activities, often together with powerful people from adjacent regions;[19] shipowners with a strong role in maritime trade (in the Mediterranean and far beyond), in the war economy (looting and plunder) and in tax farming, namely, the Hydriots, Spetsiots, and Psarians; merchants of various sorts, participating in local and international networks, granting of credit, investments in shipping, and finally a few landowners, that is, those recorded in the list of Ermoupolis.

As already mentioned, the available set of "wealthy individuals and merchants" is not exhaustive (i.e., complete). If we limit ourselves to the eight most powerful of each geographical unit (Figure 8.1),[20] we arguably end up with a more representative distribution of their economic power. We can detect the great, but still inferior "status" of the notables and merchants of the Peloponnese, compared with

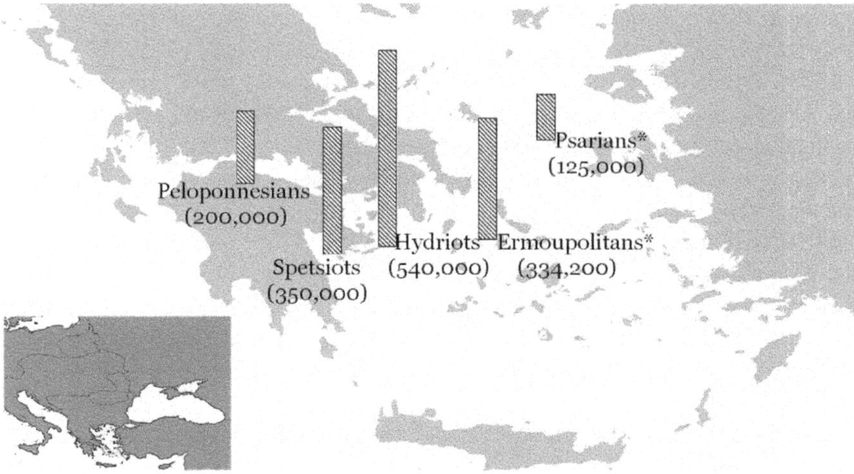

Figure 8.1 The sum of the eight highest funds divided in five geographical units (Peloponnese and the Aegean islands) in the 1820s.

Note: (*)The Psarians had abandoned their island after the disaster of 1824. Ermoupolitans from various places had fled to Syros after 1822–23.

Source: Author creation.

the others. The Hydriots and Spetsiots, who held a prominent position in the area of maritime trade, were ranked first and second; the Psarians, who had meanwhile been severely affected after the loss of their home seat in 1824, languish at the bottom of the ranking. A rising power is Ermoupolis, which hosted a diverse group of merchants and shipowners—with origins from Chios, Polis, Asia Minor, adjacent islands (Hydra, Spetses, Psara, Crete, Kasos, etc.), the Ionian Islands, and various continental regions: this was to become an important center of trade, transit, and shipping in the Eastern Mediterranean.[21]

The Distribution of Wealth at the Top and the Base of the Social Pyramid

Apart from the overall figures, the distribution of the accumulated wealth among the "wealthy individuals and major merchants" makes for an interesting perusal. What was the distribution of funds among these "138" subjects at hand? I do not deal with the *arithmetic mean*, which is not a good measure because of the asymmetrical distribution, but limit myself to the *geometric mean* which amounts to 9,000 thalers (=135,000 piastres in 1828).[22] This figure is representative across the overall landscape, although not sufficient for us to understand the diversity of the gradations: it lies at the heart of our observations.

It is more useful, for this purpose, to arrange the information into classes (statistical and here necessarily of unequal range). The most numerous—and, in this respect, the most important—class were those with up to 3,000 thalers (= 45,000 piastres in 1828). By the same criterion, this class was followed in terms of significance by that with funds ranging from 3,000 to 12,000 thalers (= 180,000 piastres in 1828). The largest funds (exceeding 12 thousand) were fewer still and associated with the most powerful segment of the major shipowners and merchants. This predictable pattern of increase, leaving any details aside, forms the three tiers of wealthy individuals and merchants that dominate the pyramid in the geographical area we review.

But, how did the gradation of economic power differ between the top and base of the social pyramid? To answer this question, I will first examine what was the order of estate size, using indicative information from Ottoman Cyprus (estate sizes) and Ottoman Crete (value of land, workshops, houses). This will show, in another way, how large the funds of these "138" subjects were in the overall area in question.

I obtained the above information from data on property confiscations that took place in these areas in the 1820s. The potential impact of the uniqueness of the circumstances and the procedure concerned on producing lower valuations must be born in mind. Auctions, in some way, "are processes for managing the ambiguity and uncertainty of value by establishing social meanings and consensus."[23] In this respect, I would say that the material available gives us a rough idea of the broader perspective.

As far as Cyprus is concerned, a small but appropriate sample of 95 properties[24] from three groups (notables, ecclesiastical and tax-paying Christians) was examined, based on their confiscated assets:[25] land, goods, livestock, cash, stocks of goods (mainly cotton and sometimes wine, pulses, grain, and wool), debts, and so on.[26] Excluding debts, their mean property was close to 190 thalers (= 1,350 piastres in 1821, or 2,850 in 1828). As it is the geometric mean that was calculated here, this result was not seriously affected by the limited significant evidence. It remains a good measure of the proportion of the mean wealth in the above sample which, as noted[27] and with some exceptions, did not involve high-value assets. We thus have an indicator that probably reflects the situation at the base of the social pyramid as well as the one in its upper parts.

To determine how realistic this scenario is, we will examine relevant data from Crete, namely, confiscations of buildings, land parcels, and shops, in the period 1822–1825.[28] Let us first look at the value of buildings from a sample of 263 cases, with the following compositions: small and large residences, with or without auxiliary and supplementary spaces (warehouses, barns, stables), urban, suburban properties, and so on.[29] The sample is heterogeneous, but it even so helps us gain a better understanding: we are talking about buildings of 55 thalers value as based on the geometric mean, or the median which was two thalers lower.[30] Most of them had a value of up to 100 thalers, but there were also those that had a very high value, to some extent due to their accessories (auxiliary spaces, courtyards, and enclosed orchards). I propose, therefore, to adopt the amount of 55 thalers (=550 piastres in 1824, or 825 in 1828) as the figure which represents the core distribution, lying as it does close to the middle of the first class, and somewhat defines the mean value of the buildings included in the sample, which of course were of some age. In fact, if we accept as probably typical the price per square meter of a number of buildings sold in the Peloponnese in 1824—using the same procedure, but as applied by the Greek authorities—this price applied to the Cretan sample reflects buildings of a total area in the main of up to 60 square meters, but also include a number of larger structures.[31]

The next asset concerns shops (wineries, commercial shops, etc.) and workshops. Based on a sample of 49 cases, a mean value of 60 thalers (geometric mean, equivalent to 600 piastres in 1824, or 900 in 1828) is obtained. Buildings with a value of up to 80 thalers represented the majority of cases. These size categories can be also found in other sources.[32] Therefore, another relevant set of information can be applied, useful in determining a smaller set of assets indicative of a household, enough to ensure all essential goods for a livelihood.

The last asset for which we will provide a breakdown of its value is land (here undifferentiated as to its type). From a sample of 149 parcels of land, confiscated during the period 1824–1825, a mean value of approximately 40 thalers (=400 piastres in 1824, or 600 in 1828) was obtained; the average area was 4 *stremma* (1,000 square meters), and the mean price was 10 thalers per *stremma*, which seems high but is reasonable, as our sample includes urban and high-quality suburban land. The bulk of the material consisted of areas whose value was up to 60 thalers, that is, up to about 6 *stremma*.[33] We therefore arrive at one more piece of information, useful in terms of the value of assets and on the basis of which we could arrive at a working assumption on the size category of a small property unit.

Based on the material from Crete, the mean value of a residence and a few *stremma* of land was close to 100 thalers. Accordingly, the value of a workshop and a separate residence and probably a property combining both functions was similar. Does then a value of 190 thalers for a medium-sized property from the material in Cyprus actually refer to the same wealth tier? In other words, to what extent do these figures reflect the gradation of properties at the base of the social pyramid, and what was approximately the range of property values at that level?

A Comparison Between Wealth and Poverty

An undated draft document, entitled "On voting," found in the Ioannis Kapodistrias' Archive, describes the minimum property and social criteria appropriate for the right to vote. It records some very interesting gradations (Table 8.4). In small settlements, owning real estate assets worth 67 thalers (≈500 piastres in 1821, or 1,000 in 1828) ensured one the right to vote, while 200 thalers' worth granted the right to be elected.[34] However, at the provincial level, representation required 2,000 thalers' worth (30,000 piastres in 1828) of real estate.[35]

The lowest tier, defined by the possession of real estate assets worth up to 67 thalers, did not necessarily involve groups with low incomes, because income formation was a result of rather more factors (cultivation of third-party land, etc.). If anything, however, this threshold reflects the very poor, that is, farmers with very little property, and others who engaged in activities without owning any property, or but little (small home-workshop, home-shop, etc.): it also embraced itinerant or settled tradesmen, poor artisans, assistants and other manual workers. Let us, therefore, focus on those who had property worth from 67 to 200 thalers.

Based on the material from Crete—as well as on evidence seen above on the value of old houses per square meter—67 thalers' worth could represent a small house and, at most, 15 *stremma* of land, assuming a price of about 2.5 thalers per *stremma* for land parcels with lower yields.[36] This area was capable of producing, after deducting sowing and taxes, sufficient to cover a part of the basic subsistence of a family of four.[37] On the contrary, an estate worth up to 200 thalers should have corresponded to a larger house and a larger land area or, alternatively, to a large home-workshop, two such separate premises, or combinations thereof including land. I would suggest that in the Peloponnese, 67–200 thalers' worth of real estate corresponded to 15–65 *stremma* of land area, and that such was enough to provide up to two times one's actual needs for living.[38]

The above information and assumptions/scenarios seem to confirm, albeit roughly, that it is real estate worth up to 200 thalers that defines the broad social base, and that a real estate of 67 talers approximates the boundary between the lowest and the upper tier of this base. It is interesting to note that 67 thalers' worth is close to the geometric mean (=75 thalers) resulting from estate assets worth between 1 and 200 thalers.

The question thus arises of how powerful were, first, these 138 "wealthy entities and merchants" in the list in question in terms of their social base and then the other intermediate tiers, based on their funds. Of course, if we dwell on individual cases, the range of internal discrepancies between each could be massive. I will therefore limit myself to a more global perspective, and attempt different sorts of comparisons, which lead to the same approximate result, namely, of how great the economic power possessed by these "138" subjects was. In numbers, based on the funds of the "138" subjects in question, the mean discrepancy of this top tier was 90 times higher than the common estate assets at its base.

The estimates of Greek officials on the ability to raise capital for the National Financial Bank provide a more sensitive understanding, as it also contains a segment of the intermediary tier. These officials had projected the amounts that they might receive from very powerful individuals and from those with a medium local economic strength (small local merchants, shop owners, local notables acting in local/secondary economic centers, etc.). To this, to represent the social base, I considered, as a fictitious contributing factor, the lowest tier of the poll tax.[39]

Considering this material and, more specifically, based on the multiple differences between the gradation of the above potential contributions, two very interesting aspects can be observed. One of these concerns is the distance between the top and the base of the social pyramid, which is still high. The above criterion reveals that the economic strength of the "138" subjects was 75 times greater than the economic power of people at the social base (Table 8.3).

Another aspect, resulting from the gradation of potential participations in the bank, concerns the middle tier of *affluent* individuals that lay between the wealthy—very wealthy, and the poor—very poor. Wealthy individuals, who pursued large-scale economic activity, appear to be 15 times more powerful on

Table 8.3 Estimates of the ability of individual groups to contribute to the capital of the National Financial Bank established in 1828 by the Greek authorities: the multiple between individual contributions.

	a. Social Base	*b-c. Affluent*	*d. Wealthy*
a. Social base[(i)]	1		
b–c. Affluent[(ii)]	5	1	
d. Wealthy[(iii)]	75	15	1

Note: [(i)] Working assumption, according to which the potential amount of contributions from the social base level was equal to the lowest tier of the poll tax. Gradation of projected contributions of the upper tiers: [(ii)] groups with limited—mainly local—power: 20, 25, 50, and 100 thalers; [(iii)] groups of economically powerful individuals at the territory level: 150, 250, 400, 800, and 2,000 thalers. Source: GSA/CSA/GS, f. 19, doc. no. 25, *same*, f. 35, doc. no 19.

Table 8.4 The multiples between the property tiers, according to draft criteria on the right to vote and to be elected in the new Greek state.

	a[(i)]	*b*[(i)]	*c*[(i)]	*d*[(i)]
a. Social base	1			
b. Affluent at settlement level	4	1		
c. Affluent at the provincial level	12	3	1	
d. Wealthy at the territory level	73	18	6	1

Note: [(i)] The gradations as described in the first column. Source: GSA/AC/KA/VARIOUS, f. 46, subf. 1, ream 5, doc. no. n/a.

average than the affluent, who mainly were involved in local activities. And this latter group, the affluent individuals, was in turn five times more powerful than the great mass at the social base. Accordingly, the affluent individuals could easily secure the goods necessary for their livelihood as well as such surpluses that ensured their unhindered social presence.

Finally, using as a criterion the minimum property, if any, for participation in the electoral college and running for an elective office—the criterion we discussed above—a scale of at least 73 to 1 emerges between the property assets of the wealthy individuals and the small property units of the social base (Table 8.4). By this way of thinking, the economic strength of the wealthy individuals was at least 6–18 times greater than that of the affluent individuals in different regions, who in turn were 4–12 times more powerful than the mass of the population at the social base. Moreover, as we saw at the beginning, the presence of middle and lower middle classes, as a percentage of the total population, was not homogeneous throughout the territories under review. The majority can be found in Hydra, Spetses, Psara (before 1824), and Ermoupolis (after 1822–23), rather than in the Peloponnese.

Differences in accumulation levels and inequalities reflect the degrees of market development operating. These relative distances manifest the different organic connections between individual social groups, in the context of production and circulation of goods, which had consequences for the distribution of income in the regions discussed here. They also indicate the significantly higher economic strength of certain groups: (a) whose activity was articulated in the structures of internationalized commercial and financial capitalism (sea and land trade in goods and funds, lending, etc.); (b) who in some cases had direct ownership of large areas of land dedicated to commodity production; and (c) who secured a part of the surplus product through tax farming and loan granting (until 1821, to the communities; after 1821, to the emerging Greek state). The area that we have focused on did not lack for funds, but it was neither entrenched from earlier times nor closed to outsiders.

Instead of an Epilogue

The funds of the "138" subjects were formed through a set of different activities and at varying rates of accumulation. The traces of these activities, in most cases, can be discerned in the late 18th century to the early decades of the 19th century, especially in the territories of the Ottoman Empire. These funds were part of estates that had been formed over the last pre-revolutionary years and which continued to grow, or remained the same after 1821 if in a more unstable context, as new possibilities were presented and various challenges faced. *However, regardless of the fluctuations that followed, the key observation is that the funds had already been accumulated.*

The degree of capital accumulation of major merchants trading by land and sea was high, and so was the wealth of the notables. The accumulated wealth was the result of economic activities conducted on land, coastal, and maritime milieux, ones that were not merely complementary, but presented also deeply established interconnections between them,[40] despite structural differences. These connections opened the way to "markets," improving the distribution of income, but at different rates: the relative inequality was clearly greater in rural areas, with the exception, I would say, of livestock farming. In contrast, in the centers of trade, the opportunities for social mobility were greater and accompanied by an improved share in the total product.

The transition from Ottoman rule to the new Greek state accompanied by the revival of the war economy in the Eastern Mediterranean with the start of the Greek Revolution produced new opportunities (wide and full access to the control of public revenue, loot and plunder, trade in supplies and internal supply, etc.), which each had their own life-span. However, the end of the 1820s was a turning point, centered on the conditions, adjustments, and transformations on which the question of accumulation depended on the new conditions, both in the sphere of trade, especially maritime trade, and in the sphere of agriculture.

There was though no shortage in funds, as was formerly widely believed, because of the industrial "backwardness" of the eastern Mediterranean and southern Balkans; it was simply that investments in other sectors had higher returns.[41] Industrialization in England "pushed" the Mediterranean economies toward an even greater specialization in other sectors (agricultural production, raw materials, services) to ensure a comparative advantage and a benefit from the differences in relative prices of goods and factors of production.[42] Thus, the interest in ship owning, trade, tax farming, usury, and agricultural production was kept active, but this did not mean that there was a lack in adjustments, transformations, and the search for opportunities in other sectors.

Archives

General State Archives (GSA)
Archives of Corfu, Capodistria Archive, Outgoing Documents (GSA/AC/CA/O)
Archives of Corfu, Capodistria Archive, Various (GSA/AC/CA/V)
Central Service Archives, Archive of Secretariat of Finance 1833–1862 (GSA/CSA/ASF)
Central Service Archives, Archive of the Ministry/Secretariat/Ministry of Religious Affairs and Education 1821–1827 (GSA/CSA/AMR)
Central Service Archives, Archive of the Ministry/Secretariat/Ministry of Finance 1821–1827 (GSA/CSA/AMF)
Gazette of the Kingdom of Greece

Notes

1 Χριστίνα Αγριαντώνη, "Οι μετασχηματισμοί της βιομηχανικής δομής της Ερμούπολης τον 19ο αιώνα [The Transformations of the Industrial Structure of Ermoupolis in the 19th Century]," in *Νεοελληνική Πόλη: οθωμανικές κληρονομιές και ελληνικό κράτος. Πρακτικά του διεθνούς συμποσίου ιστορίας* (Αθήνα: Εταιρεία Μελέτης Νέου Ελληνισμού, 1985), 606.

2 Petros T. Pizanias, *The Making of the Modern Greeks: 1400–1820* (Newcastle: Cambridge Scholars Publishing, 2020), 124–73; Τζελίνα Χαρλαύτη, "Η εισβολή της ναυτιλίας των "Γραικών' στο μεγάλο εμπόριο της Μεσογείου, 1714–1815 [The Invasion of the Shipping of the "Greeks' in the Great Trade of the Mediterranean, 1714–1815]," in *Η ναυτιλία των Ελλήνων, 1700–1821*, ed. Τζελίνα Χαρλαύτη and Κατερίνα Παπακωνσταντίνου (Αθήνα: Κέδρος, 2013), 237–41, 257, 267–68.

3 Σίμος Μποζίκης, *Ελληνική Επανάσταση και Δημόσια Οικονομία 1821–1832 [Greek Revolution and Public Economy (1821–1832)]* (Αθήνα: Ασίνη, 2020), 341–63; Ibid., "Ναυτικός αγώνας, δημόσια οικονομία και εθνική κυριαρχία το Εικοσιένα [Naval War, Public Economy and National Sovereignty in 1821]," in *Η Ναυτιλία των Ελλήνων στα χρόνια της Επανάστασης. Ο εμπορικός και πολεμικός στόλος, 1821–1831*, ed. Κατερίνα Γαλάνη and Τζελίνα Χαρλαύτη (Ηράκλειο: Πανεπιστημιακές Εκδόσεις Κρήτης, υπό έκδοση); Katerina Galani and Gelina Harlaftis, "Privateering During the Greek War of Independence (1821–1829): Issues of Legitimacy, Organization and Economics of a War-Induced Practice," in *New Perspectives on the Greek War of Independence: Myths, Realities, Legacies and Reflections*, ed. Yianni Cartledge and Andrekos Varnava (Cham: Palgrave Macmillan, 2022), 129–53.

4 Σοφία Λαΐου, "Οθωμανοί Έλληνες σαράφηδες στην Κωνσταντινούπολη του 1821 [Ottoman Greek Sarrafs in Istanbul in 1821]," *Μεσαιωνικά και Νέα Ελληνικά* 14 (2021): 217–38; Δέσποινα Βλάμη, "Πόλεμος και επιχειρήσεις: οι αδελφοί Μπουντούρη [War and Business: The Boudouri Brothers]," Ibid., 53–99.

5 Μάρθα Πύλια, "Λειτουργίες και αυτονομία των κοινοτήτων της Πελοποννήσου κατά τη δεύτερη τουρκοκρατία (1715–1821) [Functions and Autonomy of Peloponnesian

Communities During the Second Turkish Occupation (1715–1821)]," *Μνήμων* 23 (2001): 67–98.

6 Μποζίκης, *Ελληνική Επανάσταση*, 244–66, 269–328, 363–98; Σίμος Μποζίκης, "Δυναμικές και αδράνειες στη φορολογία και στο φορολογικό μηχανισμό κατά την Επανάσταση του 1821 [Dynamics and Stagnation of the Taxation and the Tax Mechanism During the Greek Revolution of 1821]," *Μνήμων* 31 (2010): 31–70; Μηνάς Αντύπας, "Οικονομικοί προσανατολισμοί των υδραίικων πλοιοκτητικών οικογενειών στη διάρκεια της Ελληνικής Επανάστασης. Η περίπτωση της οικογένειας Μπουντούρη [Financial Orientations of Hydriot Shipowing Families During the Greek Revolution: The Case of the Boudouri Family]," in *Η οικονομία στα χρόνια της Επανάστασης*, ed. Δημήτρης Δημητρόπουλος and Μαρία Χριστίνα Χατζηιωάννου (Αθήνα: Ινστιτούτο Ιστορικών Ερευνών/Εθνικό Ίδρυμα Ερευνών, 2023), 191–222; Δημήτρης Δημητρόπουλος, "Και πέραν της γεωργίας και της ναυτιλίας; Μια ψηλάφηση των παραγωγικών δραστηριοτήτων των πόλεων στα χρόνια της Ελληνικής Επανάστασης [Beyond Agriculture and Shipping? Outlining the Productive Activities in the Cities in the Years of the Greek Revolution]," Ibid., 171–90.

7 Ανδρέας Κακριδής, "Η ελληνική εκβιομηχάνιση: συνοπτική εισαγωγή [The Greek Industrialization: A Brief Introduction]," in Robert C. Allen, *Η βιομηχανική επανάσταση: συνοπτική εισαγωγή*, ed. Ανδρέας Κακριδής (Ηράκλειο: Πανεπιστημιακές Εκδόσεις Κρήτης, 2021), 178–80.

8 Source Abbreviations: GSA/AC/CA/O = General State Archives, Archives of Corfu, Capodistria Archive, Outgoing Documents; GSA/AC/CA/V = General State Archives, Archives of Corfu, Capodistria Archive, Various;

GSA/CSA/AMR = General State Archives, Central Service Archives, Archive of the Ministry/Secretariat/Ministry of Religious Affairs and Education 1821–1827; GSA/CSA/AMF = General State Archives, Central Service Archives, Archive of the Ministry/Secretariat/Ministry of Finance 1821–1827; GSA/CSA/ASF = General State Archives, Central Service Archives, Archive of Secretariat of Finance 1833–1862.

9 GSA/AC/CA/O, fold. 474, doc. no. 18. This is not the first time this source has been used, see Pizanias, *The Making*, 409–10.

10 Since our approach involves comparisons and distributions of monetary figures across different years, I have opted to retain the Spanish thaler as a more stable unit of value measurement than the piastres. If any readers wish to convert the amounts of money into Greek piastres, the mean annual exchange rate of piastres per Spanish thaler in Greece is available below: 7.1 το 1821; 7.8 το 1822; 9.5 το 1823; 10.0 το 1824; 11.0 το 1825; 12.5 το 1826; 14.2 το 1827; 15.0 το 1828; 15.0 το 1829; 15.4 το 1830; 15.8 το 1831; 17.4 το 1832; 19.0 το 1833; GSA/CSA/ASF, sub-archive 1, series 6, f. 193, doc. no. n/a. Hereinafter, wherever the word "thaler" is used, it refers to the Spanish eight real coin.

11 Μποζίκης, *Ελληνική Επανάσταση*, 93–96.

12 Μαρία Χριστίνα Χατζηιωάννου, "Οι εμποροκαπετάνιοι μετά την Επανάσταση: μερικές παρατηρήσεις [The Merchant Captains after the Revolution. Some Remarks]," in *Η Επανάσταση του 1821: Μελέτες στη Μνήμη της Δέσποινας Θεμελή-Κατηφόρη* (Αθήνα: Εταιρεία Μελέτης Νέου Ελληνισμού, 1994), 163.

13 On the continuity of maritime trade in those years, see Σοφία Λαΐου, "Εμπόριο και ναυτιλία στα χρόνια της ελληνικής επανάστασης: η οθωμανική αντίδραση [Trade and Shipping During the Greek Revolution: The Ottoman Reaction]," in *Η Ναυτιλία των Ελλήνων στα χρόνια της Επανάστασης. Ο εμπορικός και πολεμικός στόλος, 1821–1831*, ed. Κατερίνα Γαλάνη and Τζελίνα Χαρλαύτη (Ηράκλειο: Πανεπιστημιακές Εκδόσεις Κρήτης, forthcoming).

14 See also Χρήστος Λούκος, *Η Ερμούπολη της Σύρου, 1821–1950 [Ermoupolis of Syros, 1821–1950]* (Ηράκλειο: Πανεπιστημιακές Εκδόσεις Κρήτης, 2021), 30.

15 See also Pizanias, *The Making*, 409–10.

16 Note on this occasion the information from Hadjianargyrou about 60 wealthy shipping families in Hydra, and that more recent research raise this number to 220 (research

project 'Amphitrite', PI: Gelina Harlaftis [https://marehist.gr/gr/research/04.03.02https://marehist.gr/gr/research/04.03.02])—on the above information, Βλάμη, "Πόλεμος και επιχειρήσεις," 61.

17 On the number of families per province/island, Μιχάλης Χουλιαράκης, *Γεωγραφική, διοικητική και πληθυσμιακή εξέλιξις της Ελλάδος, 1821–1971 [Geographical, Administrative and Population Evolution of Greece, 1821–1971]*, vol. 1 (Αθήνα: Εθνικό Κέντρο Κοινωνικών Ερευνών, 1973), 27.

18 Pizanias, *The Making*, 325–90.

19 This does not mean that the Peloponnese lacked powerful men who were active in maritime trade, Βασίλης Κρεμμυδάς, *Αρχείο Χατζηπαναγιώτη [Hadjipanayoti Archive]*, vol. 1 (Αθήνα, 1973).

20 The amount is given in thousand thalers after the name. *Hydriots:* Koundouriotis 600, Gikas 200, Boudouris 100, D. Tsamados 60, Voulgaris 40, A. Tsamados 40, Gionis 40, Tombazis 30, Orlandos 30. *Spetsiots*: Ch. Mexis 60, G. Botasis 60, Hadjianagyrou 60, Orloff 50, Th. Mexis 40, Lazarou 40, A. Botasis 20, Christinis 20. *Psarians*: Giannitsis 30, Hadjialexandris 20, Nikolis 20, Kalaris 15, Hadjimikes 10, Mamounis 10, Monarchidis 10, Milaitis 10. *Ermoupolitans from various areas*: E. Xenos 150, Skaramangas 40, Stefanos 35.7, A. Nikas—Th. Xenou 30, Skourtis 25, Valsamakis 20, Roussos 17.5, Argentis 16. *Peloponnesians*: Poniropoulos 50, Papalexopoulos 40, Deligiannis 20, Notaras 20, Fotilas 20, Antonopoulos 20, Nikolaou 15, Kopanitsas 15. In the case of Hydra, the very high figure amassed by the Koundouriotis family was excluded, in order to focus on the more homogeneous core.

21 Pizanias, *The Making*, 407–12; Τζελίνα Χαρλαύτη, "Εμπόριο και ναυτιλία τον 19ο αιώνα. Το επιχειρηματικό δίκτυο των Ελλήνων της διασποράς. Η 'χιώτικη' φάση (1830–1860) [Trade and Shipping in the 19th Century. The Entrepreneurial Network of Greeks in the Diaspora. The Phase of Chios (1830–1860)]," *Μνήμων* 15 (1993): 69–127; Μαρία Χριστίνα Χατζηιωάννου, *Οικογενειακή στρατηγική και εμπορικός ανταγωνισμός. Ο οίκος Γερούση τον 19ο αιώνα [Family Strategy and Business Competition. The Geroussi Merchant House in the 19th Century]* (Αθήνα: Μορφωτικό Ίδρυμα Εθνικής Τραπέζης, 2003).

22 This amount was also approximated by the *median*, i.e., the size that divides 'observations' into two equal parts.

23 Charles W. Smith, *Auctions: The Social Construction of Value* (Berkeley: University of California Press, 1990), 163; Noel D. Johnson and Mark Koyama, "Standardizing the Fiscal State: Cabal Tax Farming as an Intermediate Institution in Early-Modern England and France," *MPRA*, Paper No. 40403. http://mpra.ub.uni-muenchen.de/40403/, posted 31 July 2012 20:51 UTC.

24 Calculations based on the catalogs of the following: Ιωάννης Π. Θεοχαρίδης, "Οι Κύπριοι προγραφέντες το 1821 σύμφωνα με άγνωστη οθωμανική πηγή [The Proscribed Cypriots of 1821 According to an Unknown Ottoman Source]," *Δωδώνη* 24 (1995): 67–109; Güven Dinç, "The Fate of the Properties of the Executed/Escaped Greek Cypriots of July 1821 According to Ottoman Documents," *Journal of Modern Greek Studies* 41, no. 2 (2023): 261–86.

For a comprehensive mapping of the distribution of wealth in Cyprus, Antonis Hadjikyriacou, "Inequality in Cyprus During the 1830s," in this volume. For the distribution of real property, especially property in adjacent and other areas, see among others, Martha Mundy and Richard Saumarez Smith, *Governing Property, Making the Modern State: Law, Administration, and Production in Ottoman Syria* (London: I. B. Tauris, 2007), 55–65; Nora Elizabeth Barakat, *Bedouin Bureaucrats. Mobility and Property in the Ottoman Empire* (Stanford: Stanford University Press, 2023), 124–32; Socrates D. Petmezas, "Land Tenure and Land Settlement in Vostizza from Ottoman to Venetian Rule: G.I.S. Mapping of the Venetian Cadastro of 1700," in *Ottoman Rural Societies and Economies. Halcyon Days in Crete VIII*, ed. Elias Kolovos (Heraklion: Crete University Press, 2018), 423–59; Ηλίας Κολοβός, *Όπου ην κήπος: Η μεσογειακή νησιωτική οικονομία της Άνδρου σύμφωνα με το οθωμανικό κτηματολόγιο του 1670 [There Was a Garden: The Economy of the Mediterranean Island of Andros According to the Ottoman Land and Property Survey of 1670]* (Ηράκλειο: Πανεπιστημιακές Εκδόσεις Κρήτης και Καΐρειος Βιβλιοθήκη, 2017).

25 For examples from other regions, see Abdul-Karim Rafeq, "Making a Living or Making a Fortune in Ottoman Syria," in *Money, Land and Trade. An Economic History of the Muslim Mediterranean*, ed. Nelly Hanna (London: I. B. Tauris, 2002), 110–11.

26 For more information on the composition of estates, which is examined in detail, see Dinç, "The Fate," 271–76 and throughout the text. See also corresponding information on Crete from: Βασίλης Δημητριάδης and Διονυσία Δασκάλου, eds., *Ο Κώδικας των Θυσιών: Ονόματα και δημευμένες περιουσίες των Χριστιανών αγωνιστών της Ανατολικής Κρήτης κατά την Επανάσταση του 1821 [Register of Sacrifices: Names and Confiscated Properties of Christian Combatants of Eastern Crete During the Revolution of 1821]*, trans. Βασίλης Δημητριάδης, Ελένη Καραντζίκου, Πηνελόπη Φωτεινού, Χρυσούλα Χριστοδουλάρα (Ηράκλειο: Πανεπιστημιακές Εκδόσεις Κρήτης και Βικελαία Δημοτική Βιβλιοθήκη Ηρακλείου, 2003), κβ΄-κγ΄.

27 Dinç, "The Fate," 275.

28 Δημητριάδης and Δασκάλου, *Ο Κώδικας*, 235–85.

29 Δημητριάδης and Δασκάλου, *Ο Κώδικας*, κβ΄-κγ΄.

30 For comparisons with the Syrian countryside, Mundy and Smith, *Governing Property, Making the Modern State*, 62–64.

31 This assumption is based on a price per square metre of about 0.75 thalers based on three national buildings sold in Tripolitsa in 1824; see Μποζίκης, *Ελληνική Επανάσταση*, 395. However, there is also evidence from other sources that the cost of a newly constructed building per square meter at that time was probably 10–15 times higher, GSA/CSA/AMR, f. 19, doc. no. 36.

32 Indicatively: Sell-out of 7 mills in Gastouni in 1824 at prices of 75 to 300 thalers, Μποζίκης, *Ελληνική Επανάσταση*, 395. See also Δημητρόπουλος, "Και πέραν της γεωργίας," 171–90.

33 The *stremma* mentioned here are average parcel area. For comparisons with the Dardanelles and regions of Anatolia, Reşat Kasaba, *The Ottoman Empire and the World Economy. The Nineteenth Century* (New York: Suny Press, 1988), 62.

34 It is of interest at that point that according to the property gradations established by Dinç in "The Fate of the Properties," 275, the upper limit of the first tier is placed at 500 piastres, considering the purchasing power of that currency in 1821. The equivalent of that figure in a more stable currency was 66.7 thalers. Thus, there is evidence from yet another source that 67 thalers was the threshold of the lowest property tier.

35 See GSA/AC/CA/V, f. 46, subf. 1, ream 5.

36 For the relevant evidence: Στάθης Τσοτσορός, *Οικονομικοί και κοινωνικοί μηχανισμοί στον ορεινό χώρο. Γορτυνία (1715–1828) [Economic and Social Mechanisms in the Mountain Areas. Gortynia 1715–1828]* (Αθήνα: Ιστορικό Αρχείο της Εμπορικής Τράπεζας της Ελλάδος, 1986), 134; GSA/CSA/AMF, f. 6, doc. no. n/a; *Gazette of the Kingdom of Greece*, no. 35 (November 6, 1837); Ibid., no. 12 (April 11, 1838).

37 Calculations based on grain (based on raisins the yields were clearly higher). In order to calculate the *essential survival needs* in the Greek territory in 1828, I considered the following: Robert C. Allen, *Global Economic History: A Very Short Introduction* (Oxford: Oxford University Press, 2011), 10; Süleyman Özmucur and Şevket Pamuk, "Real Wages and Standards of Living in the Ottoman Empire, 1489–1914," *The Journal of Economic History* 62, no. 2 (2002): 298; Σίμος Μποζίκης, *Χρήμα, χρέος, κράτος: νόμισμα, πίστη και εξουσία στην Ελλάδα, 1821–1832 [Money, Debt, State: Currency, Credit and Power in Greece, 1821–1832]* (Αθήνα: Ασίνη, forthcoming).

38 For similar figures in the area, Kasaba, *The Ottoman Empire*, 62.

39 Γιώργος Προγουλάκης, "Η αγροτική οικονομία κατά την οθωμανική περίοδο [The Agricultural Economy During the Ottoman Period]," in *Ιστορία των Ελλήνων: Ο ελληνισμός υπό*

ξένη κυριαρχία 1453–1821, vol. 8 (Αθήνα: Δομή, 2006), 569. For additional information on poll tax see Bruce McGowan, *Economic Life in Ottoman Europe: Taxation, Trade and the Struggle for Land, 1600–1800* (Cambridge: Cambridge University Press, 1981), 62.

40 Τζελίνα Χαρλαύτη, "Η ναυτιλία των Ελλήνων ως μοχλός ενοποίησης των αγορών. Η μεθοδολογία [Greek Shipping as a Lever for the Unification of Markets. The Methodology]," in *Η ναυτιλία των Ελλήνων*, ed. Τζελίνα Χαρλαύτη and Κατερίνα Παπακωνσταντίνου (Αθήνα: Κέδρος, 2013), 39–90; Antonis Hadjikyriacou, "Ottoman(ist)s and the Sea, Islands, and Space: An Overview of the State of the Field on the Occasion of a Recent Review Article," *Turkish Historical Review* 11 (2020): 303–23.

41 On a critical review on this matter, Κακριδής, "Η ελληνική εκβιομηχάνιση," 175–201.

42 Şevket Pamuk and Jeffrey G. Williamson, "Ottoman De-industrialization, 1800–1913: Assessing the Magnitude, Impact, and Response," *The Economic History Review* 64 (2011): 159–84.

Bibliography

Allen, Robert C. *Global Economic History: A Very Short Introduction.* Oxford: Oxford University Press, 2011.

Barakat, Nora Elizabeth. *Bedouin Bureaucrats. Mobility and Property in the Ottoman Empire.* Stanford: Stanford University Press, 2023.

Dinç, Güven. "The Fate of the Properties of the Executed/Escaped Greek Cypriots of July 1821 According to Ottoman Documents." *Journal of Modern Greek Studies* 41, no. 2 (2023): 261–86.

Galani, Katerina, and Gelina Harlaftis. "Privateering During the Greek War of Independence (1821–1829): Issues of Legitimacy, Organization and Economics of a War-Induced Practice." In *New Perspectives on the Greek War of Independence: Myths, Realities, Legacies and Reflections*, edited by Yianni Cartledge and Andrekos Varnava, 129–53. Cham: Palgrave Macmillan, 2022.

Hadjikyriacou, Antonis. "Ottoman(ist)s and the Sea, Islands, and Space: An Overview of the State of the Field on the Occasion of a Recent Review Article." *Turkish Historical Review* 11 (2020): 303–23.

Harlaftis, Gelina. "Amphitrite." Research Project. https://marehist.gr/gr/research/04.03.02.

Johnson, Noel D., and Mark Koyama. "Standardizing the Fiscal State: Cabal Tax Farming as an Intermediate Institution in Early-Modern England and France." Munich Personal Research Papers in Economics Archive (MPRA), Paper No. 40403. http://mpra.ub.uni-muenchen.de/40403/, posted July 31, 2012 20:51 UTC.

Kasaba, Reşat. *The Ottoman Empire and the World Economy. The Nineteenth Century.* New York: Suny Press, 1988.

McGowan, Bruce. *Economic Life in Ottoman Europe: Taxation, Trade and the Struggle for Land, 1600–1800.* Cambridge: Cambridge University Press, 1981.

Mundy, Martha, and Richard Saumarez Smith. *Governing Property, Making the Modern State: Law, Administration, and Production in Ottoman Syria.* London: I. B. Tauris, 2007.

Özmucur, Süleyman, and Şevket Pamuk. "Real Wages and Standards of Living in the Ottoman Empire, 1489–1914." *The Journal of Economic History* 62, no. 2 (2002): 293–321.

Pamuk, Şevket, and Jeffrey G. Williamson. "Ottoman De-industrialization, 1800–1913: Assessing the Magnitude, Impact, and Response." *The Economic History Review* 64 (2011): 159–84.

Petmezas, Socrates D. "Land Tenure and Land Settlement in Vostizza from Ottoman to Venetian Rule: G.I.S. Mapping of the Venetian Cadastro of 1700." In *Ottoman Rural Societies and Economies. Halcyon Days in Crete VIII*, edited by Elias Kolovos, 423–59. Heraklion: Crete University Press, 2018.

Pizanias, Petros T. *The Making of the Modern Greeks: 1400–1820.* Newcastle: Cambridge Scholars Publishing, 2020.

Rafeq, Abdul-Karim. "Making a Living or Making a Fortune in Ottoman Syria." In *Money, Land and Trade. An Economic History of the Muslim Mediterranean*, edited by Nelly Hanna, 101–23. London: I. B. Tauris, 2002.

Smith, Charles W. *Auctions: The Social Construction of Value*. Berkeley: University of California Press, 1990.

Αγριαντώνη, Χριστίνα. "Οι μετασχηματισμοί της βιομηχανικής δομής της Ερμούπολης τον 19ο αιώνα." In *Νεοελληνική Πόλη: οθωμανικές κληρονομιές και ελληνικό κράτος. Πρακτικά του διεθνούς συμποσίου ιστορίας*, 603–8. Αθήνα: Εταιρεία Μελέτης Νέου Ελληνισμού, 1985). [Agriantoni, Christina. "The Transformations of the Industrial Structure of Ermoupolis in the 19th Century." In *Modern Greek City: Ottoman Legacies and the Greek State. Proceedings of the International Symposium on History*, 603–8. Athens: Society for the Sturdy of Modern Hellenism, 1985.]

Αντύπας, Μηνάς. "Οικονομικοί προσανατολισμοί των υδραίικων πλοιοκτητικών οικογενειών στη διάρκεια της Ελληνικής Επανάστασης. Η περίπτωση της οικογένειας Μπουντούρη." In *Η οικονομία στα χρόνια της Επανάστασης*, edited by Δημητρόπουλος, Δημήτρης, Χατζηιωάννου, Μαρία Χριστίνα, 191–222. Αθήνα: Ινστιτούτο Ιστορικών Ερευνών/Εθνικό Ίδρυμα Ερευνών, 2023. [Antypas, Minas. "Financial Orientations of Hydriot Shipowning Families During the Greek Revolution. The Case of the Boudouri family." In *The Economy in the Years of the Revolution*, edited by Dimitris Dimitropoulos and Maria Christina Chatziioannou, 191–222. Athens: Institute of Historical Research, National Hellenic Research Foundation, 2023.]

Βλάμη, Δέσποινα. "Πόλεμος και επιχειρήσεις: οι αδελφοί Μπουντούρη." *Μεσαιωνικά και Νέα Ελληνικά* 14 (2021): 53–99. [Vlami, Despoina. "War and Business: The Boudouri Μπο." *Medievalia et Neohellenica* 14 (2021): 53–99.]

Δημητριάδης, Βασίλης, Δασκάλου, Διονυσία, eds. *Ο Κώδικας των Θυσιών: Ονόματα και δημευμένες περιουσίες των Χριστιανών αγωνιστών της Ανατολικής Κρήτης κατά την Επανάσταση του 1821*, translated by Δημητριάδης Βασίλης, Καραντζίκου Ελένη, Φωτεινού Πηνελόπη, Χριστοδουλάρα Χρυσούλα. Ηράκλειο: Πανεπιστημιακές Εκδόσεις Κρήτης και Βικελαία Δημοτική Βιβλιοθήκη Ηρακλείου, 2003. [Dimitriadis, Vasilis, and Dionysia Daskalou, eds. *Register of Sacrifices: Names and Confiscated properties of Christian Combatants of Eastern Crete During the Revolution of 1821*, translated by Vasilis Dimitriadis, Eleni Karantzikou, Pinelopi Foteinou, and Chrysoula Christodoulara. Herakleion: Crete University Press and Vikelaia Library of Heraklion, 2003.]

Δημητρόπουλος, Δημήτρης. "Και πέραν της γεωργίας και της ναυτιλίας; Μια ψηλάφηση των παραγωγικών δραστηριοτήτων των πόλεων στα χρόνια της Ελληνικής Επανάστασης." In *Η οικονομία στα χρόνια της Επανάστασης*, edited by Δημητρόπουλος, Δημήτρης, Χατζηιωάννου, Μαρία Χριστίνα, 171–90. Αθήνα: Ινστιτούτο Ιστορικών Ερευνών/Εθνικό Ίδρυμα Ερευνών, 2023. [Dimitropoulos, Dimitris. "Beyond Agriculture and Shipping? Outlining the Productive Activities in the Cities in the Years of the Greek Revolution." In *The Economy in the Years of the Revolution*, edited by Dimitris Dimitropoulos and Maria Christina Chatziioannou, 171–90. Athens: Institute of Historical Research/National Hellenic Research Foundation, 2023.]

Θεοχαρίδης, Ιωάννης Π. "Οι Κύπριοι προγραφέντες το 1821 σύμφωνα με άγνωστη οθωμανική πηγή." *Δωδώνη* 24 (1995): 67–109. [Theocharidis, Ioannis P. "The Proscribed Cypriots of 1821 According to an Unknown Ottoman Source." *Dodoni* 24 (1995): 67–109.]

Κακριδής, Ανδρέας. "Η ελληνική εκβιομηχάνιση: συνοπτική εισαγωγή." In Allen Robert C. *Η βιομηχανική επανάσταση: συνοπτική εισαγωγή*, edited by Κακριδής Ανδρέας, 178–80. Ηράκλειο: Πανεπιστημιακές Εκδόσεις Κρήτης, 2021. [Kakridis, Andreas. "The Greek Industrialization: A Brief Introduction." In Allen Robert C. *The Industrial Revolution: A Brief Introduction*, edited by Andreas Kakridis, 178–80. Herakleion: Crete University Press, 2021.]

Κολοβός, Ηλίας. *Όπου ην κήπος: Η μεσογειακή νησιωτική οικονομία της Άνδρου σύμφωνα με το οθωμανικό κτηματολόγιο του 1670.* Ηράκλειο: Πανεπιστημιακές Εκδόσεις Κρήτης και Καΐρειος Βιβλιοθήκη, 2017. [Kolovos, Elias. *There Was a Garden. The Economy of the Mediterranean Island of Andros According to the Ottoman Land and Property Survey of 1670.* Herakleion: Crete University Press and Kaireios Vivliothiki, 2017.]

Κρεμμυδάς, Βασίλης. *Αρχείο Χατζηπαναγιώτη*. vol. 1. Αθήνα: Φ. Κωνσταντινίδης και Κ. Μιχάλης, 1973. [Kremmydas, Vasilis. *Hadjipanayoti Archive*, vol. 1. Athens: Ph.Konstantinidis and K.Michalis, 1973.]

Λαΐου, Σοφία. "Εμπόριο και ναυτιλία στα χρόνια της ελληνικής επανάστασης: η οθωμανική αντίδραση." In *Η Ναυτιλία των Ελλήνων στα χρόνια της Επανάστασης. Ο εμπορικός και πολεμικός στόλος, 1821–1831*, edited by Γαλάνη, Κατερίνα, Χαρλαύτη, Τζελίνα. Ηράκλειο: Πανεπιστημιακές Εκδόσεις Κρήτης, forthcoming. [Laiou, Sophia. "Trade and Shipping During the Greek Revolution: The Ottoman Reaction." In *Greek Shipping in the Years of the Greek Revolution: Merchant Shipping and Navy, 1821–1831*, edited by Katerina Galani and Tzelina Harlaftis. Herakleion: Crete University Press, forthcoming.]

Λαΐου, Σοφία. "Οθωμανοί Έλληνες σαράφηδες στην Κωνσταντινούπολη του 1821." *Μεσαιωνικά και Νέα Ελληνικά* 14 (2021): 217–38. [Laiou, Sophia. "Ottoman Greek Sarrafs (Moneychangers) in Istanbul in 1821." *Medievalia et Neohellenica* 14 (2021): 217–38.]

Λούκος, Χρήστος. *Η Ερμούπολη της Σύρου, 1821–1950.* Ηράκλειο: Πανεπιστημιακές Εκδόσεις Κρήτης, 2021. [Loukos, Christos. *Ermoupolis of Syros, 1821–1950.* Herakleion: Crete University Press, 2021.]

Μποζίκης, Σίμος. "Δυναμικές και αδράνειες στη φορολογία και στο φορολογικό μηχανισμό κατά την Επανάσταση του 1821." *Μνήμων* 31 (2010): 31–70. [Bozikis, Simos. "Dynamics and Stagnation of the Taxation and the Tax Mechanism During the Greek Revolution of 1821." *Mnemon* 31 (2010): 31–70.]

Μποζίκης, Σίμος. "Ναυτικός αγώνας, δημόσια οικονομία και εθνική κυριαρχία το Εικοσιένα." In *Η Ναυτιλία των Ελλήνων στα χρόνια της Επανάστασης. Ο εμπορικός και πολεμικός στόλος, 1821–1831*, edited by Γαλάνη, Κατερίνα, Χαρλαύτη, Τζελίνα, Ηράκλειο: Πανεπιστημιακές Εκδόσεις Κρήτης, forthcoming. [Bozikis, Simos. "Naval War, Public Economy and National Sovereignty in 1821." In *Greek Shipping in the Years of the Greek Revolution: Merchant Shipping and Navy, 1821–1831*, edited by Katerina Galani and Tzelina Harlaftis. Herakleion: Crete University Press, forthcoming.]

Μποζίκης, Σίμος. *Ελληνική Επανάσταση και Δημόσια Οικονομία 1821–1832.* Αθήνα: Ασίνη, 2020. [Bozikis, Simos. *Greek Revolution and Public Economy (1821–1832).* Athens: Asini, 2020.]

Μποζίκης, Σίμος. *Χρήμα, χρέος, κράτος: νόμισμα, πίστη και εξουσία στην Ελλάδα, 1821–1832.* Αθήνα: Ασίνη, forthcoming. [Bozikis, Simos. *Money, Debt, State: Currency, Credit and Power in Greece, 1821–1832.* Athens: Asini, forthcoming.]

Προγουλάκης, Γιώργος. "Η αγροτική οικονομία κατά την οθωμανική περίοδο." In *Ιστορία των Ελλήνων: Ο ελληνισμός υπό ξένη κυριαρχία 1453–1821*, vol. 8, 556–89. Αθήνα: Δομή, 2006. [Progoulakis, Giorgos. "The Agricultural Economy During the Ottoman Period." In *History of the Greeks: Hellenism under Foreign Rule 1453–1821*, vol. 8, 556–89. Athens: Domi, 2006.]

Πύλια, Μάρθα. "Λειτουργίες και αυτονομία των κοινοτήτων της Πελοποννήσου κατά τη δεύτερη τουρκοκρατία (1715–1821)." *Μνήμων* 23 (2001): 67–98. [Pylia, Martha. "Functions and Autonomy of Peloponnesian Communities During the Second Turkish Occupation (1715–1821)." *Mnemon* 23 (2001): 67–98.]

Τσοτσορός, Στάθης. *Οικονομικοί και κοινωνικοί μηχανισμοί στον ορεινό χώρο. Γορτυνία (1715–1828).* Αθήνα: Ιστορικό Αρχείο της Εμπορικής Τράπεζας της Ελλάδος, 1986. [Tsotsoros, Stathis. *Economic and Social Mechanisms in the Mountain Areas. Gortynia (1715–1828).* Athens: Historical Archive of the Commercial Bank of Greece, 1986.]

Χαρλαύτη, Τζελίνα. "Εμπόριο και ναυτιλία τον 19ο αιώνα. Το επιχειρηματικό δίκτυο των Ελλήνων της διασποράς. Η 'χιώτικη' φάση (1830–1860)." *Μνήμων* 15 (1993): 69–127. [Harlaftis, Gelina. "Trade and Shipping in the 19th Century. The Entrepreneurial Network of Greeks in the Diaspora. The Phase of Chios (1830–1860)." *Mnemon* 15 (1993): 69–127.]

Χαρλαύτη, Τζελίνα. "Η εισβολή της ναυτιλίας των 'Γραικών' στο μεγάλο εμπόριο της Μεσογείου, 1714–1815." In *Η ναυτιλία των Ελλήνων, 1700–1821*, edited by Χαρλαύτη, Τζελίνα, Παπακωνσταντίνου, Κατερίνα, 223–82. Αθήνα: Κέδρος, 2013. [Harlaftis, Gelina. "The Invasion of the Shipping of the 'Greeks' in the Great Trade of the Mediterranean, 1714–1815." In *Greek Shipping, 1700–1821*, edited by Gelina Harlaftis and Katerina Papakonstantinou, 223–82. Athens: Kedros, 2013.]

Χαρλαύτη, Τζελίνα. "Η ναυτιλία των Ελλήνων ως μοχλός ενοποίησης των αγορών. Η μεθοδολογία." In *Η ναυτιλία των Ελλήνων, 1700–1821*, edited by Χαρλαύτη Τζελίνα, Παπακωνσταντίνου Κατερίνα, 39–90. Αθήνα: Κέδρος, 2013. [Harlaftis, Gelina. "Greek Shipping as a Lever for the Unification of Markets. The Methodology." In *Greek Shipping, 1700–1821*, edited by Gelina Harlaftis and Katerina Papakonstantinou, 39–90. Athens: Kedros, 2013.]

Χατζηιωάννου, Μαρία Χριστίνα. "Οι εμποροκαπετάνιοι μετά την Επανάσταση: μερικές παρατηρήσεις." In *Η Επανάσταση του 1821: Μελέτες στη Μνήμη της Δέσποινας Θεμελή-Κατηφόρη*, 157–72. Αθήνα: Εταιρεία Μελέτης Νέου Ελληνισμού, 1994. [Chatziioannou, Maria Christina. "The Merchant Captains After the Revolution. Some Remarks." In *The Revolution of 1821. Studies in Memory of Despina Themeli-Katifori*, 157–72. Athens: Society for the Study of Modern Hellenism, 1994.]

Χατζηιωάννου, Μαρία Χριστίνα. *Οικογενειακή στρατηγική και εμπορικός ανταγωνισμός. Ο οίκος Γερούση τον 19ο αιώνα.* Αθήνα: Μορφωτικό Ίδρυμα Εθνικής Τραπέζης, 2003. [Chatziioannou, Maria Christina. *Family Strategy and Business Competition. The Geroussi Merchant House in the 19th Century.* Athens: National Bank of Greece Cultural Foundation, 2003.]

Χουλιαράκης, Μιχάλης. *Γεωγραφική, διοικητική και πληθυσμιακή εξέλιξις της Ελλάδος, 1821–1971*, vol. 1. Αθήνα: Εθνικό Κέντρο Κοινωνικών Ερευνών, 1973. [Chouliarakis, Michalis. *Geographical, Administrative and Population Evolution of Greece, 1821–1971*, vol. 1. Athens: National Centre for Social Research, 1973.]

Part 3

Tanzimat and the New Economic Horizons

9 Locality and Transnational Trade

The Role of the Ottoman Greek Merchant Entrepreneur

Maria Christina Chatziioannou

Discussion on merchant capitalism is essential for understanding modernity in Southeastern Europe, given that capitalism has been considered a phenomenon in global history enhanced by transnational transactions.[1] Capitalism is a process and cannot be reduced to mere production, market exchange, or profit motives. Multiple factors must come together simultaneously. The process of capitalism is a never-ending conflict between the short-term tendency "to hoard" and the long-term stimulus to diversify economic activities and invest.

A comparative analysis of agents—not only within the same ethnic group in geographic dispersion but also between different geographic environments—presents similar characteristics. The formation of mercantile networks has been well analyzed often in a descriptive way, as well as in a linear approach to costs and benefits. Avner Greif in the 1990s insisted on social determinants of institutions enforcing cooperation instead of conflict to secure and maintain reputation.[2] My argument is that social context is a key determinant of the relationship between actors in a network, and plays an important role in securing cohesiveness and mutual objectives. International trade carried out by ethnic groups often led to the creation of commercial networks with partners dispersed in different countries which sometimes were in a hostile confrontation.[3] Therefore, a good number of "Ottoman Greek merchants," as they have often been labeled, moved both as individuals and in different groups into the Ottoman, Russian, and British Empires, motivated by the exploitation of agricultural and stock-breeding products, as well as the opportunity to meet the supply requirements of the international markets. We enrich the discussion on merchant capitalism by examining human agency in international commercial networks that went beyond national and imperial boundaries, with the locality acting as a pivotal element of self-identification. A relevant number of Greek case studies have been published up to now. Based on these and new ones, we may revisit the importance of geography and locality as a comparative example in the advent of merchant capitalism.

The Ottoman Greek merchant entrepreneur is defined here according to his place of origin in the Ottoman Empire, be that in Epirus or in Chios, and his trade know-how deriving from an experience acquired in an environment directly exposed to Ottoman and European influences. The importance of the Ottoman legacy in shaping the organization and performance of the Greek merchant entrepreneur is evident.

DOI: 10.4324/9781003500780-13

However, this know-how and economic identity was subject to different interpretations and perceptions.[4] Here the main matter is the Ottoman past as it was shaped in merchant's history and agency. We argue that the key factors in this debate can be described as the *Ottoman trade experience* in the long-19th-century commerce and its know-how and wealth accumulation arising from hoarding to multifaceted consuming practices. It is primarily the geographical advantage that enables certain agents to be familiar with the environment, ports, products, and trade know-how.

These fundamental principles were widely shared and disseminated within various migrant groups shaping commercial networks within and beyond the Mediterranean. The core subjects that will be analyzed here are essential links to the understanding and interpretation of merchant capitalism in the eastern Mediterranean. The chronological period is delineated here in this context mainly as an alternative to Hobsbawm's long-19th century, covering a period from the French Revolution (1789) to the earlier treaty of Küçük Kaynarca (1774) between Russia and the Ottoman Empire, following the end of the first Russian–Turkish war up to World War I. This was a period that drastically altered social and economic life in the Ottoman Empire, leading to the latter's dissolution.[5]

The importance of trade for the development of port cities and inland economic hubs has been widely accepted from early modern times to the contemporary era, repeatedly reflecting the shifts of global capitalism. Different regions from the Ottoman and the Russian Empires exported raw or semi-processed products in the 19th century causing long-term influences on regional development, as, for example, in Asia Minor, the ports of the Azof Sea, and elsewhere. Based on the impact of the 19th-century trade on market integration when a drop in transport costs allowed the prices of commodities in Europe and Asia to converge, it has been noted—and there is plenty of evidence—that trade was an important determinant of both long- and short-term economic development in earlier periods.[6]

Apart from the national examples consisting of state-protected merchants, chartered companies, and commercial networks originating from Venice, Genoa, Holland, France, and Britain, there were other patterns of agglomerative economies fueling the development of global capitalism from the area of the eastern Mediterranean. A number of individual cases, which are different in personal characteristics (family partnerships) and diaspora economic activities (trade, finance, land property) exemplify patterns by which the members of Greek commercial networks had the power to contest and negotiate their economic demands and to vindicate their social and economic status in the Ottoman, Russian, and British empires.

Merchants were conspicuous individuals forming elites in the Mediterranean in the 18th and 19th centuries. They offer a common ground of analysis for the advent of capitalism and corporate organization. Their structure and behavior, plus the external political and economic conditions, offer a rich ground of research to investigate their strengths and weaknesses as well as the opportunities and threats they faced in a global context. The high level of merchant performance was conditioned by an "archaic" economic environment, as in Russia in the early stages of its history: this is exemplified by the cases of Vikelas, Melas, Scaramanga, and others. Merchant houses benefitted from comparative advantages, in the high-risk and high-profit capital markets, in the Ottoman and Russian Empires and expanded their commercial networks to global markets.

We may argue also that the early and long-lasting importance of the Adriatic system of exchanges (Ragusa, Venice, Trieste, and Ancona) was overtaken by global economic developments and experienced difficulties in transcending this situation due also to its geographical position in the Mediterranean.[7] The relevant historiography usually focuses on the role of the local embeddedness of economic activities in attaining economic development; a network perspective is based on theories of value chains that are entangled in both social relations and spatial allocation. A complementary approach focusing on economic behavior may have greater importance for cultural investigations and biographical studies, thus encompassing narrations of private lives in wider perspectives leading to entangled comparisons of merchants.

The Ottoman Greek merchants presented in this paper differ from the state-supported merchants, such as the Venetian, Dutch, French, and British who were protected with state alliances established through systems of exclusive contracts and monopoly practices. The granting of privileges in the Ottoman Empire, like the *beratli*, was so vague and easily mutable, that it engendered short-term individual cases and not collective norms.[8] Nonetheless, we will deal with the accumulation of wealth, expressed and invested in various ways in land property, private finance-banking activities, and also transformed into power relations within communal and state life. The Ottoman Greek merchants entrepreneurs, although they did not form an organic part of the long-distance trade (Dutch, French, British) participated in the rise of capitalism as intermediaries by forming adaptable personal networks in the Mediterranean.

The systematic study of private fortunes, family firms, merchant houses, and trading companies can raise different methodological concerns, with the Ottoman Greek merchant and his entrepreneurial activity being a constituent part of them. The study of the internal and external development of the firm suggests that the historian must deal with aspects such as organizational structure, diversification, vertical and horizontal development, business strategies, and managerial competences.[9] The preliminary choice of theoretical frameworks that lead to explanations and interpretations of historical developments is connected to the main problem regarding the rationalization of the complexity of historical reality. The point here is to analyze and interpret the impact of individual practices adapting to the development of capitalism, and institutional frameworks from the Ottoman Empire in a new context, such as the Greek State, or Britain. The reciprocal influences and changes observed are revealed by investigating the causality between individual strategies, transnational diaspora, and economic identities.

The Overland Trade Networks: The Vikelas and Melas Merchant Houses

The multi-branched merchant families of Vikelas and Melas originated from the mountainous Epirus region in Western Greece, under Ottoman rule until the beginning of the 20th century: they developed business mainly in overland trade.[10] Through extended family relations, the Melas and Vikelas families built their fortunes (amassing gold/silver coins, precious stones, and real estate) on kin and shared values, Orthodox Christian religion, and place of origin (locality). They achieved a three-generation family network that spun a commercial web between the Ottoman, the Russian, and the British Empires, from the 18th to the 20th centuries. Finally, the Greek state supported an amalgam of Ottoman trade expertise and gentlemanly capitalism[11] in the person of Dimitrios Vikelas, who, having achieved economic independence through extensive merchant and financial activities like other diaspora Greeks, was driven for a variety of reasons toward cultural pursuits, land ownership, and national politics. In his intellectual formation, trade and education were of pivotal importance. As a third-generation member of an extended diaspora family, he became an agent of gentlemanly capitalism in the Greek state.

In the immediate family of D. Vikelas, his father came from Veroia, Macedonia,[12] and the family of his mother from Ioannina, Epirus. Both his grandfathers, Dimitrios Vikelas and George Melas, had moved at a very young age to Constantinople, where they established merchant houses in the 18th century. They acquired political expertise by managing the socio-economic relations of their communities with the Ottoman authorities' sphere, through tax farming and bequest management, though we do not know the exact nature of these bequests.

George Leon Melas' family firm also constituted a three-generation family network. He was born in Ioannina, Epirus, in 1785 and died in Constantinople in 1856, two significant economic hubs in the Ottoman Empire, the first at the periphery enjoying a loose administrative dependency with the political and economic capital of the empire. He became the head of the Constantinople house under the name "George L. Melas & Bros" after the death of his father in 1811. They traded with other houses from Ioannina and administered communal relations between the mountainous Greek city and the Ottoman capital. His commercial network extended to Moscow and Nizhny Novgorod since his brother Demetrios and his cousin Ioannis Stavrou Melas were established in Moscow. In Constantinople, G. L. Melas married Eleni M. Vasiliou, also a child of a wealthy merchant from Epirus. With this marriage he acquired social and economic access to two large and wealthy merchant houses; the Sevastopoulos and the Mavros.[13] In Constantinople, he acquired real estate property and became a member of the Filiki Etairia, a secret society that prepared the outbreak of the Greek Revolution of 1821.[14] Four out of his six children were born in Constantinople and three of them died in Athens, where the family migrated after the foundation of the modern Greek State.

Through published family narratives, we learn that they remained in Odessa for one year in 1821, then traveled to Ancona, and finally settled in Corfu. It is reported that when in dire straits, the family lived off "diamonds and precious Indian shawls" that Eleni Melas had in her possession.[15] This practice can be seen as traces of evidence of pre-modern hoarding, as observed too in Chiot case studies.[16] In the first years of the Greek state (1828–1835), George Melas traveled to Syros, Aegina, and Hydra on state appointments as a tax collector and president of the commercial court. In 1835, he returned to Constantinople and reorganized his family firm by establishing a branch in Marseille with his sons Konstantinos and Michail, while his son Vasilios set up the London branch of their merchant house. Through extended family relations based on religion, place of origin, kin, and shared values the Mela, Vasiliou, and Mavros families paved a commercial path typical of those arising from Ottoman economic practices.

Dimitrios Vikelas (born in Syros in 1835 and died in Athens in 1908) was a representative member of the Greek diaspora in the 19th century. He is a characteristic example of the great chain of migration from Epirus and at the same time an active member of a commercial family business. Vikelas himself became an influential writer who depicted the economic activities of Greek merchants—entrepreneurs and mainly those from the island of Chios during the first half of the 19th century. He was to become one of the most prominent merchants of London's Greek community around 1852 and was to be deeply influenced by the values and customs of Victorian England.[17] Vikelas produced superb descriptions of the business culture of his day as seen through the exemplary life of the commercial Greek milieu in London, where he himself worked for at least 25 years. He described the archetypal Ottoman Greek merchant, with the aim of morally educating his readers. The story of the Chiot Loukis Laras, written in the 1870s, develops the moral schema of a victim of the Chiot massacre in 1822 who yet survived financial ruin and migrated to England. It is the success story of a self-made man, a member of a distinguished local group engaged in a constant quest for business opportunities. Vikelas, although not himself from Chios, depicted the self-made local businessman of the island—a type that flourished during this period—as he was acquainted with the social milieu and had relevant personal connections and experience.[18]

His family story illustrates a typical economic path taken by merchant houses via overland routes toward Constantinople in the 18th century. Hence, these merchant houses formed commercial networks in the Ottoman, Russian, and Habsburg Empires and their case studies model the earlier stage of Greek merchant capitalism. Theirs was a typical trade itinerary of Epirote families connecting to Constantinople in the 18th and 19th centuries. Their commercial networks extended into the Russian and the Habsburg Empires and they formed case studies for the earlier stage of Greek merchant capitalism. They mobilized capital in trade and finance activities in "primitive" markets and distinguished themselves in cultural patriotism by financing Greek schools and Orthodox churches both in their Diaspora settlements and in their homeland.

The Maritime Trade Network: The Scaramanga Merchant Family

The Scaramanga members of the multi-branched merchant house become numerous indeed during the 19th century. Like so many similar cases, it is difficult to reconstruct their individual social and economic trajectories, the evolution of their firms, and the multiplicity of their partnerships featuring the management of their capitals. Despite these difficulties, through scattered family archival material and other sources, we can assemble the history of this multifarious business family of Chiot origin which gained trade expertise in the Aegean and the Adriatic based on the intra-Mediterranean economic exchanges. Members of this family established business relations through Ottoman Smyrna, the Greek port of Syros, and the Habsburg port of Trieste and expanded through horizontal diversification.

One branch of the Scaramanga family delineates a migration pattern seen during the Greek Revolution that originated on the island of Chios. Their migrations to the Aegean ports and the Azof Sea were dictated by the necessity to partake in the international wheat trade from the Black Sea to London.[19] This is the generation of Emmanuel Geo. Scaramanga (born in Chios in 1782—died in Syros in 1865), a merchant who attained commercial expertise and social capital in Ottoman markets which were bound to international trade.[20] Emmanuel belonged to a group of Chiot refugees settled in Syros, the new hub of their expatriate business. The Chiot identity was strengthened and received public attention after the Ottoman destruction and massacre of the islanders (1822), an event that generated a fervent philhellenic reaction. This played an important role in the construction and perpetuation of a distinct local identity.[21]

Migration to the Aegean was in-built into the Em. Scaramanga family history, as well as in that of his wife, Despoina Salvagou (born in Chios in 1795—died in Syros in 1871). It is also evident by the birthplace of their children, born on various Aegean islands, where the family migrated in the first half of the 19th century.[22] Out of their ten children, only the first three were born in Chios: Zannis (Chios in 1815), Fragoulis (Chios in 1817), Maria (Chios in 1822), Katerina (Syros in 1823), Georgios (Naxos in 1825), Erato (Syros in 1828), Maria (Syros in 1829), Andreas (Syros in 1831), Erato (Rhodes in 1836), and Emmanuel (Rhodes in 1839) scattered across three more islands. Theirs was a typical case of commercial migration sought after by many Chiots and Smyrniots in the Aegean Sea, an organic part of the eastern Mediterranean, during the Greek War of Independence (1821–1828), when trade, war, and politics intermingled. Em. Scaramanga lived a Chiot merchant's life at that period in Syros, preoccupied with his native island which was under Ottoman occupation, trading goods in Trieste, Costanza, the neighboring island of Andros, and Athens. Soon after the foundation of the Greek state, Em. Scaramanga was appointed as the Greek consul on the island of Rhodes—still under Ottoman occupation then—a position that he held from 1834 to 1850, when he returned to Syros and died full of honors.[23]

The economic migrations of the Scaramanga family took place over two generations and spread from the Aegean to the Habsburg (Trieste), Russian (Taganrog), and British (London) empires. The family itinerary after the Chios massacre in 1822 corresponds more or less to that of the fictional figure, Loukis Laras, in the novel by the aforementioned D. Vikelas.[24] Experience in commercial transactions in the eastern Mediterranean became valuable social capital for the Scaramanga family, facilitating their commercial and entrepreneurial expansion. The commercial network formed by the first generation was based on well-trusted trade patterns of their time, family organization, and chasing funding capital through short-term partnerships. They focused on the export of agricultural goods from the Ottoman Empire to the entrepôt ports of Syros and to Trieste, as well as on the import of manufactured goods via the same ports. They participated in small flexible partnerships in the same geographical area as those of the Gerussi merchant house, which originated from Smyrna.[25] These merchants often took initiatives supporting Greek independence and their national social and economic identity. M. Grenet argued in the case of the Greek community in Marseille that their economic and political identity resulted from the contest between the national and the communal one, and we may add here their personal agency and entrepreneurship.[26]

Although not Chiot, represents a similar pattern to the Geroussi merchant house of a family network that came into being in Ottoman Smyrna and Trieste before the 1821 Greek Revolution and that subsequently expanded to the Greek port of Syros, before finally moving to Patras, the Greek export port for currants. Its trade capital consisted of liquid assets, a network of personal relationships, and the essential know-how that had been acquired through international transactions in Smyrna and Trieste. On this sound basis, the three Geroussi brothers established their family network in the years 1823–1835. They exported between Smyrna and Trieste raw agricultural commodities (valonia, raisins, silk, sponges, cotton) and imported colonial goods and manufactures (coffee, sugar, lumber boards, nails, paper, ropes, cloth), taking advantage first of the new entrepôt port of Syros, and later the currant export port of Patras, where they acquired land property.[27]

Emmanuel Geo. Scaramanga, as one of the first and most prominent merchants of Syros, effectively organized his personal partnerships from there and participated in wider Chiot coalitions, mainly through the free port of Hapsburg Trieste in the early 19th century. His personal partnership in Trieste dealt with general import–export trade with the Ottoman Empire, similar to other Greek partnerships there.[28] In order to avoid long-lasting and delayed capital repayments and returns, they preferred to send *gruppi* of Ottoman silver coins to Trieste, so that they could easily sell them on to the local mint as precious metal. The main difference between the Scaramanga merchant house and that of the Gerussi is that the first had access to a much wider cluster of commercial affiliations and financial sources, an advantage that would facilitate faster capitalization.

The strong Chiot network was not a sedentary coalition organized on preset conditions of shared origin. Differences in economic potency and financial hierarchy in Chiot networks were apparent in their admittance procedures. The Chiot merchant Antonio Ralli in Trieste had an established commercial network spreading from there to Odessa and Smyrna, commanded by his partnership "A. Ralli and brothers" in the first decades of the 19th century. A. Ralli explicitly stated that before beginning his collaboration with his compatriot Em. Scaramanga he wished to receive solid recommendations about him. Following this informal process, an established friendship can be testified to between A. Ralli and Em. Scaramanga, based on their intense commercial correspondence between the years 1824 and 1827, parallel to the time and events of the Greek Revolution. The Ralli network was already solid and reputable, so when Em. Scaramanga was engaged at that time in legal disputes with an Italian firm, the whole Chiot group was fearful for its reputation and apprehensive about the legal proceedings, involving such as local court appearances and engaging foreign lawyers for the case. The fear and distress were expressed because of the supposed influence and advantages in the local courts the Italians might enjoy. An escape from that situation was to use Ralli's social acquaintances in Milan and so evade the legal aspects of the dispute.[29] We are still in the conflicting realm of personal trust and honor in the Mediterranean, as foreigners in the Habsburg Empire had to adapt to and survive in a different institutional framework.

The descendants of Emmanuel Geo. Scaramanga seized entrepreneurial opportunities for migrating to Britain. The London-based Scaramanga members had rightly foreseen the new opportunities that the grain trade with Russia offered, especially after the abolition of the Corn Laws in 1846 and the increase of the relevant trade. Members of the Scaramanga family were established in Taganrog already from the 1820s. Their entrance into the wheat market was accomplished through family partnerships and in collaboration with the omnipotent Chiot Ralli family network. The partnership "Ralli-Scaramanga" was operative between 1841 and 1850 in Taganrog and its capital turnover was estimated to 1,500,000 rubles.[30] Em. Scaramanga's first son, Zannis, was established in Taganrog in 1845, traded wheat with Mediterranean and British ports and shared in the high social and economic standard in the new entrepreneurial area of the Azof, from Taganrog to Rostov, where he died in 1901.[31] His relative, Zannis A. Scaramanga (born in Syros in 1829—died in Taganrog in 1902), of the Ambrose branch, was married to Virginia M. Peterocochino who was also of Chiot origin: he also traded in Taganrog. There, apart from the grain trade, he dealt with local ores and metals. His public image was highly appraised at the time, as being member of various local committees, acquiring land property and participating in various legal claims. Zannis became the Belgian consul in Taganrog, following a well-established business pattern of obtaining diplomatic positions to attain privileged access to various information channels. In his business collaborations, apart from Chiot Greeks (such as the tannery business that he had formed with the Chiot brothers Cortesi with nominal capital 30,000 rubles), he associated with Russian and Belgian partners in a metallurgy business between 1886 and 1896.[32]

Until the 1917 Russian revolution, a village with the name Scaramanga still existed in the area, covering 250,000 square meters and featuring 3,500 residents. The village included a salt mine, a brickwork factory and a tannery.[33] All these economic activities owed their early presence in an underdeveloped Russian rural area, in the remote region of the Azof Sea, following a diversified entrepreneurial pattern founded on the grain trade in international markets.[34] Scaramanga's entrepreneurship and capital accumulation was based on natural resources and small-scale manufacturing, together with the grain trade. All these doings and activities affirm the social and economic ascent of a merchant of Chiot origin from the Aegean into the upper middle class of the British society via international trade and finance, following the pattern of gentlemanly capitalism.[35]

It has been shown that a minority of foreign entrepreneurs in the Russian Empire operated in an environment of limited legal protection of their private property, unpredictable governmental regulations and casual state interference: altogether spelling an antagonistic entrepreneurial milieu until Russian economic and social institutions changed to reduce the risks of enterprise and raise the potential returns.[36] What type of entrepreneurs stemmed from these minority groups, including the Greeks? Were they taking advantage of existing profit opportunities depending on temporary disequilibria? Or, according to an economic interpretation, did they introduce combinations of Schumpeterian "creative response"?[37] Comparative studies of personal entrepreneurial activities can give us illuminating responses to these questions.

Concluding Remarks

The Ottoman economy attracted individuals from various ethnic backgrounds and religions who were engaged in trade and early financial activities. This included a significant Greek-speaking Christian Orthodox population. Greek merchants in the Ottoman lands were characterized by their mobility during the 18th and 19th centuries as they engaged in both local and international trade activities. Commercial emigration was influenced by both economic and non-economic factors. Non-economic factors included the merchant's location of origin, family reputation and networking, religion, language, moral values, and technical knowledge. Greek merchants who initially operated within the Ottoman Empire expanded into transnational trade, contributing to the emergence of capitalism in the eastern Mediterranean. These Greek merchants played a role in exploiting local agricultural products, natural resources, and manufacturing techniques, contributing to the economic development in the region they had migrated to. Merchants and their activities formulated the economy of the market, which had characteristics that at times and under certain conditions constituted and sustained a homogenous culture. This way of interpreting matters places individual and rational decision-makers at the center of analysis—acknowledging here that an ideologically driven cultural interpretation was exemplified by the very influential article by Tr. Stoianovich published some 60 years ago.[38]

Mutatis mutandis, Greek merchants, similarly to other merchants from the Ottoman Empire, exercised similar economic behavior and practices as Venetian, Genoese, Dutch, French, and British agents in the 18th and 19th centuries. They created nuclei of capitalistic modernity in the eastern Mediterranean by exploiting local agricultural products, natural resources, and manufacturing techniques. In the context of urban agglomeration sometimes, their behavior resembled quasi-colonial behavior. Networks and groups of merchants, organized along shared religious lines, often competed and sometimes collaborated in an intra-imperial economic world. This highlights the complex dynamics of trade during this period.[39] Sited between a financially unstable Ottoman Empire in the 19th century and an expanding voraciousness for capital and goods in the British Empire, Greek merchants from the Ottoman Empire had to find their place in the new equilibrium that was emerging. The reason was that the British Empire was, for the larger part of the 19th century, the world's main supplier of manufactured goods and capital.

Throughout the 19th century, merchants pursued personal itineraries, diversified their business activities, and sought social mobility by leaving the Ottoman Empire and gradually acquiring another economic identity. Many had originally formed the nuclei of their capital within the Ottoman lands. A good number of case studies underscore the dynamic and influential role played by Greek merchants within the Ottoman Empire during a period of significant economic and geopolitical change. These Ottoman Greek merchants became Greek or British citizens. Their activities not only contributed to regional economic development but also had global implications as they navigated the evolving international trade landscape of the 18th and 19th centuries.

Archives

Archdiocese of Thyatira and Great Britain, Scaramanga archival collection
National Library of Greece, Vikelas papers, vol. 911a
Penny Illustrated Paper (London), 30/5/1863

Notes

1 Jürgen Kocka, *Capitalism. A Short History* (Princeton, NJ: Princeton University Press, 2016), 1, 21. For a critical note on the phases of capitalist development, Bartolomé Yun Casalilla, " 'Localism', Global History and Transnational History. A Reflection from the Historian of Early Modern Europe," *Historisk Tidskrift* 127, no. 4 (2007): 558–678.

2 Theoretical insights on different aspects of network analysis and entrepreneurship can be found in relation to ethnicity, locality and transaction costs. For an institutional economics' view, Douglas C. North, "Transaction Costs in History," *Journal of European Economic History* 3 (1985): 557–76; Douglas C. North, "Location Theory and Regional Economic Growth," *Journal of Political Economy* 63, no. 3 (1955): 243–58. For Avner Greif articles, see, Avner Greif, "Cultural Beliefs and the Organization of Society: A Historical and Theoretical Reflection on Collectivist and Individual Societies," *Journal of Political Economy* 102, no. 5 (1994): 912–50; Avner Greif, "Contract Enforceability and Economic Institutions in Early Trade: The Maghribi Traders' Coalition," *American Economic Review* 83, no. 3 (1993): 525–48; Avner Greif, "Reputation and Coalitions in Medieval Trade: Evidence on the Maghribi Traders," *Journal of Economic History* 49, no. 4 (1989): 857–82. See also, Olga Katsiardi-Hering, "Commerce and Merchants in Southeastern Europe, 17–18th Centuries: 'Micro-Districts' and Regions," *Etudes Balkaniques* 1 (2015): 19–35.

3 From the vast bibliography on networks, Μαρία Α. Στασινοπούλου and Μαρία Χριστίνα Χατζηιωάννου, eds., *Διασπορά, Δίκτυα, Διαφωτισμός [Diaspora, Networks, Enlightment]*, Τετράδια Εργασίας 28 (Αθήνα: Ινστιτούτο Ιστορικών Ερευνών/Εθνικό Ίδρυμα Ερευνών, 2005); Ina Baghdiantz McCabe, Gelina Harlaftis, and Ioanna Pepelasis-Minoglou, eds., *Diaspora Entrepreneurial Networks: Five Centuries of History* (Oxford: Berg, 2005); Jon Stobart, "Personal and Commercial Networks in an English Port: Chester in the Early Eighteenth Century," *Journal of Historical Geography* 30, no. 2 (2004): 277–93; A. Molho et al., eds., "Réseaux Marchands," *Annales. Histoire, Sciences Sociales* 58, no. 3 (Mai-Juin 2003): 569–674; Mustafa Emirbayer and Jeff Goodwin, "Network Analysis, Culture, and the Problem of Agency," *American Journal of Sociology* 99, no. 6 (1994): 1411–54.

4 Maurits Van Boogert, "Ottoman Greeks in the Dutch Levant Trade: Collective Strategy and Individual Practice (c. 1750–1821)," *Oriente Moderno* 25 (anno 86), no. 1 (2006): 129–47; Bruce McGowan, *Economic Life in Ottoman Europe. Taxation, Trade and the Struggle for Land, 1600-1800* (Cambridge: Cambridge University Press, 1981).

5 Maria Christina Chatziioannou, *On Merchants' Agency and Capitalism in the Eastern Mediterranean 1774–1914* (Istanbul: The ISIS Press, 2017), 7–11.

6 Manuel Perez Garcia and Lucio De Sousa, eds., *Global History and New Polycentric Approaches Europe, Asia and the Americas in a World Network System* (Basingstoke: Palgrave Macmillan, 2018); Kevin H. O'Rourke and Jeffrey G. Williamson, "When did Globalization Begin?" *European Review Economic History* 6, no. 1 (2002): 23–50; Sevket Pamuk, *The Ottoman Empire and European Capitalism, 1820–1913: Trade, Investment and Production* (Cambridge and New York: Cambridge University Press, 1987).

7 For example, the Durutti merchant house as a case study of trust and dependence on the Adriatic economic system of trade and manufacturing techniques, Chatziioannou, *On Merchant's Agency*, 73–101.

8 Cihan Artunc, "The Price of Legal Institutions: The Beratli Merchants in the Eighteenth-Century Ottoman Empire," *Journal of Economic History* 75, no. 3 (2015): 720–48.

9 Geoffrey Jones, *Merchants to Multinationals: British Trading Companies in the Nineteenth and Twentieth Centuries* (Oxford and New York: Oxford University Press, 2000).

10 The main sources for Dimitrios Vikelas life are: his private archive deposited at the National Library of Greece (190 boxes); D. Vikelas, *Η Ζωή μου* (*My Life*). The first part of the autobiography was written from August to December 1898, and the second from July 1901 to March 1907, in Δημήτριος Βικέλας, *Άπαντα [Collected Works]*, ed. Άλκης Αγγέλου, vols. 1–8 (vol. 1: Autobiography; vol. 2: Literature; vol. 3: Translations. Shakespeare I; vol. 4: Translations. Shakespeare II; vol. 5: Essays; vol. 6: History; vol. 7: Travels; vol. 8: Varia) (Αθήνα: Σύλλογος Ωφέλιμων Βιβλίων, 1908); Δημήτριος Βικέλας, *Λουκής Λάρας [Loukis Laras] [1879]*, ed. Μαριάννα Δήτσα (Αθήνα: Ερμής, 1991); Αλέξανδρος Αρ. Οικονόμος, *Τρεις άνθρωποι. Β΄. Δημήτριος Βικέλας [Three Persons, vol. B, Dimitrios Vikelas]* (Αθήνα: Ελληνική Εκδοτική Εταιρεία, 1953).

11 "Gentlemanly capitalism" as defined by P. J. Cain and A.G. Hopkins is a 1980s explanatory proposal which may fit for British and Britons agents. It describes a society in which landed and commercial wealth, together with a range of service and professional interests, dominated Britain's economy after the mid-19th century. Cain and Hopkins' thesis emphasizes both the supremacy of London-based financial and commercial interests in the formation of British policy toward the empire, and the separateness of City-based "gentlemanly capitalists" from provincial mercantile and industrial interests. Peter J. Cain and Anthony G. Hopkins, "The Political Economy of British Expansion Overseas, 1750–1914," *Economic History Review* 33, no. 4 (1980): 463–90; Peter J. Cain and Anthony G. Hopkins, "Gentlemanly Capitalism and British Expansion Overseas. I. The Old Colonial System, 1688–1850" and "II. New Imperialism, 1850–1945," *Economic History Review* 39, no. 4 (1986): 501–25 and 40, no. 1 (1987): 1–26.

12 About D. Vikelas senior, Antonis Anastasopoulos, "Building Alliances: A Christian Merchant in Eighteenth-Century Karaferye," *Oriente Moderno* 25 (anno 86), no. 1 (2006): 65–75.

13 On the Mavros and Melas family businesses, Βασίλης Καρδάσης, *Έλληνες ομογενείς στη Νότια Ρωσία: 1775–1861 [Greek Diaspora in Southern Russia: 1775–1861]* (Αθήνα: Αλεξάνδρεια, 1998), 201, 203, 205, 219–23, 225, 331, 333.

14 Λέων Μελάς, *Μια οικογένεια. Μια ιστορία [One Family: One Story]* (Ηπειρωτικές μελέτες, Αθήνα: αυτοέκδοση, 1967), 201–35.

15 Λέων Μελάς, *Μια οικογένεια. Μια ιστορία [One Family: One Story]* (Ηπειρωτικές μελέτες, Αθήνα: αυτοέκδοση, 1967).

16 It is evident that diamonds were kept as security capital Βικέλας, *Λουκής Λάρας*, ζ′ and 105, 126 and θ′; Μαρία Χριστίνα Χατζηιωάννου, *Στη δίνη της χιακής καταστροφής (1822). Διασταυρούμενες ιστορίες και συλλογική ταυτότητα [Entangled Histories and Collective Identity: Narratives of the Chios Massacre (1822)]*, Ιστορική Βιβλιοθήκη 1821, αρ. 6 (Αθήνα: Ινστιτούτο Ιστορικών Ερευνών/Εθνικό Ίδρυμα Ερευνών, 2021).

17 National Library of Greece, Vikelas papers, v. 911a: Ledger covering transactions from 1855–1876. For their activities there, see: Vasilis Kardasis, *Diaspora Merchants in the Black Sea: The Greeks in Southern Russia, 1775–1861* (Lanham, MD: Lexington Books, 2001).

18 On the life and deeds of D. Vikelas, see Marie-Élisabeth Mitsou, "Négoce et transfert culturel Dimitrios Bikélas et le réseau intellectuel francogrec dans la seconde moitié du xixe siècle," *Rives méditerranéennes* 50 (2015): 13–25; Ariadni Moutafidou, "Greek Merchant Families Perceiving the World: The Case of Demetrius Vikelas," *Mediterranean Historical Review* 23, no. 2 (2008): 143–64; Μαρία Χριστίνα Χατζηιωάννου, "Ο Δημήτριος Βικέλας και ο παροικιακός ελληνισμός στην Αγγλία [Dimitrios Vikelas and the Diaspora Hellenism in England]," *Η Μελέτη*, Α΄/περίοδος Β΄ (2004): 143–63; Dimitris Tziovas, "Dimitrios Vikelas in the Diaspora: Memory, Character Formation and Language," *Κάμπος, Cambridge Papers in Modern Greek* 6 (1998): 111–33.

19 Γεώργιος Κανδύλης, *Ιστορία των οικογενειών της μεγάλης διασποράς. Σκαραμαγκά—Σκαναβή—Κανδύλη [History of the Families of the Great Diaspora. Scaramanga—Scanavi—Kandyli]* (Αθήνα: Ερμής, 1994), 10–22.

20 For the permission to study the Scaramanga archival collection kept in London in the Archdiocese of Thyatira and Great Britain, I thank the Archimandrite Theonas Bakalis and dr. George Manginis *(academic director of Benaki museum).*

21 Χατζηιωάννου, *Στη δίνη της χιακής καταστροφής*, 71–79.

22 Archdiocese of Thyatira and Great Britain, Scaramanga archival collection. See, for example, the exchange of clearing accounts from Rhodes Zorzi A. Calvocoressi to Em. G. Scaramanga in 1847.

23 The Aegean island remained in the family's memory, so much so that one of his sons residing in London at a later time, sent a subsidy to the British consul there for the relief of the local population after a destructive earthquake in 1863. *Penny Illustrated Paper*, 30/5/1863, fasc. 87, 363.

24 Δημήτριος Βικέλας, *Λουκής Λάρας [Loukis Laras]*, translated in English in 1881 by John Gennadius (Athens, 1879).

25 All relevant information on the Gerussi merchant house comes from their extended archive, Μαρία Χριστίνα Χατζηιωάννου, *Οικογενειακή στρατηγική και εμπορικός ανταγωνισμός. Ο οίκος Γερούση τον 19ο αιώνα [Family Strategy and Business Competition. The Geroussi Merchant House in the 19th Century]* (Αθήνα: Μορφωτικό Ίδρυμα Εθνικής Τράπεζας, 2003).

26 Mathieu Grenet, "Citizens Abroad—The Greek Community of Marseilles and Political Events in Greece, 1820–1830," *Inter-cultural Studies A Forum on Social Change & Cultural Diversity* 7 (2007): 39–52.

27 Χατζηιωάννου, *Οικογενειακή στρατηγική και εμπορικός ανταγωνισμός.*

28 Όλγα Κατσιαρδή-Hering, *Η ελληνική παροικία της Τεργέστης (1751–1830) [The Greek Community in Trieste, 1751–1830]*, τ. 2 (Αθήνα: Εθνικό και Καποδιστριακό Πανεπιστήμιο Αθηνών, 1986), 556–57.

29 Archdiocese of Thyatira and Great Britain, Scaramanga archival collection, Letters of A. Ralli (Trieste) to Em. G. Scaramanga (Syros), 17/2/1827; 26/2/1824; 15/7/1824; 21/9/1824; 17/10/1824; 29/10/1824; 19/10/1824; 22/12/1824; 14/3/1825; 26/4/1825; 27/7/1827; 2/11/1827; 27/12/1827.

30 A. I. Nikolaenko, "V Poiskah Skaramangi [Looking for Scaramanga]," *Vehi Taganroga* 5–6 (December 2000): 19–21.

31 Ολυμπία Σελέκου, *Η καθημερινή ζωή των Ελλήνων της Διασποράς. Δημόσιος και ιδιωτικός βίος (19ος- αρχές του 20ού αιώνα) [The Daily Life of the Diaspora Greeks; Public and Private Life (19th—Early 20th Century)]* (Αθήνα: Εθνικό Κέντρο Κοινωνικών Ερευνών, 2004), 43–69.

32 Nikolaenko, "V Poiskah Skaramangi," 19–21.

33 Nikolaenko, "V Poiskah Skaramangi,".

34 In 1886 the British consul of Taganrog mentions his name as one of the main 22 wheat exporters there, Gelina Harlaftis, "Trade and Shipping in the Nineteenth-Century Sea of Azov," *International Journal of Maritime History* 22, no. 1 (2010): 249.

35 Andrew Porter, " 'Gentlemanly Capitalism' and Empire: The British Experience since 1750?," *The Journal of Imperial and Commonwealth History* 18, no. 3 (1990): 265–95.

36 Gregory Guroff and Fred V. Carstensen, eds., *Entrepreneurship in Imperial Russia and the Soviet Union* (Princeton, NJ: Princeton University Press, 1983).
37 Joseph A. Schumpeter, "The Creative Response in Economic History," *The Journal of Economic History* 7, no. 2 (1947): 149–59.
38 For an overall discussion, see Nathan Sussman, "A Medieval Homo Economicus?" *Capitalism: A Journal of History and Economics* 2, no. 2 (2021): 527–66; Francesco Boldizzoni, *The Poverty of Clio: Resurrecting Economic History* (Princeton, NJ: Princeton University Press, 2011); Greif, "Cultural Beliefs and the Organization of Society," 912–50. The most influential article on Greek merchants was probably: Traian Stoianovich, "The Conquering Balkan Orthodox Merchant," *Journal of Economic History* 20, no. 2 (1960): 234–313.
39 For a case of Muslim and Christian economic collaboration, see Sophia Laiou, "Economic Networks in the Eastern Mediterranean: Kâtiboğlu Mehmed Efendi of Izmir and his Christian Partner," *Mediterranean Historical Review* 34, no. 2 (2019): 181–94.

Bibliography

Anastasopoulos, Antonis. "Building Alliances: A Christian Merchant in Eighteenth-Century Karaferye." *Oriente Moderno* 25 (anno 86), no. 1 (2006): 65–75.
Artunc, Cihan. "The Price of Legal Institutions: The Beratli Merchants in the Eighteenth–Century Ottoman Empire." *Journal of Economic History* 75, no. 3 (2015): 720–48.
Boldizzoni, Francesco. *The Poverty of Clio: Resurrecting Economic History.* Princeton, NJ: Princeton University Press, 2011.
Cain, Peter J., and Anthony G. Hopkins. "The Political Economy of British Expansion Overseas, 1750–1914." *Economic History Review* 33, no. 4 (1980): 463–90.
Cain, Peter J., and Anthony G. Hopkins. "Gentlemanly Capitalism and British Expansion Overseas. I. The Old Colonial System, 1688–1850." *Economic History Review* 39, no. 4 (1986): 501–25.
Cain, Peter J., and Anthony G. Hopkins. "Gentlemanly Capitalism and British Expansion Overseas. II. New Imperialism, 1850–1945." *Economic History Review* 40, no. 1 (1987): 1–26.
Casalilla, Bartolomé Yun. " 'Localism,' Global History and Transnational History. A Reflection from the Historian of Early Modern Europe." *Historisk Tidskrift* 127, no. 4 (2007): 558–678.
Chatziioannou, Maria Christina. *On Merchants' Agency and Capitalism in the Eastern Mediterranean 1774–1914.* Istanbul: The ISIS Press, 2017.
Emirbayer, Mustafa, and Jeff Goodwin. "Network Analysis, Culture, and the Problem of Agency." *American Journal of Sociology*, 99/6 (1994): 1411–54.
Garcia, Manuel Perez, and Lucio De Sousa, eds. *Global History and New Polycentric Approaches Europe, Asia and the Americas in a World Network System.* Basingstoke: Palgrave Macmillan, 2018.
Greif, Avner. "Reputation and Coalitions in Medieval Trade: Evidence on the Maghribi Traders." *Journal of Economic History* 49, no. 4 (1989): 857–82.
Greif, Avner. "Contract Enforceability and Economic Institutions in Early Trade: The Maghribi Traders' Coalition." *American Economic Review* 83, no. 3 (1993): 525–48.
Greif, Avner. "Cultural Beliefs and the Organization of Society: A Historical and Theoretical Reflection on Collectivist and Individual Societies." *Journal of Political Economy* 102, no. 5 (1994): 912–50.
Grenet, Mathieu. "Citizens Abroad—The Greek Community of Marseilles and Political Events in Greece, 1820–1830." *Inter-cultural Studies A Forum on Social Change & Cultural Diversity* 7 (2007): 39–52.
Guroff, Gregory, and Fred V. Carstensen, eds. *Entrepreneurship in Imperial Russia and the Soviet Union.* Princeton, NJ: Princeton University Press, 1983.

Harlaftis, Gelina. "Trade and Shipping in the Nineteenth-Century Sea of Azov." *International Journal of Maritime History* 22, no. 1 (2010): 241–51.

Jones, Geoffrey. *Merchants to Multinationals. British Trading Companies in the Nineteenth and Twentieth Centuries.* Oxford and New York: Oxford University Press, 2000.

Kardasis, Vasilis. *Diaspora Merchants in the Black Sea: The Greeks in Southern Russia, 1775–1861.* Lanham, MD: Lexington Books, 2001.

Katsiardi-Hering, Olga. "Commerce and Merchants in Southeastern Europe, 17–18th Centuries: 'Micro-districts' and Regions." *Etudes Balkaniques* 1 (2015): 19–35.

Kocka, Jürgen. *Capitalism. A Short History*. Princeton, NJ: Princeton University Press, 2016.

Laiou, Sophia. "Economic Networks in the Eastern Mediterranean: Kâtiboğlu Mehmed Efendi of Izmir and his Christian Partner." *Mediterranean Historical Review* 34, no. 2 (2019): 181–94.

McCabe, Ina Baghdiantz, Gelina Harlaftis, and Ioanna Minoglou Pepelasis, eds. *Diaspora Entrepreneurial Networks: Five Centuries of History.* Oxford: Berg, 2005.

McGowan, Bruce. *Economic Life in Ottoman Europe. Taxation, Trade and the Struggle for Land, 1600–1800.* Cambridge: Cambridge University Press, 1981.

Mitsou, Marie-Élisabeth. "Négoce et transfert culturel Dimitrios Bikélas et le réseau intellectuel francogrec dans la seconde moitié du xixe siècle." *Rives méditerranéennes* 50 (2015): 13–25.

Molho, Anthony, Diogo Ramada Curto, Francesca Trivellato, Maria Fusaro, Daviken Studnicki-Gizbert, and David Hancock, eds. "Réseaux Marchands." *Annales. Histoire, Sciences Sociales* 58, no. 3 (Mai–Juin 2003): 569–674.

Moutafidou, Ariadni. "Greek Merchant Families Perceiving the World: The Case of Demetrius Vikelas." *Mediterranean Historical Review* 23, no. 2 (2008): 143–64.

Nikolaenko, A. I. "V Poiskah Skaramangi (Looking for Scaramanga)." *Vehi Taganroga* 5–6 (December 2000): 19–21.

North, Douglas C. "Location Theory and Regional Economic Growth." *Journal of Political Economy* 63, no. 3 (1955): 243–58.

North, Douglas C. "Transaction Costs in History." *Journal of European Economic History* 3 (1985): 557–76.

O'Rourke, Kevin H., and Jeffrey G. Williamson. "When did Globalization Begin?" *European Review Economic History* 6, no. 1 (2002): 23–50.

Pamuk, Sevket. *The Ottoman Empire and European Capitalism, 1820–1913: Trade, Investment and Production.* Cambridge and New York: Cambridge University Press, 1987.

Porter, Andrew. "'Gentlemanly Capitalism' and Empire: The British Experience since 1750?" *The Journal of Imperial and Commonwealth History* 18, no. 3 (1990): 265–95.

Schumpeter, Joseph A. "The Creative Response in Economic History." *The Journal of Economic History* 7, no. 2 (1947): 149–59.

Stobart, Jon. "Personal and Commercial Networks in an English Port: Chester in the Early Eighteenth Century." *Journal of Historical Geography* 30, no. 2 (2004): 277–93.

Stoianovich, Traian. "The Conquering Balkan Orthodox Merchant." *Journal of Economic History* 20, no. 2 (1960): 234–313.

Sussman, Nathan. "A Medieval Homo Economicus?" *Capitalism: A Journal of History and Economics* 2, no. 2 (2021): 527–66.

Tziovas, Dimitris. "Dimitrios Vikelas in the Diaspora: Memory, Character Formation and Language." *Κάμπος, Cambridge Papers in Modern Greek* 6 (1998): 111–33.

Van Boogert, Maurits. "Ottoman Greeks in the Dutch Levant Trade: Collective Strategy and Individual Practice (c. 1750–1821)." *Oriente Moderno* 25 (anno 86), no. 1 (2006): 129–47.

Vikelas, Dimitrios. *Loukis Laras*, translated in English in 1881 by John Gennadius. Athens (1879).

Βικέλας, Δημήτριος. *Άπαντα*, edited by Αγγέλου Άλκης, vols. 1–8. Αθήνα: Σύλλογος Ωφέλιμων Βιβλίων, 1908. [Vikelas, Dimitrios. *Collected Works*, edited by Alkis Angelou, vols. 1–8. Athens: Syllogos Ofelimon Vivlion, 1908.]

Βικέλας, Δημήτριος. *Λουκής Λάρας (1879)*, edited by Δήτσα Μαριάννα. Αθήνα: Ερμής, 1991. [Vikelas, Dimitrios. *Loukis Laras (1879)*, edited by Ditsa Marianna. Athens: Hermes, 1991.]

Κανδύλης, Γεώργιος. *Ιστορία των οικογενειών της μεγάλης διασποράς. Σκαραμαγκά—Σκαναβή—Κανδύλη*. Αθήνα: Ερμής, 1994. [Kandylis, Georgios. *History of the Families of the Great Diaspora. Scaramanga—Scanavi—Kandyli*. Athens: Hermes, 1994.]

Καρδάσης, Βασίλης. *Έλληνες ομογενείς στη Νότια Ρωσία: 1775–1861*. Αθήνα: Αλεξάνδρεια, 1998. [Kardasis, Vasilis. *Greek Diaspora in Southern Russia: 1775–1861*. Athens: Alexandreia 1998.]

Κατσιαρδή-Hering, Όλγα. *Η ελληνική παροικία της Τεργέστης (1751–1830)*, τ. 2. Αθήνα: Εθνικό και Καποδιστριακό Πανεπιστήμιο Αθηνών, 1986. [Katsiardi-Hering, Olga. *The Greek Community in Trieste (1751–1830)*, vol. 2. Athens: National and Kapodistrian University of Athens, 1986.]

Μελάς, Λέων. *Μια οικογένεια. Μια ιστορία*. Ηπειρωτικές μελέτες. Αθήνα: αυτοέκδοση, 1967. [Melas, Leon. *One Family, One Story*. Ipeirotikes meletes. Athens: Self-published, 1967.]

Οικονόμος, Αλέξανδρος Αρ. *Τρεις άνθρωποι. Β΄. Δημήτριος Βικέλας*. Αθήνα: Ελληνική Εκδοτική Εταιρεία, 1953. [Oikonomos, Alexandros Ar. *Three Persons. v. Β΄. Dimitrios Vikelas*. Athens: Helliniki Ekdotiki Etaireia, 1953.]

Σελέκου, Ολυμπία. *Η καθημερινή ζωή των Ελλήνων της Διασποράς. Δημόσιος και ιδιωτικός βίος (19ος- αρχές του 20ού αιώνα)*. Αθήνα: Εθνικό Κέντρο Κοινωνικών Ερευνών, 2004. [Selekou, Olympia. *The Daily Life of the Diaspora Greeks; Public and Private Life (19th—Early 20th Century)*. Athens: National Centre for Social Research, 2004.]

Στασινοπούλου, Μαρία Α., Χατζηιωάννου, Μαρία Χριστίνα, eds. *Διασπορά, Δίκτυα, Διαφωτισμός*, Τετράδια Εργασίας 28. Αθήνα: Ινστιτούτο Ιστορικών Ερευνών/Εθνικό Ίδρυμα Ερευνών, 2005. [Stasinopoulou, Maria A., and Maria Christina Chatziioannou, eds. *Diaspora, Networks, Enlightenment*, Tetradia Ergasias 28. Athens: Institute of Historical Research/National Hellenic Research Foundation, 2005.]

Χατζηιωάννου, Μαρία Χριστίνα. "Ο Δημήτριος Βικέλας και ο παροικιακός ελληνισμός στην Αγγλία." *Η Μελέτη*, Α΄/περίοδος Β΄ (2004): 143–63. [Chatziioannou, Maria Christina. "Dimitrios Vikelas and the Diaspora Hellenism in England." *I Meleti*, Α΄/period Β΄ (2004): 143–63.]

Χατζηιωάννου, Μαρία Χριστίνα. *Οικογενειακή στρατηγική και εμπορικός ανταγωνισμός. Ο οίκος Γερούση τον 19ο αιώνα*. Αθήνα: Μορφωτικό Ίδρυμα Εθνικής Τράπεζας, 2003. [Chatziioannou, Maria Christina. *Family Strategy and Business Competition. The Geroussi Merchant House in the 19th Century*. Athens: National Bank of Greece Cultural Foundation, 2003.]

Χατζηιωάννου, Μαρία Χριστίνα. *Στη δίνη της χιακής καταστροφής (1822). Διασταυρούμενες ιστορίες και συλλογική ταυτότητα*. Ιστορική Βιβλιοθήκη 1821, αρ. 6. Αθήνα: Ινστιτούτο Ιστορικών Ερευνών/Εθνικό Ίδρυμα Ερευνών, 2021. [Chatziioannou, Maria Christina. *Entangled Histories and Collective Identity: Narratives of the Chios Massacre (1822)*. Historical Library of the 1821, n. 6. Athens: Institute of Historical Research/National Hellenic Research Foundation, 2021.]

10 Businesses and Investment Strategies in the Cigarette Industry of the Eastern Mediterranean, Late 19th to Early 20th Centuries

Thanasis Betas

Introduction

A complex web of interests grew up across the globe around tobacco from the 19th century and indeed had started even earlier: tobacco as an agricultural product, as a commodity, as an industry, and as a taxable object.[1] Tobacco is a smoking product and the raw material for one of the most popular consumer goods, the cigarette. The hand-rolled and, later, from the late 19th and whole of the 20th centuries, the industrially manufactured cigarette.[2] In the late 19th century, the tobacco industry was labor-intensive and a monopoly—wherever it existed—and so required the concentration of production in an integrated space to prevent tax theft. This can be observed not only in the Ottoman Empire during this period but also in European countries, such as France, Spain, and Italy, where the tobacco industry was based on monopolies. In these cases, production was centralized for budgetary reasons, as there was no technological innovation available to justify the concentration of production in large factories. The "French model" was thus adopted in such cases, which entailed this same concentration of production and of women's labor.[3] In contrast, in countries where the tax system did not impose a monopoly, cigarette production in the late 19th and early 20th centuries was primarily done by small- and medium-sized enterprises, some of which subsequently grew into large tobacco companies. The skilled cigarette rollers were men who, given their expertise, were much in demand.

Until 1885, the year in which the cigarette-rolling machine was invented, the handmade cigarette was an expensive smoking product aimed primarily at the upper classes, with Egypt, and specifically Cairo, being the main center of cigarette making. This situation quickly changed, with the cigarette becoming a product of mass consumption and a popular habit for the poorer classes.[4] This change was largely due to the gradual fall in its price as a result of the mass production of cigarettes, thanks to the invention of the cigarette-rolling machine, as well as to the new business strategies adopted by the companies. These last had begun to expand into this new industrial sector and systematically promoted the product, advertising it via the mass media of the day, thereby shaping new habits and consumer behaviors.[5] Cigarette advertising was advanced by the tobacco industries as an "answer"

DOI: 10.4324/9781003500780-14

to the market expansion of the late 19th century and to the competition between businessmen and merchants to "conquer" ever more of these markets. Technological changes and the adoption of better business management techniques resulted in an increase of production capacity to levels that required a continuous increase in demand in order for the "wheels" of the industry to keep turning. The cigarette industry thus represents one of the first business sectors where companies attempted to expand their international sales by adopting practices that enabled the implementation of both technological and organizational innovations and of advertising strategies. The impetus was provided by the competition between British and American companies, as both sought to expand their markets beyond their national borders.[6]

In the USA in the late 19th century, a new form of industrial and organizational structure developed, based on the professional management of the enterprise. In contrast to the traditional company, which had hitherto prevailed in industrialized countries, the modern company was designed to manage rapid changes in the sphere of production and to develop organizational structures capable of disseminating management know-how for a previously unimaginable range of commercial activities. Such organizational structures enabled these American companies to grow rapidly in the late 19th century. The center of the global cigarette industry was to change very quickly, and in the coming decades, the companies that were to dominate the global cigarette market came to be based in the USA and Britain.[7]

In the late 19th century, tobacco and tobacco products such as cigarettes were transformed into a globalized, highly profitable commercial and industrial activity with a customer base that was not only stable but was expanding. A business activity that was subject to state intervention and an oligopolistic market structure. Within this framework, not only each company but each state also had the ability and opportunity to multiply its revenue. In the Ottoman Empire, approximately 400 companies were active in tobacco cutting and the production of handmade cigarettes until 1873, when the domestic production of tobacco products, a significant source of revenue, was monopolized by the public sector. Private tobacco merchants and producers of tobacco products (industrialists, blenders, cigarette rollers) were then forced to emigrate, mostly to Egypt, Samos, Central Europe, and the USA.[8]

In Greece, unlike in other regions, a significant preindustrial/handicraft sector did not develop in the field of the production of tobacco products. The history of the hand-rolled cigarette industry in the country, although very brief, can be traced to the period from the late 19th century until approximately the mid-1920s. Apart from the two years 1885–1887, in the period 1883–1892, small family enterprises specialized in making hand-rolled cigarettes were compelled to remain within the sphere of the public tobacco factories.[9] After 1892, tobacco processing—cutting and cigarette rolling—ceased to be the exclusive prerogative of the state and private tobacco factories were permitted to operate, albeit under the supervision of the directors of the public tobacco factories and their employees.[10] Hand-rolled cigarettes had to be made within the public tobacco factories but by artisans (cigarette rollers) who were selected exclusively by the manufacturers.

In this chapter, I trace the investment strategies and initiatives in the cigarette production "market" in various regions of the eastern Mediterranean in the late

19th to early 20th centuries, investigating the factors that caused them and the features they developed to exist. I start from the general position that the choices of the people and companies active in the "market" are guided by personal ambitions, social and ideological factors, and the regulations imposed by public authorities. These then shape the institutional environment in specific time periods and local frameworks, as well as being affected by the features of the global "market" for the product in each instance. I thus argue that business activity in the cigarette "market," the form and characteristics it took in the periods and local frameworks under study, was the product of these complex and interdependent factors, and not of spontaneous economic initiatives.[11]

The chapter is divided into two parts. In the first, a general presentation is given of the frameworks in which these business efforts were carried out in the cigarette-production sector in Egypt in the late 19th and early 20th centuries. I investigate the factors that led to the establishment of Greek tobacco manufacturers and cigarette makers in Egypt and the investment initiatives and work they undertook there. In the second part, the core of the article, I turn my gaze to a business attempt to establish a tobacco and cigarette company in Greece in the early 20th century with financing from the Bank of Athens. This proposal caused intense controversy and led to open conflict between its supporters and opponents. It occurred during an era that has been described as the "Belle Époque" of the Greek capital when Greek companies led by banks assumed a leading role in the organization of capitalism throughout the Eastern Mediterranean. The signing of the contract and the impending establishment of the company led to the creation of two rival groups, which, depending on how they perceived their interests, were either for or against its establishment, thus highlighting—among other things—the divisions within Greek society of the day. The "reasons" and strategies of the stakeholders around this project will be explored in the second and largest part of the article.

In Search of New Markets

In the Ottoman Empire, the tobacco monopoly was granted in 1884 to Régie (*Régie co-intéressée des Tabacs de l'Empire Ottoman*). The Ottoman government sought to control tobacco revenues to service its foreign debt, to which purpose (with the participation of Ottoman and foreign banks) it founded Tobacco Régie, which had a monopoly on the purchase, export, and sale of tobacco.[12] The establishment of the State Tobacco Monopoly (Régie) in the Ottoman Empire resulted in the departure of many Greek tobacco merchants and artisans who left and settled in Egypt, where they worked in the tobacco trade and cigarette production, opening the first workshops and cigarette factories.[13] It has been convincingly demonstrated that the reasons for this choice were due to the formation of an important and dynamic cigarette market, thanks to the presence of the British occupation army, the European colonies, and a large number of travelers moving to and from the East. The addiction of these consumers, who eventually returned to their homelands, created the conditions for significant cigarette exports to European countries. The success and relative longevity of the Greek-owned cigarette industry in Egypt was because these companies had easy access to and, to a certain degree, controlled the production of the raw material, oriental tobaccos, which gave them a comparative advantage over their local competitors. Along with the low level of automation in the sector, this was the reason for the proliferation of factories, as initial investment in fixed overheads was also low.[14] Relli Shechter, commenting upon the Egyptian government's policy for the tobacco industry in relation to the changes taking place in the Ottoman Empire during the same period, observes that the creation of a free market without restrictions, which promised significant profits thanks mainly to the export character of the cigarette industry, attracted both Greek tobacco manufacturers and cigarette makers.[15]

The Greek-owned cigarette factories of Egypt were of varying calibers. Mechanization of production was uneven and machines were used only in certain initial stages of production, such as cutting the tobacco. Filling and, later, rolling cigarettes were done by hand until the late 19th century.[16] Christos Hadziiossif aptly observes that "it was precisely at this stage of production that the Greek tobacco manufacturers had a great comparative advantage because, apart from the oriental tobaccos, they also imported a cheap and skilled workforce in the form of Greek cigarette makers."[17] Even so, this advantage was not due solely to the skilled labor of the male cigarette makers, but also from the use or, more accurately, the exploitation of a more extensive labor force that included both women and children.

These Greek-owned cigarette companies were unable, however, to cope with the new international competition in the cigarette industry ushered in by the mechanization of the industry in the 1880s. In the following years, they were bought out by German, English, and American businessmen and related companies.[18] This was because the Greek factory owners lacked two basic factors that could have allowed them to continue operating their factories themselves: the social predisposition and the necessary bank support. In Egypt in 1907, the British American Tobacco Co. (BAT) and later the Eastern Tobacco Co. bought Maspero Frères Limited, the only English firm operating in Egypt, gradually followed by the Greek companies S.A. des Tabacs et Cigarettes Papatheologos and S. Mavridis Ltd., and the Armenian companies Gamsaragan, Melkonian, Soussa, and Kivork Ipekian Ltd. The remaining Greek companies continued to make cigarettes by hand, with the exception of the Koutarellis brothers' factory, which installed cigarette-rolling machines to make it more competitive in the domestic market.[19]

The Koutarellis brothers' tobacco company was founded in Alexandria, Egypt, in 1890 by Konstantinos, Dimitrios, and Alkiviades Koutarellis. The Koutarellis brothers were from Drakeia in Pelion, a mountain village in central Greece. The factory employed approximately 2,000 people, with a daily production of over 3,000 *okas* (approximately 3,900 kg) and was the only company that could compete with EASTERN Co. S.A.E., which gradually absorbed almost all Greek and Armenian tobacco companies in Egypt.[20] In the early 20th century, the company modernized its machinery and its building facilities: in 1920, it built its own factory, installing a large number of modern cigarette-rolling machines and special tobacco-cutting machines and increasing its technical staff. The factory underwent continuous enhancement from the 1920s and had expanded to an area of 5,000 square meters on the eve of World War II.[21] However, the tax measures taken in the countries of settlement, combined with the general climate of economic nationalism in the interwar period and, in Germany, the Nazi rise to power which forced the closure of Greek businesses, gradually led to the "disappearance" of the Greek-owned cigarette factories from the international market.[22]

Some Greek tobacco merchants and artisans who had gone to Egypt, however, returned to their places of origin and became active in the tobacco trade and the production of hand-rolled cigarettes. Manolis Karathanassis from Samos, for example, went to Egypt—when and for how long is unknown—in order to "specialise" in hand-rolled cigarette production.[23] He returned to his homeland when it was an autonomous Principality in the Ottoman Empire and, along with his brother Stamatis Carathanassis, founded in Vathy in 1882 the company known as M.C. Carathanassis & Co. This tobacco company, which both traded and produced hand-rolled cigarettes, operated until 1943.[24] The company made a name for itself in cigarette production and became one of the most important tobacco trading firms on Samos. It developed trade with European markets (United Kingdom, Austria, Germany, Netherlands, Hungary, Denmark, etc.) and the markets of the Far East (China, Japan, Indochina), South Africa, and America. The firm was rewarded for the quality of its cigarettes, winning a gold medal and an honorary award at the International Exhibition of Athens in 1903, and an honorary award at the Panama International Exposition in 1915.[25]

In any case, the success of the expatriate tobacco merchants and cigarette manufacturers of Egypt did not go unnoticed in Greece. Indeed, it attracted the interest of the country's business world, leading to profound discussions about the prospect of establishing a cigarette industry in Greece with an outward-facing character. I will trace these discussions in the second part of this chapter.

"Tobacco and Cigarette Company"

It is a fact that at the turn of the 20th century, industry was not often a subject of current affairs in a Greece that was swamped with national questions and the central concerns of the economy: raisins, public finances, and immigration. Nonetheless, the prospect of a cigarette industry in Greece with an outward-facing character was an issue that preoccupied, even in passing, not only some columnists and commentators of the day, but, as we shall see, the business world as well. We can observe an early interest in the cigarette industry, which was also one of the unknown, perhaps premature—and ultimately fruitless—hopes for the country's industrialization.

Thus, in 1899, there was discussion on the need to develop the cigarette industry in Greece, just as in Egypt. A columnist for *Empros* criticized the Theotokis government, which had been formed a few months earlier—on 12 April 1899—for negligence and indifference toward the possibility of developing a monopoly in the cigarette industry. Praising the work of Greek tobacco manufacturers in Egypt, he notes that the law on cigarette paper made it impossible to develop the cigarette industry in Greece and expresses strong support for the tobacco sellers' demand that it be abolished.[26] In a front-page article in *Empros* titled "Το μονοπώλιο του καπνού σήμερα" [The tobacco monopoly today], we read:

> Isn't it ludicrous that Greek tobacco merchants and Greek tobacco must relocate to Egypt, from where it has been made easy for them to export the cigarettes they make abroad? Isn't it possible for these merchants to use their own means to develop the export of this product from the original point of its production? . . . But the government prefers to import [cigarette paper] of a terrible quality and protect the cigarette paper factory in the Prime Minister's home town . . . The advocates of this despicable regime say that the restriction of cigarette paper ensures the restriction of illegal cutters.[27]

The abolition of the tax on cigarette paper and its free production and use in Greece were therefore necessary conditions for tobacco sellers in order for the Greek cigarette manufacturing industry to grow.

In 1902, an attempt was made to create a tobacco and cigarette company in Greece with funding from the Bank of Athens. The Bank of Athens had begun its operations in the capital in 1894 under Antonios Kallergis and, in 1896, acquired the private bank of Ioannis Pesmazoglou in Alexandria, which became its first branch abroad. The following year, Pesmazoglou, sidelining Kallergis, became general manager of the Bank of Athens, which evolved into a deposit bank active among the Greek expatriate community in the southeastern Mediterranean. The emergence of a new class of Greek merchants in the communities of the Eastern Mediterranean and the provinces of the Ottoman Empire contributed to the policy of expanding the newly established bank beyond the borders of the Greek state. Its main objectives were both to attract small depositors and to finance businesses—although, as has been pointed out, the Bank was not consistent when it came to financing small entrepreneurs. On the contrary, its focus was confined to a closed circle of big businessmen, who were, as a rule, shareholders and members of the Bank's Board of Directors, as is confirmed by the case of the cigarette industry presented here.[28] This particular proposal, then, was an arena of intense disagreements and open conflict between the supporters of the effort and its opponents, during an era that has been described as the "Belle Époque" of the Greek capital when Greek companies, led by the banks, undertook—especially after 1905—a supervisory role over the organization of capitalism throughout the Eastern Mediterranean.

At the beginning of 1902, a contract was signed between the Greek government—represented by the Minister of Finance, Phokion Negris—and the Bank of Athens—represented by its director Ioannis Pesmazoglou—which was conventionally known as the "Cigarette Manufacturing Contract." With this contract, the Bank of Athens undertook to establish a company with the aim of supporting tobacco production and developing the trade of tobacco leaves, in exchange for the prerogative of establishing tobacco cutting and cigarette factories, both for the domestic market and for export. In an open letter to the newspaper *Skrip* on 22 January 1902, Pesmazoglou presented the aims and objectives of this Company.

The "Ελληνική Εταιρεία προς ανάπτυξιν της παραγωγής και εμπορίας των καπνών" [Greek company for the development of the production and marketing of tobacco] and the "Εταιρεία Καπνού και Σιγαρέττων" [Tobacco and Cigarettes Company] with a startup capital of 2,500,000 drachmas and a further 5,000,000 drachmas subsequently and with secured credit of 2,000,000 drachmas from the Bank of Athens were to be active in three areas: tobacco sales, cigarette manufacturing, and tobacco production.[29]

In the trade of tobacco, the Company's aim, according to Pesmazoglou, was to modernize the trade of tobacco leaves, which was in a "*primordial state*" due to "*the meagre means generally available to tobacco merchants*" and "*the lack of specialist knowledge,*" and which functioned only "*as a source of large profits for tobacco merchants in Egypt.*" At the same time, as a credit institution, it could secure loans to tobacco producers on favorable terms "*instead of the current loan sharks.*"[30] The company's main area of activity, however, was to establish cigarette factories in Greece.

> The Company wishes to establish a large cigarette factory on the model of the Egyptian ones, in time setting up large factories that will employ thousands of male and female workers and in which it wishes gradually to concentrate . . . a large part of the wealth-producing labour, which is today utilised exclusively in Egypt . . . the Company . . . in organising such a factory . . . wishes through it to provide abundant, permanent and well-paid work for hundreds of families . . . in the manufacture of Egyptian cigarettes, completely excluding the use of any machinery.[31]

In Pesmazoglou's words, we can discern some of his views on industry, work, and the country's economy more generally. Indirectly, he suggests that in the Greece of the early 20th century, the conditions were in place for the development of industry—at least in this particular sector of industry. First, the human resources are available to whom the "thousands" of jobs will be offered. Second, the capital is also available, as the Bank had managed to raise "the large amounts of capital required for [the project's] success." The Bank of Athens' plan promised "*abundant, permanent and well-paid work.*" The implicit association is not difficult to draw. The promised, future *abundant, permanent and well-paid work* implies both its current lack and the rise in unemployment at the time when Pesmazoglou was writing the letter, as well as the typical features of wage labor in Greece of the day: casual and poorly paid.

The promise to secure abundant work for thousands of families was made during a period of intensive rural flight, mainly in the form of overseas migration, a problem that was plaguing the country at the time. It implied the provision of work for all family members, including female and child labor, which, after all, already existed in the handmade cigarette sector, inside both public and private tobacco-cutting factories. Besides, Pesmazoglou himself and the expatriate investors came from an environment—Egypt—where the presence of the female workforce in tobacco factories was a given and contributed, along with that of the artisan cigarette makers, to a flourishing domestic cigarette industry. If to the above we add his explicit commitment to exclude any machinery ("*the manufacture of Egyptian cigarettes, completely excluding the use of any machinery*"), then we can assume that the model of growth that the director of the Bank of Athens and the capital investors had in mind was labor-intensive rather than capital-intensive. In this case too, the main factor of labor, the human factor, was more than essential for the growth of the company. With this guarantee, Pesmazoglou wanted to reassure the skilled craftsmen, the cigarette makers. Of course, businesses of this type relied mainly on the rest of the workforce, the part that was considered unskilled and complementary and—therefore—low-cost, such as "unskilled" female workers and children.

Indicative, finally, of the predominant ideologies of the day were Pesmazoglou's references to the "nation" and the "country." The Bank "*has adequately performed its duty to the country,*" Pesmazoglou underlined, and the project that it was planning was "*exceedingly national,*" as, among other things, it would improve Greek tobaccos, "*so that instead of buying the commodity there [Egypt] at the paltriest prices . . . without the . . . Greek tobacco planter being able to recover from the low prices at which he sells and which just about cover the annual cultivation costs.*" He was thus addressing multiple audiences: the newspaper's readers, that is, "public opinion," the project's critics, and the state. Among the project's critics were the country's tobacco merchants who, for obvious reasons, opposed the establishment of a large, competitive company in the tobacco and cigarettes sector. With the reference to a national project, he was attempting to mitigate or disguise the pursuit of profit, as the aim—according to Pesmazoglou—was the development of "national production," while the company, as he wrote, "*sees itself as being misunderstood and at risk of being considered as pursuing a completely simple profit-making enterprise.*"

The discourse of a "national project" also attempted to disguise business competition, any of the—horizontal and vertical—contradictions and conflicts generated by an entrepreneurial effort, in keeping with the dominant ideology of "national solidarity." Finally, Pesmazoglou reminded the state that the Bank has done its own duty to the country and therefore the success of the project is also dependent on the state. Pesmazoglou's letter gives the flavor of the day and reflects the ideological obsession with the development of "national production," business aims, and competition while also containing allusions to the role and attitude of the state regarding industrial policy. At the same time, however, the idea itself of the formation of the company and the involvement of the Bank of Athens indicates attempts to concentrate capital and create a monopoly—features found not only in the cigarette-making sector but also in many other sectors, especially in 1906–1914.[32] On the contrary, the banking sector's willingness to become involved in industry was a particularly rare phenomenon in the period under study.

The signing of the contract and the imminent establishment of the Company led to the creation of two conflicting groups, which, depending on how they perceived their interests, were either for or against its establishment, highlighting in this way—among other things—the disagreements within Greek society of the day.

The tobacco farmers in the large tobacco-producing areas of the country (Agrinio, Lamia, the plain of Thessaly) were in favor of the contract, considering it a "lifeline" that would enhance production. The inhabitants of these regions, through open letters to the press or to the members of the visiting parliamentary committee responsible for assessing the contract, positively proclaimed their support while at the same time declaring the dire economic situation in which they found themselves due to the unaccountability of the tobacco traders: "*although the province of Agrinio produces one-and-a-half million okas (kilos) of tobacco, only 200,000 okas (kilos) are sold, while the rest remains practically unsold or is sold at a paltry price.*"[33] Such statements appeared regularly in the press in 1902 and not only demonstrate the type and scale of the problems of rural society in the tobacco-producing areas but also testify to the conflicting interests of the social groups active in the tobacco sector, in other words, the class dimension of Greek society.

On the other side, the tobacco merchants and tobacco sellers of Athens, Piraeus, and other urban centers around the country expressed, through their associations, their profound displeasure at the Cigarette Manufacturing Contract. Of particular interest is a memorandum by tobacco sellers of Corfu published in the press, not only because it reflects the positions of those who disagreed but also because its language reflects the way in which the mentalities, behaviors, and interests of the Greek bourgeoisie, namely, merchants and businessmen, were intertwined with gendered social perceptions and attitudes.

The tobacco sellers of Corfu, then, openly criticized the contract, as they perceived it as an attempt to monopolize the cigarette-making sector: "*because the Company, through its large amounts of capital . . . wishes to exclude within a short space of time all other manufacturers, merchants and tobacco buyers.*"[34] Tobacco merchants, like Pesmazoglou earlier, however, seemed to have been dressing up the economic confrontation, namely, the clash of business interests and strategies revolving around cigarettes and tobacco, in the guise of "public and national interest," that is, the dominant—national—discourse of the day: "*No one else is hiding a tobacco monopoly, and especially one exercised not in favour of the State, but in the interests of a few capitalists.*"[35] The tobacco merchants and sellers of Corfu left the most interesting argument against the establishment of the Company till last. The transition from a small craft to the cigarette-making industry—which the Company heralded—would lead to the mass entry of women into wage labor, and this posed—according to the tobacco merchants—a double threat: both for men, the skilled craftsmen and cigarette makers, as well as society as a whole, as—due to the proletarianization of women—social relations and institutions outside the space of production would be disrupted too.

This perhaps encapsulates the spirit of the social group of small craftsmen and small entrepreneurs, in other words, a segment of the Greek petty bourgeoisie. The large company is presented as a factor that is corrosive for social cohesion and peace, as it challenges stable and established values and—gendered—social roles. The true cause of the tobacco merchants' dissatisfaction toward the creation of the company, however, was none other than the threat of their professional extinction if large firms were established, which would usher in different terms for the operation of the tobacco and cigarette market. The same tobacco merchants—who in 1902 and 1903 appeared as passionate supporters and protectors of the cigarette makers against the industrialization of the sector—a little while later, when the "danger" of the creation of the company had receded, would take the lead in the mechanization of cigarette making, now altering their rhetoric and views.[36]

In sum, the Bank of Athens' plan for tobacco and cigarette making was an early indicator of the Bank's intentions to become actively involved in production, both agricultural and industrial. The Bank partially implemented this plan a little later with the establishment of the Privileged Company for the Protection and Distribution of Corinthian Currants [Προνομιούχο Εταιρεία για την Προστασία και τη Διάδοση της Κορινθιακής Σταφίδας], which effectively controlled the entire currant industry. Moreover, in August 1906, the Bank also founded the Wines and Spirits Company [Εταιρεία Οίνων και Οινοπνευμάτων], which benefitted from the "withholding."[37] These plans by the Bank were also connected to the Winemaking and Industrial Agricultural Company [Εταιρεία Οινοποιίας και Γεωργικής Βιομηχανίας] (formerly Zannos, Ross & Co), which had been founded in 1901 also with the participation of the Bank of Athens.[38] Ultimately, the cigarette manufacturing contract was not implemented. We do not know the details as to why, but it is likely that Parliament did not vote for it during the government of Alexandros Zaimis, and it may have been annulled by the government of Theodoros Deligiannis, which emerged from the elections of November 1902.

Conclusions

The establishment in the Ottoman Empire of the State Tobacco Monopoly resulted in many Greek tobacco merchants and cigarette rollers abandoning it and settling in Egypt, where they worked in the tobacco trade and cigarette rolling, opening the first cigarette workshops and factories. The formation of a free market without restrictions, which promised significant profits, mainly thanks to the export character of the cigarette industry, attracted Greek tobacco manufacturers. Initial investment in fixed installations was low, due to the low level of automation in the cigarette industry. The low investment costs combined with the fact that these companies had easy access to the raw material, oriental tobacco, made them competitive against their local counterparts. Concerning the "Tobacco and Cigarette Company," the foundation of a cigarette company in Greece shows that the cigarette manufacturing sector—in addition to commercial tobacco processing in the early 20th century, as happened elsewhere—attracted the interest of the business world, both domestic and expatriate, and bank credit. It could also be argued that it foreshadowed the growth of the Greek cigarette industry, which was to take place a few years later. But it also portended to a degree the more general direction and orientation that domestic industry was to follow, in which the production of consumer goods along with the electricity, chemicals and building materials sectors was to play a leading role.

Archives

Hellenic Literature and Historical Archive (Thessaloniki), Karathanasis Archive, folder 20

Καπνική Επιθεώρησις [Kapniki Epitheorisis], 102 (April 1955)

Εμπρός [*Empros*] (gazette)

Σκριπ [*Skrip*] (gazette)

Notes

1 See Allan Kulikoff, *Tobacco, and Slaves: The Development of Southern Cultures in the Chesapeake 1680–1800* (Chapel Hill: University of North Carolina Press, 1986). On the tobacco industries, see Eric W. Zitzewitz, "Competition and Long-Run Productivity Growth in the UK and US Tobacco Industries, 1879–1939," *The Journal of Industrial Economics* 51, no. 1 (March 2003): 1–33; Robert Fitzgerald and Takashi Hira, "Reappraising Corporate Failure in Britain: Labor Management in the Tobacco Industry Before 1939," *The Business History Review* 79, no. 2 (Summer 2005): 305–37.

2 On the tobacco industry, see Howard Cox, *The Global Cigarette, Origins and Evolution of British-American Tobacco, 1880–1945* (Oxford and New York: Oxford University Press, 2000); Melvyn Read, *The Politics of Tobacco: Policy Networks and the Cigarette Industry* (Ashgate: Farnham 2000); Howard Cox, "International Business, the State and Industrialization in India: Early Growth in the Indian Cigarette Industry, 1900–1919," *Indian Economic and Social History Review* 27, no. 3 (1990): 289–312.

3 For the Spanish tobacco monopoly, see Lina Galvez Munoz, "Engendering the Experience of Wages: The Evolution of the Piecework System at the Spanish Tobacco Monopoly, 1800–1930s," in *Experiencing Wages, Social and Cultural Aspects of Wage Forms in Europe Since 1500*, ed. Peter Scholliers and Leonard Schwarz (New York and Oxford: Berghahn Books, 2003), 201–27. For the relationship between technology and gender in the Spanish tobacco industry, see for further details Lina Galvez Munoz, *Compania Arrendataria de Tabaccos. Cambio Technológico y Empleo Feminino, 1887–1945* (Madrid: Lid, 2000).

4 The invention of the cigarette rolling machine by James A. Bonsack was an important turning point in the history of tobacco production, as it marked the transition from handmade cigarettes to industrially produced cigarettes. The first tobacco factory immediately to install Bonsack's machine, thus establishing large-scale cigarette production, was the Wills Company in the United Kingdom. Patrick G. Porter, "Origins of the American Tobacco Company," *Business History Review* 43 (1969): 59–76. These two countries, the USA and Great Britain—especially the former, the "birthplace" of the first cigarette rolling machine—were to dominate the global tobacco industry market throughout the 20th century.

5 On the advertising practices of the tobacco industries of Egypt and the ways in which they intersected with questions of "identity," see Relli Shechter, "Reading Advertisements in a Colonial/Development Context: Cigarette Advertising and Identity Politics in Egypt, 1919–1939," *Journal of Social History* 39, no. 2 (Winter 2005): 483–503. On the same issue in the USA and Great Britain in the early 20th century, see Mathew Hilton, *Smoking in British Popular Culture, 1800–2000* (New York: Manchester University Press, 2000), 83–113. See also the somewhat older study on the early steps of the American cigarette industry in Patrick G. Porter, "Advertising in the Early Cigarette Industry: W. Duke, Sons & Company of Durham," *The North Carolina Historical Review* 48, no. I (1971): 31–43.

6 Cox, *The Global Cigarette*, 338–41. On this issue, see also Maurice Corina, *Trust in Tobacco: The Anglo-American Struggle for Power* (London: Michael Joseph, 1975).

7 Cox, *The Global Cigarette*, 331–47. On tobacco industries in Britain, see Bernard Alford, "Penny Cigarettes. Oligopoly, and Entrepreneurship in the UK Tobacco Industry in the Late Nineteenth Century," in *Essays in British Business History,* ed. Barry Supple (Oxford: Oxford University Press, 1977), 49–68.

8 Σωκράτης Πετμεζάς, "Οι βαλκανικές κοινωνίες την εποχή του καπνού ή αλλιώς το πρόβλημα της εθιστικής εξάρτησης από ένα παγκοσμιοποιημένο περιβάλλον [Balkan Societies in the Tobacco Era or Else the Problem of Addictive Dependence on a Globalized Environment]," in *Ο καπνός στην ιστορία. Οικονομικές, κοινωνικές και πολιτισμικές προσεγγίσεις*, ed. Άγγελος Παληκίδης, *Πρακτικά Συνεδρίου, Καβάλα, 7–9 Δεκεμβρίου 2018* (Καβάλα: Ινστιτούτο Κοινωνικών Κινημάτων και Ιστορίας Καπνού, 2020), 40–67.

9 In 1885, the Deligiannis government closed the public tobacco factories and sold all their tools to the tobacco merchants, simultaneously ending the monopoly on cigarette paper, thus marking a return to the "free market." This situation lasted only two years. In 1887, the new Trikoupis government reopened the public tobacco factories, thus bringing tobacco processing—cutting and cigarette rolling—back into the state monopoly regime that had existed in the period 1883–1885. Theologos Labrianidis, "Industrial Location in Capitalist Societies: The Tobacco Industry in Greece, 1880–1980" (Unpublished PhD diss., LSE, 1982), 125.

10 Ιωάννης Σερραίος, *Περί εισαγωγής Μονοπωλίου καπνού εν Ελλάδι [On the Introduction of a Tobacco Monopoly in Greece]* (Αθήνα: Εθνικό Τυπογραφείο, 1934), 14 and Ευάγγελος Πρόντζας, "Ο χωρικός, ο καπνός και το κράτος. Η ελληνική αγορά καπνού (1887–1939) [The Peasant, the Tobacco and the State. The Greek Tobacco Market (1887–1939)]," *Τα Ιστορικά* 17 (1992): 275–300.

11 On these issues, see Christina Agriantoni, Leda Papastefanaki, and Maria Christina Chatziioannou, "Introduction," in *Markets and Politics. Private Interests and Public Authority (18th–20th Centuries)*, ed. Christina Agriantoni, Leda Papastefanaki, and Maria Christina Chatziioannou (Volos: University of Thessaly Press, 2016), 21–31, with the relevant bibliography.

12 Gulhan Balsoy, "Gendering Ottoman Labor History: The Cibali Regie Factory in the Early Twentieth Century," *International Review of Social History* 54 (2009): 53. Régie had the monopoly over tobacco revenues and consequently purchased the tobacco from the producers and managed its sale, processing, and export.

13 One of the most recent and complete studies on the cigarette industry of Egypt is that by Relli Shechter, *Smoking, Culture and Economy in the Middle East: The Egyptian Tobacco Market 1850–2000* (London: I. B Tauris & Co. Ltd., 2006). On the cigarette industry of Egypt, see also Relli Shechter, "Selling Luxury: The Rise of the Egyptian Cigarette and the Transformation of the Egyptian Tobacco Market, 1850–1914," *International Journal of Middle East Studies* 35, no. 1 (February 2003): 51–75; Joel Beinin, *Workers and Peasants in the Modern Middle East* (Cambridge: Cambridge University Press, 2001); Joel Beinin and Zachary Lockman, *Workers on the Nile: Nationalism Communism, Islam, and the Egyptian Working Class, 1882–1954* (Princeton, NJ: Princeton University Press, 1987), 49–57. Among Greek historians, see Χρήστος Χατζηιωσήφ, *Η Γηραιά Σελήνη, Η βιομηχανία στην ελληνική οικονομία 1830–1940 [The Old Moon, Industry in the Greek Economy 1830–1940]* (Αθήνα: Θεμέλιο, 1993), 366–68.

14 Χατζηιωσήφ, *Γηραιά Σελήνη*, 366–67.

15 Shechter, "Selling Luxury," 51–75.

16 Χατζηιωσήφ, *Γηραιά Σελήνη*, 368.

17 Χατζηιωσήφ, *Γηραιά Σελήνη*. On the Greek-owned cigarette factories in Egypt during the interwar period, see also Alexander Kitroeff, *The Greeks in Egypt, 1919–1937: Ethnicity and Class* (London: Ithaca Press, 1987), 96–111.

18 A typical example is that of the factory of Georgios Giasmatzis in Dresden, which was bought out by an American company in 1907 for 1.5 million marks. See Χατζηιωσήφ, *Γηραιά Σελήνη*, 368.

19 *Καπνική Επιθεώρησις [Kapniki Epitheorisis],* 102 (April 1955).
20 See Απόστολος Γ. Κωνσταντινίδης, *Οι Πηλιορείται εν Αιγύπτω [The Peliorites in Egypt],* vol. 1 (Αλεξάνδρεια: Σύλλογος Ζαγοράς, 1936), 60–61.
21 Thanks to the constant upgrading and expansion of its machinery, during the war, the company was able to supply cigarettes not only to the Egyptian market but also to the allied troops of the Middle East and to continue operating in the post-war period. See *Καπνική Επιθεώρησις,* 102 (April 1955).
22 Χατζηιωσήφ, *Γηραιά Σελήνη*, 368–69. As E. Papastratos points out, a "victim" of German nationalism and chauvinism was the Hellas-Zigaretten Fabrik, founded by the Papastratos family in Berlin in 1933 and which was forced to close three years later. See Ευάγγελος Παπαστράτος, *Η δουλειά και ο κόπος της [The Work and Its Effort]* (Αθήνα: Gema, 1964).
23 Hellenic Literature and Historical Archive (Thessaloniki), Karathanasis Archive, folder 20.
24 Hellenic Literature and Historical Archive (Thessaloniki), Karathanasis Archive, folder 20.
25 On the Karathanassis cigarette company, see also Χρυσούλα Αναγνωστοπούλου, " 'Βιομηχανία σιγαρέττων εν Σάμω': Όψεις της επιχειρηματικότητας του καπνεμπορικού οίκου των αδελφών Μ. και Σ. Καραθανάση στη Σάμο (1887–1916) [Cigarette Industry in Samos': Aspects of the Entrepreneurship of the Tobacco Trading House of M. and S. Karathanassis Brothers]," in *Ο καπνός στην ιστορία. Οικονομικές, κοινωνικές και πολιτισμικές προσεγγίσεις*, ed. Άγγελος Παληκίδης, *Πρακτικά Συνεδρίου, Καβάλα, 7–9 Δεκεμβρίου 2018* (Καβάλα: Ινστιτούτο Κοινωνικών Κινημάτων και Ιστορίας Καπνού, 2020), 225–37.
26 Law ΑΡΚΔ΄/1883, "On the imposition of a privilege on cigarette paper."
27 *Εμπρός [Empros],* 19/11/1899 (gazette).
28 Χρήστος Χατζηιωσήφ, "Η Μπελ Επόκ του κεφαλαίου [The Belle Époque of Capital]," in *Ιστορία της Ελλάδας του 20ου αι.,* ed. Χρήστος Χατζηιωσήφ, vol. A1 (Αθήνα: Βιβλιόραμα, 2002), 326–31.
29 *Σκριπ* [*Skrip*], 22/1/1902 (gazette). The contract was published in full in *Εμπρός* on 24/1/1902.
30 *Σκριπ,* 22/1/1902.
31 *Σκριπ,* 22/1/1902.
32 Χριστίνα Αγριαντώνη, "Βιομηχανία [Industry]," in *Ιστορία της Ελλάδας του 20ου αι.,* ed. Χρήστος Χατζηιωσήφ, vol. A1 (Αθήνα: Βιβλιόραμα, 2002), 206–7.
33 *Σκριπ,* 29/3/1902.
34 *Εμπρός*, 5/2/1902.
35 *Εμπρός*, 5/2/1902.
36 *"Bear in mind that 5,000 people who live from this work will be thrown into the streets with the ratification of the contract, as not only will tobacco merchants and sellers be ruined but the cigarette makers too, as, according to article 5 of the Contract, the Company is permitted to procure machines for the most efficient execution of the work."* Committee of tobacco merchants and tobacco sellers of Athens-Piraeus and provinces. *Εμπρός*, 24/3/1902. The vice-chairman of this committee was the tobacco merchant K. Varkas, who a few years later was to introduce cigarette-rolling machines.
37 On these issues, see Σωκράτης Πετμεζάς, "Αγροτική Οικονομία [Agricultural Economy]," in *Ιστορία της Ελλάδας του 20ου αι.,* ed. Χρήστος Χατζηιωσήφ, vol. A1 (Αθήνα: Βιβλιόραμα, 2002), 64–73.
38 For the Winemaking and Industrial Agricultural Company, see Αγριαντώνη, "Βιομηχανία," 211–12.

Bibliography

Agriantoni, Christina, Leda Papastefanaki, and Maria Christina Chatziioannou. "Introduction." In *Markets and Politics. Private Interests and Public Authority (18th-20th*

Centuries), edited by Christina Agriantoni, Leda Papastefanaki, and Maria Christina Chatziioannou, 21–31. Volos: University of Thessaly Press, 2016.

Alford, Bernard. "Penny Cigarettes. Oligopoly, and Entrepreneurship in the UK Tobacco Industry in the Late Nineteenth Century." In *Essays in British Business History*, edited by Barry Supple, 49–68. Oxford: Oxford University Press, 1977.

Balsoy, Gulhan. "Gendering Ottoman Labor History: The Cibali Regie Factory in the Early Twentieth Century." *International Review of Social History 54* (2009): 45–68.

Beinin, Joel. *Workers and Peasants in the Modern Middle East.* Cambridge: Cambridge University Press, 2001.

Beinin, Joel, and Zachary Lockman. *Workers on the Nile: Nationalism Communism, Islam, and the Egyptian Working Class, 1882–1954.* Princeton, NJ: Princeton University Press, 1987.

Corina, Maurice. *Trust in Tobacco: The Anglo-American Struggle for Power*. London: Michael Joseph, 1975.

Cox, Howard. "International Business, the State and Industrialization in India: Early Growth in the Indian Cigarette Industry, 1900–1919." *Indian Economic and Social History Review* 27, no. 3 (1990): 289–312.

Cox, Howard. *The Global Cigarette, Origins and Evolution of British-American Tobacco, 1880–1945.* Oxford and New York: Oxford University Press, 2000.

Fitzgerald, Robert, and Takashi Hira. "Reappraising Corporate Failure in Britain: Labor Management in the Tobacco Industry Before 1939." *The Business History Review* 79, no. 2 (Summer 2005): 305–37.

Hilton, Mathew. *Smoking in British Popular Culture, 1800–2000.* New York: Manchester University Press, 2000.

Kitroeff, Alexander. *The Greeks in Egypt, 1919–1937: Ethnicity and Class.* London: Ithaca Press, 1987.

Kulikoff, Allan. *Tobacco, and Slaves: The Development of Southern Cultures in the Chesapeake 1680–1800.* Chapel Hill: University of North Carolina Press, 1986.

Labrianidis, Theologos. "Industrial Location in Capitalist Societies: The Tobacco Industry in Greece, 1880–1980." Unpublished PhD diss., LSE, 1982.

Munoz, Lina Galvez. *Compania Arrendataria de Tabaccos. Cambio Technológico y Empleo Feminino, 1887–1945.* Madrid: Lid, 2000.

Munoz, Lina Galvez. "Engendering the Experience of Wages: The Evolution of the Piecework System at the Spanish Tobacco Monopoly, 1800–1930s." In *Experiencing Wages, Social and Cultural Aspects of Wage Forms in Europe since 1500*, edited by Peter Scholliers and Leonard Schwarz, 201–27. New York and Oxford: Berghahn Books, 2003.

Porter, Patrick G. "Origins of the American Tobacco Company." *Business History Review* 43 (1969): 59–76.

Porter, Patrick G. "Advertising in the Early Cigarette Industry: W. Duke, Sons & Company of Durham." *The North Carolina Historical Review* 48, no. I (1971): 31–43.

Read, Melvyn. *The Politics of Tobacco: Policy Networks and the Cigarette Industry.* Ashgate: Farnham, 2000.

Shechter, Relli. "Selling Luxury: The Rise of the Egyptian Cigarette and the Transformation of the Egyptian Tobacco Market, 1850–1914." *International Journal of Middle East Studies* 35, no. 1 (February 2003): 51–75.

Shechter, Relli. "Reading Advertisements in a Colonial/Development Context: Cigarette Advertising and Identity Politics in Egypt, 1919–1939." *Journal of Social History* 39, no. 2 (Winter 2005): 483–503.

Shechter, Relli. *Smoking, Culture and Economy in the Middle East: The Egyptian Tobacco Market 1850–2000.* London: I. B. Tauris & Co. Ltd., 2006.

Zitzewitz, Eric W. "Competition and Long-Run Productivity Growth in the UK and US Tobacco Industries, 1879–1939." *The Journal of Industrial Economics* 51, no. 1 (March 2003): 1–33.

Αγριαντώνη, Χριστίνα. "Βιομηχανία." In *Ιστορία της Ελλάδας του 20ου αι.*, edited by Χατζηιωσήφ Χρήστος, vol. A1, 173–221. Αθήνα: Βιβλιόραμα, 2002. [Agriantoni, Christina. "Industry." In *History of Greece in the 20th Century*, edited by Christos Chatziiosif, vol. A1, 173–221. Athens: Vivliorama, 2002.]

Αναγνωστοπούλου, Χρυσούλα. " 'Βιομηχανία σιγαρέττων εν Σάμω': Όψεις της επιχειρηματικότητας του καπνεμπορικού οίκου των αδελφών Μ. και Σ. Καραθανάση στη Σάμο (1887–1916)." In *Ο καπνός στην ιστορία. Οικονομικές, κοινωνικές και πολιτισμικές προσεγγίσεις*, edited by Παληκίδης Άγγελος, Πρακτικά Συνεδρίου, Καβάλα, 7–9 Δεκεμβρίου 2018, 225–37. Καβάλα: Ινστιτούτο Κοινωνικών Κινημάτων και Ιστορίας Καπνού, 2020. [Anagnostopoulou, Chrysoula. " 'Cigarette Industry in Samos': Aspects of the Entrepreneurship of the Tobacco Trading House of M. and S. Karathanassis Brothers in Samos (1887–1916)." In *Tobacco in History. Economic, Social and Cultural Approaches*, edited by Angelos Palikidis, *Conference Proceedings, Kavala, December 7–9, 2018*, 225–37. Kavala: Institute of Social Movements and Tobacco History, 2020.]

Κωνσταντινίδης, Απόστολος Γ. *Οι Πηλιορείται εν Αιγύπτω*, vol. 1. Αλεξάνδρεια: Σύλλογος Ζαγοράς, 1936. [Konstantinidis, Apostolos G. *The Peliorites in Egypt*, vol. 1. Alexandreia: Syllogos Zagoras, 1936.]

Παπαστράτος, Ευάγγελος. *Η δουλειά και ο κόπος της*. Αθήνα: Gema, 1964. [Papastratos, Evangelos. *The Work and Its Effort*. Athens: Gema, 1964.]

Πετμεζάς, Σωκράτης. "Αγροτική Οικονομία." In *Ιστορία της Ελλάδας του 20ου αι.*, edited by Χατζηιωσήφ Χρήστος, vol. A1, 41–85. Αθήνα: Βιβλιόραμα, 2002. [Petmezas, Sokratis. "Agricultural Economy." In *History of Greece in the 20th Century*, edited by Christos Chatziiosif, vol. A1, 41–85. Athens: Vivliorama, 2002.]

Πετμεζάς, Σωκράτης. "Οι βαλκανικές κοινωνίες την εποχή του καπνού ή αλλιώς το πρόβλημα της εθιστικής εξάρτησης από ένα παγκοσμιοποιημένο περιβάλλον." In *Ο καπνός στην ιστορία. Οικονομικές, κοινωνικές και πολιτισμικές προσεγγίσεις*, edited by Παληκίδης Άγγελος, Πρακτικά Συνεδρίου, Καβάλας, 7–9 Δεκεμβρίου 2018, 40–67. Καβάλα: Ινστιτούτο Κοινωνικών Κινημάτων και Ιστορίας Καπνού, 2020. [Petmezas, Sokratis. "Balkan Societies in the Tobacco Era or else the Problem of Addictive Dependence on a Globalized Environment." In *Tobacco in History. Economic, Social and Cultural Approaches*, edited by Angelos Palikidis, *Conference Proceedings, Kavala, December 7–9, 2018*, 40–67. Kavala: Institute of Social Movements and Tobacco History, 2020.]

Πρόντζας, Ευάγγελος. "Ο χωρικός, ο καπνός και το κράτος. Η ελληνική αγορά καπνού (1887–1939)." *Τα Ιστορικά* 17 (1992): 275–300. [Prontzas, Evangelos. "The Peasant, the Tobacco and the State. The Greek Tobacco Market (1887–1939)." *Ta Istorika* 17 (1992): 275–300.]

Σερραίος, Ιωάννης. *Περί εισαγωγής Μονοπωλίου καπνού εν Ελλάδι*. Αθήνα: Εθνικό Τυπογραφείο, 1934. [Serraios, Ioannis. *On the Introduction of a Tobacco Monopoly in Greece*. Athens: National Printing House, 1934.]

Χατζηιωσήφ, Χρήστος. "Η Μπελ Επόκ του κεφαλαίου." In *Ιστορία της Ελλάδας του 20ου αι.*, edited by Χατζηιωσήφ Χρήστος, vol. A1, 309–49. Αθήνα: Βιβλιόραμα, 2002. [Chatziiosif, Christos. "The Belle Époque of Capital." In *History of Greece in the 20th Century*, edited by Christos Chatziiosif, vol. A1, 309–49. Athens: Vivliorama, 2002.]

Χατζηιωσήφ, Χρήστος. *Η Γηραιά Σελήνη, Η βιομηχανία στην ελληνική οικονομία 1830–1940*. Αθήνα: Θεμέλιο, 1993. [Chatziiosif, Christos. *The Old Moon, Industry in the Greek Economy 1830–1940*. Athens: Themelio, 1993.]

11 Motifs of Primary Accumulation in the Ottoman Empire

The Bankers of Galata and the Case of Andreas Syngros

Dimitrios Stergiopoulos

Introduction

In September 1867, Andreas Syngros traveled to Athens to ensure that his business interests in the Ottoman Empire were supported by the Greek government. Although this incident seems inconspicuous, it was one of the first signs of a process that would deeply affect life in Greece in the following decades; it signaled the influx of capital holders and capital from abroad. These men of capital introduced a series of modern economic concepts and processes to a relatively backward and impoverished country and allied themselves to the emerging political program of modernization personified by Charilaos Trikoupis.

Often it is assumed that the source for these advanced methods and techniques was the financial markets of Western Europe. To a certain extent, this view can even be found in the words and memoirs of these historical actors themselves. However, the life and career of Syngros until 1872, when he returned to Greece, reveals that identifying this source of influence is a much more complicated process. By putting the socioeconomic life of the Ottoman Empire at the center of our inquiry, we can identify some of the indigenous banking and money-lending traditions of the region and trace their transformation through regular contacts with the emerging capitalist world system in Western Europe.

The main source of my inquiry is the *Memoirs* of Syngros. They were written in 1894–1899 and were published in 1908, nine years after his death.[1] They cover the first 43 years of his life, alongside two small chapters that focus on events in 1893–1894 and 1897. They were edited by the authors Dimitrios Vikelas and Georgios Drosinis while the article "Study on the current position of Hellenism" (Μελέτη επί της σημερινής θέσεως του Ελληνισμού), published anonymously in 1877 in Estia magazine by Syngros, was also included to the memoirs.[2] Additionally, a short biography of Syngros was published by E. Oistridis in 1899.[3]

In the context of Ottoman studies, the study of the *Banque Impériale Ottomane* (BIO) and the interactions between the financiers of Istanbul, the Sublime Porte, and the European stock markets have drawn the interest of most scholars. However, their research mainly focuses on matters of state borrowing. The Ottoman bankers are seen as agents of the empire's debt dependency, while the broader social and political significance of this class remains largely unrecognized.[4] Among scholars

DOI: 10.4324/9781003500780-15

of modern Greece, a series of very important works were published including the 1998 edition of the *Memoirs*.[5] Often, the framework of diaspora and diasporic capital lies at the center of these analyses. Although extremely innovative and informative, it also imposes certain limitations on our understanding of that era because it considers as its main point of reference a broader Greek world, with the Greek Kingdom at its center.[6] This viewpoint leads it to offer only limited connections between the historical actors under study and the countries in which they were living, while it stresses the links between these diasporic communities. We should also recognize that this is not just a perspective imposed on that era by present scholarship. Some of these very same historical actors tended to hold these ideas, or post-ipso facto to stress that these ideas were always part of their identity. In any case, the socioeconomic context in which these *homme d'affaires* accumulated their wealth allows us to trace some of the distinguishing characteristics of doing business in the East and reveals the importance of this business culture in the modernizing reformist agendas of the region.

Syngros' Business Activities in the Ottoman Empire

Syngros the Trader

According to his *Memoirs*, we can divide his professional activities into two broad periods: the first was between 1845 and 1860, when he learned the trade of the merchant, and the second was between 1860 and 1873, when he was primarily active as a banker. Since the early modern period, mercantile networks were usually established and maintained through intermarriages and extended families. This was also the case for Syngros' family, even though his father, Domenico or Kyriakos Tsingros, was not a merchant.[7] Syngros' grandfather was a wine and cotton merchant from a small village on the island of Chios and his great uncle was a low-ranking clergyman. The family must have been modestly wealthy, and it was expected that D. Tsingros would become a priest and inherit the position and fortune of his childless uncle. However, after graduating from Chios' middle school, D. Tsingros rejected this career and studied medicine in Pisa and Paris with a loan from the prominent Rodocanachi family from Chios. With the outbreak of the 1821 revolution, D. Tsingros and his wife Mondini (Nikoleta) Tsingrou, nee Nomikou, managed to escape from the island and migrate to Istanbul. There, their two children, Georgios and Andreas, were born. Although D. Tsingros managed to become the personal physician of Ottoman royals and high-ranking officials, in 1831, the whole family moved first to Andros and then to Syros, the most important commercial center in Greece after Athens.[8]

In the 1840s, some of the bankers and moneylenders of Istanbul had started to move from Phanar and other neighborhoods in the old part of the city, to Galata and Pera, on the other side of the Golden Horn.[9] At the same time, European diplomats had established their residences in the same area and socialized with the financiers.[10] These neighborhoods became the epicenter of Western cultural norms, known as Alafranga in Ottoman parlance, while the sultan himself resided in the

Dolmabahçe Palace in neighboring Beşiktaş. By contrast, the old part of the city served as a hub of Alaturka cultural norms. Some of the major bankers in Galata were the Baltatzis family (Evangelos, Theodoros, and Emmanouil), the Camondo family (Abraham Salomon, Rafael, Abraham Behor, and Nissim), Christakis Zografos, and Georgios Zarifis. In 1847, Baltatzis together with Jacques Alléon opened the first joint-stock Ottoman bank and, albeit short-lived, this act initiated a new period in Ottoman socioeconomic life.[11]

In 1845, Andreas Syngros moved to Istanbul to work as an apprentice in the merchant house of Nikolaos Damianos and Sia. The 15-year-old Syngros managed to rise in the hierarchy. In 1847, when the firm's first secretary and accountant decided to switch jobs, Syngros took the opportunity to take over his duties, even if he barely knew how to keep the books and look after the business correspondence. In 1849, when his boss, Nikolaos Damianos, died unexpectedly, Syngros became the acting director of the shop. In 1852, having already secured one of the highest salaries among all clerks in Istanbul's trading houses, he became a partner of the firm, with a 4% share even though he lacked the necessary capital to buy it. Instead, he secured the money through a loan from the firm, at a 6% interest. In 1854, his share increased to 7%, and in 1859, when he visited the general director of the trading firm in Marseille, he was its second most important director.[12] This meteoric rise from complete obscurity to the helm of one of the major trading firms in Istanbul reveals his unquestionable talent for this job, as well as the opportunities that existed for certain individuals in the mid-1800s.

When Syngros started his career in that merchant house, he became part of a well-established pattern of doing business whose origins can be traced back to at least the 18th century.[13] Usually, trading houses were formed by a group of brothers, brothers-in-law, and other relatives who opened their shops in various economically strategic locations, usually ports. They established a firm, took advantage of the strong trust between the partners, and exchanged products on favorable terms with limited capital requirements. N. Damianos was a partner in a trading firm that had two shops in Istanbul, and one shop apiece in Galanti, Varna, Trieste, Manchester, London, and Marseille, which served as the headquarters. The trading firm also cooperated with a more extensive network of brokers and associates in locations such as Izmir, Amasya, Syros, Zakynthos, (probably) Athens, Berdiansk, Burgas, Vienna, Antwerp, and Liverpool. The firm's main enterprises were the export of grain from the Black Sea region through Istanbul; the export of silk and other agricultural products from the Ottoman Empire to Marseille; and the import of textiles, iron nails, pins, and colonial products, including coffee and sugar, to the Ottoman Empire. The in-depth analysis of price patterns in all these markets through regular and constant correspondence between the various shops and associates, their local connections with small-scale producers, merchants, and brokers, and their knowledge on how to do business in institutionally different environments were some of the main reasons for the competitiveness of these firms. The business partners tended to live quite modestly; they kept the operational costs of their shops to the absolute minimum, while they constantly reinvested their profits into the business.[14]

According to Syngros' own narrative, his ability to predict the busts and booms of trade, as well as his flexibility to try new trading opportunities, appeared to be among his talents. His first contact with such a bust was in the winter of 1847–1848. In previous years, European economies had experienced a series of crises accompanied by a shortage of grain and other foodstuffs. The merchants in Istanbul responded by buying increasingly larger quantities of grain from Russia and the Danube and shipping them to Marseille.[15] However, French produce in 1848 was abundant while huge quantities of wheat had already been imported during the winter. This led to the collapse of prices and the bankruptcy of many merchants in Istanbul. This turbulence also gave Syngros his opportunity for promotion: the previous first secretary chose to work for another merchant who offered him a higher salary.[16]

Syngros' narrative also reveals some of the challenges faced by this type of trade. Istanbul served as a transit center for the products that were exchanged between the eastern and western parts of the Mediterranean Sea, with Marseille as its western counterpart. The trade treaties of the 1830s and 1840s between the Ottoman Empire and the Great Powers significantly enhanced this trade. However, the subsequent widespread use of steamships, telegrams, and, eventually, railroads changed this pattern. The large wholesale importers and exporters in Marseille and London were soon able to make deals directly with small traders in the various entrepots. Thus, Istanbul was gradually losing its importance. The industries in Europe started to exercise increasingly direct control over their supply chains, and according to Syngros, the formerly strong mercantile community of Istanbul had disappeared almost completely by the 1890s.[17] However, it should be kept in mind that this did not mean that international trade between the Ottoman Empire and Europe was decreasing. On the contrary, according to one estimate, it grew by 15% per year.[18] This process, which was observed by Syngros, can be described as peripheralization which refers to

> the relative diminution of the state's ability to interfere with the flows of factors of production in the world economy; on the other, it means specialization in certain products, improving the means of transportation, creation of a more efficient bureaucracy, and the transfer of new technologies and information into these areas.[19]

Syngros the Banker

In 1859, after 14 years of working constantly as a merchant in Istanbul, Syngros decided to take a vacation and travel to major cities in Europe. However, his plan had one more aim, namely, to speak, for the first time, face to face with the general director of the trading firm, Georges Petrokokkinos, and present to him the next investment opportunity—lending money to the Ottoman state.

Until the Crimean War, the sultan had avoided direct contacts with the capital markets in Europe. The story by one of his advisors about the British fleet's bombardment of the port of Athens because Greece had defaulted its loan payments made him even more reluctant.[20] Instead, he preferred that the bankers of Galata lent money to the High Porte at a 12–20% interest rate. This was significantly higher than the one he could have got abroad but it allowed him to avoid direct contact with European financiers and their states. Moreover, the Ottoman state covered its budget deficits by paying its officials and contractors with various types of orders of payment, called *havale, esham*, and *sergi*. Instead of waiting to receive their money from the treasury, these employees preferred to sell these orders of payment to the Galata bankers at a lower price (called discounting in banking parlance). These bankers would then bribe the high-ranking officials so that their orders would be redeemed faster. Thus, privileged access to the higher echelons of power was a prerequisite for a successful banking and money-lending enterprise in Istanbul. Moreover, the need to bribe explains why the price of capital—in other words, the interest rates and the premiums and fees attached to it—was much higher in the Ottoman Empire and why bankers bought the orders of payment for significantly lower prices.[21] The *sergi* were *notes of indebtedness* issued by various government departments, while *havale* were *promissory notes* issued by Ottoman officials stationed in distant provinces in which future revenues from that province were assigned to the recipients of these notes. The holder of this note, usually a banker, who had acquired it at a lower value than the nominal value, obtained the right to receive the revenues of a specific tax, usually the tithe, from a certain province for a period of 3–10 years. This method of tax farming was extremely profitable and formed the main mechanism through which many Ottoman merchants and bankers made their fortune.[22] Syngros wanted to become part of this industry.

To specialize in such activities, advanced banking techniques were essential for a successful merchant house in the East. These houses were faced with the task of raising significant capital through their partners, associates, and bankers in the West, to buy large quantities of agricultural products from the East, transfer them to the West, sell them to manufacturers and other wholesale importers, and repatriate their profits. This circle of money meant that, for large periods, they had extremely limited liquidity. However, the broader public had to be kept unaware of their periodic difficulties, because preserving the reputation of their merchant firm as financially healthy was their upmost concern. Any rumors of such difficulties would undermine their ability to raise capital through bills of exchanges. These were the main means for raising capital in a region with a severe scarcity of capital and lack of other financial instruments and institutions such as checks and large state-backed banks. In its simplest form, the banker or merchant drew a bill of exchange which was to be paid in three months' time. Then he sent this bill to one of his partners abroad who encashed it or got it discounted at one of the merchant bankers in France and Great Britain. However, for all this to happen, the original drawer and the intermediate payees had to be deemed trustworthy, a fee had to be paid to the banker, while these bills themselves carried interest. When the client was seen as reliable, the banks and financiers were happy to refinance their debt by accepting new bills of exchange in the place of that which had matured.[23]

Since the 1860s, more and more of these merchants focused on banking and state loans, while they raised capital through the discounting of bills of exchange and the floating of Ottoman securities in the European capital markets. The most lucrative options were the lending of money to the Sublime Porte and supplying the Ottoman troops at 12–20% interest. However, this interest would be only one source of their profits. In exchange for the loan, they would receive *promissory notes* (*havale*) as collateral. Given that these promissory notes were used extensively by the authorities whenever they were short of cash, they did not carry their nominal value. Thus, the banker would negotiate the actual value of these notes during negotiations with the Ottoman Ministry of Finance (*Maliye Nezareti*) or other governmental departments. These notes could end up losing up to half of their value, due to the difficulties and time-consuming processes of collecting these taxes from faraway provinces and transferring the funds to the capital. Finally, large amounts of these loans were paid in *kaime*, an interest-bearing banknote, that the Ottoman government had started to issue since the Crimean War. However, these banknotes circulated only in the capital, while their actual value was also significantly lower than the nominal value. By contrast, the silver species (known as *kuruş* or *piastre*) used in the provinces preserved most of their value. Therefore, the banker tried to pay the loans in banknotes at close to their nominal value while receiving taxes on gold and silver species. If the banker had supplied the Ottoman troops, then his profit margin would have further increased because he could find these materials at below the market prices. Overall, a bank loan of 100,000 kuruş could even return a profit of 170,000 kuruş, a profit margin of 62%. According to the numbers provided by Syngros in his memoirs and my calculations, this was more than double the profit margin for most of the other activities of the trading firm in the previous years.[24] Initially, G. Petrokokkinos was reluctant to allocate the necessary capital, but he was persuaded by the instincts of his young director.[25]

In 1861, the trading firm in which Syngros had been working since 1845 was closed. The various partners had different opinions on how to overcome the diminishing profits of most of the shops. Two notable exceptions were the one in Istanbul, directed by Syngros, and the one in Marseille, directed by G. Petrokokkinos. Times had changed too. Since the late 1850s, the various bankers, financiers, and moneylenders of the Ottoman capital had started to cooperate and establish larger banking houses. One of the first major new banking institutions was the *Société Ottomane de l'Empire Ottoman* where most of the major bankers and financiers were among its shareholders. The bank was a subsidiary of the BIO, the main banking institution of the Ottoman Empire which had been founded by British and French interests and enjoyed special privileges in the Ottoman domains.[26]

In 1861, Syngros opened his own banking and trading shop, which specialized in currency exchange, tax farming, money lending, and loans to the Sublime Porte. In 1868, after a series of conflicts and disagreements with some other bankers, Syngros, with two more partners, opened a brokerage firm with powerful bankers, like the Camondo Bank and Zarifis-Zafeiropoulos, participating as limited liability partners. The Camondo Brothers wanted a middleman for their dealings with the Sublime Porte and preferred the favors and bribes channeled to Ottoman officials not to be conducted through their large and respectable bank. However, Syngros knew the right person for this job: his close friend and old schoolmate, Georges

Koronios. After three years, this brokerage firm was transformed into the Banque de Constantinople, a Société Anonyme, which also had the monetary support of several bankers in Istanbul. This period was particularly lucrative for all of them, including Syngros. Between 1868 and 1871, he managed to increase his fortune six fold.[27]

An article by *The Times* in 1880 also confirms Syngros' depiction of these intricate and performative in nature negotiations.[28] In 1880, the Ottoman Empire had been at default for five years, but its lack of access to the financial markets was not catastrophic. The domestic bankers and financiers (described as usurers by the newspaper) provided short-term loans that secured the empire's survival, while their behavior was hailed as an exemplary case of patriotic duty by the public. In these five years, the Ministry of Finance had stopped paying most of its debtors, internal and external, with the notable exception of some state contractors and bankers who were sufficiently important for the state to meet its basic needs. This situation also meant that the actual building of the Ministry of Finance was constantly besieged by large numbers of people who tried to redeem their orders of payment to receive their salaries. *The Times*' article offers us an interesting depiction of the Ottoman social hierarchy, observing the proximity of the guests to the minister, with the bankers of Galata being at the top.

First, in the court of the building, the journalist encounters a group of women who try to get into the building and who are being paid by the office for small salaries and pensions. Some wait patiently and some others "*complain loudly of the way they are treated, and express themselves in very unparliamentary language to any of the officials who have the misfortune to come within hearing distance.*" This gendered depiction of women as impatient but forceful is contrasted to "*the old blind man in thread bare civil uniform, who is led by a pale faced, bright-eyed little girl, and wanders about the outskirts of the crowd.*" On the corridors of the second floor, crowds of contractors and businessmen also impatiently wait for their orders to be redeemed. In the office of the Minister of Finance, Abdüllatif Suphi Pasha, some of the more important guests are also waiting to speak with him. Most are also creditors who could not encash their *notes* issued by provincial treasuries. The local agents of these creditors, an indispensable part of the Ottoman way of banking, had failed to redeem these notes, so they had sent them to their partners in the capital who had close contacts with the ministry. Such interactions between Ottoman officials, moneylenders, contractors, and merchants were occurring throughout the empire and formed the main mechanism that provided liquidity to the Ottoman economy and secured the transfer of agricultural products to the internal and external markets.[29]

The narrative of the London Times journalist also offers us one of the best in-person descriptions of the interactions between the bankers and the Sublime Porte:

> *Foiled in his efforts he (the minister) is obliged to have resource to the money-lenders, so he sends for two or three Galata bankers. These gentlemen on arriving notice that his Excellency is more than usually amiable,*

> *and accordingly they harden their hearts and assume at once a defensive attitude. In reply to the suggestion that they should make a small advance to the Treasury for a few weeks, they object that all their available capital is already invested, by far the greater part of it in Government securities which are very much below their nominal value. Pressed a little more, they inquire about the security now proposed, and on learning that they will get havallehs, or assignments on the sheep-tax, or tithes of some distant province, they shake their heads and decline the offer. . . . There are certain safer revenues that can be mortgaged, or, the bankers might be allowed to sell at the market value some depreciated securities which they hold as a deposit, and on such basis an arrangement can be made. The amount of the advance is then discussed. The Treasury requires, let us suppose 100,000 pounds, and the bankers declare that such a sum surpasses their available resources. After much higgling the sum of 60,000 pounds is agreed to; but there is no possibility, it is said, of giving the whole amount in hard cash, and here appears for the first time the plan which the bankers have from the outset determined to propose. Their main object in advancing more money is to recover some of their previous claims, so they make the following arrangement. 40,000 pounds will be paid in hard cash and 20,000 will be given in Treasury paper which is already in their possession. That paper could not be sold except at 30 or 40 per cent discount and they give it to the Treasury at its full nominal value. Thus, by exacting a safe guarantee for the advance, they not only recover in a few months the amount they actually paid, but they also obtain full payment for old claims, which, if they closed now their current account with the Treasury, they would be obliged to write off as bad debts or sell to other at a ruinous discount. It is the prospect of thus realizing on most advantageous terms some of the depreciated Government paper already in their possession, and not the offer of 10 or 12 per cent on the actual advance, which induces them to entertain the new proposal. The Minister understands perfectly the nature of the arrangement . . . [but] he is obliged to submit and reluctantly signs the contract.*

Conclusions

The previous cases reveal that doing business in the East in the second half of the 19th century entailed that these *homme d'affaires* partake in a business culture different than the one in Western and Central Europe and one that demanded time and effort to acquire. The dealings with the Sublime Porte were particularly challenging and involved a whole set of behaviors and norms that the banker had to know so as to provide these loans on extremely profitable terms. An aspect of this different business culture was also that most of the profits were not mentioned in the contracts signed with the Ministry of Finance. A large part of it came from lending money to the state in the form of banknotes in their nominal value instead of their actual market value.

Examples of this culture were provided by Syngros in his *Memoirs*. When he had visited his partners in Marseille, he was amazed by the easiness with which trade deals were concluded. In contrast, in Istanbul, it demanded constant bargaining with various agents, officials and employees in a variety of languages where even the smallest amounts of money were subject of intense negotiations. Similarly, he was surprised at how easy and cheap it was to encash a bill of exchange in one of the merchant bankers of London.[30] In contrast, the discounting of state *notes* and merchant *bills* had been the foundation of the Ottoman banking and remained more than profitable at least until 1881, when the creation of the Ottoman Public Debt Administration led the BIO to become the strongest banking institution in the empire. All in all, this indigenous business culture in trade and finance was an indispensable part of the region's transformation in the 19th century: it formed the main component in the modernizing and reformist agendas that characterized its politics.

Archives

The Times (London), *The Times Digital Archive*, https://go.gale.com/ps/dispBasicSearch.do?userGroupName=ucsandiego&prodId=TTDA.AccessedMarch 7, 2024.

Notes

1 Ανδρέας Συγγρός, *Απομνημονεύματα [Memoirs]*, vols. I–III (Εν Αθήναις: Βιβλιοπωλείον της Εστίας, 1908).

2 We know that the editor Drosinis, with the help of Syngros' wife, Ifigeneia Mavrokordatou—Syngrou, removed several negative and sarcastic comments about prominent figures who were still alive in 1908. The original manuscript was never found. We assume that Syngros' personal archive was also lost. Άλκης Αγγέλου and Μαρία Χριστίνα Χατζηιωάννου, "Εισαγωγή [Introduction]," in *Απομνημονεύματα [Memoirs]*, by Ανδρέας Συγγρός (Αθήνα: Εστία. Νέα Ελληνική Βιβλιοθήκη, 1998), 28, 37, 40.

3 E. I. Οιστρίδης, *Ο Μέγας Εθνικός Ευεργέτης, Ανδρέας Συγγρός [The Nation's Great Benefactor, Andreas Syngros]* (Εν Αθήναις: Εκ του Κεντρικού Βιβλιοπωλείου Δράκου Δ. Παπαδημητρίου, 1899). Also see Sotiroula Vasileiou, "Profiling the 'Greek Genius': Nineteenth-Century Biographies of Illustrious Greeks," in *Demon Entrepreneurs: Refashioning the 'Greek Genius' in Modern Times*, ed. Basil C. Gounaris and Ioannis D. Stefanidis (London and New York: Routledge, 2022), 128. The biography by Oistridis is quite short, contains several factual mistakes, and mentions events that cannot be confirmed by other sources.

4 Murat Birdal, *The Political Economy of Ottoman Public Debt: Insolvency and European Financial Control in the Late Nineteenth Century* (London: Tauris Academic Studies, 2010); Christopher Clay, *Gold for the Sultan: Western Bankers and Ottoman Finance, 1856–1881* (London and New York: I. B. Tauris, 2000); Nurhan Davutyan, "The Penetration of European Banking into Ottoman Lands During the Second Half of the Nineteenth Century," *Journal of Balkan and Near Eastern Studies* 25, no. 3 (2022): 322–39; M. Şükrü Hanioğlu, *A Brief History of the Late Ottoman Empire* (Princeton, NJ: Princeton University Press, 2008); Nurdan İpek, *Selanik ve İstanbul'da Yahudi Bankerler [The Jewish Bankers of Thessaloniki and Istanbul]* (İstanbul: Yeditepe Yayınevi, 2011); Huri Islamoğlu-Inan, *The Ottoman Empire and the World-Economy* (Cambridge: Cambridge

University Press, 1987); Reşat Kasaba, *The Ottoman Empire and the World Economy: The Nineteenth Century* (New York: Suny Press, 1988); Haydar Kazgan, *Galata Bankerleri Cilt I [The Bankers of Galata, vol. I]* (Ankara: Orion Yayınevi, 2005/1991); Haydar Kazgan, *Galata Bankerleri Cilt İİ [The Bankers of Galata, vol. II]* (Ankara: Orion Yayınevi, 2006); Emine Kıray, *Osmanlı'da Ekonomik Yapı ve Dış Borçlar [The Ottoman Economic Structure and Foreign Debts]* (İstanbul: İletişim Yayınları, 1995); Roger Owen, *The Middle East in the World Economy, 1800–1914* (London: I. B. Tauris, 1993); Sevket Pamuk, *A Monetary History of the Ottoman Empire* (Cambridge: Cambridge University Press, 2000). There is one relatively short mention of Syngros actions in Murat Hulkiender, *Bir Galata Bankerinin Portresi: George Zarifi [The Portrait of a Galata Banker: George Zarifi]* (İstanbul: Osmanlı Bankası Arşiv ve Araştırma Merkezi, 2003), 82–83.

5 Αγγέλου and Χατζηιωάννου, "Εισαγωγή," 31–32. Some of these works are Χρήστος Χατζηιωσήφ, "Εμπορικές παροικίες και ανεξάρτητη Ελλάδα: ερμηνείες και προβλήματα [Commercial Communities and Independent Greece: Interpretations and Problems]," *Ο Πολίτης* 62 (1983): 28–34; Γεώργιος Β. Δερτιλής, *Το ζήτημα των τραπεζών. Οικονομική και πολιτική διαμάχη στην Ελλάδα του ΙΘ΄ αιώνα [The Central-Bank Question. Economy and Politics in Nineteenth Century Greece]* (Αθήνα: Μορφωτικό Ίδρυμα Εθνικής Τραπέζης, 1989); Χάρης Εξερτζόγλου, *Προσαρμοστικότητα και πολιτική ομογενειακών κεφαλαίων. Έλληνες τραπεζίτες στην Κωνσταντινούπολη: Το κατάστημα "Ζαρίφης και Ζαφειρόπουλος," 1871–1881 [Adaptability and Policy of the Capital of Expatriate Greeks. Greek Bankers in Constantinople: The "Zariphis-Zapheiropoulos" Company, 1871–1881]* (Αθήνα: Ίδρυμα Έρευνας και Παιδείας της Εμπορικής Τράπεζας της Ελλάδος, 1989); Ioanna Minoglou Pepelasis, "Ethnic Minority Groups in International Banking: Greek Diaspora Bankers of Constantinople and Ottoman State Finances, C. 1840–81," *Financial History Review* 9, no. 2 (2002): 125–46; Μαρία Χριστίνα Χατζηιωάννου, "Εθνικοί ευεργέτες: Τα πρότυπα και η ιστορία τους. Από τους αδελφούς Ζωσιμά στον Ανδρέα Συγγρό [National Benefactors: Their Role Models and Their History: From the Zosima Brothers to Andreas Syngros]," in *Μνήμη Άλκη Αγγέλου. Τα άφθονα σχήματα του παρελθόντος* (Θεσσαλονίκη: University Studio Press, 2004), 401–12; Maria Christina Chatziioannou and Gelina Harlaftis, "From the Levant to the City of London: Mercantile Credit in the Greek International Commercial Networks of the Eighteenth and Nineteenth Centuries," in *Centres and Peripheries in Banking. The Historical Development of Financial Markets*, ed. Philip L. Cottrell et al. (London: Routledge, 2007), 13–40; Maria Christina Chatziioannou and Dimitris Kamouzis, "From a Multiethnic Empire to Two National States: The Economic Activities of the Greek Orthodox Population of Istanbul, Ca. 1870–1939," in *The Economies of Urban Diversity: Ruhr Area and Istanbul*, ed. Darja Reuschke, Monika Salzbrunn, and Korinna Schönhärl (New York: Palgrave Macmillan, 2013), 117–43; Katerina Galani, "The Galata Bankers and the International Banking of the Greek Business Group in the 19th Century," in *Istanbul and the Black Sea Coast: Shipping and Trade (1770–1920)*, ed. Edhem Eldem-Sophia Laiou (Istanbul: The Isis Press, 2018), 49–74; Catherine Bregianni, "Migrating Economic Identities in the Ottoman Empire: Regional Expressions of the Global Market in the Greek Banker's Andreas Syngros Autobiography," in *Population Displacements and Multiple Mobilities in the Late Ottoman Empire*, ed. Catherine Horel and Bettina Severin-Barboutie (Leiden and Boston: Brill, 2023), 147–70.

6 For a concise summary of this approach, see Basil C. Gounaris, "Greece, a Nation of Commercial and Other Geniuses in a State fir for Petty Traders and Poor Devils: An Introduction," in *Demon Entrepreneurs: Refashioning the 'Greek Genius' in Modern Times*, ed. Basil C. Gounaris and Ioannis D. Stefanidis (London and New York: Routledge), 2–3.

7 His father's name sounds Italian, so we could assume that his family must have been among the Catholic inhabitants of Chios and, at some point, became Orthodox Christians. Andreas Syngros and his brother Georgios do not have the same last name as

their father because at some point, they must had decided to "Hellenize" it. However, in Chios, his name continued to be pronounced as Tsingros.

8 Συγγρός, *Απομνημονεύματα*, I, 24, 27–29, 40, 43–44, 57.

9 Merih Erol, *Greek Orthodox Music in Ottoman Istanbul: Nation and Community in the Era of Reform* (Bloomington: Indiana University Press, 2015), 33.

10 Roderic H. Davison, *Reform in the Ottoman Empire, 1856–1876* (Princeton, NJ: Princeton University Press, 1963), 71–72, footnote 71.

11 Pamuk, *A Monetary History*, 203.

12 Συγγρός, *Απομνημονεύματα*, I, 138, 166, 170, 218–20, 281, 346.

13 Kasaba, *The Ottoman Empire and the World Economy,* 19. For more information on banking and trading in the 18th and early 19th centuries, see Sophia Laiou, "The Ottoman State and the Black Sea Trade, 18th—Beginning of the 19th Century," in *The Economic and Social Development of the Port-Cities of the Southern Black Sea Coast and Hinterland, Late 18th—Beginning of the 20th Century*, ed. Edhem Eldem, Sophia Laiou, and Vangelis Kechriotis (Corfu: The ISIS Press, 2017), 1–16; Σοφία Λαΐου, "Οθωμανοί Έλληνες Σαράφηδες στην Κωνσταντινούπολη του 1821 [Ottoman Greek Sarrafs (Moneychangers) in Istanbul in 1821]." *Μεσαιωνικά και Νέα Ελληνικά* 14 (2021): 217–38.

14 Συγγρός, *Απομνημονεύματα*, I, 121–22, 143–48.

15 At that time, the import of grain from North America had been quite modest and Russia was still the main source.

16 Συγγρός, *Απομνημονεύματα*, I, 138–41. Also see Helge Berger and Mark Spoerer, "Economic Crises and the European Revolutions of 1848," *The Journal of Economic History* 61, no. 2 (2001): 293–326.

17 Συγγρός, *Απομνημονεύματα*, I, 349–52.

18 Pamuk, *A Monetary History*, 205.

19 Birdal, *The Political Economy of Ottoman Public Debt*, 9.

20 Kasaba, *The Ottoman Empire and the World Economy,* 53.

21 Birdal, *The Political Economy of Ottoman Public Debt*, 24, 31–32.

22 Minoglou Pepelasis, "Ethnic Minority Groups in International Banking," 131–34.

23 The bill of exchange, alongside the bankers' draft and the letter of credit, had been the initial instruments through which capital was transferred between different localities. Among others, see Landes, *Bankers and Pashas,* 3–4; Edhem Eldem, *French Trade in Istanbul in the Eighteenth Century* (Leiden: Brill Publishing, 1999).

24 Anything above 10% was considered an adequate profit margin, while in very lucrative deals, such as the trade of silk cocoons to France in 1858–1861, their profit margin was similar to the one obtained by state loans.

25 Συγγρός, *Απομνημονεύματα*, I, 352–55.

26 Συγγρός, *Απομνημονεύματα,* II, 15–19, 28–29, 79; Minoglou Pepelasis, "Ethnic Minority Groups in International Banking," 130–31.

27 Συγγρός, *Απομνημονεύματα*, II, 158–59, 168, 174–79, 202–3, 317; Ibid., III, 6–7, 28–29.

28 *The Times* (London), December 16, 1880, 3–4: "The Financial Condition of Turkey."

29 Davutyan, "The Penetration of European Banking," 323–24.

30 Συγγρός, *Απομνημονεύματα,* I, 346–48; Ibid., II, 243–44.

Bibliography

Berger, Helge, and Mark Spoerer. "Economic Crises and the European Revolutions of 1848." *The Journal of Economic History* 61, no. 2 (2001): 293–326.

Birdal, Murat. *The Political Economy of Ottoman Public Debt: Insolvency and European Financial Control in the Late Nineteenth Century*. London: Tauris Academic Studies, 2010.

Bregianni, Catherine. "Migrating Economic Identities in the Ottoman Empire: Regional Expressions of the Global Market in the Greek Banker's Andreas Syngros Autobiography."

In *Population Displacements and Multiple Mobilities in the Late Ottoman Empire*, edited by Catherine Horel and Bettina Severin-Barboutie, 147–70. Leiden and Boston: Brill, 2023.

Chatziioannou, Maria Christina, and Gelina Harlaftis. "From the Levant to the City of London: Mercantile Credit in the Greek International Commercial Networks of the Eighteenth and Nineteenth Centuries." In *Centers and Peripheries in Banking. The Historical Development of Financial Markets*, edited by Philip L. Cottrell, Even Lange, Ulf Olsson, and Iain L. Fraser, 13–40. London: Routledge, 2007.

Chatziioannou, Maria Christina, and Dimitris Kamouzis. "From a Multiethnic Empire to Two National States: The Economic Activities of the Greek Orthodox Population of Istanbul, Ca. 1870–1939." In *The Economies of Urban Diversity: Ruhr Area and Istanbul*, edited by Darja Reuschke, Monika Salzbrunn, and Korinna Schönhärl, 117–43. New York: Palgrave Macmillan, 2013.

Clay, Christopher. *Gold for the Sultan: Western Bankers and Ottoman Finance, 1856–1881*. London and New York: I. B. Tauris, 2000.

Davison, Roderic H. *Reform in the Ottoman Empire, 1856–1876*. Princeton, NJ: Princeton University Press, 1963.

Davutyan, Nurhan. "The Penetration of European Banking into Ottoman Lands during the Second Half of the Nineteenth Century." *Journal of Balkan and Near Eastern Studies* 25, no. 3 (2022): 322–39.

Eldem, Edhem. *French Trade in Istanbul in the Eighteenth Century*. Leiden: Brill Publishing, 1999.

Erol, Merih. *Greek Orthodox Music in Ottoman Istanbul: Nation and Community in the Era of Reform*. Bloomington: Indiana University Press, 2015.

Galani, Katerina. "The Galata Bankers and the International Banking of the Greek Business Group in the 19th Century." In *Istanbul and the Black Sea Coast: Shipping and Trade (1770–1920)*, edited by Edhem Eldem-Sophia Laiou, 49–74. Istanbul: The Isis Press, 2018.

Gounaris, Basil C. "Greece, a Nation of Commercial and Other Geniuses in a State Fit for Petty Traders and Poor Devils: An Introduction." In *Demon Entrepreneurs: Refashioning the 'Greek Genius' in Modern Times*, edited by Basil C. Gounaris and Ioannis D. Stefanidis, 1–22. London and New York: Routledge, 2022.

Hanioğlu, M. Şükrü. *A Brief History of the Late Ottoman Empire*. Princeton, NJ: Princeton University Press, 2008.

Hulkiender, Murat. *Bir Galata Bankerinin Portresi: George Zarifi [The Portrait of a Galata Banker: George Zarifi]*. İstanbul: Osmanlı Bankası Arşiv ve Araştırma Merkezi, 2003.

İpek, Nurdan. *Selanik ve İstanbul'da Yahudi Bankerler [The Jewish Bankers of Thessaloniki and Istanbul]*. İstanbul: Yeditepe Yayınevi, 2011.

Islamoğlu-Inan, Huri. *The Ottoman Empire and the World-Economy*. Cambridge: Cambridge University Press, 1987.

Kasaba, Reşat. *The Ottoman Empire and the World Economy: The Nineteenth Century*. New York: Suny Press, 1988.

Kazgan, Haydar. *Galata Bankerleri Cilt I [The Bankers of Galata Volume I]*. Ankara: Orion Yayınevi, 1991/2005.

Kazgan, Haydar. *Galata Bankerleri Cilt İİ [The Bankers of Galata Volume II]*. Ankara: Orion Yayınevi, 2006.

Kıray, Emine. *Osmanlı'da Ekonomik Yapı ve Dış Borçlar [Ottoman Economic Structure and Foreign Debts]*. İstanbul: İletişim Yayınları, 1995.

Laiou, Sophia. "The Ottoman State and the Black Sea Trade, 18th—Beginning of the 19th Century." In *Istanbul and the Black Sea Coast: Shipping and Trade, 1770–1920*, Istanbul: The ISIS Press, 2018.

Minoglou Pepelasis, Ioanna. "Ethnic Minority Groups in International Banking: Greek Diaspora Bankers of Constantinople and Ottoman State Finances, C. 1840–81." *Financial History Review* 9, no. 2 (2002): 125–46.

Owen, Roger. *The Middle East in the World Economy, 1800–1914*. London: I. B. Tauris, 1993.

Pamuk, Sevket. *A Monetary History of the Ottoman Empire*. Cambridge: Cambridge University Press, 2000.

Vasileiou, Sotiroula. "Profiling the 'Greek Genius': Nineteenth-Century Biographies of Illustrious Greeks." In *Demon Entrepreneurs: Refashioning the 'Greek Genius' in Modern Times*, edited by Basil C. Gounaris and Ioannis D. Stefanidis, 125–38. London and New York: Routledge, 2022.

Δερτιλής, Γεώργιος Β. *Το ζήτημα των τραπεζών. Οικονομική και πολιτική διαμάχη στην Ελλάδα του ΙΘ΄ αιώνα*. Αθήνα: Μορφωτικό Ίδρυμα Εθνικής Τραπέζης, 1989. [Dertilis, George B. *The Central-Bank Question. Economy and Politics in Nineteenth Century Greece*. Athens: Cultural Foundation of the National Bank of Greece, 1989.]

Εξερτζόγλου, Χάρης. *Προσαρμοστικότητα και πολιτική ομογενειακών κεφαλαίων. Έλληνες τραπεζίτες στην Κωνσταντινούπολη: Το κατάστημα "Ζαρίφης και Ζαφειρόπουλος," 1871–1881*. Αθήνα: Ίδρυμα Έρευνας και Παιδείας της Εμπορικής Τράπεζας της Ελλάδος, 1989. [Exertzoglou, Haris. *Adaptability and Policy of the Capital of Expatriate Greeks. Greek Bankers in Constantinople: The "Zariphis-Zapheiropoulos" Company, 1871–1881*. Athens: Foundation for Research and Education of the Commercial Bank of Greece, 1989.]

Λαΐου, Σοφία. "Οθωμανοί Έλληνες σαράφηδες στην Κωνσταντινούπολη του 1821." *Μεσαιωνικά και Νέα Ελληνικά* 14 (2021): 217–38. [Laiou, Sophia. "Ottoman Greek Sarrafs (Moneychangers) in Istanbul in 1821." *Medievalia et Neohellenica* 14 (2021): 217–38.]

Οιστρίδης, Ε. Ι. *Ο Μέγας Εθνικός Ευεργέτης, Ανδρέας Συγγρός*. Εν Αθήναις: Εκ του Κεντρικού Βιβλιοπωλείου Δράκου Δ. Παπαδημητρίου, 1899. [Oistridis, E. I. *The Nation's Great Benefactor, Andreas Syngros*. Athens: Bookshop of Drakou D. Papadimitriou, 1899.]

Συγγρός, Ανδρέας. *Απομνημονεύματα*, introduction by Αγγέλου Άλκης, Χατζηιωάννου Μαρία Χριστίνα. Αθήνα: Εστία. Νέα Ελληνική Βιβλιοθήκη, 1998. [Syngros, Andreas. *Memoirs*, Introduction by Alkis Angelou and Maria Christina Chatziioannou. Athens: Hestia. New Greek Library, 1998.]

Συγγρός, Ανδρέας. *Απομνημονεύματα*, vols. I–III. Εν Αθήναις: Βιβλιοπωλείον της Εστίας, 1908. [Syngros, Andreas. *Memoirs*, vols. I–III. Athens: Hestia Bookshop, 1908.]

Χατζηιωάννου, Μαρία Χριστίνα. "Εθνικοί ευεργέτες: Τα πρότυπα και η ιστορία τους. Από τους αδελφούς Ζωσιμά στον Ανδρέα Συγγρό." In *Μνήμη Άλκη Αγγέλου. Τα άφθονα σχήματα του παρελθόντος*, 401–12. Θεσσαλονίκη: University Studio Press, 2004. [Chatziioannou, Maria Christina. "National Benefactors: Their Role Models and Their History: From the Zosima Brothers to Andreas Syngros." In *Memoriam of Alkis Angelou: The Abundant Shapes of the Past*, 401–12. Thessaloniki: University Studio Press, 2004.]

Χατζηιωσήφ, Χρήστος. "Εμπορικές παροικίες και ανεξάρτητη Ελλάδα: ερμηνείες και προβλήματα." *Ο Πολίτης* 62 (1983): 28–34. [Chatziiosif, Christos. "Commercial Communities and Independent Greece: Interpretations and Problems." *O Politis* 62 (1983): 28–34.]

Part 4

Land Possession and Entrepreneurship

12 Capital and Wealth in the Ottoman Balkans at the Turn of the 19th Century

Some Evidence From Salonica

Yücel Terzibaşoğlu

Introduction

Social and economic origins of wealth, and inequality in the generation and distribution of wealth have been issues central to the founding and critique of classical political economy ever since the 18th century. It is no coincidence that Adam Smith's 1776 book was titled "The Wealth of Nations," whereas the critique of that political economy was called "Capital." Since then, the difference between the two concepts has remained fundamental in socially and historically contextualizing wealth. Karl Marx argued that not any stock of wealth—be that land left unattended or gold under the pillow, and so on—was capital, for capital was first and foremost a social relationship that required certain historical and social relations to sustain and generate itself. This critique reflected a concern to prioritize the generation of wealth (rather than the ex-post distribution of it), and the dynamics that gave rise to wealth accumulation which were inherently inequality-generating, irrespective of how that wealth was then distributed.

In the same spirit, this chapter aims to differentiate between wealth and capital in our historical understanding of the social and economic dynamics of the Ottoman Balkans at the turn of the 19th century. Following an initial clarification of the terms such as wealth, income, capital, surplus, and so on, historical evidence from turn-of-the-19th-century Salonica will be used to analyze the social and economic conditions of wealth generation and distribution at this part of the empire. It will conclude with some long-term consequences of such dynamics.

In recent studies on wealth and inequality, a similar difference of perspective to that outlined above has become manifest. Mainstream approaches generally tend to emphasize how initial—almost inevitable—wealth differences and inequalities tend to smooth themselves out as "economic growth" accelerates (the Kuznets Curve), reproducing a variation of the modernization school arguments of the 1950s.[1] In contrast, there have been strong arguments based on historical and contemporary global data on how wealth inequalities perpetuate themselves in a vicious cycle of wealth accumulation and ever more wealth and income inequality, rather than its correction, through economic growth.[2]

In looking at flows (rather than stock) of income and potential sources of capital in a historical business enterprise, this chapter will depart from recent studies

DOI: 10.4324/9781003500780-17

of Ottoman wealth which seem to prefer the first approach outlined above. The article will treat the economic activities of one patrician household in Salonica as a business enterprise and will analyze the annual (for the year 1765) income and expenses related to a plethora of economic activities of the household members. As such, it will be deliberately blind to assumed peculiarities of the setting (e.g., Eastern versus Western business practices or ethnic and/or religious division of labor, etc.) and will analyze the budget for what it is, that is, a summary account of business activities and flows of money in and out of a gentry household's business concerns. It is not that such peculiarities may be unimportant (for understanding the class structure and social dynamics of the turn of the century Salonica, for one thing). Rather, it seems that such assumptions (very common in mainstream historiography, whether arising consciously or unconsciously) have been over-emphasized in contemporary historical studies to such an extent that a singular focus on such assumed cultural attributes has distracted attention from some fundamental features of the region's capitalist transformation and the integration of its study into a comparative perspective with other parts of the world, not to speak of the rest of the Eastern Mediterranean, the entire Mediterranean world, or eastern Europe.

Wealth and Capital in Salonica: The Numan Paşa Household

Numan Paşa was the head of a vizirial household in Salonica, with his brothers, sons, and their wives holding substantial urban and rural properties in and out of the city (in fact, in several other places in the empire). He served in many administrative and military posts in different parts of the empire throughout his lifetime until his death in 1753.[3] The accounting documents found in the Ottoman archive's Central Accounting Department (*Baş Muhasebe Kalemi*) in İstanbul indicate the status of the family (as the descendants of a bureaucrat-administrator-soldier). What is more important for the present purposes is that these accounting books, containing budgets of the domestic household as well as its business concerns in and around Salonica, were documented in such a way that we not only have the personal income and wealth of family members made clear but also possess knowledge of a joint family/household income and wealth of a patrician family, as a single unit.[4] The data therefore are in important ways more comprehensive, and reflect a different logic of compilation, than the probate inventories or inheritance records issued after the death of taxable subjects of the empire, a data source that has been used exclusively in studies of wealth.[5] One of the important ways the data here differ from probate inventories is that, being income and expenditure statements of the household enterprise, they show flows of money rather than stock of assets, unlike in the probate inventories. The importance of the difference between flows and stock cannot be overemphasized in that the flows of money show us the dynamics of investment preferences and the accumulation of capital and the sources of surplus. This understanding is rather difficult, if not impossible, to discern in an inventory of asset stocks frozen at the time of death (the completeness of which is itself in some doubt as the relevant literature indicates).

There is one potential complication here in that sole reliance on money transactions assumes a fully monetarized economy and thus may conceal the potential for capital accumulation in the "natural economy" (non-monetized transactions such as sharecropping contracts).[6] The dual nature of the late 18th-century Balkan rural economy will be discussed at the end of the article. Accordingly, the overall intention here will be to try to figure out the logic behind the family enterprise, that is, whether or not a political logic (in other words, non-capitalist concerns) prevailed over the economic (capitalist) concern of profit making and capital accumulation, and also what were the potential obstacles facing the latter option, even if profit making was intended.

The sources of wealth for the household consisted of a portfolio of income-generating assets the family members, characteristically similar to many other wealthy families, possessed: rent extraction from urban real estate and rural landholdings, involvement in credit networks and relations, agriculture, and animal husbandry. The overall income and expenses of the household in the year 1765 are given in Table 12.1.

Urban Property and Rent

In urban Salonica, the family held both residential and commercial urban property. Residential property included three mansions (the "konak," the "saray," and the house of the *kadın efendi*). One of the mansions was next to the mosque and its public bath, together with a public fountain in another part of the city, the maintenance of which was undertaken by the family, and which most probably was part of a *vakıf*—indeed, the connection of the family with the Evrenos family and its extensive urban and rural *vakıf* properties requires further research.

Commercial property in the city was made up of a large number and variety of shops, warehouses, manufactories, and other business and residential premises which were all rented out. The urban rent collected from such real estate (in 57 units) came to an annual total of 353,512 akçes. The highest rents were collected from the sheepfolds in the city (13,200 akçes), the mill (7,200 akçes), linseed oil press (10,800 akçes), 2 *hans* (36,000 akçes each), the public bath (13,200 akçes),

Table 12.1 Total budget (in akçes) for 1765.

	Income	*Expenses*	*Profit/–Loss*
Urban rent	353,512	140,737	212,775
Interest	28,042	174,000	–145,958
Animal husbandry	14,750	65,000	–50,250
Agriculture (*çiftliks*)	688,604	397,996	290,608
Household expenses	–	575,861	–575,861
Total	1,084,908	1,353,594	–268,686
	Receivables	Payables	Balance
Loan/debt	504,804	1,410,840	–906,036

and various konaks that were rented out to private individuals and to the local city administration (116,000 akçes). The range of real estate included manufactories (oil presses and mills, carpenters, silk workshops), khans (three in different locations in the city), coffee houses, warehouses, artisanal shops (barbers, tailors, shoemakers), one public bath, and two vegetable gardens within the city (*bostan*). Some of these urban properties were leased by the family mostly in the form of *mukataa* (tax farm) and from various *vakıfs* (e.g., the khans, various shops, and the vegetable gardens). These properties, with nominal rents, were then sublet. The total rent the family paid for these leased properties amounts to an annual total of 18,950 akçes for the same year. The accounting for the real estate in the city shows that in addition to the nominal rent, the family spent 121,787 akçes for the upkeep and maintenance of the real estate portfolio, leaving a net profit of 212,775 akçes from the real estate business.

Credit Network and Debt

The family extended credit to village communities (to a total of 5 villages) and to Greek communal leaders from the *vakıf* of the mosque they held, at the nominal interest rate of 5.5 per cent. The total loans extended from this source amounted to 171,000 akçes (with an annual expected interest income of 9,500 akçes), a standard amount of18,000 akçes was extended to each village, and an amount of 45,000 akçes was loaned to the Greek communal leaders on an annual basis. Additionally, there were the loans extended individually by family members to the cultivators at the *çiftlik*s the family held: Abdurrahman Bey loaned 45,000 akçes to cultivators at the Sene *çiftlik* (with 2,500 akçes in interest); Hamide Hanım extended 27,000 akçes (with 1,500 akçes in interest) to the Kireç *çiftlik* and 36,000 akçes to the Ravne *çiftlik* (with 2,000 akçes in interest); Zübeyde Hanım gave 33,804 akçes to the Kireç *çiftlik* inhabitants (with 1,878 akçes in interest) and 18,000 akçes to the Zagliver *çiftlik* (with 1,000 akçes ins interest); Sadullah Bey extended 12,000 akçes to the Tona *çiftlik* cultivators (with 664 akçes in interest) and 18,000 akçes to the Zagliver *çiftlik* (with 1,000 akçes in interest); Fatma Hanım gave 45,000 akçes to the Galaca *çiftlik* (with 2,500 akçes in interest); Dilaver Kadın 18,000 akçes to the Edremelde *çiftlik* (with 1,000 akçes in interest); Zeyneb Hanım 63,000 akçes to the Gölge *çiftlik* (with 3,500 akçes in interest); Zeliha Hanım 18,000 akçes to the Gölge *çiftlik* (with 1,000 akçes in interest). These loans extended individually amounted annually to a total of 333,804 akçes with an expected interest income of 18,542 akçes (calculated at a 5.5% interest rate). Overall, the total loans extended amounted to 504,804 akçes, with a total expected interest income of 28,042 akçes.

The loans borrowed by the family within the year, in contrast, had considerably higher and variable interest rates. There were four loans from money lenders totaling l,410,840 akçes with interest rates ranging from around 10% (three loans) to 20% (one loan). This borrowing and its cost were substantially higher (nearly three times) than the amount of the loans extended (and the interest income from) to the rural and urban communities in and around Salonica by the family. The interest payable on the loans totaled 174,000 akçes (more than six times the interest income). Accordingly, the family had accrued a net total debt of 906,036 akçes within a single year.

Household Expenditures

The reason for this debt at least partly lay in the high household expenses. The total expenses of the household members came to a substantial amount of 575,861 akçes, complete with a banquet at the Zagliver *çiftlik* (5,072 akçes). In addition to monthly food expenses averaging 7,750 akçes, there were lump sum expenses of the women of the household (Hamide Hanım 5,780 akçes, Zekiye Hanım 32,750 akçes, etc.), for the purchase of female slaves (28,000 akçes), public bath expenses (38,500 akçes), and 83,910 akçes for various clothing items. The total wage bill for the domestic servants, housekeepers, and clerks came to a total of 2,880 akçes in the year for the family. Most of the expenses indicate a level and type of consumption reflecting a patrician family's status, prestige, and the need for the demonstration of the same, with plenty of ceremonial effects. In addition, the charitable functions the family had committed themselves to for public works in the city should also be taken into account. The costs of maintaining and running public baths, fountains, and mosques (as listed above) should also be added to the almost compulsory prestige expenditures of the family, which taken together must have diminished the funds available for investment in agricultural production or urban property.[7]

Animal Husbandry

One other business activity is animal husbandry. From a general perspective as an enterprise that connected rural (landed estates, winter and summer pastures, barns, and associated labor force) and urban (sheepfolds in the city, transport, production of wool, processing of hides, and sale of the same), the family was losing money. Total expenses (excluding the purchase of oxen for the *çiftlik*s) included the rent paid for winter and summer pastures for the sheep, the cost of fodder, and the wages of the shepherds, which amounted to a total of about 65,000 akçes. The revenues from the sale of wool and hides were only 14,750 akçes, representing a total annual loss of 50,250 akçes.

Rural Rent and Agricultural Production

In rural Salonica, the Numan Paşa family held and directly operated a total of seven *çiftlik*s in the vicinity of Salonica in the 1760s. There are indications (common use and transfer of seed, stock, animals, and labor force between them) in the budgets (Table 12.2) prepared for these seven *çiftlik*s that they were managed and operated not as individual units but as a single enterprise. The power of the landowner family, however, reached well beyond these seven *çiftlik*s since, as indicated above, they also extended loans to at least five more *çiftlik*s and their cultivators as well as to other villages, which might signal contractual arrangements for the purchase of

Table 12.2 *Çiftlik* budgets in 1765 (in akçes).

Year 1181 (1765)	*estate1 Sana*	*estate2 Zagliver*	*estate3 Kireç*	*estate4 Böemtçe*	*estate5 Sungurlar*	*estate6 Durmuşlu*	*estate7 Langaza*
1. Income in money	59,494	249,930	89,825	80,917	94,015	31,115	83,308
2. Expenditure in money	31,583	69,614	130,141	51,655	39,351	33,543	42,109
3. Profit in money (1–2)	27,911	180,316	–40,316	29,262	54,664	–2,428	41,199
4. Annual profit rate per akçe expended (3/2)	0.88	2.59	–0.30	0.57	1.39	–0.07	0.99

the produce. There are further indications of rural land acquisitions (through purchase and/or debt bondage) by the family in the hinterland of Salonica, as will be discussed in the following. Taken together, therefore, the credit relations and other landed interests suggest that the family's involvement with rural land was much more extensive than the direct operation of seven *çiftlik*s, most probably extending their landholdings and control over the peasantry through sharecropping contracts which do not show up in the budgets, as these last were prepared primarily to show monetary flows of income and expenditures.

Even in this monetary form alone, the *çiftlik* operation seen as a unified enterprise was the single highest earner for the family, the annual income from the landed estates even exceeding the total rent from urban property holdings. Total income from the operation of the seven *çiftlik*s reached 688,604 akçes in the year 1765, with a total profit of 290,608 akçes, after the deduction of total expenses of 397,996 akçes. Yet a closer look at the individual *çiftlik*s making up the whole *çiftlik* enterprise and the profitability of the enterprise produces a different picture.

Two out of the seven *çiftlik*s were in the red in 1765: Kireç *çiftlik* made a loss of 40,316 akçes (this appears to be primarily a mining estate with a large limestone quarry, and hence its agricultural operations were secondary), and Durmuşlu a loss of 2428 akçes. The *çiftlik* with the highest profit in money was Zagliver with 180,316 akçes (note that this is the *çiftlik* where a feast was held). What is more significant than a simple comparison of cash income and outlays is the profitability of the *çiftlik*s as a business enterprise. The annual profit rate per akçe expended (profit in money/expenditure in money)[8] exceeds one (profitable) in only two of the *çiftlik*s (Zagliver and Sungurlar), the rest of the *çiftlik*s are not profitable enterprises (the annual profit rate per akçe expended being less than one). On average, taking the seven *çiftlik*s as one enterprise, the profitability falls to a rate of 0.86, showing an overall loss-making enterprise in terms of profitability. One striking feature in the cost structure of the *çiftlik*s is the high level of labor costs (wages) in the total expenses of the landed estates. For those five (out of the seven) *çiftlik*s where wage labor is used, the total labor costs (including wage labor in agriculture and animal husbandry as well as for transport and construction works) in three of them is about half to three-quarters of total costs. Only in two *çiftlik*s, does the wage bill fall to about one-fifth of the total expenses. Another major expenditure item at least for some individual *çiftlik*s is the total taxes paid to the state which range from

3.6% of total expenditures to 60%. Note also that where wage labor cost is higher the tax burden seems to be lower. This link between labor form (wage labor) and taxes suggests a trade-off in the choice of the type of labor employed in the estate (for there were both wage laborers and sharecroppers employed), but this opinion requires further research to establish the reasoning of the trade-off.

What is more evident, however, is the positive relationship between profitability and the recourse to sharecropping as the dominant labor form employed in the estates. A comparison of the income structure of the two estates, the profitable Zagliver *çiftlik* (with 2.59 profit rate per akçe expended), and the Langaza *çiftlik* (Table 12.3), which was just about floating (with 0.99 profit rate per akçe expended) show that when cultivation was carried out by sharecroppers the total agricultural income from the sale of produce in the estate (mostly wheat) made up 59% of the total revenues. In Langaza, where there were no sharecroppers and cultivation was carried out through wage labor, the share of total agricultural income in total income of the estate was less than half (42%), the rest coming from lease income (of houses, gardens, mulberry trees, etc.). In the absence of sharecroppers,

Table 12.3 Comparison of income and expenditure of Zagliver and Langaza *çiftlik*s in 1765 (in akçes).

	Zagliver	*Langaza*
Income		
Agricultural income from sale of wheat	73,733 52% of total agr. income; 29% of total income	27,988 79% of total agr. income; 34% of total income
Total agricultural income	140,730 56% of total income	35,278 42% of total income
Income from lease	37,200 15% of total income	46,320 56% of total income
Money rents (from tenant cultivators)	72,000 29% of total income	
Service fees collected		1,710
Total income	249,930	83,308
Expenditure		
Compulsory provisions and taxes	69,614	726
Wage labor		17,198
Shepherds		3,920
Transporters		2,874
Other wage labor		1,020
Repair costs		3,213
Agricultural implements		1,742
Construction labor		1,800
Purchase of oxen		3,000
Provisions to laborers		2,965
Total wage labor		29,777 71% of total expenditures
Total expenditures	69,614	42,052
Profit/loss	180,316	41,256

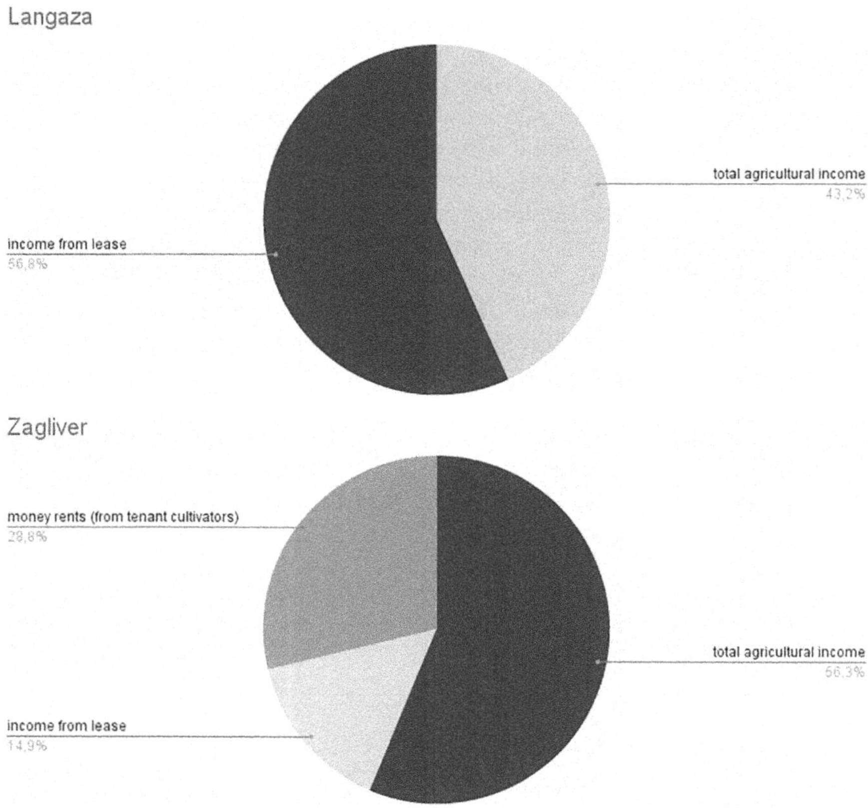

Figure 12.1 Comparison of income structures of Zagliver and Langaza *çiftliks*.

the landowner seemed to have switched to monopoly rent extraction in the face of high-wage labor costs (Figure 12.1).

Indeed, a land register[9] from the year 1773, which listed the lands for three interconnected *çiftliks* belonging to Numan Paşa (Büyük *çiftlik*, Alaca Hıtay, and Küçük *çiftlik*) in Langaza shows the outline of a pattern of acquisition or appropriation of peasant land by the landlord. Each plot of land (mostly fields) listed in the register under each *çiftlik* was described with the names of landowners of the surrounding fields as well as with geographical markers. The register also occasionally specified the names of peasant household heads or other landowners that that particular parcel of land was acquired from. In the land register, the piecemeal acquisition of land is apparent in the patchy layout of the *çiftliks*. In other words, the *çiftlik* was not a unified piece of land on the lines of a plantation or a farm, but rather, was an agglomeration of separate parcels of land of different magnitude, over which the landlord exercises different forms of control.[10] The evidence points to a process of consolidation of these separated plots of land into a larger (and in time most probably, a more uniform) estate. In fact, the process very much looks like an outright process of enclosure on the ground. It should also be noted that the fact that one part of the consolidated estates was referred to as the *beylik çiftlik* (or the demesne) points toward such a process of consolidation. Consolidation of land in this context therefore appears to be the landowner's solution to low profitability in the direct operation of the land. Unable to increase the surplus from agrarian production (low profitability), the landowner turned to agglomeration of ground rent and maximizing his monopoly rent extraction as an alternative strategy of agrarian surplus accumulation.

Conclusion

Land turns out to be by far the most important form of capital among the sources of wealth (other potential sources being rent from urban property and credit) for this urban patrician family. Given the importance of agricultural land as capital, it is no wonder that urban-based families of different levels of wealth accumulated more and more agricultural land in the countryside at this time. We know that it was not only elite families who were investing heavily in agricultural land then. Many urban dwellers, wealthier peasants, and *vakıf*s had roots in the countryside and invested in land also. Land ownership in the countryside was a substantial source of rent extraction and capital accumulation. What worked against this patrician family in the further accumulation of land and capital was the level of household conspicuous consumption and other charitable functions the family had assumed through the *vakıf*s. The dilemma was that that level of consumption was in fact necessary in order that the family members could maintain their social and economic status through securing their continued share in the political distribution of economic resources such as property grants (e.g., *mukataa*) and possibly rural and urban *vakıf* properties. This situation was further complemented by their apparent lack of control over credit and finance. Access to credit was also crucial for securing the award of state contracts for cheap land and urban property. This as we saw led to indebtedness in the face of high interest rates charged by the money lenders.

In this respect, from a long-term perspective, wealth was thought of as rural and urban surpluses, and their accumulation was structurally difficult to maintain, let alone expand, within the social and political context to which the family owed its wealth and status. In other words, given the social and economic constraints (high levels of politically motivated consumption, high levels of debt, high wage labor costs), it looked like it was difficult, if not impossible, to have an investible surplus above subsistence levels through the retained earnings of estates (agrarian profit), and landed and urban property income (ground rent).

It may be worth taking an overview of the studies on wealth in Ottoman history at this point. In the recent secondary literature, wealth is usually taken to be the stock of assets listed in the probate inventories or inheritance records of wealthy deceased persons whose inventories were taken through and recorded by the kadı court. Although there is ample appreciation that such inventories may be lacking and deficient in many ways, they are still used to make generalizations, given the assumed absence of alternative data sources especially amenable for constructing datasets. Yet these admitted deficiencies are disregarded once the dataset is constructed and it is then almost taken for granted that the only source of wealth for the individual concerned might be the list recorded by the court.

In addition to this general problem in the use of data in model building which is by now characteristic of "new economic history," a yet more substantial problem arises when wealth understood as stock of assets is conflated with capital and income. As a result, with some notable exceptions, there has been remarkably little interest (or possibility of finding out, because of the nature of the data source used) in what the wealth actually consisted of, on its nature, and how it might have accumulated within a specific historical and geographical context. In other words, wealth remains a "black box," an abstraction divorced from the society within which it was generated, as if wealth is a pre-cooked dish, existing in a vacuum. The remedy to this is to focus on individuals, groups, localities, and regions, without however falling into various forms of cultural relativisms or parochialisms, and try to relate these more focused analyses to larger trends and contexts, general patterns, and problems.

The last point is pertinent for this chapter as well: to what extent are the economic activities of the Numan Paşa family, an old patrician family, representative of the general trends in the capitalist development or underdevelopment of the region, for example? The fact that land consolidation at the expense of small peasant ownership was one of the means open to the family intent on pursuing a potentially profitable agrarian production in wheat for the market, combined with sharecropping as an increasingly dominant labor form, suggests comparisons and potential paths of development. On the one hand, pre-capitalist landed property and labor forms (bonded labor) combined with agricultural production for the market, represent an eastern European path.[11] And on the other hand, the creation of a scattered landed-estate pattern by urban landholders at the expense of an independent small peasantry, dominated by a "sharecropping landscape," represents a southern European path.[12] At the turn of the century Salonica, there were indeed urban-based and profit-oriented entrepreneurs active economically both in the town and in the countryside with links to finance and to merchant and industrial capital.[13] Which, if either, of these two paths proved feasible or possible, and so was taken up under the given social and economic context at the turn of century in the region is the subject of further research.

Archives

Başbakanlık Osmanlı Arşivi (Prime Ministry Ottoman Archives) (BOA), Istanbul, Turkey

D.BŞM.d 3478, 3895, 3962, 4168, 4193, 4358, 4437, 5673, 41337

D.BŞM.MHF.d 12640

D.HSK.d 25779

Notes

1 More recently, Jan Luiten van Zanden ("Tracing the Beginning of the Kuznets Curve: Western Europe During the Early Modern Period," *Economic History Review* 48, no. 4 (1995): 643–64) introduced a modification of this classic formulation, arguing that since "modern economic growth" predated the Industrial Revolution (i.e., "the industrious revolution") wealth inequalities were to be expected in pre-industrial societies also. There are some studies carried on Ottoman wealth data which use the Kuznetsian argument as amended by van Zanden in a more nuanced and somewhat critical spirit, for example, see Boğaç A. Ergene, Atabey Kaygun, and Metin M. Coşgel, "A Temporal Analysis of Wealth in Eighteenth-Century Ottoman Kastamonu," *Continuity and Change* 28, no. 1 (2013): 1–26; Hülya Canbakal, "Reflections on the Distribution of Wealth in Ottoman Ayntab," *Oriens* 37 (2009): 237–52. Yet the van Zanden amendment does not touch on the essence of the argument which assumes linearity of economic growth given the right institutional fix, it merely pulls the whole process earlier in time from the industrial to the pre-industrial period. The implication for the present context of this modification is the unspectacular argument that wealth inequalities are also to be expected under conditions of stagnant growth.

2 Thomas Piketty, *Capital in the Twenty-First Century* (Cambridge: Harvard University Press, 2014).

3 His inheritance record could be found in BOA (Ottoman Archives) D.BŞM.MHF.d 12640. He is referred to as the governor of the Province of Salonica (Selanik Sancağı Mutasarrıfı Numan Paşa) in the document. His connection to the Evrenos dynasty is highly likely.

4 The budgets and income and expenditure statements used in this article are compiled from the following documents: BOA D.BŞM.d 3478, 3895, 3962, 4168, 4193, 4358, 4437, 5673, and 41337.

5 Works which in different ways used the inheritance records (tereke defterleri) are too numerous to be listed fully here but start with the pioneering works of Ömer L. Barkan, especially, "Edirne Askeri Kassamı'na ait tereke defterleri (1545–1659) [The Inheritance Registers of the Edirne Military Inheritance Officials (1545–1659)]," *Belgeler* 5–6 (1966): 235–377. For a selective sample, in no particular order, see—in addition to the two works cited in footnote 1: Rossitsa Gradeva, "Towards a Portrait of 'the Rich' in Ottoman Provincial Society: Sofia in the 1670s," in *Provincial Elite in the Ottoman Empire*, ed. Antonis Anastasopoulos (Rethymno: Crete University Press, 2006), 152–63; Şevket Pamuk, "Osmanlı Zenginleri Servetlerini Nasıl Kullanıyorlardı [How the Ottoman Rich Used their Wealth]," in *Osmanlı Ekonomisi ve Kurumları, Seçme Eserler I* (Istanbul: İş Bankası Kültür Yayınları, 2007), 147–54; Nicolai Todorov, "La différenciation de la population urbaine au XVIII s., d'aprè des registres de cadis de Vidin, Sofia et Ruse. La ville balkanique XV-XIX siecles," *Studia Balcanica* 3 (1970): 45–62; Hristiyan Atanasov, "Property Trends among the Urban Population of Rumelia in the 18th Century as Indicated by Inheritance Inventories from Russe, Sofia and Vidin—a First Glance," *Bulgarian Historical Review* 41, no. 3–4 (2013): 33–59. And, of course, for Salonica, there is the extensive work of D. Papastamatiou who studied the 18th century inheritance records from Salonica (the inheritance records of the household of the present study are not recorded among these): Dimitris Papastamatiou and Phokion Kotzageorgis, "Wealth Accumulation in an Urban Context. The Profile of the Muslim Rich of Salonica in the 18th Century," *Turkish Historical Review* 5, no. 2 (2014): 165–99; Dimitris Papastamatiou, *Wealth Distribution, Social Stratification and Material Culture in an Ottoman Metropolis. Thessaloniki According to the Probate Inventories of the Muslim Court (1761–1770)* (Istanbul: The ISIS Press, 2017); Ibid., "The Structure, the Content and the Development of Large Estates in the Environs of Salonica During the Period 1697–1770," in *Festschrift in Honor of Ioannis P. Theocharides. II. Studies on the Ottoman Empire and Turkey*, ed. Evangelia Balta, Georgios Salakidis, and Theoharis Stavrides (Istanbul: The ISIS Press, 2014), 375–402.

6 Witold Kula, *An Economic Theory of the Feudal System: Towards a Model of the Polish Economy, 1500–1800* (London: NLB, 1976).

7 Richard Busch-Zantner, "Agrarverfassung," in *Gesellschaft und Siedlung in Südosteuropa unter besonderer Berücksichtigung der Türkenzeit (Beiheft zur dreiziger Viertels jahrschrift für Südosteuropa, 3 dio, Leipzig 1938, VI. str. 158)* (Leipzig: Otto Harrassowitz, 1938), 46–47.

8 Here I adopt the profitability calculation of W. Kula on Polish landed estates. Kula, *An Economic Theory*.

9 BOA D.HSK.d 25779.

10 This evidence on a patchy *çiftlik* pattern coincides with Papastamatiou's findings on the *çiftlik* formations in the Salonican countryside at this time, which he describes as "ensemble of land parcels" (Papastamatiou, "The Structure," 378).

11 Johannes Nichtweiss and Gwyn Seward, "The Second Serfdom and the So-Called 'Prussian Way': The Development of Capitalism in Eastern German Agricultural Institutions," *Review (Fernand Braudel Center)* 3, no. 1 (Summer 1979): 99–140.

12 Giuliana Biagioli, "The Evolution of Property Rights in Tuscany, from the End of the Middle Ages to the Nineteenth Century," in *Contexts of Property in Europe: The Social Embeddedness of Property Rights in Land in Historical Perspective*, ed. Rosa Congost and Santos Rui (Turnhout: Brepols Publishers, 2010), 61–82. In fact, the Tuscan sharecropping landscape has striking parallels with the *çiftlik* pattern in the Salonican countryside (both in terms of the dominance of sharecropping and the increasing investment in land of a new urban landholding class). See Papastamatiou, "The Structure." A similar pattern is also observed by S. Laiou in Thessaly; see Sophia Laiou, "Some Considerations Regarding Çiftlik Formation in Western Thessaly, Sixteenth-Nineteenth Centuries," in *The Ottoman Empire, the Balkans, the Greek Lands: Toward a Social and Economic History. Studies in Honor of John C. Alexander*, ed. Elias Kolovos, Phokion Kotzageorgis, Sophia Laiou, and Marinos Sariyannis (Istanbul: The ISIS Press, 2007), 255–78.

13 For a recent analysis discussing these links, see Costas Lapavitsas and Pinar Çakıroğlu, *Capitalism in the Ottoman Balkans: Industrialization and Modernity in Macedonia* (London: I. B. Tauris, 2019).

Bibliography

Atanasov, Hristiyan. "Property Trends among the Urban Population of Rumelia in the 18th Century as Indicated by Inheritance Inventories from Russe, Sofia and Vidin—a First Glance." *Bulgarian Historical Review* 41, no. 3–4 (2013): 33–59.

Barkan, Ömer L. "Edirne Askeri Kassamı'na ait tereke defterleri (1545–1659) [The Inheritance Registers of the Edirne Military Inheritance Officials (1545–1659)]." *Belgeler* 5–6 (1966): 235–377.

Biagioli, Giuliana. "The Evolution of Property Rights in Tuscany, from the End of the Middle Ages to the Nineteenth Century." In *Contexts of Property in Europe: The Social Embeddedness of Property Rights in Land in Historical Perspective*, edited by Rosa Congost and Santos Rui, 61–82. Turnhout: Brepols Publishers, 2010.

Busch-Zantner, Richard. "Agrarverfassung." In *Gesellschaft und Siedlung in Südosteuropa unter besonderer Berücksichtigung der Türkenzeit (Beiheft zur dreiziger Viertels jahrschrift für Südosteuropa, 3 dio, Leipzig 1938, VI. str. 158)*. Leipzig: Otto Harrassowitz, 1938.

Canbakal, Hülya. "Reflections on the Distribution of Wealth in Ottoman Ayntab." *Oriens* 37 (2009): 237–52.

Ergene, Boğaç A., Atabey Kaygun, and Metin M. Coşgel. "A Temporal Analysis of Wealth in Eighteenth-Century Ottoman Kastamonu." *Continuity and Change* 28, no. 1 (2013): 1–26.

Gradeva, Rossitsa. "Towards a Portrait of 'the Rich' in Ottoman Provincial Society: Sofia in the 1670s." In *Provincial elite in the Ottoman Empire*, edited by Antonis Anastasopoulos, 147–97. Rethymno: Crete University Press, 2006.

Kula, Witold. *An Economic Theory of the Feudal System: Towards a Model of the Polish Economy, 1500–1800.* London: NLB, 1976.

Laiou, Sophia. "Some Considerations Regarding Çiftlik Formation in Western Thessaly, Sixteenth-Nineteenth Centuries." In *The Ottoman Empire, the Balkans, the Greek Lands: Toward a Social and Economic History. Studies in Honor of John C. Alexander*, edited by Elias Kolovos, Phokion Kotzageorgis, Sophia Laiou, and Marinos Sariyannis, 255–78. Istanbul: The ISIS Press, 2007.

Lapavitsas, Costas, and Pinar Çakıroğlu. *Capitalism in the Ottoman Balkans: Industrialization and Modernity in Macedonia.* London: I. B. Tauris, 2019.

Nichtweiss, Johannes, and Gwyn Seward. "The Second Serfdom and the So-Called 'Prussian Way': The Development of Capitalism in Eastern German Agricultural Institutions." *Review (Fernand Braudel Center)* 3, no. 1 (Summer 1979): 99–140.

Pamuk, Şevket. *Osmanlı Ekonomisi ve Kurumları, Seçme Eserler I [The Ottoman Economy and its Institutions, Collected Works I].* Istanbul: İş Bankası Kültür Yayınları, 2007.

Papastamatiou, Dimitris. "The Structure, the Content and the Development of Large Estates in the Environs of Salonica During the Period 1697–1770." In *Festschrift in Honor of Ioannis P. Theocharides. Studies on the Ottoman Empire and Turkey*, edited by Evangelia Balta, Georgios Salakidis, and Theoharis Stavrides, 375–402. Istanbul: The ISIS Press, 2014.

Papastamatiou, Dimitris. *Wealth Distribution, Social Stratification and Material Culture in an Ottoman Metropolis. Thessaloniki According to the Probate Inventories of the Muslim Court (1761–1770).* Istanbul: The ISIS Press, 2017.

Papastamatiou, Dimitris, and Phokion Kotzageorgis. "Wealth Accumulation in an Urban Context. The Profile of the Muslim Rich of Salonica in the 18th Century." *Turkish Historical Review* 5, no. 2 (2014): 165–99.

Piketty, Thomas. *Capital in the Twenty-First Century.* Cambridge: Harvard University Press, 2014.

Todorov, Nicolai. "La différenciation de la population urbaine au XVIII s., d'après des registres de cadis de Vidin, Sofia et Ruse. La ville balkanique XV-XIX siècles." *Studia Balcanica* 3 (1970): 45–62.

Van Zanden, Jan Luiten. "Tracing the Beginning of the Kuznets Curve: Western Europe During the Early Modern Period." *Economic History Review* 48, no. 4 (1995): 643–64.

13 Çiftlik Holdings in Western Anatolia

The Karaosmanoğlu Family and the Baltazzi Family in the 18th–19th Centuries[1]

Alp Yücel Kaya

Introduction: *Çiftlik* Holdings and a New Entrepreneurial Class

The "*Çiftlik* debate" is one of the important and fundamental topics in the sphere of Ottoman economic history. It is centered on three approaches that seek to interpret the formation of *çiftlik*s.[2] The first is the Marxist approach that sees the formation of *çiftlik*s as a transition from feudalism to capitalism with the formation of capitalist entrepreneurship and wage labor.[3] The second involves the theory of peripheralization following the theoretical premises of the World-System Theory: this associates the emergence of *çiftlik*s with the impetus of foreign trade in the capitalist world system and the re-organization of agricultural production by means of the enserfment of peasants on large-scale holdings.[4] The third approach, the Ottomanist theory that takes issue with the first two approaches, emphasizes the internal dynamics in the formation of *çiftlik*s: the "breakdown" of the *timar* system and the subsequent emergence of the *mukataa-iltizam* system that generated the tax-collecting entrepreneurs who established private property on miri or mevat lands.[5] We would like here to focus on the entrepreneur *çiftlik* owner, who cuts across all three approaches. Thus, it is the entrepreneurial *çiftlik* ownership, emerging first in the 18th century, which İnalcık puts down to a combination of different factors, that is our starting point:

> Along with their control as lease-holder of the lands under the old *çift-hane* system, the *ayan*s also emerged as a new type of "entrepreneur" in land reclamation and expansion of plantation-like farms. They were economically motivated to maximize their revenues under both the impact of an expanding external market, and under the pressure of pecuniary needs in order to sustain their position as tax farmers and heads of local mercenary forces.[6]

This "new type of entrepreneur" in pursuit of investment and profit is none other than the capitalist who came to rule the countryside through agricultural production. Stoianovich similarly discusses the transformation of the *Grundherr*, whose military duties were at the forefront rather than his economic activities, into the *Gutsherr*, who, conscious of his economic activities, turned the land within the

DOI: 10.4324/9781003500780-18

estate he controlled into his own property in the 17th and 18th centuries.[7] Gandev also emphasizes the emergence of capitalist *çiftlik* owners who, in addition to agricultural production, invested in real estate in the urban space in the 18th century, established commercial companies for grain exports, invested in shipping and product warehouses, and were also active in credit markets. According to Gandev, who also takes into account the dispossession of the peasant population, what happened in Vidin in the 18th century is not much different from what happened in England in the 17th century![8]

The chapter will examine the *çiftlik*-holding entrepreneurs in Western Anatolia in the 18th and 19th centuries. Unlike the studies that have so far focused on a particular period, region, or an entrepreneurial family through one specific set of archival material, we will examine two prominent families, Karaosmanoğlu and Baltazzi, who rose as successive big *çiftlik* holders in Western Anatolia. To do so, first, we will analyze in a more detailed way the character of the new entrepreneurs and the subsequent transformation in the class configuration of the Ottoman governing classes. In the later part of the article, we will study the histories of the Karaosmanoğlu and then the Baltazzi families, with a special focus on their *çiftlik*-holding practices.

Transformation in Class Configuration in the 18th and 19th Centuries

As is agreed in the literature on Ottoman economic history concerning the emergence of a new "entrepreneurial" class in the Ottoman Empire in the 18th century,[9] entrepreneurship was not something new in the Ottoman territories; what was new in the 18th century was the change in the nature of the entrepreneur. The new entrepreneurial class, coming mostly from among the local notables and created by the tax-farming system, began to overtake the old entrepreneurial class, which in the 15th–18th centuries had consisted of the ruling classes associated with the central bureaucracy. These old and new entrepreneurs did not develop independently of each other; what tied them together, especially the latter set, was the proliferation of the tax farming and the *malikâne* systems that emerged when some *mukataa*s began to be farmed out on a lifetime basis. "The *malikâne* owners were a group of bureaucrats, soldiers and ulemas, the majority of whom resided in Istanbul, numbering around 1,000, and whose connection with the central authority was close to the point of identity."[10] However, the owners of the *malikâne* did not undertake the management of the *mukataa* themselves, but farmed them out; in this way, the tax farmers in the system consisted of the notables of the provinces in the *mukataa* region, working within multi-layered subcontracting relationships and networks. One pole of this relationship is composed of a capitalist class in the making, which we would call bourgeois-bureaucrats (composed of pashas depending on the central bureaucracy and being in office either in the center or in the provinces), whose "connection with the central authority was close to the degree of identity." The other pole is composed of yet another capitalist class in the making, which we would call the provincial bourgeoisie (composed of local notables coming from local dynasties or parvenus), which develops as a "new type of entrepreneur" in the provinces. In sum, the tax-farming system played a decisive role in the transformation of the entrepreneurial classes and the emergence of the bourgeoisie in the Ottoman territory. However, this system, which made capitalist development possible, also harbored intra-class conflict dynamics within the emerging capitalist classes.[11] The dynamics of the conflict and struggle between them are quite clearly revealed by Mehmet Genç:

> As a highly integrated social group identified with the central authority and capable of acting jointly in terms of unity of interests, communication and solidarity, the owners of the *malikâne*, determined their proportional share of the tax revenue at the end of a struggle with the tax-farmer notables, another group that had influence in local social relations and made extensive use of this influence in terms of efficiency in taxation, such as knowing the region, receiving information and being able to use appropriate personnel cheaply. [12]

The first effective intervention of the bourgeois-bureaucrats to regain the economic and political power that was slipping out of their hands was the reforms introduced under the heading of *Nizam-ı Cedid* at the end of the 18th century. In this, the large and highly profitable *mukataa*s were removed from the *malikâne* system, and at the same time, an attempt was made to prevent the second-hand farming out of *mukataa*s. It should also be stressed that the number of *çiftlik*s gradually began to increase among the *mukataa*s that were seized and administered by the Imperial Treasury in the 1780s.[13] In this way, both the economic resources of the provincial bourgeoisie began to shrink and a new investment portfolio (consisting of *çiftlik*s) for the bourgeois-bureaucrats began to emerge. This development ensured that investments of the bourgeois-bureaucrats in *çiftliks* would be especially significant in the *Tanzimat* period starting from 1839. These and similar unsettling interventions resulted in the mobilization of the provincial bourgeoisie and the signing of a settlement called the *Sened-i İttifak* in 1808, which emphasized their partnership with the central power. This power partnership was short-lived as Bayraktar Mustafa Paşa, who served as the grand vizier and the representative of provincial bourgeoisie, was killed in the uprising that broke out in the same year. Afterward, the interventions of bourgeois-bureaucrats became more dominant.

The real blow to the notables in the provinces came with the granting of *mukataa*s to the bourgeois-bureaucrats. The *mukataa*s, the control of which was transferred to the central treasury, began to be granted to centrally appointed governors, trustees, and voivodes from 1811 to 1839.[14] The process that began with *Nizam-ı Cedid* should also be seen as the bourgeois-bureaucrats changing their skins. In the seventeenth and eighteenth centuries, the entrepreneurial bourgeois-bureaucrats dependent on the "households" of viziers and pashas and who rose through the ownership of *malikâne* were replaced by individual bourgeois-bureaucrats who rose through farming out *mukataa*s (and holding *esham*s).[15] As a result of this process,

> the central state and those acting on its behalf, which became the sole distributor of all tax-farms in the first half of the 19th century, succeeded in controlling to a great extent the rents previously received by the *malikâne* owners and provincial notables.[16]

However, as this control was not fully achieved, the bourgeois-bureaucrats declared (with the Edict of Gülhane in 1839) that the system of tax-farming was "nothing but injustice and cruelty . . . for those who look after their own interests." By abolishing the system in 1839, they essentially cut off the branch they themselves were sitting on. Of course, the fiscal and financial crisis of 1840–1842 led to a compromise with the political situation, and tax farming was reintroduced in 1842, again under the reins of the bourgeois-bureaucrats.[17]

Capitalist development specific to the Ottoman lands was dependent on the financial sector accessed through public finance. In this context, we should not forget the banker-merchants who played a key role in the tax-farming system and financed the investments of the bourgeois factions. However, the banker-merchants representing the financial bourgeoisie remained in the shadow of other bourgeois factions. The struggle was primarily between the bourgeois-bureaucrats and the provincial bourgeoisie, and the fate of the banker-merchants depended on whom they cooperated in the struggle for power.

It could be argued that the intra-class struggle was between the urban and rural bourgeoisie, if one accepts that the bourgeois-bureaucrats and financial-commercial bourgeoise were associated with urban capital and the provincial bourgeoisie with rural capital. Nevertheless, as both factions engaged in tax farming, we argue that urban and rural characters of bourgeois factions became blurred; to conquer and survive the provincial bourgeoisie had to urbanize itself, just as the bourgeois-bureaucrats and financial-commercial bourgeoisie needed provincial connections to succeed.

Within this context defined by the dynamics of uneven and combined development, we distinguish first the *Nizam-ı Cedid* period and reforms in the Ottoman Empire at the end of the 18th century and then the *Tanzimat* period and reforms in 1839 as manifestations of intra-class conflict. After 1839, the *Tanzimat* period emerged as a period in which the competition within the bourgeoisie increased in intensity and the bourgeois-bureaucrats along with the financial-commercial bourgeoisie attempted to suppress the competing bourgeois faction in the provinces. At this point, we will concentrate on Western Anatolia where the Karaosmanoğlu family represented *par excellence* the provincial bourgeoisie and the Baltazzi family the financial-commercial bourgeoisie in close collaboration with the bourgeois-bureaucrats.

Karaosmanoğlu Family

The Karaosmanoğulları is the name of a well-known *ayan* family that dominated Western Anatolia, especially during the 18th century of the Ottoman Empire. The family of Karaosmanoğlu originated from Yayaköy from the *kaza* of Manisa.[18] According to the *muhallefat defteri* of 1644, the family was managing oil mills and engaging in farming by employing male and female slaves, and in husbandry and transportation activities by means of camels.[19] Mehmed Çavuş (?–1644), in whose name a house was registered in 1630, was the first member to appear in the archives.[20] His son, Kara Osman (?–1706), was in 1666 the *emin* of *mukataa* of Bahadırlı that was connected to the *mukataa* of the vakıf of Mosque of Murad II. Being the *kethüda* of the Rodoslu Ali Ağa and *Beyt-ül Mal-i Amme*, and the *emin* of the *mukataa* of the *Hassa* of Manisa in 1676, he became responsible for the registration of the *cizye* of the Greeks of İzmir and Aydın in 1687.[21]

After the death of Kara Osman in 1706, his eldest son, Hacı Mustafa Ağa, already the *emin* for the *Beyt ül Mal-i Amme* and for the *mukataa* of the Hassa in Manisa, was appointed in 1743 as the *mütesellim* of Saruhan where he remained in office until 1755.[22] During this period, he had strengthened his political, economic, and social influence over the entire *sancak* through farming out of the *mukataa* of *bedel-i sancağ-ı Saruhan.* This comprised for the most part of the *mukataa*s, *timar*s, *zeamet*s, and *çiftlik*s of the *sancak* on the one hand and on the other of the *mukataa*s of *Koru-ı Cebel-i* Manisa and Turgutlu, comprising several *timar*s and *zeamet*s in the Gediz plain. The first *mukataa* was owned as *malikâne* by Yeğen Ali, the *arpa emini* of the Topkapı Palace and future *vali* of the Anadolu and Rumeli provinces, and by his partners; the other *mukataa*s were held as *malikâne* by the İvaz Paşazade Halil Ağa, future grand vizir, and his partners; it was Hacı Mustafa Ağa who sub-contracted both.[23]

Farming out *timar* and *zeamet* villages in the Gediz plain led the Hacı Mustafa Ağa (and other successive members of the family) to convert some of them into *çiftlik*s.[24] The *muhallefat defterleri* of 1755 and 1756, in registering the wealth of Hacı Mustafa Ağa, provides detailed data about two such converted *çiftlik*s, Durasallı and Yeni. In the *çiftlik* of Durasallı, there worked seven female and three male slaves (probably in addition to sharecroppers) using 10 farm instruments and 15 plows to cultivate in particular cotton and to a certain extent sesame; they also bred and maintained 69 horses, 25 donkeys, 93 water buffalos, and 157 bovines. In the Yeni *çiftlik*, there were also slaves (whose number was not recorded) to cultivate cotton, operate two olive oil mills, and look after 96 horses, 18 donkeys, and 355 bovines. Although they were not recorded within these *çiftlik*s, it is worth noting that Hacı Mustafa Ağa had also 4,766 sheep and 667 goats in the *Koru-ı Cebel-i Manisa* which consisted of mainly coppices and pastures: this was a way of encroachment practiced by the *çiftlik*s (already existing or in the making).[25]

Hacı Mustafa Ağa was executed in 1755 by a Sultan's edict issued, based on complaints that were sent from local inhabitants to İstanbul claiming ongoing over-taxation. An edict issued in 1756 tells us though that the over-taxation was closely tied into the fierce struggle between Hacı Mustafa Ağa and the *malikâne* owner Yeğen Ali Paşa over the revenues of *bedel-i sancağ-ı Saruhan.* Hacı Mustafa Ağa, who farmed out the *mukataa* in question by engaging to pay an amount that would triple the value of the tax farming held by Yeğen Ali Paşa, actually collected an amount that quadrupled it.[26] Mustafa Ağa's execution did not, however, interrupt the family's influence in the region. His eldest son, Ataullah Ağa, succeeded soon after in farming out *bedel-i sancağ-ı Saruhan* and therefore becoming *mütesellim* of Saruhan. Nevertheless, in 1761, he was dismissed for conflict with local notables and seditions committed during his term of office. Among these events, his dispute with Araboğlu was based on his intrusion on the *mukataa* of Mamaklı village that was sub-contracted by the *voyvoda* of Menemen from *voyvoda* of Bergama, namely, Araboğlu himself. The central government also dispatched a punitive force against Ataullah Ağa after his conflict with Araboğlu, who had also played a part in bringing about his father's execution. Ataullah Ağa was defeated in the subsequent struggle and died in 1766 a fugitive, pursued by the forces of the government.[27] The wealth of Ataullah was then subject to confiscation; the real property and *çiftlik*s held by him, together with animals, produce, and tools found in them, were, however, not sold but farmed out (in addition to *timar*s he had farmed out himself) under the supervision of *mütesellim* of Manisa. The *muhallefat defteri* of Ataullah Ağa registered, in addition to *çiftlik* of Durasallı and Yeni *çiftlik* inherited from his father, the *çiftlik*s of Papaslı, Mihail and Burunören, all found as were the others in the Gediz plain within the *Koru-ı Cebel-i Manisa*.[28] In these three *çiftlik*s, cereal cultivation and animal husbandry (250 bovines, 60 horses, 80 camels) were dominant; wıth 15,000 sheep, sheep breeding was also significant.[29]

Despite the government's continuous declarations to prohibit the grant of *iltizam* right and the office of *mütesellim* to the Karaosmanoğlu family, yet soon after the death of Hacı Mustafa Ağa and Ataullah Ağa, the government was forced (in the context of war with Russia) to grant the family again both the right and the office. The headship of the family soon afterward passed to Hacı Mustafa Ağa's other son, Ahmed Ağa, who succeeded in 1769 in becoming *voyvoda* of İzmir and then in 1773 *mütesellim* of the sancak of Saruhan.[30] His successors as *mütesellim* of Saruhan were (Kara Mütesellim) Hacı Mehmed Ağa (nephew of Hacı Mustafa Ağa) between 1776 and 1796 and then Hacı Hüseyin Ağa (son of Ahmet Ağa) between 1796 and 1816.[31]

Although the wealth of Ataullah Ağa had been confiscated and his *çiftliks* farmed out to bidders, from the analysis of *muhallefat* defterleri, we learn that his brother Hacı Ahmet Ağa regained the possession of the *çiftliks* of Mihaili and Burunören and his son Hacı Osman Ağa, voyvoda of Menemen, and his grandsons, Ebubekir Ağa and Ali Ağa, that of the *çiftlik* of Papaslı and Yeni *çiftlik*.[32] Research by Nagata does not give information on the faith of the *çiftlik* of Durasallı, but the *temettüât defter*s of 1845 let us know that the *çiftlik* felt under the control of the Tavaslızade's, a notable family reigning in Denizli and Menteşe region.[33] From this circulation of *çiftlik* holdings, we argue that the tax farming and the office correlated with it had control over the *çiftlik* holding and not vice versa. Behind such hegemony, there is first a political motive: in the context of the intra-class struggle, only if you continued as a tax farmer and an officeholder, did you obtain enough political power to be able to hold firmly onto your property; otherwise, your possession became very fragile. Second, there is a motive partly political, partly economical: tax farmers became almost the sole creditor in the region where they operated in such a way as to establish their political and economic authority.[34]

Third, there is a purely economic motive: tax farming was economically more profitable than *çiftlik* holding; for example, the profit that Hacı Hüseyin Ağa got from tax farming was almost two times higher than that from *çiftlik* holding.[35]

Nagata categorizes four paths in the formation of *çiftliks*: formation of *çiftliks* in the *timar* villages; purchase of *çiftliks* from another notable family; formation of *çiftliks* on the common lands (coppices and pastures); and formation of *çiftliks* on farming out the vakıf lands.[36] Just as the second and third paths were entrepreneurial operations of an economic nature, so the first and fourth paths were consequent on and the result of tax-farming operations. To sum up, tax farming was *sine qua non* at the heart of *çiftlik* formation and its operation.

After the Russian War of 1787–92, the Karaosmanoğlu family not only governed the sancak of Saruhan but its sphere of influence was also enlarged as far as Aydın in the south and Bergama in the north. Various members of the family became, respectively, *mütesellim* of Aydın and Isparta and *voyvoda*s of Turgutlu, Menemen, Bergama, and Gelenbe. When the *Sened-i İttifak* was signed in Istanbul in 1808 between Sultan Mahmut II and *ayan*s in Anatolia and the Balkans, Hacı Ömer Ağa (nephew of Hacı Mustafa Ağa), who had ended the rule of the Araboğulları in Bergama by being made the *voyvoda* of Bergama in the 1780s, represented the family at the agreement. According to Nagata, the period when Hacı Ömer Ağa (*voyvoda* of Bergama between the 1780s and 1812) and Hacı Hüseyin Ağa (*mütesellim* of Saruhan between 1796 and 1816) were in office was the zenith for the Karaosmanoğlu family both from the political and economic standpoints. Farming out *mukataa*s going with the offices of *mütesellim* and *voyvoda* led the family members to enlarge their investment in *çiftlik*s within and beyond the Gediz plain.[37]

As Nagata underlines, in contrast to the dominant argument in Ottoman historiography that privileges investments of urban capital in the formation of *çiftlik*s, in the case of Karaosmanoğlu family, it was the wealth generated in the rural areas that was channeled to the urban, and not vice versa.[38] In other words, it was not financial-commercial capital generated in the sphere of exchange, but that of agrarian capital generated in the sphere of production that was steering the economic activities of the family. Nevertheless, as we discussed above, owing to the particularities of the economic and political evolution of the Ottoman society, investments in *çiftlik*s definitely needed the protection afforded by financial-commercial (i.e., tax farming) and political (i.e., office holding) capital. Otherwise, such productive investments were suffocated largely by financial-commercial-political investments.

At the turn of the 18th century, the political ascendance of the Karaosmanoğlu family was accompanied by an amplification in the number of *çiftlik*s in which they invested. Looking closer at the *çiftlik*s, according to the *muhallefat* defteri of Hacı Hüseyin Ağa dated 1816, some observations can be made: as the value of one *dönüm* of land is equivalent of one to two sheep, the sheep is therefore more valuable in the market than the land is.[39] In total terms, the value of *çiftlik*s was nearly equivalent to the value of total number of sheep and goats[40]; the value of agricultural produce (cotton and cereals) was nearly double that of income raised from the animals (excluding the income from produce—cheese and other milk products—of animals bred in the *çiftlik*s as there is no information on them).[41] In the three *çiftlik* where cotton was cultivated, the cultivated area dedicated to cotton (13.2%) was limited compared with that given over to cereal (86.6%)[42]; oil mills (26) and olive groves (29,671 trees) recorded as vakıf investments of the Karaosmanoğlu family were also remarkable.[43] In the context of suffocation of productive investments, what was striking was the imposing dominance exercised by sheep and goat breeding and olive and olive oil production over the other agricultural products.

After the death of Hacı Ömer Ağa in 1812 and Hüseyin Ağa in 1816, the central government intended to confiscate the properties they left and to utterly destroy the family's influence in the region. No other member of the family was appointed in their place, but, instead, the posts regressed to the government. In 1829 though, a rebellion led by Atçalı Kel Mehmed struck the Aydın province; to repress the disturbance, the central government appointed Küçük Mehmet Ağa to the post of *mütesellim* of Saruhan and Hacı Eyüp Ağa to the post of *voyvoda* of the Tire district in Aydın province.

The attenuation in the economic and political power of the family was closely linked to the transformation of *malikâne* and *mukataa* system. The *Nizam-ı Cedid* reforms increasingly transferred the control of *mukataa*s to the central treasury that then started to grant tax units not in wholesale (as *malikâne*s) but in retail (as *mukataa*s and even as *eshams*); in this new context, the Karaosmanoğlu family lost their quasi-monopoly control over tax units in the region where they were paramount.[44] Additionally, starting from 1811, the central treasury began to grant *mukataa*s to centrally appointed governors, trustees, and voivodes.[45] Such a transfer impacted directly on the economic and political power of the provincial bourgeoise whose power was based primarily on tax farming. In this context, we observe that the Karaosmanoğlu family, to continue the tax-farming activities, choose to hold onto power, but as officials dependent now on the central bureaucracy.[46]

Yetim Ahmed Ağa was the first member of the family who worked as an official in the Ottoman provincial bureaucracy: he was *mütesellim* of Isparta in 1822, *voyvoda* of Bolu and Viranşehir in 1824, *mütesellim* of Antalya in 1825, and *muhassıl* of Aydın in 1830. It was Hacı Eyüp Ağa who replaced him in Aydın to continue work as an official in the provincial bureaucracy. In 1833, Hacı Eyüp Ağa became *mütesellim* of Manisa and two years later achieved the rank of *İstabl-i amire müdürü*; he was *muhassıl* of Manisa between 1839 and 1842 and died in 1845 while he was the *kaymakam* of Aydın. His brother Yakup Paşa who was many times *vali* of Aydın (1833–6, 1841, 1845–7) was appointed to the governorship of Rumeli in 1842; when he died in 1854, he was the governor in Jerusalem. His son, Sadık Bey, was at various times *kaymakam* of Aydın and, like his father, became *İstabl-i amire müdürü*. With his death in 1861, the influence of the Karaosmanoğlu family in the *sancak*, already weakened, faded altogether.[47]

According to the *muhallefat defteri* of 1861, Sadık Bey had 6,089 sheep and nine *çiftliks* (Burunören, Mütevelli, Koldere, Çobanisa, Karaağaçlı, Çavuşoğlu, Tatar, Hasırcı, and Kıylı). The *çiftliks* of Mütevelli and Koldere passed to his son Arif Bey upon the death of Karaosmanoğlu Sadık Bey in 1861. When Arif Bey, who seems to have been a spendthrift without any occupation, wanted to sell them to pay off his debts owed to various merchants, it was a merchant family from

Izmir, the Cousinery family, who demanded the *çiftliks* in settlement of what was owed. But the family later declined its offer. In the 1870s, Grand Vizier Rüşdü Paşa bought the *çiftliks* and then sold them to the Balyozyans, another merchant and industrialist family of Izmir, about 15 years later. One year after this sale, in 1889, the *çiftliks* were bought by the *Hazine-i Hassa Nezareti*.[48]

The Baltazzi Family

In 1862, Spiridone Baltazzi (son of Manolaki Baltazzi) bought the estate called Tatar, from Arif Bey, son of Karaosmanoğlu Sadık Bey, in the Sart (Sardis) district of the Saruhan province.[49] In the same year, he bought the *çiftlik* of Makaronya (composed of 28,000 dönüm) in the Dikili district from Kulaksız and Karaosmanoğlu families.[50] These two investments in landed estates signaled the shift in power in rural Izmir: The Karaosmanoğlu family, which had ruled the region since the 18th century, was replaced by the Baltazzi. It should be noted, however, that the Baltazzis as entrepreneurs began acquiring landed property by purchase as early as the 1840s. According to 1845 *temettüât defterleri*, Manolaki Baltazzi, an "esteemed merchant" (*tacir-i müteberan*) was the "owner of the estate" (*ashab-ı çiftlikat*) of Arap Çiftliği (composed of 5,000 dönüm of land); he leased an additional land of 1,500 dönüm and also 500 sheep.[51] He was also the "owner of the estate" of the Ali Ağa Çiftliği, neighboring Arap Çiftliği. He held 2,600 dönüm of cultivated land, 1,000 dönüm of fallow land, 1,200 dönüm of pasture and 500 sheep, and in the company of his two associates Hacı Mehmed Ağa and Hasan Ağa, held 3,200 dönüm of sharecropped cultivated land, 900 dönüm of fallow land and 200 sheep.[52]

A testimonial from 1856 provides information on the acquisition of Arap Çiftliği and Ali Ağa:

> The farm of Arab-Tchiftilick was purchased by the father of the present proprietor, fifteen years ago, for £ 1000. It contains about ten thousand acres, four thousand of which are now in cultivation. There are two villages on the estate- on the south and the other on the north side of a promontory; the population of the two together is about fifteen hundred. The village on the north side is the more flourishing on account of its position, it being situated on the shores of the Bay of Ali-Agha.[53]

Comparing the surface areas owned over time (9,800 dönüm in 1845 and 40,000 dönüm in 1856) tells us that the *çiftliks*' lands had almost quadrupled. The hypothesis is that Manolaki Baltazzi bought the land he leased from Arap Çiftliği, that of Hacı Mehmed Ağa and Hasan Ağa (and probably that of many others), as well as additionally undertaking land clearing.

An account from 1856 also tells the story of the purchase of a large estate on the Menemen plain, one controlled largely by the members of Karaosmanoğlu family:

> There are now in cultivation about 40,000 acres. A great part of this plain [Menemen] belongs to the family of Baltazzi, who have laid out much

money in redeeming it from the inroads of the sea. They purchased the land ten years ago at 30 s. an acre; it is now worth £ 10 and yields a good rental to the proprietor.[54]

Temettüât Defterleri tells us that, by 1840, Manolaki Baltazzi (a 50-year-old, Austro-Hungarian subject, living in Izmir's commercial heartland, the Kasab Hızır district) was well established in the city. He had a hotel opening onto the sea (*frenkhane*) with three stores on the first floor, a house with a shoemaker's store on the first floor, a stable in a han, a han (*rumhane)*, and five stores in his house.[55] The same goes for his brother Yorgaki (45), who had a house, a garden, nineteen warehouses, four stores, and a stable in the same district, but in different locations.[56] They exported olive oil from Izmir to Marseille in the 1830s and 1840s, and the stores and warehouses were used by their own trading house.[57] Dimitri Baltazzi (32 years old) was also in the same neighborhood but had no property other than his residence.[58] Based in Marseille, his trading house depended on that of Izmir.[59]

On the contrary, Theodoraki Baltazzi was one of Istanbul's great financiers (*sarraf*), advancing considerable sums to the tax authorities for customs and market duties in İzmir in 1840[60] and for tithes in the provinces of Aydın in 1841.[61] As a financier, he resided in Istanbul and had two associates in Izmir, his brothers Manolaki and Yorgaki. The two Smyrniot merchants in turn provided bills of exchange to the provincial administration for the transfer of revenues to the central treasury in 1841.[62]

The history of the Baltazzi family is closely linked to the history of tax farming in the Ottoman Empire of the *Tanzimat*. Events followed one another swiftly during the Baltazzis' accelerated rise: although tax farming was denounced and abolished following the *Tanzimat* tax reforms of 1839, all reforms failed in the face of the financiers' order. Tax revenues remained blocked, and a financial crisis broke out in 1841. The leasing system was reintroduced in 1842, but its management was entrusted to two companies, the Company of Anatolia, made up of seven financiers, and the Company of Rumelia, made up of six financiers; it is worth noting that Theodoraki Baltazzi was a member of the Company of Rumelia.[63] Having such a hegemonic position in finance, the Baltazzis developed an entrepreneurial spirit during the decades of 1840 and 1850, obtaining almost every year the lease of the customs and market duties of Izmir and the *öşr* (notably those of olive oil) of most of the western provinces of Anatolia.

It should be noted that merchants were indeed part of the tax-farming circuit. Indeed, as local agents of the tax farmers, they were an essential part of the fiscal and economic chain: taxes were often paid in kind, and it was the merchants who collected, stored, and transported the products concerned. Yet, with the vertical integration of their businesses, the Baltazzi's entrepreneurship is exceptional. The financier, the tax farmer, and the merchant were all part of a single family or trading house; they advanced capital to the tax authorities to acquire a locality's tax farms, collected taxes on the ground, and engaged in the commerce of olive oil collected in kind.

In the early 1870s, the heyday of the Baltazzi business that had begun in the early 1840s began to come to an end. We posit that the acceleration in their rise was made possible by their alliance with the reformist party personified in the *Tanzimat* bourgeois-bureaucrat trio, Mustafa Reşid Paşa, Fuad Paşa, and Ali Paşa. This trio assumed the office of prime minister several times and governed the Ottoman Empire in an almost hegemonic manner between 1839 and 1871 (the death of the last living member of the trio, Ali Paşa). They were heavily involved in the business world and were representatives *par excellence* of the bourgeois-bureaucrats; the biggest name of the *Tanzimat*, the leader of the trio, Mustafa Reşid Paşa owned several estates in the Empire.[64] What evidence is there of their relationship with the Baltazzi? Looking for a suitable landed property to grant to Lamartine in 1850, Mustafa Reşid Pacha turned directly to Manolaki Baltazzi, who offered him his *çiftliks* in Tire.[65]

The fact that the Baltazzis, as Austro-Hungarian subjects, had almost no administrative and legal problems acquiring the leasing of *öşr* and various rights and also landed property in urban and rural spaces between 1839 and 1871 leads us to conclude that they were also collaborators and protégés of the *Tanzimat* trio. But the atmosphere changed in the 1870s: first Manolaki Baltazzi's obligations, then those of Theodoraki and Aristide, began to preoccupy the family: this situation lasted for a long time to come. In 1874, the Ministry of Foreign Affairs asked for Manolaki's debt obligations, dated 1850.[66] Worse still, by the 1880s, this type of obligation led them to lose their agrarian roots in the Izmir hinterland. Aristid Baltazzi lost his *çiftliks* in Tire and in Torbalı. It was *Hazine-i Hassa Nezareti* who appropriated them.[67] In conclusion, capitalist entrepreneurship has no chance of survival if political power does not support it, particularly in the countryside.

Conclusion

The conflict among the bourgeoisie intensified between 1839 and 1871, the bourgeois-bureaucrats together with merchants and banker-merchants as part of their inner circle (an example par excellence is the Baltazzi family) left their mark on the period in keeping with their economic interests. The tax-farming system still played a key role at this point, but the important factor that facilitated the investments of this class in the provinces was that the central administration by the end of the 18th century started to seize the *çiftlik*s held by the notables. These *çiftlik*s, called "imperial *çiftlik*s" (*çiftlikât-ı hümayun*), were auctioned or sold to suitors by the Ministry of Finance; they began to constitute an important investment portfolio, especially with the seizure of Tepedelenli Ali Paşa's *çiftliks* in the 1820s. When dividing the intra-bourgeoisie struggle into phases, it would be more accurate to extend the period from the 1820s to 1876, taking in the beginning of Abdülhamid II's rule. The Sultan took the *çiftliks*, usually controlled by the bourgeois-bureaucrats, under his own hand by means of the Ministry of Sultan's Treasury (*Hazine-i Hassa Nezareti*). The Ministry no longer tendered out the *çiftliks* as it had done in the past but began to operate them under its own management, removing them as a source of income for the bourgeois-bureaucrats. However, the Ministry was not content with this and expanded its *çiftlik* portfolio by adding new ones. In this context, one should note well that the Sultan's Treasury seized in the 1880s many of the *çiftliks* of the Baltazzi family who had close relationships with the bourgeois-bureaucrats and also those once held by Karaosmanoğlu family. Behind Abdülhamid II's policy of taking the *çiftliks* into his control and extending them was the crucial need to cut off the economic leg of a possible political rival. Furthermore, in the period after the 1870s, the Ministry of Finance started to farm out of the *öşr* revenues to smaller units and local tax farmers.[68] Such a change in the direction of tax farming dealt a blow to the financial bourgeoisie (banker-merchants) and the bourgeois-bureaucrats allied with them. Thus, the economic base of the pashas, both through the Sultan's Treasury and the tax farming of *öşr* revenues, almost dried up. 1876 then is the date that spells the end to the investments of the bourgeois-bureaucrats. The dominance of the financial bourgeoisie, in collaboration with the bourgeois-bureaucrats, was extinguished with the establishment of the Ottoman Public Debt Administration in 1881 (when foreign capital began to control domestic and foreign borrowing in Ottoman public finance, following the debt default in 1875). Thus, an era in the intra-class struggle came to a complete end.

On the contrary, as the Sultan's *çiftliks* expanded after 1876 and the tenders for the tax farms changed addresses, the provincial bourgeoisie began to gain relative strength from the elimination of their competitors and the opening up of a new investment area for themselves. Their ranks tightened with the inclusion of the newly emerging entrepreneurs among them. In the period after 1876, the landowning groups were joined by those who flourished within the commercial bourgeoisie and by foreign capitalists seeking investment opportunities in different places. Both capitalist groups carved out an important place for themselves, especially with the increasing agricultural investments in Western Anatolia.[69]

Archives

Başbakanlık Osmanlı Arşivi (BOA), Istanbul, Turkey

A.M. 3/95

A.O. HR.H 379/15

A.O. HR.H 495/8

A.O. *Kamil Kepeci Tasnifi, Muhassıllık Defterleri*, 5789 (14 March 1841–24 March 1842)

A.O. Maliye Nezareti Mektubi Kalemi Defterleri, 25 (3 March 1840-14 September 1840)

A.O. ML.VRD.TMT 1486

A.O. ML.VRD.TMT 16115

A.O. ML.VRD.TMT 1940

A.O. ML.VRD.TMT 2028

A.O. MVL 848/34

Notes

1 The research for this article is funded by a grant from TÜBİTAK (Project entitled "Çiftlik Holding and Its Transformation in the Western Anatolia, 1740–1914", no 219K145, 2020–2023).

2 Gilles Veinstein, "Çiftlik Tartışması Üzerine [On the Çiftlik Debate]," in *Osmanlı Toprak Mülkiyeti ve Ticari Tarım*, ed. Çağlar Keyder and Faruk Tabak (İstanbul: Tarih Vakfı Yurt Yayınları, 1998), 36–38.
3 Christov Gandev, "L'apparition des rapports capitalistes dans l'économie rurale de la Bulgarie du nord ouest au cours du XVIIIe s.," *Études historiques*, vol. 1 (Sofia: Éditions de l'Académie Bulgare des Sciences, 1960).
4 Immanuel Wallerstein, "The Ottoman Empire and the Capitalist World-Economy: Some Questions for Research," in *Social and Economic History of Turkey, 1071–1920*, ed. Halil İnalcık and Osman Okyar (Ankara: Meteksan, 1980), 389–98.
5 Halil İnalcık, "Çiftliklerin Doğuşu: Devlet, Toprak Sahipleri ve Kiracılar [Emergence of Big Farms, Çiftliks: State, Landholders and Tenants]," in *Osmanlı Toprak Mülkiyeti ve Ticari Tarım*, ed. Çağlar Keyder and Faruk Tabak (İstanbul: Tarih Vakfı Yurt Yayınları, 1998), 17–35.
6 İnalcık, "Çiftliklerin Doğuşu," 23.
7 Traian Stoianovich, "Land Tenure and Related Sectors of the Balkan Economy, 1600–1800," *The Journal of Economic History* 13, no. 4 (1953): 410.
8 Gandev, "L'apparition."
9 Özer Ergenç, "18. Yüzyılda Osmanlı Taşrasında Yerel İlişkilerin Yeniden Şekillenmesi [Transformation of Local Relations in the 18th Century Ottoman Provinces]," 21. CIEPO Symposium, Budapest, October 7–11, 2014, Unpublished Paper.
10 Mehmet Genç, *Osmanlı İmparatorluğunda Devlet ve Ekonomi [State and Economy in the Ottoman Empire]* (İstanbul: Ötüken Neşriyat, 2000), 167.
11 Rifa'at Ali Abou-el-Haj, *Modern Devletin Doğası, 16. Yüzyıldan 18. Yüzyıla Osmanlı İmparatorluğu [Formation of the Modern State: The Ottoman Empire, Sixteenth to Eighteenth Centuries]*, trans. Oktay Özel and Canay Şahin (Ankara: İmge Kitabevi Yayınları, 2000), 121.
12 Genç, *Osmanlı İmparatorluğunda*, 168.
13 Yavuz Cezar, *Osmanlı Maliyesinde Bunalım ve Değişim Dönemi (XVIII: yüzyıldan Tanzimat'a Mali Tarih) [Depression and Transformation in the Ottoman Finances, Fiscal History from XVIIIth Century to the Tanzimat]* (İstanbul: Alan Yayıncılık, 1986), 102–3.
14 Mehmet Genç, "İltizam [Tax-Farming]," *Türkiye Diyanet Vakfı (TDV) İslam Ansiklopedisi*, vol. 22 (İstanbul: Türkiye Diyanet Vakfı, 2000), 157. Yavuz Cezzar gives however the date 1813, Cezar, *Osmanlı Maliyesinde,* 242–43.
15 Rifa'at Ali Abou-el-Haj, "The Ottoman Vezir and Pasha Households 1683–1703: A Preliminary Report," *Journal of the American Oriental Society* 89, no. 3 (1974): 467–75.
16 Genç, "İltizam," 157.
17 Alp Yücel Kaya, "In the Hinterland of Izmir: Mid-Nineteenth Century Traders Facing a New Type of Fiscal Practice," in *Merchants in the Ottoman Empire*, ed. Suraiya Faroqhi and Gilles Veinstein (Leuven: Peeters, 2008), 261–79.
18 Yūzō Nagata, *Tarihte Ayanlar, Karaosmanoğulları Üzerine Bir İnceleme [Notables in History: A Research on Karaosmanoğulları]* (Ankara: Türk Tarih Kurumu, 1997), 26.
19 Çağatay Uluçay, "Karaosmanoğullarına Ait Bazı Vesikalar [Certain Documents on Karaosmanoğulları]," *Tarih Vesikaları* 2, no. 9 (1942): 205, n. 15.
20 Çağatay Uluçay, "Karaosmanoğullarına Ait Bazı Vesikalar [Certain Documents on Karaosmanoğulları]," *Tarih Vesikaları* 2, no. 9 (1942): 197.
21 Çağatay Uluçay, "Karaosmanoğullarına Ait Bazı Vesikalar [Certain Documents on Karaosmanoğulları]," *Tarih Vesikaları* 2, no. 9 (1942): 199.
22 Nagata, *Tarihte Ayanlar*, 26.
23 Nagata, *Tarihte Ayanlar*, 61–72.
24 Nagata, *Tarihte Ayanlar*, 68.
25 Yūzō Nagata and Feridun Emecen, "Bir âyânın doğuşu: Karaosmanoğlu Hacı Mustafa Ağa'ya ait belgeler [Genesis of a Notable: Documents on Karaosmanoğlu Hacı Mustafa Ağa]," *Belgeler* 25–29 (2005): 19–20, 26–29; Nagata, *Tarihte Ayanlar,* 99–102.

26 Nagata, *Tarihte Ayanlar*, 69–70.
27 Nagata, *Tarihte Ayanlar*, 31–32; Fikret Yılmaz, "Kara Osman-Oğlu Ataullah Ağa'ya Ait Malların Müsaderesi ve Bir Kira Defteri [Confiscation of Property Pertaining to Kara Osman-Oğlu Ataullah Ağa and A Register of Rents]," *Tarih İncelemeleri Dergisi* 5 (1990): 241–44.
28 Nagata, *Tarihte Ayanlar,* 32–33, 66–68, 102, 106, 108.
29 Yılmaz, "Kara Osman-Oğlu," 250.
30 Nagata, *Tarihte Ayanlar*, 35.
31 Nagata, *Tarihte Ayanlar*, 39, 46.
32 Nagata, *Tarihte Ayanlar*, 108–9.
33 A.O. ML.VRD.TMT, 1486.
34 Nagata, *Tarihte Ayanlar*, 75–79.
35 Nagata, *Tarihte Ayanlar*, 73.
36 Nagata, *Tarihte Ayanlar*, 94–105.
37 Nagata, *Tarihte Ayanlar*, 40–52.
38 Nagata, *Tarihte Ayanlar*, 89–91.
39 Nagata, *Tarihte Ayanlar*, 121–22.
40 Nagata, *Tarihte Ayanlar*, 139.
41 Nagata, *Tarihte Ayanlar*, 139.
42 Nagata, *Tarihte Ayanlar*, 135–36.
43 Nagata, *Tarihte Ayanlar*, 152–53.
44 Nagata, *Tarihte Ayanlar*, 79–80.
45 Genç, "İltizam," 157; Cezar, *Osmanlı,* 242–43.
46 Nagata, *Tarihte Ayanlar*, 79–86.
47 Nagata, *Tarihte Ayanlar*, 52, 58.
48 Umut Gündoğdu, "19. Yüzyılda Gediz Ovasında Büyük Toprak Sahipliği ve Köylü İsyanları [Large Landholding and Peasant Revolts in the Gediz Plain in the 19th Century]," Paper presented at the 17th Congress of Türk Sosyal Bilimler Derneği, Ankara, ODTÜ, February 1–3, 2023.
49 A.O. MVL, 848/34.
50 A.O. HR.H, 495/8, 19.
51 A.O. ML.VRD.TMT, 1940, 1.
52 A.O. ML.VRD.TMT, 2028, 20, 23.
53 "A Visit to a Model Farm in Asia Minor," *Fraser's Magazine for Town and Country* 55 (January–June 1857): 60.
54 "A Visit to a Model Farm in Asia Minor," *Fraser's Magazine for Town and Country* 55 (January–June 1857): 59.
55 A.O. ML.VRD.TMT, 16115, 37.
56 A.O. ML.VRD.TMT, 16115, 13.
57 *Journal de jurisprudence commerciale et maritime* 17 (1838): 260–63; *Journal de jurisprudence commerciale et maritime* 23 (1844): 100–8; A.M. 3/95.
58 A.O. ML.VRD.TMT, 16115, 12.
59 Marie-Carmen Smyrnelis, "La diaspora marchande grecque méditerranéenne (XVIIIe-XIXe siècles) à travers le parcours d'une famille: les Baltazzi," in *Grecs et Arméniens en diaspora: approches comparatives*, ed. Michel Bruneau et al. (Athènes: l'École française d'Athènes, 2007), 85–92.
60 A.O., *Kamil Kepeci Tasnifi, Muhassıllık Defterleri*, 5789 (14 March 1841–24 March 1842).
61 Onnik Jamgocyan, *Osmanlı İmparatorluğu'nda Sarraflık, Rumlar, Museviler, Frenkler, Ermeniler [Bankers in the Ottoman Empire, Grecs, Jews, Franks, Armenians]* (İstanbul: Yapı Kredi Yayınları, 2016), 83, 103.
62 A.O., Maliye Nezareti Mektubi Kalemi Defterleri, 25 (3 March 1840–14 September 1840).
63 Araks Şahiner, "The Sarrafs of İstanbul: Financiers of the Empire" (MA thesis, University of Boğaziçi, 1995), 50–55, 84; Smyrnelis, "La diaspora marchande grecque."

64 Alp Yücel Kaya, "On the Çiftlik Regulation in Tırhala in the Mid Nineteenth Century: Economists, Pashas, Governors, Çiftlik-Holders, Subaşıs and Sharecroppers," in *Ottoman Rural Societies and Economies: Halcyon Days in Crete VIII A Symposium Held in Rethymno, January 13–15, 2012*, ed. Elias Kolovos (Rethymno: Crete University Press, 2015), 333–79.
65 Alex Baltazzi, "Lamartine, Tire et les Baltazzi," in *Actes du colloque international Lamartine, 8–10 Juin 2004, Tire*, ed. Gertrude Durusoy (İzmir: Ege Üniversitesi Yayınları, 2004), 297–98.
66 HR.H, 379/15, 23.
67 Aysun Sarıbey Haykıran, "Aydın Vilayeti'nde Çiftlikler (1839–1918) [Large Estates in the Aydın Province 1839–1918)]" (Unpublished PhD diss., Ege Üniversitesi, 2013), 107–11.
68 Nadir Özbek, *Tanzimat'tan Cumhuriyet'e Aşar Vergisi ve Tahsilatı Ekseninde Toplum ve Siyaset, 1839–1925 [Society and Politics in the Axis of Tithe Tax and its Collection from Tanzimat to the Republic 1839–1925]* (TÜBİTAK Proje No: 113K142, 2016), 113–38.
69 Orhan Kurmuş, *Emperyalizmin Türkiye'ye Girişi [The Entry of Imperialism into Turkey]* (İstanbul: Yordam Yayınları, 1974/2007).

Bibliography

"A Visit to a Model Farm in Asia Minor." *Fraser's Magazine for Town and Country* 55 (January–June 1857): 59–63.

Abou-el-Haj, Rifa'at Ali. "The Ottoman Vezir and Pasha Households 1683–1703: A Preliminary Report." *Journal of the American Oriental Society* 89, no. 3 (1974): 438–47.

Abou-el-Haj, Rifa'at Ali. *Modern Devletin Doğası, 16. Yüzyıldan 18. Yüzyıla Osmanlı İmparatorluğu [Formation of the Modern State: The Ottoman Empire, Sixteenth to Eighteenth Centuries]*, translated by Oktay Özel and Canay Şahin. Ankara: İmge Kitabevi Yayınları, 2000.

Baltazzi, Alex. "Lamartine, Tire et les Baltazzi." In *Actes du colloque international Lamartine, 8–10 Juin 2004, Tire*, edited by Durusoy Gertrude, 297–98. İzmir: Ege Üniversitesi Yayınları, 2004.

Cezar, Yavuz. *Osmanlı Maliyesinde Bunalım ve Değişim Dönemi (XVIII. yüzyıldan Tanzimat'a Mali Tarih) [Depression and Transformation in the Ottoman Finances, Fiscal History from XVIIIth Century to the Tanzimat]*. İstanbul: Alan Yayıncılık, 1986.

Ergenç, Özer. "18. Yüzyılda Osmanlı Taşrasında Yerel İlişkilerin Yeniden Şekillenmesi [Transformation of Local Relations in the 18th Century Ottoman Provinces]." 21. CIEPO Symposium, Budapest, October 7–11, 2014, Unpublished Paper.

Gandev, Christov. "L'apparition des rapports capitalistes dans l'économie rurale de la Bulgarie du nord ouest au cours du XVIIIe s." In *Études historiques*, vol. 1. Sofia: Éditions de l'Académie Bulgare des sciences, 1960.

Genç, Mehmet. "İltizam [Tax-Farming]." In *Türkiye Diyanet Vakfı* (TDV) *İslam Ansiklopedisi*, vol. 22, 154–58. İstanbul: Türkiye Diyanet Vakfı, 2000a.

Genç, Mehmet. *Osmanlı İmparatorluğunda Devlet ve Ekonomi [State and Economy in the Ottoman Empire]*. İstanbul: Ötüken Neşriyat, 2000b.

Gündoğdu, Umut. "19. Yüzyılda Gediz Ovasında Büyük Toprak Sahipliği ve Köylü İsyanları [Large Landholding and Peasant Revolts in the Gediz Plain in the 19th Century]." Paper presented at the 17th Congress of Türk Sosyal Bilimler Derneği, Ankara, ODTÜ, February 1–3, 2023.

Haykıran, Aysun Sarıbey. "Aydın Vilayeti'nde Çiftlikler (1839–1918) [Large Estates in the Aydın Province (1839–1918)]." Unpublished PhD diss., Ege Üniversitesi, 2013.

İnalcık, Halil. "Çiftliklerin Doğuşu: Devlet, Toprak Sahipleri ve Kiracılar [Emergence of Big Farms, Çiftliks: State, Landholders and Tenants]." In *Osmanlı Toprak Mülkiyeti ve*

Ticari Tarım [Ottoman Landholding and Commercial Agriculture], edited by Çağlar Keyder and Faruk Tabak, 17–35. İstanbul: Tarih Vakfı Yurt Yayınları, 1998.

Jamgocyan, Onnik. *Osmanlı İmparatorluğu'nda Sarraflık, Rumlar, Museviler, Frenkler, Ermeniler [Bankers in the Ottoman Empire, Grecs, Jews, Franks, Armenians]*. İstanbul: Yapı Kredi Yayınları, 2016.

Kaya, Alp Yücel. "In the Hinterland of Izmir: Mid-Nineteenth Century Traders Facing a New Type of Fiscal Practice." In *Merchants in the Ottoman Empire*, edited by Suraiya Faroqhi and Gilles Veinstein, 261–79. Leuven: Peeters, 2008.

Kaya, Alp Yücel. "On the Çiftlik Regulation in Tırhala in the Mid Nineteenth Century: Economists, Pashas, Governors, Çiftlik- Holders, Subaşıs and Sharecroppers." In *Ottoman Rural Societies and Economies: Halcyon Days in Crete VIII A Symposium Held in Rethymno, January 13–15, 2012*, edited by Elias Kolovos, 333–79. Rethymno: Crete University Press, 2015.

Kurmuş, Orhan. *Emperyalizmin Türkiye'ye Girişi [The Entry of Imperialism into Turkey]*. İstanbul: Yordam Yayınları, 1974/2007.

Nagata, Yūzō. *Tarihte Ayanlar, Karaosmanoğulları Üzerine Bir İnceleme [Notables in History: A Research on Karaosmanoğulları]*. Ankara: Türk Tarih Kurumu, 1997.

Nagata, Yūzō, and Feridun Emecen. "Bir âyânın doğuşu: Karaosmanoğlu Hacı Mustafa Ağa'ya ait belgeler [Genesis of a Notable: Documents on Karaosmanoğlu Hacı Mustafa Ağa]." *Belgeler* 25–29 (2005): 1–72.

Özbek, Nadir. *Tanzimat'tan Cumhuriyet'e Aşar Vergisi ve Tahsilatı Ekseninde Toplum ve Siyaset, 1839–1925 [Society and Politics in the Axis of Tithe Tax and Its Collection from Tanzimat to the Republic 1839–1925]*. TÜBİTAK Proje No: 113K142, 2016.

Şahiner, Araks. "The Sarrafs of İstanbul: Financiers of the Empire." MA thesis, University of Boğaziçi, 1995.

Smyrnelis, Marie-Carmen. "La diaspora marchande grecque méditerranéenne (XVIIIe–XIXe siècles) à travers le parcours d'une famille: les Baltazzi." In *Grecs et Arméniens en Diaspora: Approches Comparatives*, edited by Michel Bruneau, Ioannis Hassiotis, Martine Hovanessian, and Claire-Marie Mouradian, 85–92. Athènes: l'École française d'Athènes, 2007.

Stoianovich, Traian. "Land Tenure and Related Sectors of the Balkan Economy, 1600–1800." *The Journal of Economic History* 13, no. 4 (1953): 398–411.

Uluçay, Çağatay. "Karaosmanoğullarına Ait Bazı Vesikalar [Certain Documents on Karaosmanoğulları]." *Tarih Vesikaları* 2, no. 9 (1942): 193–207.

Veinstein, Gilles. "Çiftlik Tartışması Üzerine [On the Çiftlik Debate]." In *Osmanlı Toprak Mülkiyeti ve Ticari Tarım [Ottoman Landholding and Commercial Agriculture]*, edited by Çağlar Keyder and Faruk Tabak, 35–56. İstanbul: Tarih Vakfı Yurt Yayınları, 1998.

Wallerstein, Immanuel. "The Ottoman Empire and the Capitalist World-Economy: Some Questions for Research." In *Social and Economic History of Turkey, 1071–1920*, edited by Halil İnalcık and Osman Okyar, 389–98. Ankara: Meteksan, 1980.

Yılmaz, Fikret. "Kara Osman-Oğlu Ataullah Ağa'ya Ait Malların Müsaderesi ve Bir Kira Defteri [Confiscation of Property Pertaining to Kara Osman-Oğlu Ataullah Ağa and A Register of Rents]." *Tarih İncelemeleri Dergisi* 5 (1990): 239–52.

14 Wealth Inequality, *Çiftliks*, and the Question of Agrarian Capitalism in Cyprus During the 1830s

Antonis Hadjikyriacou

Wealth inequality has recently attracted increased attention in Ottoman economic history.[1] This has partly been the result of the regeneration of interest in Ottoman quantitative sources. The advent of the "cultural turn" has made historians highly skeptical of the positivistic claims based on cliometrics and related methods—not without good reason. Pointing out their limitations, as well as earlier problematic readings of these sources, scholars have lost interest in quantitative economic history methods since the 1990s. Yet, the addition of cultural critique to the methodological toolbox of economic historians means that such sources can be taken less as accurate recordings of reality and more as proxy data conducive to gradually putting together the bigger picture to identify broader trends and patterns.[2] Any general dismissal of Ottoman quantitative data on account of their problems runs the risk of discarding a body of sources limited though it may be—as is the case anyway with any type of historical source—that nonetheless carries significant potential. The challenge is to maximize this potential without uncritically taking them at face value.[3]

The above discussions can be situated in what has been termed "the return of economic history" in Ottoman studies.[4] Contributing to this growing corpus of work, the present essay examines a rare moment for which systematic and relatively comprehensive quantitative data are available for Cyprus. This is the 1832/33 property survey, recording the possessions of some 23,000 people living across the island.

The temporal limitations of the dataset mean that this essay cannot aspire to significantly engage in the broader discussions in the field of long-term wealth inequality, as recent scholarly works have done for various parts of the Ottoman world. It does, however, aim to contribute toward understanding the *cause* and *effect* of wealth inequality in the specific temporal and spatial setting. Wealth inequality is something that existed in different periods; it is crucial to understand why it has increased at one point in time and what were its economic and social consequences. This essay tests the hypothesis of whether a noteworthy unequal distribution of wealth in Cyprus in the 1830s can be connected to discussions on capitalist transformations in the Ottoman world. It thus provides a broader framework where future inquiries over longer spans of time and phasing can make a contribution toward the study of inequality.

DOI: 10.4324/9781003500780-19

To do so, the essay will open with a short presentation of the source at hand and then procced to the quantitative analysis of wealth inequality-related data. Having established the increased polarization of Cypriot society at the time, it seeks the correlations between inequality in landholding and the proliferation of *çiftlik*s on the island. It therefore revisits the question of whether *çiftlik*s constituted agrarian capitalism, a critical question in Ottomanist historiography.[5] Having provided some evidence for a differentiated mode of organization of *çiftlik*s that would maximize efficiency and cost reduction, arguing that the hypothesis of agrarian capitalism cannot be dismissed, at least from the third decade of the 19th century onward. Finally, it demonstrates that poverty was more pronounced in settlements in the vicinity of *çiftlik*s, a condition that theoretically should increase the availability of labor with which to run such larger economic units, illustrating the complex social and economic dynamic of the phenomenon.

The 1832/33 Cyprus Land and Property Survey

Cataloged under the *temettüât* series of the Ottoman Archives in Istanbul, registers ML.VRD.TMT.d.16152–16155 concern a survey of Cyprus. The particular survey was conducted almost a decade before the inauguration of the *temettüât* (there is an 1834 survey from Kayseri also cataloged as *temettüât*).[6] The title in the cover of the register itself makes it clear that the survey does not record the *temettü* tax, but that it is confined to land and property (*Emlâk ve arazi defteri*), while the preamble in each of the four volumes makes no mention of taxation in the survey; it only records what it states in the title. Yet, only one of several studies by historians examining the survey points out that it is *not* a *temettüât*.[7]

It is reasonable to assume that this was an *ad hoc* pilot project that foreshadowed the *temettüât*: in that it records property holders and four broad categories of property—lands, trees, buildings, and animals. Given that there is no mention of taxation, the figures recorded cannot but be taken to refer to the official value of these properties. Thus, this was probably a pilot survey that needs to be differentiated from a *temettüât* proper. At the same time, the survey clearly manifests the (loosely speaking) shift in the Ottoman fiscal mind from production to property and (decisively) from collective to individual assessment. In other words, it represents a moment of transition that was preceded by earlier experiments which had consolidated to this form.[8]

One question concerns the way individual property entries are recorded across the island. Property holders are sometimes marked as "*. . . emlâki,*" other times as "*. . . malı,*" and less often as "*. . . emlâk ve malı.*" "*Emlâk*" and "*mal*" are both synonyms for property, so the distinction is not entirely clear. One may suppose that *emlâk* may refer to private property (*mülk*), as opposed to *mal*, which may imply some sort of leasehold. That this distinction is made in the survey and that properties are categorized among these groups is evocative of the significance it places on private property.[9]

Wealth Inequality

The analysis of the distribution of wealth among the 23,000 registered property holders of Cyprus in 1832/33 reveals a highly polarized society. The top 20 property holders (0.08%) control 5.4% of the wealth. Many individuals or institutions appearing in this list are monasteries, Islamic endowments, or individuals from well-known business families that acted collectively, such as the Mattei or Lapierre families. If we consolidate these multiple entries (e.g., all the monasteries and local parish churches within the Church of Cyprus, or all the Islamic pious endowments), the top 20 list changes dramatically. They control 10.07% of the total wealth; almost double the amount than when they were treated as individual entities.[10]

Furthermore, the percentage of the top 20 holders (0.08%) in the total is misleading, as it is calculated on property holders: the survey does not record propertyless individuals. In 1831, a male population survey recorded 44,882 males.[11] This figure, however, includes subsequent newborns and minors. If we allow one-third for the underage,[12] this would leave us with an estimate of 29,921 adult males. A year later, the land and property survey records 17,940 male property holders. This means that 11,981 males held no property, that is, about 27%. While only an exact matching of the adult males in both surveys would allow a precise calculation of the figure of those who hold property and those who do not, this rough estimate, even with a generous margin error, remains significantly high. In turn, this would imply that these landless individuals, who do not even appear as holding a house to live in, would need to exchange their labor in order to survive.

Another indicator of wealth inequality is the Gini coefficient, which is estimated here at 0.60. Again, the figure should be considerably higher if we were to add propertyless males and females. The figure, then, would increase to 0.84, which is quite a jump. Comparison is the only way to make better sense of this figure. Yet, it is next to impossible to achieve this unless the exact same set of data is available for another region.

Given that this is an *ad hoc* survey, there are not many comparable sources of data. The closest match is *temettüât* surveys. A study of the *temettüât* survey of Koçana in the province of Skopje calculated the Gini coefficient at 0.45.[13] Burcu Işıl also employs *temettüât* survey data for the regions of Manastır, İştip, and Pirlepe in the mid-1840s. Her calculations, however, concern the distribution of land ownership, as opposed to the total value of property. This makes comparison difficult. For what it is worth, the Gini coefficient she calculated for the villages of Manastır was 0.67, but the sample is much smaller than Cyprus. Comparisons with probate registers would make little sense, given the different nature of the data.

Much more enlightening of the nature of wealth inequality in Cyprus are Tables 14.1 and 14.2. Separating the total number of property holders into five numerically equal groups (centiles) according to the total value of the property, we see that the top 20% controls slightly over 60% of the total value of properties in Cyprus, while the bottom 20% holds less than 2% (Table 14.1). More revealing of the polarized nature of the society is the calculation of the percentile difference between categories, which shows how much the value of the property of a person in one group would need to rise in order to move to the next higher category. A person in the bottom 20% group would need to almost triple the value of their property (184%), while a person in the second to top group (61–80%) would need

Table 14.1 Quintiles of unequal distribution of properties.

Population Category	*Percentage Over Total Value of Properties*	*Percentage Change Between Categories*
0–20%	1.93	184.46
21–40%	5.49	101.22
41–60%	11.01	81.37
61–80%	20.03	218.93
81–100%	61.55	

Table 14.2 Centiles of unequal distribution of properties.

Population Category	*Percentage Over Total Value of Properties*	*Percentage Change Between Categories*
0–10%	0.63	105.51
11–20%	1.30	68.79
21–30%	2.19	50.53
31–40%	3.30	41.38
41–50%	4.65	36.93
51–60%	6.36	34.24
61–70%	8.56	33.67
71–80%	11.47	40.42
81–90%	16.19	196.93
91–100%	45.35	

to more than triple (219%) the value of their property to move to the top category. Less startling are the differences between the in-between categories, that is, 101% and 81%, respectively.

The discrepancy between the top and bottom groups with the in-between ones becomes much more lucid when we divide them into centiles, that is, in ten equal groups (Table 14.2). Individuals at the poorest end of the chart would need to double (105.5%) their property to move to the next group, while those among the 81–90% aspiring to reach the exclusive highest group would need to triple their property (196.9%). Correspondingly, this would mean increasing their group share of the total wealth of the island from 16% to 45%. Equally significant is the observation that almost half of the value of properties of the island were held by the top 10%.

What was the significance of this highly polarized distribution of wealth? This property survey comes in the midst of the most turbulent period in Cypriot history since at least the late medieval era,[14] being characterized by constant crises, revolts, socio-political tensions, and an overall redistribution of wealth and power—reflecting the overall conditions in many parts of the Ottoman world. Indeed, the survey itself—as mentioned above, an *ad hoc* one that was unprecedented and never repeated—was the Ottoman state's response to the dire socio-economic conditions on the island, in part the result of environmental and climatic pressures (droughts, locusts, famines). Istanbul-based bureaucrats took the mass migration of impoverished Cypriots to the nearby coastlines of Anatolia, Greater Syria, and Egypt as a red flag, and took measures by producing knowledge that would help them better understand and alleviate the situation.[15] Indeed, the subsequent decades saw the systematic surveying of the island and a consistent policy that bore fruit in the recovery of the island.[16] As a result, Cyprus was in a much better condition when delivered to the British.

*Çiftlik*s and Agrarian Capitalism

The above discussion reveals that Cyprus in the 1830s was an extremely polarized society, with a high degree of landlessness and poverty. The implication is that peasant smallholding, by all accounts *the* key characteristic of the Ottoman economy, no longer carried the same weight as it hitherto did. At stake is a redistribution of resources, leading to the concentration of land to fewer hands. According to the 1832/33 survey, much of this land was part of *çiftlik*s, while sizeable fields (even up to 1,000 *dönüm*) were not registered as part of a *çiftlik*.

This narrative, tentative though it may be, goes against the grain of the current consensus on the *çiftlik* debate.[17] It calls for a reconsideration, and perhaps revision, of some of the premises of the prevalent interpretation.

*Çiftlik*s were large farms, once considered as channels of raw materials to the industrializing centers of Western Europe, thus part of capitalist world-system periphery in the Wallersteinian line of thinking.[18] The current consensus argues that *çiftlik*s did not constitute units that played a significant role in agrarian capitalism and that peasant small-holding remained dominant. This consensus notwithstanding, a great deal of imponderabilia still remains. Veinstein, whose views appear to have "put an end to the debate,"[19] was careful enough to repeatedly point out the lack of knowledge on the functioning of the *çiftlik*s. No matter how authoritative his arguments are currently considered, he calls them "initial impressions" that need "to be confirmed by a more extensive study of the available historical sources."[20] True, his opinions were supported by subsequent studies.[21] Despite his skepticism of an Ottoman integration into a global capitalist economy, evidence on the actual functioning of *çiftlik*s remains scarce—even almost two-and-a-half decades after the publication of a volume where the most consistent debate on the topic has taken place. In other words, how possible is it to reach a definitive conclusion without having a reasonably comprehensive knowledge of the evidence? For example, Yuzo Nagata had reported as early as 1987 the existence of *çiftlik* account registers in the Topkapı Palace archives.[22] Indeed, there have been a few voices that continue to see a connection between *çiftlik*s and capitalism.[23]

The case of Cyprus is particularly conducive to such an inquiry, because of the history of how it switched from Venetian feudal commercial agriculture to Ottoman peasant smallholding. This transition was a long-drawn process stretching well into both sides of 1571. It entailed neither the complete abolition of *corvée* labor upon the inauguration of Ottoman rule nor the abandonment of a lower status (albeit, not legally speaking) for serfs. By the closing decades of Venetian presence on the island, scores of serfs were being freed in the face of population pressure and social unrest.[24] Regarding post-conquest conditions, a recent study corroborated the earlier arguments posited by Arbel and Veinstein on the economic and social transition to Ottoman rule.[25] More importantly, serfs were originally employed in sugar plantations on the island, one of the most important suppliers of sugar to Europe before the 17th century, playing a key role in the development of capitalism.[26] Once not as profitable, sugar was gradually being substituted by cotton.[27] While the former was cultivated by serf labor, smallholding sufficed for the latter. When cotton had replaced sugarcane on the island in the 17th century, Cypriot cotton seeds had been sown by African slaves in the American colonies.[28]

All this is important because, by the 19th century, large landholding had returned on the island. Discussing Cyprus in the 1830s, Marc Aymes identifies "a certain degree of 'commercial agriculture,' if not outright 'agrarian capitalism.'"[29] The proliferation of *çiftlik*s and the consequent concentration of the factors and means of production in fewer hands for the purposes of channeling the agricultural surplus of the island (cotton, silk, cereals, wine) to the ports and warehouses of the main port cities (Larnaka and the rising competitor of Limassol) were a key dynamic for Aymes. While there is ample evidence to support such a conclusion, research is still necessary to demonstrate the degree to which production methods have been intensified through irrigation works, land reclamation, or more efficient fertilization. Yet, significant elements pointing toward the more efficient administration of agrarian businesses are evident in the historical record.

For example, the use of accounting methods akin to double-entry bookkeeping in *çiftlik* administration has been documented in 1833,[30] indicating a transitionary process toward this more efficient and profit-maximizing system. Three decades later, the lease-holder of a *çiftlik* recorded that "my bookkeeping was perfect, and in it was the secret of my control as to results."[31] Far from an isolated phenomenon, double-entry bookkeeping was practiced in the Greek world by the 1810s, as evidenced by a manual taught in the Kaplaneion School of Ioannina (Yanya).[32] The implication is that the appearance of this practice has to be dated some decades earlier before it was taught in commercial schools. Indeed, the earlier extant such manual is from the 1790s.[33]

What other *economic* means existed to reduce costs? The analysis of the account books of two *çiftlik*s in different parts of Cyprus in the 1830s demonstrates the steady annual decline in the cost of labor and the waning of reliance on wage labor in favor of sharecropping.[34] No matter how circumstantial this evidence is, it is worth comparing with other examples. Nagata convincingly demonstrated that a similar *çiftlik* account register in north-western Anatolia, possibly Çanakkale, from the mid-18th century did not engage in market-oriented agriculture. He calculated the cost of labor at 70%, unfortunately without an annual breakdown and with some data missing.[35] One Cypriot *çiftlik*-account register reports the cost of labor starting at 28%, falling to 20% after three years, while another from 71% to 54% after four years. The same applies in absolute figures: from 15,000 to 11,667 piasters (kuruş) and from 14,503 to 7,981 *piasters*—the latter cutting labor costs almost at half.[36] What this indicates is the more efficient administration of *çiftlik*s in 1830s Cyprus than in mid-18th-century Çanakkale. Could this mean that the 18th century was a transitional period, whereas, in the 1830s, there is evidence of more efficient management strategies? While there is no certainty as to how prolific these practices were, such indications for their existence point to the need for further research, rather than the abandonment of the hypothesis. What other evidence is there?

In his memoirs, the previously mentioned *çiftlik* lease-holder describes his ten year-long administration of the *çiftlik*, the investments he made, and the more efficient cultivation methods he implemented. Having received it at a poor state, by the end of the lease, he increased the amount of arable land by 1,320%, while, after seven years, the per acre productivity of wheat and barley, the two most revenue-yielding crops, had increased by 40%, despite two years of drought and four years of locusts. He describes his annual monitoring of rainfall, or how he maximized efficiency. One way he did so was by using indigenous wheat seeds in years of drought instead of imported foreign seeds, to maximize productivity (the latter were less accustomed to local climate), following the advice of his steward, a former African slave who had lived most of his life on the island.[37]

Like elsewhere, *çiftlik*s in Cyprus appear on the morrow of Ottoman rule, with the most profitable of former Venetian estates being granted to members of the royal family.[38] By the 17th century, they appeared as a prominent factor in the struggle for the agricultural surplus—a clear turning point;[39] it was not until the closing decades of the 18th century, however, that new *çiftlik*s were formed and we can observe some qualitative changes in their functioning.[40] Still, at that time, coercion as an extra-economic means seems to have been a key factor for this process, as is evidenced by a *muhassıl*'s arbitrary redirection of *vakıf* water resources meant to serve public needs to his own *çiftlik*s.[41] Half a century later, such practices do not appear as prominent in the historical record, without excluding the possibility.

Other purely economic means of capital accumulation not directly related to the *çiftlik* phenomenon are documented in 18th- and 19th-century Cyprus. Prominent is the institution of advance purchase, be it within the confines of Islamic law (*selem*/*salam*),[42] or in more informal practices like in-kind payments of monetary debts. Such contracts entailed the agreement of a price between merchants and producers prior to the yield, in anticipation of the market price. Merchants were hoping to secure production at a lower price without having to negotiate at the marketplace, while producers sought payment in cash when this was necessary and hopefully a better price depending on future conditions. Advance purchase was widespread throughout the empire, and was particularly studied by Beshara Doumani in Palestine as a key mechanism that transformed urban/rural relations, facilitating the concentration of production, and as part of the transition to capitalism more generally.[43] The system appears prolific in Cyprus, with several examples providing evidence of how it was widely used in transactions between merchants and producers.[44] In the cases where differentials between the price agreed in advance and the export market price could be calculated, these had reached a level of 266%.[45] Extraordinary or not, such price differentials secured handsome profits for merchants.

In the grand scheme of things, Cyprus was a microcosm of the empire. Every single fiscal and administrative system had been applied and repeatedly tested; the features of local agriculture, manufacturing, or finance do not diverge from Ottoman economic trends; the island follows the ebbs and flows of imperial fortunes, while larger Ottoman- as well as Mediterranean-wide processes are locally reflected.[46] On their own, none of these attributes are exclusive to Cyprus. Taken together, they represent a miniature version of the bigger picture—as other regions that I know less well would most probably do.

To the above list, we should also add *çiftlik*s and their role in the economy and society of the empire—obviously at a much bigger scale. Thus, while it was not before the 1830s or 1840s that one might argue confidently of agrarian capitalism conditions in key regions of the empire, this was a long-term process the early foundations of which were set in the 17th century. At that time, global interconnectedness changed gear and the character of international trade was transformed quantitatively and qualitatively. Izmir appeared as a port city of note in the Eastern Mediterranean, substituting Bursa as a key Anatolian entrepôt. Salonica channeled goods into the Balkans, while at the eastern end of the Mediterranean Tripoli was the most important port in the Syrian coast. In Cyprus, the diversion of the spice trade meant that the splendor that the east-coast port city of Famagusta enjoyed until the 16th century was long lost. Larnaka was a rising Eastern Mediterranean port by the 17th century, when Venetian, Dutch, French, and English merchants congregated to compete for the rural surplus of grain, cotton, and silk.

In the century that followed, Alexandretta, Sidon, and Jaffa switched places on the Syrian coast. The 18th century saw the unparalleled rise of Izmir, while Salonica continued to increment its importance. Regional notables in Anatolia, the Black Sea, the Balkans,[47] and Greater Syria took advantage of the conditions of the Age of Revolutions to consolidate and channel production to ports on the way to Europe, and to provision Ottoman or European troops during the Napoleonic wars or many a Russo-Ottoman conflict. Samsun and Trabzon, for instance, were key nodes for connecting the Black Sea with the Anatolian hinterland. All these changes cannot be accounted for by an unchanging smallholding-based production model.

The 19th century, however, was a different animal. Alexandria, a historically important Eastern Mediterranean port notwithstanding, did not regain its ancient glory before the 1820s. During the following decade, Mersin was founded under Egyptian control to dominate the Levantine cotton export market. By mid-century, the star of Beirut rose phenomenally, followed by Haifa and Gaza. The changing cartography of international commerce in the Eastern Mediterranean, particularly so on the Syrian coast with its constant shifts in entrepôts of note, necessitated changes in the production of the goods traded to meet the demand of industrializing Europe and its rapidly growing urban populations. They not only needed to be clothed in cotton or wool; they needed to be cleansed by soap made of olive oil and, most importantly, to be fed: grain, dried figs, or raisins provided vital (and by then, cheap) sources of protein, carbohydrates, calories, and other nutrients.

If earlier arguments about the centrality of external demand in the proliferation of *çiftlik*s were put to question, putting emphasis on internal dynamics, a mutually exclusive understanding of the two factors obscures more than it reveals. Important though it may be to underline "socio-organizational and political realities" in challenging a view that presumes a West-imposed historical process,[48] it is difficult to discard the role of trade in generating additional demand that significantly contributed to, but perhaps may not have determined, the resulting transformations in Ottoman political economy. For example, Veinstein posits that *çiftlik*-revenue constituted a small section of the activities of some of the regional notables.[49] This does not necessitate that market-oriented agricultural output was negligible.

Linked to the earlier discussion on the long-term transformation of the relationship between landholding and labor in Cyprus, I have argued that peasant smallholding had, by the 19th century, diminished, with a significant section of the peasantry remaining landless or with minimal land (see also the subsequent section). Crucial, in this phenomenon, was the trend among the lower strata to register as "destitute" (what in Ottoman documentation appears as *gureba*), that is, too poor to pay taxes. An 1818 encyclical of the Archbishop of Cyprus excoriated the mass tendency to acquire the status of a "servant" (*doulos*) in *tekke*s, monasteries, or *çiftlik*s, thereby escaping their tax burden, with the declaration that tax exemptions would no longer apply to this category. Any disobedience was threatened with excommunication, as well as violence by Ottoman authorities.[50] The abovementioned *ciftlik* account registers make a clear distinction between regular wage laborers, sharecroppers, and "servants."[51]

That this was a widespread phenomenon in Cyprus cannot but raise the possibility of something akin to the broader European phenomenon of "second serfdom." Faruk Tabak has argued that *çiftlik*-agriculture constituted the Ottoman reflection—but not in absolute ways—of second serfdom: "The Ottoman *çiftlik*s, however, should not be seen as poor replicas of the 'second serfdom,' but as a manifestation of the basic ecological and economic traits of the Mediterranean landscape during the seventeenth and eighteenth centuries,"[52] observing that in Odessa "the ability of the nobility to utilize coerced labor—under the second serfdom—was a result of the region's growing incorporation into the world-economy."[53] If this were true in the Cypriot case, this would not have been the result of a *de jure* return of serfdom, but rather a *de facto* one that did not require the change of the legal status of peasants; it was the result of *economic* coercion. It is important to note that, in the Wallersteinian scheme of things, the distinction between an industrializing core and a raw materials-supplying agricultural periphery did not entail the latter not being capitalist; part of the *same* capitalist world economy, core, and periphery simply performed different roles.

Historians still lack a detailed understanding of how *çiftlik*s functioned, especially in comparison to European developments as discussed in the context of the Brenner debate.[54] What often escapes attention are the many lacunae in the European story of agrarian capitalism,[55] with a great deal of presumptions and questionable statistics.[56] The received wisdom is that equivalent lacunae in Ottomanist knowledge mean that agricultural production in the Ottoman world did not take a capitalist form. Are Ottoman data so inadequate? And if so, does this preclude the existence of agrarian capitalism, let alone commercial agriculture?

Method is crucial to extracting more meaningful information from available evidence, as long as one is willing to look.

Poverty and *Çiftlik*-Labor

The geo-spatial analysis offers a better understanding of the dynamics between wealth distribution and the availability of labor in settlements near *çiftlik*s. Figure 14.1 shows the 51 geo-coded (i.e., identified and given geographic coordinates) *çiftlik*s out of a total of 76 recorded in the 1832/33 survey.

Figure 14.2 shows all settlements within a five-km radius from *çiftlik*s, assuming that this is a reasonable, but minimum, distance to cover on foot in about an hour and 15 minutes twice a day. The hypothesis tested in this exercise is whether there is a correlation between people dwelling in settlements near *çiftlik*s and a more unequal distribution of wealth that would compel those in the poorer strata to offer their labor to those.

Table 14.3 shows the descriptive statistics for the whole dataset of property holders. Of the total of about 23,000 across the island, 4,076 (17.5%) live in 172 settlements (23%) within a five-km range of *çiftlik*s. While the median for

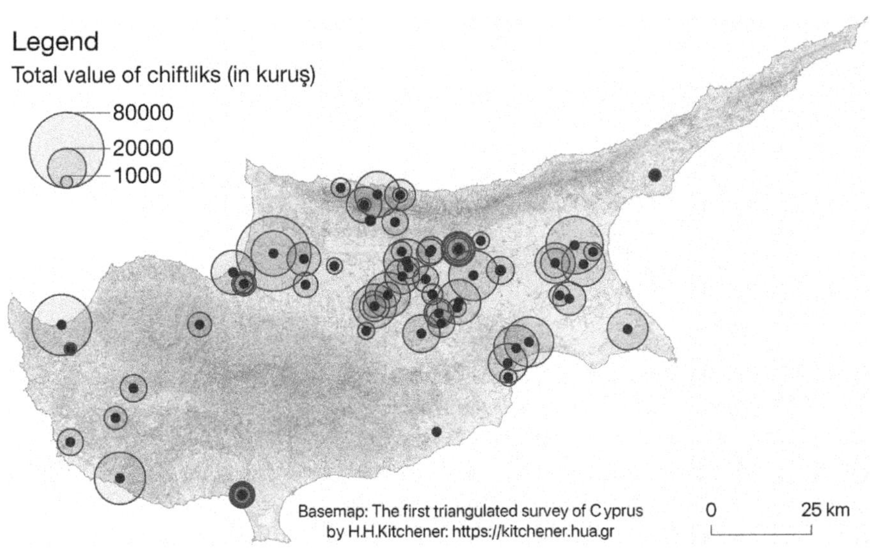

Figure 14.1 Map showing geo-located *çiftlik*s and their value. The 1883 Kitchener map of Cyprus and geodata from the "EcoLand: Environment, Economy, and Landscape in the Cypriot longue durée" project are used with the permission of the Sylvia loannou Charitable Foundation. Copyright © 2024 Sylvia loannou Charitable Foundation. Map designed by Christophoros Vradis.

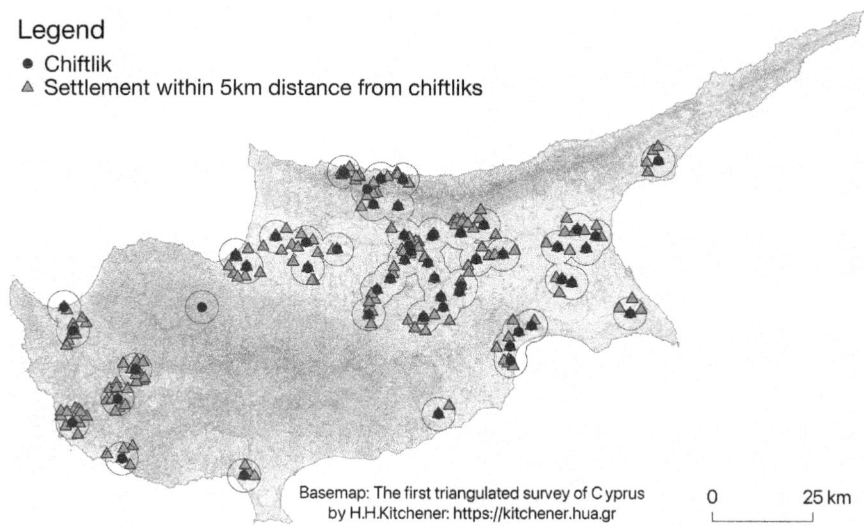

Figure 14.2 Map showing settlements within a 5-km range of geo-located *çiftlik*s.

Table 14.3 Descriptive statistics for dataset of property holders in Cyprus (value of property in *piasters*).

Mean	1,027.45
Median	555
Mode	100
Minimum	2.50
Maximum	122,127
Sum	23,298,359.72

the whole of Cyprus is 555 *piasters*, the corresponding median for those living close to *çiftlik*s is 225, that is, less than half. This demonstrates a much higher concentration of poverty in settlements near *çiftlik*s. That the mode for both the whole dataset and the sample is the same, namely, 100 *piasters*, is explicable by the fact that this was the most common value for a house. In turn, this indicates that about 2,725 individuals, that is, 12% of the property-holding population, held either just a house, or a cheaper house and a small piece of property. It is reasonable to assume that these properties would be inadequate to sustain oneself. This figure only concerns those holding property; it should be added to the number of propertyless population. If the above estimate of 27% of the male population being propertyless is correct, then almost 40% were poor enough to seek work

Table 14.4 Percentage of property holders below different thresholds of total value for the whole dataset and for the sample of settlements near *çiftliks*.

Threshold	*Dataset (Whole of Cyprus)*	*Sample (Settlements Near çiftliks)*
<555 *piasters*	50%	37.8%
<200 *piasters*	23.4%	41%
<150 *piasters*	17.9%	42.2%
<100 *piasters*	11.9%	43.8%

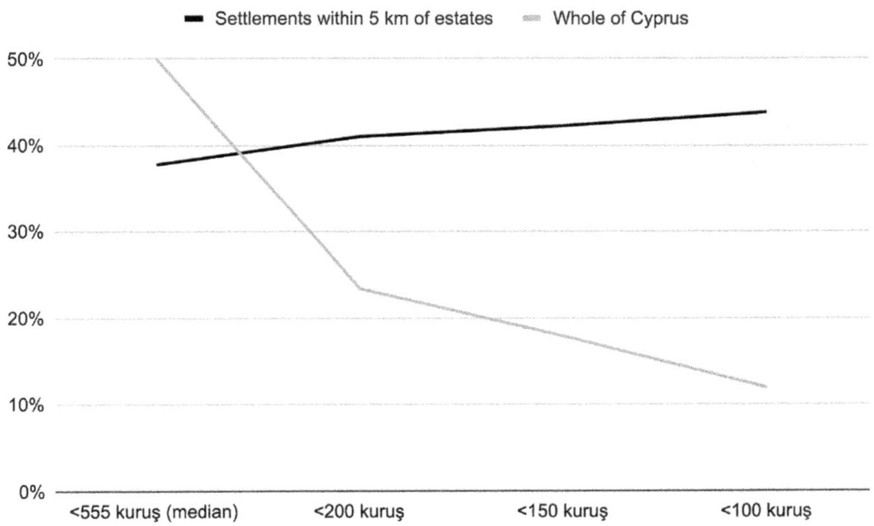

Figure 14.3 Percentage of property holders below certain values in settlements of the whole dataset and the sample.

at *çiftliks*. Even a generous downward rectification of this estimate still makes it considerable, to say the least.

While the percentage of property holders below the 555 *piasters* median for the whole dataset is naturally 50%, for the sample of those living near *çiftliks*, it is 37%. Once we set lower thresholds of 200, 150, and 100 *piasters*, amounts closer to what we can assume as the poverty line, we see the corresponding rise of the percentage for the sample, and the opposite trend for the whole dataset (see Table 14.4). Particularly so for those holding property valued at 100 *piasters*, the percentage for the whole island is only 12%, while, for the sample, it is at 43%. Figure 14.3 illustrates the opposing directions in each case, showing how settlements in close proximity to *çiftliks* demonstrate a very different distribution of wealth, with much larger segments of their population having little enough of their own, thereby having increased incentives to seek work at these farms.

In Lieu of a Conclusion

While convincingly demonstrating the higher concentration of poverty around *çiftlik*s, the above findings generate more questions than they answer. This essay's point of departure was wealth inequality; this has led to an examination of how it correlates to *çiftlik*s, to better understand the role played by large-scale property holding, a key process in the transition to capitalism. In turn, this has prompted an analysis of the value of property holding and how it may relate to labor in *çiftlik*s. As such, this is but a preliminary result of an early-stage research into Ottoman landed estates and the extent to which their functioning constituted agrarian capitalism.

Be that as it may, the present analysis of quantitative data on property holding verifies what seems obvious and makes perfect sense: that poor peasants are likely to work in *çiftlik*s. This, however, poses another question for further analysis: what are the profiles of poor smallholders in terms of the kind of properties they held, and how may that contribute to their incentive to supplement their income by exchanging their labor, other than proximity to a *çiftlik*? And to return to the bigger question at the heart of the present volume, how is capitalism related to these processes?

These questions are important in the context of one of the most long-lasting debates in Ottomanist historiography, namely, the *çiftlik*. The same questions are equally valuable for the bigger picture of Cypriot history. The century-long period between the 1770s and 1870s, within which the present study is contextualized, immediately precedes British colonial rule, generally considered as the inauguration of capitalist transformation and modernization on the island. These processes should not be seen as an exclusively British development, but as phenomena stretching back into the Ottoman period.

Archives

Başbakanlık Osmanlı Arşivleri (BOA), Istanbul, Turkey
A.DVN.KBŞ 1/17, 1/20, 1/40
C.ADL.1508
C.HR. 5791
C.ML. 22683
D.BŞM.d. 3825, 4094, 4099, 4172, 4177, 4258, 4263, 4284, 4285, 4450
HAT 16918, 36516

Notes

Research for this essay was funded by the Sylvia Ioannou Charitable Foundation in the context of the *Economy, Environment, and Landscape in the Cypriot* longue durée project (https://ecoland.hua.gr/en/), hosted at Harokopeio University, Athens, jointly coordinated by Professor Christos Chalkias and myself. Christophoros Vardis was the IT consultant of the project (and who also designed the maps), and Evangelos Papadias was responsible for geo-informatics analysis. The data-entry team was composed of Zeynep Akçakaya, Dimitris Giagtzoglou, Nesli Ruken Han, Yener Koç, and Sefer Soydar. This essay has benefited from the critical reading of Alp Yücel Kaya and Sophia Laiou, to whom I am thankful. Any shortcomings are, naturally, my sole responsibility.

1 For a review of the literature, see Hülya Canbakal and Alpay Filiztekin, "Wealth Inequality in Northwestern Anatolia under the Ottomans, 1460–1870." Unpublished paper presented online in Third Seminar of Greek Economic History Association, February 6, 2023.
2 Antonis Hadjikyriacou, "Economic Geographies," in *Doing Spatial History*, ed. Riccardo Bavaj, Konrad Lawson, and Bernhard Struck (London and New York: Routledge, 2021), 252–73.
3 Metin M. Cosgel, "Ottoman Tax Registers (Tahrir Defterleri)," *Historical Methods* 37, no. 2 (2004): 89.
4 Ulaş Karakoç and Alp Yücel Kaya, eds., *İktisat Tarihinin Dönüşü: Yeni Yaklaşımlar ve Tartışmalar [The Return of Economic History: New Approaches and Debates]* (Istanbul: İletşim, 2021).
5 See the more recent review of the literature in Yannis Spyropoulos, Stefanos Poulios, and Antonis Anastasopoulos, "*Çiftliks*, Landed Elites, and Tax Allocation in Eighteenth-Century Ottoman Veroia," *European Journal of Turkish Studies* [online] (2022). https://doi.org/10.4000/ejts.6647; Antonis Anastasopoulos, Stefanos Poulios, and Yannis Spyropoulos, "The Spread of *Çiftliks* (Large Estates) in the Eighteenth-Century Ottoman Balkans: The Case of the District of Veroia," in *History, Culture and Research*, ed. Dumitru-Cătălin Rogojanu and Gherghina Boda, vol. 3 (Târgovişte: Cetatea de Scaun, 2019), 90–109.
6 İsmet Demir, ed., *Kayseri Temettüât Defteri (H. 1250/M. 1834 Tarihli)* (Kayseri, 1998). I am indebted to Alp Yücel Kaya for informing me of this register.
7 Marc Aymes, *A Provincial History of the Ottoman Empire: Cyprus and the Eastern Mediterranean in the Nineteenth Century* (Routledge: Abingdon, 2013). For the other studies, Yusuf Sarınay, ed., *Osmanlı İdaresinde Kıbrıs: Nüfusu-Arazi Dağılımı ve Türk vakıfları [Cyprus under Ottoman Rule: Population-Land Distribution and Turkish Endowments]* (Ankara: T. C. Başbakanlık Devlet Arşivleri Genel Müdürlüğü, Osmanlı Arşivi Daire Başkanlığı, 2000), 129–97; Vahdettin Atik, ed., *Belgelerle Osmanlı Yönetiminde Kıbrıs [Based on Documents Cyprus under the Ottoman Rule]* (Istanbul: Cumhurbaşkanliği Devlet Arşivleri Başkanliği 2020), 79–246; Evangelia Balta, ed., *Registering Life in a Multicultural City. Late Ottoman Nicosia* (Baden-Baden: Orient-Institut Istanbul, 2022); Evangelia Balta, ed., *Ottoman Chrysochou (Mid-19th Century)* (Istanbul: Libra, 2019); Evangelia Balta, ed., *Ottoman Paphos. Population, Taxation and Wealth (Mid-19th Century)* (Istanbul: The ISIS Press, 2016); Evangelia Balta, Mustafa Oğuz, and Ali Efdal Özkul, *Kouklia in Nineteenth Century Cyprus: On the Ruins of an Once Glorious Paphos* (Istanbul: The ISIS Press, 2015); Evangelia Balta et al., "Temettuat Defteri #16153 (ML.VRD.TMT.#16153)." Transcribed dataset, accessed August 17, 2021, http://helios-eie.ekt.gr/EIE/handle/10442/8703?locale=el.
8 For such examples from the eighteenth century which could be considered part of this genealogy, see Ottoman Archives (OA)—Başbakanlık Osmanlı Arşivleri (BOA), D.BŞM.d. 3825, 4094, 4099, 4172, 4177, 4258, 4263, 4284, 4285, 4450. I am indebted to İrfan Kokdaş and Yahya Araz for informing me of the existence of these surveys.
9 The database of the survey is available at "The 1832/33 Ottoman property survey of Cyprus," accessed December 12, 2023, https://cyprus1833.hua.gr/en/. As of that time, the data entry and curating procedures required to create 231,935 entries across 1,094 taxonomic categories, has involved 215,644 user actions, and taken 9,752 hours of work on the database by the aforementioned data-entry team of the project.
10 Αντώνης Χατζηκυριακού, *Χερσαίο νησί. Η Μεσόγειος και η Κύπρος στην οθωμανική εποχή των επαναστάσεων [Peninsular Island: Cyprus and the Mediterranean in the Ottoman Age of Revolutions]* (Θεσσαλονίκη: Ψηφίδες, 2023), 190–200.
11 Atik, *Belgelerle Osmanli Yönetiminde Kıbrıs,* 49.
12 I am calculating this figure using the 1857 census of Spain as proxy, being the temporally closest available dataset with comparable socio-economic conditions. The proportion of those below fifteen years of age was 35%. *Resumen general. Censo de 1857* (Fondo documental del Instituto Nacional de Estadística), accessed December 14, 2023,

www.ine.es/inebaseweb/pdfDispacher.do?td=192687&ext=.pdf. I am indebted to historical demographer Dácil Juif for her assistance.
13 Gökay Karaduman and Ahmet Tabakoğlu, "19. Yüzyıl Temettuat Defterleri'ne Göre Üsküp/Koçana Kazası'nın Lorenz Eğrisi ve Gini Katsayısı ile Gelir Dağılımının Analizi [Analysis of Income Distribution of Skopje/Koçana District with Lorenz Curve and Gini Coefficient According to 19th Century Temettuat Registers]," *Eskişehir Osmangazi Üniversitesi İİBF Dergisi* 16, no. 1 (2021): 146–65.
14 Χατζηκυριακού, *Χερσαίο νησί*, 65.
15 Χατζηκυριακού, *Χερσαίο νησί*, 119–28.
16 George Hill, *A History of Cyprus*, vol. 4: *The Ottoman Province, the British Colony*, ed. Harry Luke (Cambridge: Cambridge University Press, 1952), 263.
17 Spyropoulos, Poulios, and Anastasopoulos, "*Çiftliks*."
18 See indicatively, Immanuel Wallerstein, *The Modern World-System*, vols. 1–4 (New York: Academic Press: 1974–1989); Huri Islamoğlu, ed., *The Ottoman Empire and the World Economy* (Cambridge: Cambridge University Press, 1987). Earlier forms of the argument came from Marxist traditions of thought, discussed in Gilles Veinstein, "On the Çiftlik Debate," in *Landholding and Commercial Agriculture in the Middle East*, ed. Cağlar Keyder and Faruk Tabak (Albany: State University of New York Press, 1991), 35–54.
19 Nicolas Vatin, "A Day of Tribute to Gilles Veinstein," *La lettre du Collège de France* [online] 9 (2015). https://doi.org/10.4000/lettre-cdf.2218.
20 Veinstein, "On the Çiftlik Debate," 53.
21 See endnotes 6 and 17.
22 Yūzō Nagata, "Notes on the Managerial System of a Big Farm (*Çiftlik*) in the Mid-18th Century Turkey," in *Studies on the Social and Economic History of the Ottoman Empire*, ed. Yūzō Nagata (Izmir: Akademi Kitapevi, 1995), 83–101.
23 Alp Yüvel Kaya, "On the Çiftlik Regulation in Tırhala in the Mid-Nineteenth Century: Economists, Pashas, Governors, Çiftlik-holders, Subaşıs, and Sharecroppers," in *Ottoman Rural Societies and Economies, Halcyon Days in Crete VIII. A Symposium Held in Rethymno, January 13–15, 2012*, ed. Elias Kolovos (Rethymnon: Crete University Press, 2015), 333–79; Yücel Terzibaşoğlu, "Landed Estates, Rural Commons and Collective Agriculture in Ottoman Niş and Leskofçe in the Nineteenth Century," *Turkish Historical Review* 13, no. 3 (2022): 343–71; Yücel Terzibaşoğlu, "Privatisation of Land, Criminalisation of Custom, and Land Disputes in 19th-Century Anatolia," in *Les acteurs des transformations fonciéres autour de la Méditerranée au XIXe siècle*, ed. Vanessa Guéno and Didier Guignard (Paris: Karthala and Maison Méditerranéenne des Sciences de l'Homme, 2013), 25–47.
24 Benjamin Arbel, "Cypriot Population under Venetian Rule (1473–1571): A Demographic Study," in *Cyprus, the Franks, and Venice, 13th–16th Centuries* (Aldershot: Ashgate, 2000), v, 187.
25 Mehmet Demiryürek, "The Story of the Parici: Fiscal Transformation and Social Reconstruction in Ottoman Cyprus (1572–1672)," *Turkish Historical Review* 14, no. 1 (2023): 1–25; Benjamin Arbel and Gilles Veinstein, "La fiscalité Vénéto-chypriote au miroir de la législation ottomane: le *qânûnnâme* de 1572," *Turcica* 18 (1986): 7–51; Halil İnalcık, "Ottoman Policy and Administration in Cyprus After the Conquest," in *Milletlerarası Birinci Kıbrıs Tetkikleri Kongresi (14–19 Nisan 1969). Türk Heyeti Tebliğleri* (Ankara: Türk Kültürünü Araştırma Enstitüsü Yayınları, 1971), 59–77.
26 Ulbe Bosma, *The World of Sugar: How the Sweet Stuff Transformed Our Politics, Health, and Environment over 2,000 Years* (Cambridge, MA: Harvard University Press, 2023), 4, 26–36.
27 Χατζηκυριακού, *Χερσαίο νησί*, 109–10, 139.
28 Sven Beckert, *Empire of Cotton: A Global History* (New York: Vintage, 2014), 101.
29 Aymes, *A Provincial History*, 95.

30 Κυπριανός Δ. Λούης, "Μορφές οικονομικών σχέσεων στην Κύπρο (1817–1839): ο Γεωργάκης Μαρκαντωνίδης και τα τσιφλίκια Μόρφου και Derviş Efendi [Forms of Economic Relations in Cyprus (1817–1839): Georgakis Markantonides and the Çiftliks of Morphos and Derviş Efendi]" (PhD diss., Πανεπιστήμιο Ιωαννίνων, 2006), 63.
31 Robert Hamilton Lang, *Cyprus: Its History, Its Present Resources, and Future Prospects* (London: Macmillan, 1878), 360.
32 Γεώργιος Παπαγεωργίου, *Ο εκσυγχρονισμός του Έλληνα πραγματευτή σύμφωνα με τα ευρωπαϊκά πρότυπα (τέλη 18ου—αρχές 19ου αι.). Ένα μαθηματάριο εμπορίου του Αθανασίου Ψαλίδα [The Modernization of the Greek Trader According to European Standards (Late 18th—Early 19th Century). A Trade Manual by Athanasios Psalidas]* (Αθήνα: Εκδόσεις Αφοί Τολίδη, 1990), 18–19, 72–86, 126–27.
33 Γεώργιος Παπαγεωργίου, *Ο εκσυγχρονισμός του Έλληνα πραγματευτή σύμφωνα με τα ευρωπαϊκά πρότυπα (τέλη 18ου—αρχές 19ου αι.). Ένα μαθηματάριο εμπορίου του Αθανασίου Ψαλίδα [The Modernization of the Greek Trader According to European Standards (Late 18th—Early 19th Century). A Trade Manual by Athanasios Psalidas]* (Αθήνα: Εκδόσεις Αφοί Τολίδη, 1990), 8.
34 Κυπριανός Δ. Λούης, "Η εκμετάλλευση του τσιφλικιού της Πύλας [Exploitation of the Pyla *Çiftlik*]," *Επετηρίδα Κέντρου Επιστημονικών Ερευνών* 30 (2004): 334–35; Kyprianos D. Louis, *Entrepreneurship and Economic Strategy in Cyprus in the First Half of the 19th Century: The Case of Georgakis Markantonides* (Nicosia: Cyprus Research Centre, 2022), 190–91.
35 Nagata, "Notes," 87.
36 Λούης, "Η εκμετάλλευση του τσιφλικιού της Πύλας," 334–35; Louis, *Entrepreneurship and Economic Strategy*, 190–91.
37 Lang, *Cyprus*, 356–69.
38 İnalcık Halil, Yıldırı Mehmet and Kadıoğlu Songül, eds., *Kıbrıs Tahrir Defterleri: Mufassal, İcmal ve Derdest. Tıpkıbasım [Cyprus Tahrir Registers: Mufassal, Incmal and Derdest. Reprint]* (Ankara: T. C. Çevre ve Şehirlik Bakanlığı, Tapu ve Kadastro Genel Müdürlüğü, Arşiv Dairesi Başkanlığı, 2013), 153–56.
39 Θεόδωρος Παπαδόπουλος, "Το άσμα των Διερμηνέων [The Song of the Translators]," *Κυπριακαί Σπουδαί* 45 (1981): 78.
40 BOA. A.DVN.KBŞ 1/20; A.DVN.KBŞ 1/17; HAT 36516; C.HR. 5791; C.ADL.1508; HAT 16918; C.ML. 22683.
41 BOA. A.DVN.KBM. 1/40.
42 John Derek Latham, art. "Salam," in *Encyclopaedia of Islam2*, ed. Peri Bearman, et al. Consulted Online February 20, 2024, http://dx.doi.org/10.1163/1573-3912_islam_SIM_6519; Mehmet Zeki Pakalin, art. "Selem," in *Osmanlı Tarih Deyimleri ve Terimleri Sözlüğü*, vol. 3 (Istanbul: Maarif Basımevi, 1954), 160–61; Bilal Aybakan, art. "Selem," *TDVİA* 36 (2009): 402–5.
43 Beshara Doumani, *Rediscovering Palestine: Merchants and Peasants in Jabal Nablus, 1700–1900* (Berkeley and Los Angeles: University of California Press, 1995).
44 Antonis Hadjikyriacou, "Society and Economy on an Ottoman Island: Cyprus in the Eighteenth Century" (PhD diss., School of Oriental and African Studies, University of London, 2011), 209–35.
45 Antonis Hadjikyriacou, "Society and Economy on an Ottoman Island: Cyprus in the Eighteenth Century" (PhD diss., School of Oriental and African Studies, University of London, 2011), 232.
46 Hadjikyriacou, "Society and Economy on an Ottoman Island."
47 Ali Yaycioglu, *Partners of the Empire: The Crisis of the Ottoman Order in the Age of Revolutions* (Stanford: Stanford University Press, 2016).
48 Ariel Salzmann, *Review of Landholding and Commercial Agriculture in the Middle East*, ed. Çağlar Keyder and Faruk Tabak (Albany: State University of New York Press, 1991)," *Turkish Studies Association Bulletin* 16, no. 2 (1992): 289.

49 Veinstein, "On the Çiftlik Debate," 52.
50 Κωνσταντίνος Θ. Δημαράς, "Αθησαύριστο έγγραφο του Αρχιεπισκόπου Κύπρου Κυπριανού [Unrecorded Document of Archbishop Cyprian of Cyprus]," in *Πρακτικά του πρώτου διεθνούς Κυπρολογικού συνεδρίου, Λευκωσία 14–19 Απριλίου 1969*, ed. Θεόδωρος Παπαδόπουλος and Μενέλαος Χριστοδούλου, vol. 3, no. I: *Ιστορία-Γεωγραφία* (Λευκωσία: Εταιρεία Κυπριακών Σπουδών, 1973), 55–61.
51 Λούης, "Η εκμετάλλευση," 334–35; Louis, *Entrepreneurship and Economic Strategy*, 190–91.
52 Faruk Tabak, *The Waning of the Mediterranean, 1550–1870: A Geohistorical Approach* (Baltimore: Johns Hopkins University Press, 2007), 223.
53 Faruk Tabak, *The Waning of the Mediterranean, 1550–1870: A Geohistorical Approach* (Baltimore: Johns Hopkins University Press, 2007), 213.
54 Trevor Aston and Charles H. E. Philpin, eds., *The Brenner Debate: Agrarian Class Structure and Economic Development in Pre-Industrial Europe* (New York: Cambridge University Press, 1985).
55 Rodney Howard Hilton, "A Crisis of Feudalism," in *The Brenner Debate: Agrarian Class Structure and Economic Development in Pre-Industrial Europe*, ed. Trevor Aston and Charles H. E. Philpin (New York: Cambridge University Press, 1985), 136.
56 See indicatively, Robert C. Allen, *The British Industrial Revolution in Global Perspective* (Oxford: Oxford University Press, 2009).

Bibliography

"The 1832/33 Ottoman Property Survey of Cyprus." Accessed December 12, 2023, https://cyprus1833.hua.gr/en/.

Allen, Robert C. *The British Industrial Revolution in Global Perspective*. Oxford: Oxford University Press, 2009.

Anastasopoulos, Antonis, Stefanos Poulios, and Yannis Spyropoulos. "The Spread of Çiftliks (Large Estates) in the Eighteenth-Century Ottoman Balkans: The Case of the District of Veroia." In *History, Culture and Research*, edited by Dumitru-Cătălin Rogojanu and Gherghina Boda, vol. 3, 90–109. Târgovişte: Cetatea de Scaun, 2019.

Arbel, Benjamin. "Cypriot Population under Venetian Rule (1473–1571): A Demographic Study." In *Cyprus, the Franks, and Venice, 13th-16th Centuries*. Aldershot: Ashgate, 2000.

Arbel, Benjamin, and Gilles Veinstein. "La fiscalité Vénéto-chypriote au miroir de la législation ottomane: le qânûnnâme de 1572." *Turcica* 18 (1986): 7–51.

Aston, Trevor, and Charles H. E. Philpin, eds. *The Brenner Debate: Agrarian Class Structure and Economic Development in Pre-industrial Europe*. New York: Cambridge University Press, 1985.

Atik, Vahdettin, ed. *Belgelerle Osmanlı Yönetiminde Kıbrıs [On the Basis of Documents Cyprus under the Ottoman Rule]*. Istanbul: Cumhurbaşkanliği Devlet Arşivleri Başkanliği, 2020.

Aybakan, Bilal. Art. "Selem." Türkiye Diyanet Vakfı (TDV) İslam Ansiklopedisi, vol. 36, 402–5. İstanbul: Türkiye Diyanet Vakfı, 2000.

Aymes, Marc. *A Provincial History of the Ottoman Empire: Cyprus and the Eastern Mediterranean in the Nineteenth Century*. Routledge: Abingdon, 2013.

Balta, Evangelia, ed. *Ottoman Paphos. Population, Taxation and Wealth (Mid-19th Century)*. Istanbul: The ISIS Press, 2016.

Balta, Evangelia, ed. *Ottoman Chrysochou (Mid-19th Century)*. Istanbul: Libra, 2019.

Balta, Evangelia, ed. *Registering Life in a Multicultural City. Late Ottoman Nicosia*. Baden-Baden: Orient-Institut Istanbul, 2022.

Balta, Evangelia, et al. "Temettuat Defteri #16153 (ML.VRD.TMT.#16153)" [The Temettuat Register 16513]. Transcribed dataset. http://helios-eie.ekt.gr/EIE/handle/10442/8703?locale=el

Balta, Evangelia, Mustafa Oğuz, and Ali Efdal Özkul. *Kouklia in Nineteenth Century Cyprus: On the Ruins of a Once Glorious Paphos*. Istanbul: The ISIS Press, 2015.
Beckert, Sven. *Empire of Cotton: A Global History*. New York: Vintage, 2014.
Bosma, Ulbe. *The World of Sugar: How the Sweet Stuff Transformed Our Politics, Health, and Environment over 2,000 Years*. Cambridge, MA: Harvard University Press, 2023.
Canbakal, Hülya, and Alpay Filiztekin. "Wealth Inequality in Northwestern Anatolia under the Ottomans, 1460–1870." Unpublished paper presented online in 3rd Seminar of Greek Economic History Association, February 6, 2023.
Cosgel, Metin M. "Ottoman Tax Registers (Tahrir Defterleri)." *Historical Methods* 37, no. 2 (2004): 87–100.
Demir, İsmet, ed. *Kayseri Temettuat Defteri (H. 1250/M. 1834 Tarihli) [The Temettual Register of Kayseri (H.1250/M.1834)]*. Kayseri: Kayseri Ticaret Odası, 1998.
Demiryürek, Mehmet. "The Story of the Parici: Fiscal Transformation and Social Reconstruction in Ottoman Cyprus (1572–1672)." *Turkish Historical Review* 14, no. 1 (2023): 1–25.
Doumani, Beshara. *Rediscovering Palestine: Merchants and Peasants in Jabal Nablus, 1700–1900.* Berkeley and Los Angeles: University of California Press, 1995.
Hadjikyriacou, Antonis. "Society and Economy on an Ottoman Island: Cyprus in the Eighteenth Century." PhD diss., School of Oriental and African Studies, University of London, 2011.
Hadjikyriacou, Antonis. "Economic Geographies." In *Doing Spatial History*, edited by Riccardo Bavaj, Konrad Lawson, and Bernhard Struck, 252–73. London and New York: Routledge, 2021.
Hill, George. *A History of Cyprus*, vol. 4: *The Ottoman Province, the British Colony*, edited by Harry Luke. Cambridge: Cambridge University Press, 1952.
Hilton, Rodney Howard. "A Crisis of Feudalism." In *The Brenner Debate: Agrarian Class Structure and Economic Development in Pre-industrial Europe*, edited by Trevor Aston and Charles H. E. Philpin, 119–37. New York: Cambridge University Press, 1985.
İnalcık, Halil. "Ottoman Policy and Administration in Cyprus After the Conquest." In *Milletlerarası Birinci Kıbrıs Tetkikleri Kongresi (14–19 Nisan 1969). Türk Heyeti Tebliğleri [First International Cyprus Studies Congress (April 14–19, 1969). Proceedings of the Turkish Delegation]*, 59–77. Ankara: Türk Kültürünü Araştırma Enstitüsü Yayınları, 1971.
Islamoğlu, Huri, ed. *The Ottoman Empire and the World Economy*. Cambridge: Cambridge University Press, 1987.
Karaduman, Gökay, and Ahmet Tabakoğlu. "19. Yüzyıl Temettuat Defterleri'ne Göre Üsküp/Koçana Kazası'nın Lorenz Eğrisi ve Gini Katsayısı ile Gelir Dağılımının Analizi [Analysis of the Income Distribution of Skopje/Koçana District with Lorenz Curve and Gini Coefficient Based on the Temettuat Registers of the 19th Century]." *Eskişehir Osman Gazi Üniversitesi İİBF Dergisi [Eskişehir Osman Gazi University Journal of Economics and Administrative Sciences]* 16, no. 1 (2021): 146–65.
Karakoç, Ulaş, and Alp Yücel Kaya, eds. *İktisat Tarihinin Dönüşü: Yeni Yaklaşımlar ve Tartışmalar [The Return of Economic History: New Approaches and Debates]*. Istanbul: İletşim, 2021.
Kaya, Alp Yüvel. "On the Çiftlik Regulation in Tırhala in the Mid-Nineteenth Century: Economists, Pashas, Governors, Çiftlik-holders, Subaşıs, and Sharecroppers." In *Ottoman Rural Societies and Economies, Halcyon Days in Crete VIII. A Symposium Held in Rethymno, January 13–15, 2012*, edited by Elias Kolovos, 333–79. Rethymnon: Crete University Press, 2015.
İnalcık, Halil, Yıldırı Mehmet, and Kadıoğlu Songül, eds. *Kıbrıs Tahrir Defterleri: Mufassal, İcmal ve Derdest. Tıpkıbasım [Cyprus Tahrir Registers: Mufassal, Icmal and Derdest. Reprint]*. Ankara: T. C. Çevre ve Şehirlik Bakanlığı, Tapu ve Kadastro Genel Müdürlüğü, Arşiv Dairesi Başkanlığı, 2013.
Lang, Robert Hamilton. *Cyprus: Its History, Its Present Resources, and Future Prospects.* London: Macmillan, 1878.

Latham, John Derek. Art. "Salam." In *Encyclopaedia of Islam*, edited by Peri Bearman, Thierry Bianquis, Edmund Bosworth, E. J. Donzel, and Wolfhart Heinrichs. http://dx.doi.org/10.1163/1573-3912_islam_SIM_6519

Louis, Kyprianos D. *Entrepreneurship and Economic Strategy in Cyprus in the First Half of the 19th Century: The Case of Georgakis Markantonides*. Nicosia: Cyprus Research Centre, 2022.

Nagata, Yūzō. "Notes on the Managerial System of a Big Farm (*çiftlik*) in the Mid-18th Century Turkey." In *Studies on the Social and Economic History of the Ottoman Empire*, edited by Yūzō Nagata, 83–101. Izmir: Akademi Kitapevi, 1995.

Pakalin, Mehmet Zeki. Art. "Selem." In *Osmanlı Tarih Deyimleri ve Terimleri Sözlüğü [Dictionary of Ottoman History Expressions and Terms]*, vol. 3, 160–61. Istanbul: Maarif Basımevi, 1954.

Resumen general. Censo de 1857. Fondo documental del Instituto Nacional de Estadística. www.ine.es/inebaseweb/pdfDispacher.do?td=192687&ext=.pdf

Salzmann, Ariel. Review of "*Landholding and Commercial Agriculture in the Middle East*, edited by Çağlar Keyder and Faruk Tabak (Albany: State University of New York Press, 1991)." *Turkish Studies Association Bulletin* 16, no. 2 (1992): 264–71.

Sarınay, Yusuf, ed. *Osmanlı İdaresinde Kıbrıs: Nüfusu-Arazi Dağılımı ve Türk Vakıfları [Cyprus under Ottoman Rule: Population-Land Distribution and Turkish Endowments]*. Ankara: T. C. Başbakanlık Devlet Arşivleri Genel Müdürlüğü, Osmanlı Arşivi Daire Başkanlığı, 2000.

Spyropoulos, Yannis, Stefanos Poulios, and Antonis Anastasopoulos. "*Çiftliks*, Landed Elites, and Tax Allocation in Eighteenth-Century Ottoman Veroia." *European Journal of Turkish Studies* [online] (2022). https://doi.org/10.4000/ejts.6647

Tabak, Faruk. *The Waning of the Mediterranean, 1550–1870: A Geohistorical Approach*. Baltimore: Johns Hopkins University Press, 2007.

Terzibaşoğlu, Yücel. "Privatisation of land, criminalisation of custom, and land disputes in 19th-century Anatolia." In *Les acteurs des transformations fonciéres autour de la Méditerranée au XIXe siècle*, edited by Vanessa Guéno and Didier Guignard, 25–47. Paris: Karthala and Maison Méditerranéenne des Sciences de l'Homme, 2013.

Terzibaşoğlu, Yücel. "Landed Estates, Rural Commons and Collective Agriculture in Ottoman Niş and Leskofçe in the Nineteenth Century." *Turkish Historical Review* 13, no. 3 (2022): 343–71.

Vatin, Nicolas. "A Day of Tribute to Gilles Veinstein." *La lettre du Collège de France* [online] 9 (2015). https://doi.org/10.4000/lettre-cdf.2218

Veinstein, Gilles. "On the Çiftlik debate." In *Landholding and Commercial Agriculture in the Middle East*, edited by Cağlar Keyder and Faruk Tabak, 35–54. Albany: State University of New York Press, 1991.

Wallerstein, Immanuel. *The Modern World-System*, vols. 1–4. New York: Academic Press, 1974–1989.

Yaycioglu, Ali. *Partners of the Empire: The Crisis of the Ottoman Order in the Age of Revolutions.* Stanford: Stanford University Press, 2016.

Δημαράς, Κωνσταντίνος Θ. "Αθησαύριστο έγγραφο του Αρχιεπισκόπου Κύπρου Κυπριανού." In *Πρακτικά του πρώτου διεθνούς Κυπρολογικού συνεδρίου, Λευκωσία, 14–19 Απριλίου 1969*, edited by Παπαδόπουλος Θεόδωρος, Χριστοδούλου Μενέλαος, 3/I: *Ιστορία-Γεωγραφία*, 55–61. Λευκωσία: Εταιρεία Κυπριακών Σπουδών, 1973. [Dimaras, Konstantinos Th. "Unrecorded document of the Archbishop Cyprian of Cyprus." In *Proceedings of the First International Conference on Cyprology, Nicosia, April 14–19, 1969*, edited by Theodoros Papadopoulos and Menelaos Christodoulou, vol. 3, no. 1: *History-Geography*, 55–61. Nicosia: Society for Cypriot Studies, 1973.]

Λούης, Κυπριανός Δ. "Η εκμετάλλευση του τσιφλικιού της Πύλας." *Επετηρίδα Κέντρου Επιστημονικών Ερευνών* 30 (2004), 305–45. [Louis, Kyprianos D. "Exploitation of the Pyla Çiftlik." *Yearbook of the Scientific Research Center* 30 (2004), 305–45.]

Λούης, Κυπριανός Δ. "Μορφές οικονομικών σχέσεων στην Κύπρο (1817–1839): ο Γεωργάκης Μαρκαντωνίδης και τα τσιφλίκια Μόρφου και Derviş Efendi." PhD diss., Πανεπιστήμιο Ιωαννίνων, 2006. [Louis, Kyprianos D. "Forms of Economic Relations in Cyprus (1817–1839): Georgakis Markantonides and the Çiftliks of Morphos and Derviş Efendi." PhD diss., University of Ioannina, 2006.]

Παπαγεωργίου, Γεώργιος. *Ο εκσυγχρονισμός του Έλληνα πραγματευτή σύμφωνα με τα ευρωπαϊκά πρότυπα (τέλη 18ου—αρχές 19ου αι.). Ένα μαθηματάριο εμπορίου του Αθανασίου Ψαλίδα.* Αθήνα: Εκδόσεις Αφοί Τολίδη, 1990. [Papageorgiou, Georgios. *The Modernization of the Greek Trader According to European Standards (Late 18th—Early 19th c.). A Trade Manual by Athanasius Psalida.* Athens: Tolidis Publications, 1990.]

Παπαδόπουλος, Θεόδωρος. "Το άσμα των Διερμηνέων." *Κυπριακαί Σπουδαί* 45 (1981): 55–141. [Papadopoulos, Theodoros. "The Song of the Translators." *Kypriakai Spoudai* 45 (1981): 55–141.]

Χατζηκυριακού, Αντώνης. *Χερσαίο νησί. Η Μεσόγειος και η Κύπρος στην οθωμανική εποχή των επαναστάσεων.* Θεσσαλονίκη: Ψηφίδες, 2023. [Hadjikyriacou, Antonis. *Peninsular Island: Cyprus and the Mediterranean in the Ottoman Age of Revolutions.* Thessaloniki: Psifides, 2023.]

15 Stephan Spartalian

An Armenian Entrepreneur in the Age of "National Economy" of the Young Turk Period

Yaşar Tolga Cora

In the middle of August 1918, while the Great War was marching toward its conclusion, the Armenian language press in the Ottoman capital gave the news of the passing away of Stephan Spartalian in his summer residence on Prinkipo. Mr. Spartalian was a former deputy of the imperial parliament and a well-known businessman of the late Ottoman Istanbul.

Mr. Spartalian's funeral turned into a performative meeting for the Armenian community of Istanbul, which was kept exempt from the death marches. The service was held in the main cathedral of the city, led by the deputy patriarch—as the patriarch was exiled at the time—and attended by the leading Armenian figures, directors of various orphanages which Mr. Spartalian had supported financially, alongside "Turkish and foreign esteemed personalities."[1] Among the Greek visitors was the Orthodox Archbishop of Smyrna, the hometown of the Spartalians, and among the Turkish figures were Ziya Bey, the president of the Maritime Commercial Tribunal, Nazif Bey, the former president of the Military Tribunal, and Nuzhet Bey, the second chamberlain of the imperial palace. On top of the list of Turkish guests stood Ali Cevat Bey, the director of the Incirli Estate Development and Construction Joint-Stock Company (*İncirli Çiftliği İmarat ve İnşaat Osmanlı Anonim Şirketi*, IEDCC).[2] The Armenian businessman had recently established the company to transform his meadows in the district of Incirli near Makriköy (Bakırköy) into a new suburb away from the impoverished and over-populated city.

IEDCC was an early example of an urban development company; one of the least studied phenomena in the economic and urban history of the imperial capital, although the role of such institutions in the making of the imperial cities and the metropoles in the colonies has been widely acknowledged in the scholarship.[3] As a recent collection of studies has shown, land speculation by investing in rural land around the city was in the portfolio of entrepreneurs of different ethnic and religious backgrounds in 19th-century Istanbul.[4] However, the different ways in which these entrepreneurs accumulated land, the role of family and personal relations in such accumulation, and their dealings with state officials are still less known aspects of this type of investment. This chapter aims to establish a ground for addressing these questions by examining Stephan Spartalian's various business activities with a particular focus on his plans for the Incirli Estate. By examining a case of investment in land, the chapter will contribute to the existing scholarship on

DOI: 10.4324/9781003500780-20

Christian capital owners and entrepreneurs who are depicted primarily as owners of financial or mercantile capital. It also aims to criticize the widespread assumption that Christian and Jewish merchants are primarily actors within and primarily under the auspices of the networks of their own ethno-religious communities and with European capital.[5] Investigating urban development projects such as the one in Incirli will demonstrate that Christian entrepreneurs acted in a broader network of actors which included businessmen of different ethno-religious backgrounds and state officials.

Mr. Spartalian's project in Incirli began in 1911 whereas he established the IEDCC at the end of 1917. This period was crucial for the urban history of the imperial capital as it was a period of constant warfare. The city was impoverished, the inflation rate was the highest among all belligerent states by 1918; the city was overcrowded with waves of refugees, first the Muslims after the Balkan Wars, and then by subjects of the empire from all communities and the refugees outside the empire.[6] As will be discussed in the following, in an advertorial piece in 1914, Mr. Spartalian's project was depicted as an opportunity to find cheap housing in a suburb. Yet, it was probably "cheap" for those who could afford it. Likewise, when IEDCC began to sell lands in the last year of the war, it was the elite who benefitted from the opportunity and invested in suburban land, away from the city of migrants.

Mr. Spartalian's investments took place in a period identified as the National Economy (*Milli İktisat*) policies of the Young Turk rule.[7] The scholarship on the subject has highlighted the role of the state in supporting Turkish/Muslim entrepreneurs and their joint-stock companies.[8] The chapter aims to complicate the focus of the current scholarship on these policies by focusing on the activities of an Armenian entrepreneur in Istanbul in that period. Like many Muslim counterparts, Mr. Spartalian established a joint-stock company and had close relations with the state officials. Thus, the activities of a leading Christian entrepreneur will provide a nuanced picture of the "National Economy" during the Great War. Needless to say, this focus does not deny the process of Turkification in economy. Indeed, like most of the Christian subjects of the empire, the Spartalian family lost their lands, as well. Moreover, in the 1930s, Mr. Spartalian's suburban project in Incirli was revitalized by the political-military elite of Republican Turkey, without hinting at the memory of its former Armenian founder.

Stephan Spartalian: Family Relations and Political Background of an Entrepreneur

Stephan Spartalian was born in Smyrna in 1853 as one of four sons of Agop Spartalian, the founder of the giant commercial house of the Spartalians. During the time of the Agop, the Spartalians turned into one of the leading merchants of Smyrna, the booming port city in the mid-19th century.[9] The Spartalian commercial house joined the ranks of the Ottoman Armenian commercial houses in Manchester in the late 1860s.[10] Their success in trade was also translated into philanthropic activities and received appreciation from the Sultan for their commercial and communal activities.[11] Moreover, commercial success meant close ties with political power. Agop Spartalian was known to be a very good friend of Hüseyin Avni Paşa, the grand vizier of the tremulous years of 1874–75 and a mastermind of the Ottoman Constitution of 1876. Agop Spartalian served as a deputy of Izmir in the first Ottoman parliament.[12]

By the turn of the late 19th and early 20th centuries, the four Spartalian brothers began to separate to establish their own business houses. First, the eldest brother Takavor Spartalian formed his own company specializing in the booming carpet business in 1897. Then, Yervand Spartalian departed to open his business in fabrics in 1903. Following those breakups, the Spartalian company began to be led by Stephan and Zareh.[13]

Yet, in that period, Spartalians had moved away from the heydays of the past. By late 1907, Stephan and Zareh Spartalian had to declare bankruptcy in the middle of the Great Panic.[14] Although the consequences of the Panic on the Ottoman markets are still not known, news and rumors about economic contraction circulated widely during the period. The Spartalians were among the prime examples.[15] Stephan Spartalian had lost enormous sums in speculative acts in the Paris stock exchange during the Panic, yet the commercial house was more affected when the Bank of England began to collect its loose credits as a financial measure during the Panic. By late 1907, the Spartalian company had goods value of 50.000 Turkish Liras and had 21.000 TL to be collected from the market whereas it was 70.000 TL in debt. The investigator created a payment plan of the 70.000 Liras to be paid within two years. In that liquidation plan, Stephan Spartalian's immovable assets were also mentioned, however, not included in the payment plans.[16]

In addition to the businesses, Mr. Spartalian invested in politics, too, like his father. The term "investment" seems to be an apt one as his engagement in politics went hand in hand with major business dealings. He had been always a part of local politics; a member of the Provincial Administrative Assembly of Aydın province in the late 1890s and received an honorary rank from Sultan Abdülhamid II for his services.[17]

After the Constitutional Revolution of 1908, a few months after his bankruptcy, Stephan Spartalian was elected to the imperial parliament as an "independent" deputy from Izmir.

His election was rather dubious; one Turkish deputy resigned right after being elected to leave his seat to him.[18] Mr. Spartalian served in the Ottoman Parliament until 1912. He did not take the floor except for a few but important cases. One of such cases was his suggestions about the reform in the Eastern provinces while the other was about the activities of the foreign firms. In the latter, he suggested the parliament create legislation that would force foreign firms to adapt themselves to the Ottoman laws and to work toward the cancellation of some of the privileges that they held due to their foreign status.[19] Mr. Spartalian's views, although limited in scope and number, are still important as they show how a leading businessman brought some of its economy-oriented concerns onto the discussion floor of the parliament.

Some of the views in this proposal aimed to diminish the power of the foreign firms and thus might be regarded as serving the Ottoman businessmen to have

Figure 15.1 Stephan Spartalian as the deputy of Izmir/Smyrna 1908.

Source: Salt Research, FFT730052, https://archives.saltresearch.org/handle/123456789/25123

some competitive power against the foreign firms. Yet, Mr. Spartalian was a representative of global firms, which may be due to his connections in the UK as well as his position as a deputy of the parliament.

Among such firms were two British firms that formed a consortium to get the concessions to run some of the lines between various ports of the empire.[20] Some of the ferry lines of Istanbul were run by the *İdare-i Mahsusa* during the reign of Sultan Abdülhamid II. Both the performance of the company administration and the condition of its fleet were under attack after the 1908 Revolution. Mr. Stephanian's application was a result of the attempts to privatize it by the post-revolutionary government with the condition that the majority of the shares would be held by Ottoman subjects. However, the concession could not be materialized despite the support of the Ministry of Public Works.[21]

Personal connections were as important as the official ones in obtaining such concessions and Stephan Spartalian was quite rich in them. He was married to Polin Maksudzade, the daughter of Simon Maksudzade. Simon Maksudyan, who carried the title "bey" and was called Maksudzade (the -zade ending normally reserved for the Muslim prominent figures), was the most important Armenian figure of the Hamidian era; he was the president of the Assembly of the Armenian community and one of the closest to the Sultan Abdülhamid II. As a result of these relations, Simon Bey indeed was seen as a traitor and there was an attempt on his life in 1894 by a group of Armenian revolutionaries.[22] Although Simon Bey preferred to step back from politics after the assassination, he remained one of the most trustworthy Armenians in the eyes of the Sultan. For instance, he was one of the two Armenians summoned to Abdülhamid II's palace to put a halt to the activities of the revolutionaries in the summer of 1895. What is even more interesting is that it was no other than Gabriel Noroudiakian, the future minister of Public Works of the Young Turk era, who counseled them for the course of proper action.[23] These ties illustrate how the Armenian elite were connected to each other both before and after the Revolution, and thus demonstrate some of the continuities at the top echelons in the Armenian community.[24] The family ties and personal relations were especially crucial because they were transformed into economic capital.

Stephan Spartalian: Urban Land Developer

In August of 1911, Mr. Spartalian applied to various offices this time with another project, namely, transforming parts of his lands in Incirli into residential urban land. The land was more than 2.360 *dönüms*, namely, 2,300,000 m^2. Some sections would be used for roads, sidewalks, and public buildings including mosques, churches, synagogue, a school, and a police station, the remaining lands would be divided into plots of no less than 1,000 *arşın*, approximately 550 m^2. The houses would have gardens; thus, the goal was to build a suburb following the examples of garden cities developing in Europe and the USA at the time.[25]

An advertorial essay from 1914 well highlighted the project's suburban characteristics. Those who purchased the land plot would build houses either on their own budget or Mr. Spartalian would construct houses and the owners would pay in installments. There was an emphasis on the gardens in each house as that would form the characteristic of the settlement. The essay also promoted the availability of fresh air and the good view at the complex (such as the Prince Islands); it also emphasized its convenient location for transportation (its proximity to the suburban railroad and the macadam road connecting Istanbul to the provinces). Indeed, a streetcar was proposed to connect the settlement to the railway station at Makriköy, and before its completion, buses would be operated. The settlement would have public facilities and a club (*gazino*) which was already built.[26]

Stephan Spartalian's project was not unique in Istanbul, there were individual attempts and companies to build housing in Istanbul in the period. Moreover, in the nearby district of today's Zeytinburnu, east of Incirli, a savings and building company was established in the 1880s with a similar goal of creating a suburban settlement. The goal of that company, *Arewelyan Tntesakan Miutiwn* (Oriental Savings Association, OSA), was to purchase and divide a large piece of land into smaller plots and sell them to its members through installments and allow them to build their houses while the company would undertake the infrastructure and public facilities.[27] They facilitated a form of capitalist urbanization while business calculations were on the basis of the development of the urban centers both in the European capitals as well as various colonial centers in the period.[28] Mr. Spartalian openly framed his project as a step to solve the housing problem by providing cheap housing—a dubious claim—and also as a contribution to the treasury by generating revenues by turning a meadow into a settlement.[29]

The project of Stephan Spartalian shared another characteristic with other urban projects of the time, namely, the use of vakıf lands. Nineteenth-century Istanbul witnessed the diminishing role of the Islamic vakıfs in urban life as not only many of their functions were taken over by the state but also their lands and properties in the city and outside the city walls changed hands through market transactions.[30] In these transactions, the vakıf properties kept their status mostly in name as the new proprietor (*mutasarrıf*) of land paid a certain and usually a symbolic annual fee to the vakıf while the value of the land increased based on the demands of the market.

While this process opened up "new" land in and around the city for construction, it also allowed different groups including Christian and Jewish entrepreneurs to invest by obtaining the rights of proprietorship of these vakıf lands—not to say "own" to keep the fiction of the nonalienation of Islamic vakıf properties. Moreover, some of these belonged to the imperial vakıfs which were established by the previous sultans or the members of their households. Thus, the political power holders, the palace, and the bureaucracy in the nineteenth century were in the position to decide on their fate. The lands in the projects of Stephan Spartalian were indeed lands of such imperial vakıfs that changed hands over time and they necessitated some ties with the holders of the political power.

The lands he proposed for the Incirli housing project were the lands of Sultan Beyazid Vakıf. They passed into his hands in July 1911, only a few months before his initial application to the state offices. More importantly, they were previously held by Simon Bey Maksudzade, who was in the closest circle of Sultan Abdülhamid II and Stephan Spartalian's father-in-law. The lands first had passed into the

Table 15.1 The value of vakıf lands which were converted to residential areas, and the yearly fees paid for them.

Register the Number of the Deed	*Size (dönüm+ zira)*		*Value (in Piasters)*	*Yearly Fee (in Piasters) Mukâtaa*
	Dönüm (1 dönüm was app. 918 m²)	Zira (1 zira was app. 0.57 m²)		
64	395	505	195,000	146.10
65	476	616	1,500,000	1,125
66	245	20	375,000	281.10
67	189	1000	375,000	281.10
68	240	586	720,000	540
69	819	244	1,635,000	1,226.10
Total	2,366	171	4,800,000	3,600

Source: B.O.A., Ş.D., 81–4, no.17.

hands of the son of Simon Bey, Maksud, and his daughter Polin, Mr. Spartalian's wife. The siblings sold the land, which was recorded as a meadow, to Mr. Spartalian in April 1911 while they were in Paris through their deputy Nshan Andonian in Istanbul. Mr. Spartalian obtained the official approval of the Council of the State which changed the status of the meadow into residential land in July 1911.[31]

In addition to the legal transaction of the land, Mr. Spartalian prepared the maps and plans of the land which was a crucial step in the transformation of its status. These maps were essential as they formed the basis of the cadastral knowledge. They delineated the borders of different plots which would be later divided into smaller individual plots and sold in the market.[32] As we will see in the following, these maps and plans themselves carried exchange value in the market by themselves, too.

When the status of the land changed and gained a new market value, Mr. Spartalian was obliged to set a new amount to be paid to the treasury of the vakıf. However, this was a symbolic amount of 75/100,000 piasters (kuruş) (Table 15.1). Neither the potential increase in the value of the land was taken into account in the calculations of the yearly fees.

Despite the elaborated plans, the project had not progressed by 1914. The constantly changing political, social, and demographic world of the late Ottoman Empire might be a reason for this. In the middle of World War I, in December 1917, Mr. Spartalian once again tried to revitalize the project, this time by establishing a joint-stock company, Incirli Estate Development and Construction Joint-Stock Company (IEDCC) for a period of 25 years.[33]

The Foundation of IEDCC

Joint-stock companies in the late Ottoman Empire, particularly those established during World War I, are considered as the founding blocks of the "national economy" of the era. The governing Committee of Union and Progress aimed to create a nascent Muslim-Turkish bourgeoise through supporting their entrepreneurial activities, to regulate the market, and to provide the provisioning of the cities during the war.[34] The companies were also instrumental in the use of the confiscated properties of non-Muslims, as the founding capital of many of these companies, particularly those in the provinces often came through the confiscation and transfer of properties during the Armenian Genocide.[35] This process of capital accumulation and Turkification of the economy was seen as the backbone of the economy of the republican period, too.[36]

Yet, as the recent critical scholarship underlined, this widely accepted definition of "national economy" might mislead on different grounds despite its explanatory power.[37] For instance, the case of IEDCC shows the vivid activities of Armenian businessmen in Istanbul in the period of Turkification. The founders of the company were Armenians and Muslims, figures from both bureaucratic offices and financial circles. The founders of the company were Ahmed Salim Beyefendi, the former president of the Office of Administrative and Educational Affairs of the Council of the State, and Stephan Spartalian who used the title "the former deputy of Izmir." The other five members of the seven-membered Board of Directors were Cevad Beyefendi, a member of the executive board of the Imperial Ottoman Bank, Nüzhed Beyefendi, the second chamberlain of the imperial palace, Military Doctor Aziz Paşa, retired with the rank of a brigadier, Takavor Sukasyan Efendi, president of the Ottoman Commercial Bank, and K. Hosrovyan Efendi, a prominent merchant.[38] The ethnic composition of the directors of the IEDCC does not fit into the mainstream understanding of the national economy of the period.

Yet, there are other aspects of the company which complicate the understanding of the national economy. The Turkification of the economy was depicted as a necessary step toward the broader goal of foundation of the Turkish nation-state. This position which prioritizes the political goals over the economic ones, overshadows the discussions of not only the ethnic composition of the companies but also the personal and profit-oriented motivations of many entrepreneurs, Muslim and Christian alike, of the period. Most of the market-oriented activities that may contradict the political goals of the Union and Progress Party are still understudied.

Ahmet Salim's position as partner of Stephan Spartalian illustrates these points. He was the former president of the Office of Administrative and Educational Affairs of the Council of the State but by the time the IEDCC was established, he had already lost this prestigious position. Interestingly enough, he had been insistently petitioning his former office to have a position fitting his past services.[39] Thus, Ahmet Salim Beyefendi's role as the co-founder of the IECDD was not a result of a close affiliation with the ruling party but rather a result of his attempt to make money through the prestige and connections of his former position. In Ahmet Salim's case, however, there is more that challenges the primary role attributed to political power and ideology in the establishment of such joint-stock companies in the period. Ahmet Salim Beyefendi was one of the signatories in the Council of the State that approved Stephan Spartalian's initial application to transform the meadows into residential areas in 1911. In other words, his path had crossed with

Mr. Spartalian long before the foundation of IEDCC thanks to his bureaucratic position not through his connection with the governing party. Bureaucratic power and business had merged in the case of IEDCC, but it did so in a way that has not been examined in the scholarship on the national economy.

The idiosyncrasies of the IEDCC do not end there. The founding capital of the IEDCC, 80,000 Ottoman Liras, was provided by the sale of Mr. Spartalian's lands and the related projects to his own company. According to the contract signed by Stephan Spartalian, this amount included both the 2,037,588 zira land and all the plans and projects he had commissioned, including, in his words "particularly the plan for the construction of the street car running between Makriköy and Incirli" which amounted to 60,000 Liras "as assessed by the company."[40] The company purchased further land from Mr Spartalian, amounting to 267,000 zira (130 donum) for 30,000 Liras, thus possessed land which worthed 110,000 Liras in total.

However, the question of whether there was any money that changed hands remains a curious one. As, on 1 December 1918, only 8,000 Liras were paid to Stephan Spartalian's account in the Ottoman Commercial Bank as a downpayment. The remaining 72,000 were claimed to be deposited in the treasury of the IEDCC on 5 December.[41] Likewise, the second purchase of land which worthed 30,000 Liras was claimed to be paid, again, to the treasury of the company on 15 July 1918. The second transaction took place while Mr. Spartalian was on his deathbed on Prinkipo. In the second transaction, Mr. Spartalian was represented by his deputy, Levon Hacian, who was, not surprisingly, the treasurer of the IEDCC.[42] Through these rather dubious transactions of the sale of his lands to the company, Mr. Spartalian provided the capital for his company, whereas the company obtained immovable property which was necessary to undertake the project.

Stephan Spartalian and IEDCC felt the need to resort to such dubious transactions because of the laws regarding joint-stock companies. According to the Ottoman law on joint-stock companies, a joint-stock company could issue stocks at a predetermined proportion of its initial capital. In the case of IEDCC, it was 80,000 TL and the company issued 16,000 stocks worth 5 liras each.

In other words, this amount which was equal to the sale of lands, 80,000 Liras, was shown as the necessary initial capital to issue stocks. Moreover, the company applied to sell further stocks to increase its capital in November 1918. During the application process, the capital of the company and its immovable property were asked to be calculated in order to be presented as a voucher for issuing new stocks. The calculation of the company administration was as follows: the company had sold the land of 53,000 zira for a value of approximately 1,100,000 piasters in the first year following its establishment. Thus, as it still possessed lands over 2,250,000 zira, while each zira would worth between 15 and 30 piasters. Moreover, the company argued that the value of land would increase when the proposed streetcar project would be materialized. Thus, the company claimed to have a value of at least 330,000 Liras, thus applied to issue new bonds worth of 50,000 Liras.[43] According to an official document prepared by the Office of Title Deeds at Makrikoy, the company had lands worth 29,780,000 piasters, as each zira of land was calculated at the rate of 15 piasters in March 1919.[44] Upon examination, the

Figure 15.2 The stock of IEDCC worth of 25 Liras, dated 1 January 1918.

Source: Personal collection of the author.

Council of the State approved the application of the IEDCC to issue stocks in total of 40,000 TL in April 1919.[45]

In these correspondences, the company provided the lists of individual plots bought from Stephan Spartalian. According to these lists, Spartalian's lands were already divided into four smaller districts. Three of the districts were named after Ottoman historical figures, namely, after the ruling Sultan Mehmet V Reşad, Ertuğrul Bey who was the father of Sultan Osman, and after Sultan Orhan. The fourth district was named simply the "Park." The neighborhoods of Reşadiye and Ertuğrul, however, had second names, too, Garden City and Health City, respectively. Thus, these districts together with the "the Park" district show that the project of indeed closely followed the European examples of suburbanization as indicated in the advertorial text of 1914.

The company also provided lists of buyers in its application for issuing new stocks. It had sold 29 plots of land of around 53,000 zira to 31 buyers between April and November 1918. Most of those sales were carried out while Stephan Spartalian was still alive. The sales were concentrated in the Reşadiye (the Garden City), whereas the largest plots sold were located in the district of Ertuğrul (the Health City) where a certain Melahat Hanım, a Muslim woman, purchased a plot of 4,265 ziras and Andrea and Nikola Manol and Nikola Vasil Mavrivasil purchased a plot of 4,220 ziras. There was no demand for the district of Orhaniye which was not divided into plots and made up of one large land of 384,586 zira.[46]

The project was attractive as the 31 buyers came from all ethno-religious groups and both sexes. In a period of hyperinflation, reaching around 600% already in 1917, many of the Ottoman elite might have wanted to invest in land which looked like a more secure investment tool. This choice may be also related to the fact that life in the older districts of the imperial capital has been changing drastically as the war prolonged and conditions of life deteriorated. Thus, they might have found the project of a suburban life quite attractive. The IEDCC had a promising start; thus, Stephan Spartalian, although did not live long enough to see the materialization of this project, had initiated one of the earliest examples of suburban garden city projects of late Ottoman Istanbul.

Conclusion: From Garden City to Bahçeli Evler

Various practices of the war period, including confiscation of Christian (former) Ottoman citizens' properties continued after the war, especially during the first decades of the republican Turkey as some of these practices were legalized through law.[47] Mr. Spartalian's lands had a similar fate. As early as 1922, the lawyer of the Spartalian's descendants, no other than Nshan Andonyan, lawyer of the Maksudian family, submitted a protest to the Governorate of Istanbul with the claim that the Spartalians were being removed forcefully from their land in Incirli by the sub-governorate of Bakırköy, and the quarries which were located within the area were being auctioned out, too. The lawyer stated that the Spartalian family possessed the title deeds of the land which showed that the land had been under the proprietorship by different people for two hundred years and had passed to the

Spartalian family since the 1877–78 Russo-Ottoman War. This was an important claim as it claimed a continuity both in the practice of proprietorship of a vakıf land over the centuries by different owners and the Spartalians was the last one in that chain as well as in terms of the land's transition from the Maksudian family to the Spartalian family in 1911.[48]

The investigation revealed that the villagers of a nearby village encroached on the meadow only for grazing their animals; thus, they were removed, and the rights of the Spartalian family were said to be preserved.[49] It is interesting that such an encroachment took place in the first place as the land was known to be Spartalian's land for decades, and that was known by the locals, too. This may indicate the tense political atmosphere in Istanbul under Allied occupation in the early 1920s and such incidents becoming a possibility, and then turning into regular and irreversible incidents.

The history of the lands of the broader Incirli Estate is relatively better known as they turned into the district of Bahçelievler (literally Houses with Gardens), which was one of the first suburbs of Istanbul in the late 1930s. The cadastral survey of the land was carried out once again and the stone quarries which were mentioned in the letter of protest in 1922 were auctioned by the state in this period, which shows that Mr. Spartalian's lands indeed had been confiscated, too.[50] The process of that confiscation is not known yet it was a step in the formation of the new district. Bahçelievler, just like Mr. Spartalian's project of Garden City, involved the use of political power for land speculation. In the late 1930s, Fikret Yüzatlı who was a former cavalry captain (hence the surname "with 100 horses"), an associate of İsmet İnönü, and a deputy of the ruling Republican People's Party was informed by a friend of his top-ranking bureaucrat brother that the government in Ankara was planning to auction out the lands of the Incirli Estate. After purchasing the land, he founded the İncirli Bahçelievler Construction Company which turned into today's district carrying the same name. It has to be mentioned that Yüzatlı was even more ambitious than his predecessor Mr. Spartalian in his project; he had Henri Prost draw the plans for the suburban district.[51]

The previous history of the Incirli Estate and the role of the IEDCC in the foundation of the Bahçelievler are not revealed in the histories of the district which heavily rely on oral testimonies of the descendants of its founders.[52] The only aspect that "reminds" the Armenian connection in this history, to add insult to injury, is the name of the main boulevard of the district, Talat Pasha, the chief perpetrator of the Armenian Genocide.

Yet, the naming hides more than it reveals, as this chapter showed there were complex relationships between the Christian entrepreneurs and various offices and those who held political power in the late Ottoman Empire. Talat Pasha was the prime minister when the IEDCC was established through shady transactions as a joint-stock company in late 1917. This was only one of the many layers in the history of Stephan Spartalian's various entrepreneurial activities including the projects regarding the Incirli Estate. Mr. Spartalian who had come from a business magnate family from Smyrna and turned into a politician cum businessman after 1908 shows how blurred the lines between politics and business could be for Christian entrepreneurs, too, in the period of Turkification. Mr. Spartalian was involved in various projects, the projects regarding the Incirli Estate and then the foundation of the IEDCC were simply magnanimous in their size for the period and his vision of forming a garden city was ahead of its time. These characteristics of the IEDCC deserve to be noted in the histories of Istanbul alongside the central role that politics, shady transactions, and land speculation cases played in the urbanization of the imperial capital.

Archives

Başbakanlık Osmanlı Arşivi (BOA), Istanbul, Turkey

BEO, 3983/298724
DH.İ.UM, 7–1, no. 2, 4
I. Duit, 121–26, no. 3.
Ş.D. 3138–28
Ş.D. 3141–29
Ş.D., 1260–26, no 4, 6, 7, 9, 12, 15, 17
Ş.D., 81–4, no 1, 15

Meclis-i Mebusan Zabıt Ceridesi. Ankara: Türkiye Büyük Millet Meclisi Matbaası, 1986.

Gazettes

Arewelyan Mamul [Eastern Press] (Izmir)
Manzume-i Efkar [Row of Thoughts] (Istanbul)
Hayrenik [Homeland] (Watertown, Massachusetts)
Jamanak [Time] (Istanbul)
Moda [Fashion] (Istanbul)
Son Posta [The Last Post] (Istanbul)
Haber [News] (Istanbul)

Notes

I would like to thank Ali Sipahi, Evren Çakıl, and Başak Gemüsel for their comments.

1 *Moda*, no. 1 (4–17 August 1918), 11: "Mah: Stepan Efendi Spartalıi [Death of Stepan Efendi Spartalı]."

2 *Jamanak*, no. 3263 (2–15 August 1918): "Hugharkaworutiwn S. Spartali Efendi [Funeral of S. Spartali Efendi]." *Hayrenik*, no. 98 (29 July to 11 August 1918): "Tsavali Mahagoyzh [Painful Funeral]."

3 For a study of investment of elite in urban property, see: Lorans İzabel Baruh, "The Transformation of the "Modern' Axis of Nineteenth-Century Istanbul: Property, Investments and Elites from Taksim Square to Sirkeci Station" (PhD diss., Boğazici University, 2009).

4 Ümit Fırat Açıkgöz, "Capitalistic Urbanization in Late Ottoman Istanbul: Armenian Agencies," *YILLIK: Annual of Istanbul Studies* 5 (2023): 9–21.

5 Bedross Der Matossian, "The Armenian Commercial Houses and Merchant Networks in the 19th Century Ottoman Empire," *Turcica* 39 (2007): 147–74; Haris Exertzoglou,

"The Development of a Greek Ottoman Bourgeoisie: Investment Patterns in the Ottoman Empire, 1850–1914," in *Ottoman Greeks in the Age of Nationalism,* ed. Dimitri Gondicas and Charles Issawi (Princeton: Darwin Press, 1999), 89–115.

6 For devastation of the war for empire, see Yiğit Akın, *When the War Came Home: The Ottomans' Great War and the Devastation of an Empire* (Stanford: Stanford University Press, 2018).

7 Zafer Toprak, *Türkiye'de Milli İktisat, 1908–1918 [National Economy in Turkey, 1908–1918]* (İstanbul: Doğan Kitap, 2012).

8 Toprak, *Türkiye'de Milli İktisat,* 175 f.

9 Reşat Kasaba, "Izmir," *Review (Fernand Braudel Center)* 16, no. 4 (1993): 387–410.

10 Haroutiun K. Mermerian, *Turkahayots Hin Vajarakanutiwn yew Vajarakank: 1740–1890 [The Old Trade and Merchants of Turkish Armenians: 1740–1890]* (Istanbul: Sakayan, 1908), 74.

11 *Arewelyan Mamul*, 37–39 (September 26, 1907), 967–72: "Yelewmtakan Ardi Tagnape [The Present Financial Crisis]."

12 Elke Hartmann, "The "Loyal Nation' and Its Deputies: The Armenians in the First Ottoman Parliament," in *The First Ottoman Experiment in Democracy*, ed. Christoph Herzog and Malek Sharif (Würzburg: Ergon, 2010), 199–200.

13 *Arewelyan Mamul*, 970: "Yelewmtakan Ardi Tagnape."

14 Yaşar Tolga Cora, "'It is Contraction Not Crisis': The Panic in the Ottoman Markets in 1906–1908," Unpublished paper presented at the CIEPO-Comité International des Études Pré-Ottomanes et Ottomanes Conference, Thessaloniki, June 21–25, 2022.

15 *Manzume-i Efkar*, no. 1898 (August 23/September 5, 1907): "Stepan Spartalyan Tunı [The House of Stepan Spartalyan]." *Manzume-i Efkar* was originally a newspaper publishing in Turkish in Armenian letters and by the time of this news only in Armenian.

16 *Arewelyan Mamul*, 971: "Yelewmtakan Ardi Tagnape"; *Manzume-i Efkar*, no. 1930 (September 29/October 12, 1907): "Izmiri Spartalian Vajaratune."

17 Serhan Kemal Saygı, "İzmir'de II. Meşrutiyet Döneminde Ermeni Cemaati ve Meclis-i Mebusan'daki Temsilcileri [Armenian Community of Izmir and Their Representatives in the Parliament During the Second Constitutional Period]," *Tarih Okulu Dergisi* 8, no. 24 (2015): 630.

18 Serhan Kemal Saygı, "İzmir'de II. Meşrutiyet Döneminde Ermeni Cemaati ve Meclis-i Mebusan'daki Temsilcileri [Armenian Community of Izmir and Their Representatives in the Parliament During the Second Constitutional Period]," *Tarih Okulu Dergisi* 8, no. 24 (2015): 630, fn. 36.

19 *Meclis-i Mebusan Zabıt Ceridesi [Minutes of the Parliament]*, 2–39 (February 19, 1324) (Ankara: Türkiye Büyük Millet Meclisi Matbaası, 1986), 224.

20 B.O.A, BEO, 3983/298724.

21 Ali Akyıldız, "Osmanlı İstanbul'unda Deniz Ulaşımı (Modern Dönem) [Sea Lines in Ottoman Istanbul (Modern Period)]," in *Antik Çağ'dan XXI. Yüzyıla Büyük İstanbul Tarihi* [History of Istanbul from the Ancient Period to the 21st Century], ed. M. Akif Aydın and Coşkun Yılmaz, vol. 6 (İstanbul: IBB Kültür A.Ş., 2016), 441.

22 Varak Ketsemanian, "The Hunchakian Revolutionary Party and The Assassination Attempts Against Patriarch Khoren Ashekian and Maksudzade Simon Bey in 1894," *International Journal of Middle East Studies* 50, no. 4 (2018): 735–55.

23 Gabriel Noradounghian, "Extraits des mémoires recueillis par Aram Andonian," trans. Raymond H. Kévorkian, *Revue d'histoire contemporaine arménienne* 1 (1995): 199–245.

24 For the "micro revolution" of each community in that period, see: Bedross Der Matossian, "Formation of Public Sphere(s) in the Aftermath of the 1908 Revolution among Armenians, Arabs, and Jews," in *"L'ivresse de la liberté" La Revolution de 1908 dans l'Empire Ottoman*, ed. François Georgeon (Paris: Peeters, 2012), 189–219.

25 There is a vast literature on the garden suburbs. Robert A. M. Stern, David Fishman, and Jacob Tilove, eds., *Paradise Planned: The Garden Suburb and the Modern City*

(New York: The Monacelli Press, 2013); Michel Geertse, "The International Garden: City Campaign: Transnational Negotiations on Town Planning Methods 1913–1926," *Journal of Urban History* 42, no. 4 (2016): 733–52.

26 "Hayatî bir Mesele: Ucuz Meskenler [A Vital Issue: Cheap Housing]," *Nevsal-i Milli* (Dersaadet: Artin Asaduryan ve Mahdumları Matbaası, 1330 [1914]), 508–9; Şehnaz Yaren and Acar Şinasi draws attention to this project based on the news piece in Nevsal-i Milli. Şehnaz Yaren and Acar Şinasi "Tarihten Bir Yaprak: Asır Öncesi Planlanan Bir Uydukent Projesi [A Page from History: A Satellite City that was Planned a Century Ago]," *PLANLAMA: Journal of the Chamber of City Planners* 52 (2012): 76–78.

27 Yaşar Tolga Cora, "The Failed Housing Cooperative Project of the Oriental Savings Association: Housing and Urban Rent in Istanbul in the 1880s and 1890s," *YILLIK: Annual of Istanbul Studies* 5 (2023): 47–65.

28 Açıkgöz, "Capitalistic Urbanization," 12–13.

29 "Hayatî bir Mesele: Ucuz Meskenler," *Nevsal-i Milli*, 509.

30 Cora, "The Failed Housing Cooperative," 50–51.

31 B.O.A., Ş.D., 81–84, no.1 and no.15.

32 Burcu Arıkan, "A Mode of Space Production in the Nineteenth Century: Parceling (İfraz) as a Method of Land Commodification and Urbanization in Late Ottoman Empire," *Geographies, Planning & Tourism Studios* 3, no. 1 (2023): 7–23.

33 The company was ratified in January 1918. Ramazan Balcı and İbrahim Sırma, eds., *Ticaret ve Ziraat Nezareti: Memalik-i Osmaniye'de Osmanlı Anonim Şirketleri [Ministry of Commerce and Agriculture: Ottoman Joint Stock Companies in the Ottoman Lands]* (Istanbul: İstanbul Ticaret Odası (İTO), 2012), 314–17; Ali Akyıldız, *Osmanlı Dönemi Tahvil ve Hisse Senetleri* [Ottoman Securities] (Istanbul: Türk Ekonomi Bankası (TEB), 2001), 278.

34 Toprak, *Türkiye'de Milli İktisat,* 467 f.

35 Oya Gözel Durmaz, "The Distribution of the Armenian Abandoned Properties in an Ottoman Locality: Kayseri (1915–18)," *Middle Eastern Studies* 51, no. 5 (2015): 838–53.

36 Ayhan Aktar, "Economic Nationalism in Turkey: The Formative Years, 1912–1925," *Boğaziçi Journal, Review of Social and Administrative Studies* 10, no. 1–2 (1996): 263–90; Bedross Der Matossian, "The Taboo within the Taboo: The Fate of "Armenian Capital' at the End of the Ottoman Empire," *European Journal of Turkish Studies* [online] (2011). https://doi.org/10.4000/ejts.4411.

37 For an in-depth analysis of the mainstream understanding of National Economy, see: Ezgi Akyol, "Kapitalizmin Tarihyazımında Türkiye'de Milli İktisat [National Economy in Turkey in the History-writing of Capitalism]," *Tarih ve Toplum: Yeni Yaklaşımlar* 21 (2023): 271–95.

38 Nizamname of the IEDCC, B.O.A., Ş.D., 1260–26, no 15.

39 B.O.A., Ş.D. 3138–28; Ş.D. 3141–29.

40 B.O.A., Ş.D., 1260–26, no. 6.

41 B.O.A., Ş.D., 1260–26, no. 17.

42 B.O.A., Ş.D., 1260–26, no. 12.

43 B.O.A., Ş.D., 1260–26, no. 9

44 B.O.A., Ş.D., 1260–26, no. 7.

45 B.O.A., I. Duit, 121–26, no. 3. The demand was ratified on May 8, 1919.

46 B.O.A., Ş.D., 1260–26, no. 4.

47 Taner Akçam and Ümit Kurt, *Kanunların Ruhu: Emval-i Metruke Kanunlarında Soykırımın İzini Sürmek [Spirit of Laws: Tracing the Genocide in the Laws of Abandoned Properties]* (İstanbul: İletişim Yayınları, 2012).

48 B.O.A., DH.İ.UM, 7–1, no. 2.

49 B.O.A., DH.İ.UM, 7–1, no. 4.

50 *Son Posta,* no. 2061 (29 April 1936); *Haber*, no. 1765 (13 December 1936).

51 Erdem Üngür, "Kentsel Bir Altyapının Biyopolitikası: D-100 Karayolu [Biopolitics of an Urban Infrastructure: D-100 Highway]" (PhD diss., Istanbul Technical University, 2017), 61–62.

52 As an exception to positive evaluation of such accounts, a resident of Bahçelievler would criticize them as heroic narratives of land speculation. Mustafa Necati Yıldırım, *Buralar Vaktiyle Çayırlıktı Usta: Bahçelievler [Master, These Lands were Meadows Once: Bahçelievler]* (İstanbul: Heyamola Yayınları, 2010), 93.

Bibliography

n.a. "Hayatî bir Mesele: Ucuz Meskenler [A Vital Issue: Cheap Housing]." In *Nevsal-i Milli [National Almanac]*, 508–9. 1330; Dersaadet: Artin Asaduryan ve Mahdumları Matbaası, 1330 [1914].

Açıkgöz, Ümit Fırat. "Capitalistic Urbanization in Late Ottoman Istanbul: Armenian Agencies." *YILLIK: Annual of Istanbul Studies* 5 (2023): 9–21.

Akçam, Taner, and Ümit Kurt. *Kanunların Ruhu: Emval-i Metruke Kanunlarında Soykırımın İzini Sürmek [Spirit of Laws: Tracing the Genocide in the Laws of Abandoned Properties].* İstanbul: İletişim Yayınları, 2012.

Akın, Yiğit. *When the War Came Home: The Ottomans' Great War and the Devastation of an Empire*. Stanford: Stanford University Press, 2018.

Aktar, Ayhan. "Economic Nationalism in Turkey: The Formative Years, 1912–1925." *Boğaziçi Journal, Review of Social and Administrative Studies* 10, no. 1–2 (1996): 263–90.

Akyıldız, Ali. *Osmanlı Dönemi Tahvil ve Hisse Senetleri [Ottoman Securities].* Istanbul: Türk Ekonomi Bankası (TEB), 2001.

Akyıldız, Ali. "Osmanlı İstanbul'unda Deniz Ulaşımı (Modern Dönem) [Sea Lines in Ottoman Istanbul (Modern Period)]." In *Antik Çağ'dan XXI. Yüzyıla Büyük İstanbul Tarihi* [History of Istanbul from the Ancient Period to the 21st Century], edited by M. Akif Aydın and Coşkun Yılmaz, vol. 6, 436–79. İstanbul: IBB Kültür A.Ş., 2016.

Akyol, Ezgi. "Kapitalizmin Tarihyazımında Türkiye'de Milli İktisat [National Economy in Turkey in the History-writing of Capitalism]." *Tarih ve Toplum: Yeni Yaklaşımlar [History and Society: New Approaches]* 21 (2023): 271–95.

Arıkan, Burcu. "A Mode of Space Production in the Nineteenth Century: Parceling (İfraz) as a Method of Land Commodification and Urbanization in Late Ottoman Empire." *Geographies, Planning & Tourism Studios* 3, no. 1 (2023): 7–23.

Balcı, Ramazan, and İbrahim Sırma, eds. *Ticaret ve Ziraat Nezareti: Memalik-i Osmaniye'de Osmanlı Anonim Şirketleri [Ministry of Commerce and Agriculture: Ottoman Joint Stock Companies in the Ottoman Lands].* Istanbul: İstanbul Ticaret Odası (İTO), 2012.

Baruh, Lorans İzabel. "The Transformation of the 'Modern' Axis of Nineteenth-Century Istanbul: Property, Investments and Elites from Taksim Square to Sirkeci Station." PhD diss., Boğazici University, 2009.

Cora, Yaşar Tolga. "'It is Contraction Not Crisis': The Panic in the Ottoman Markets in 1906–1908." Unpublished paper presented at the CIEPO-Comité International des Études Pré-Ottomanes et Ottomanes Conference, Thessaloniki, June 21–25, 2022.

Cora, Yaşar Tolga. "The Failed Housing Cooperative Project of the Oriental Savings Association: Housing and Urban Rent in Istanbul in the 1880s and 1890s." *YILLIK: Annual of Istanbul Studies* 5 (2023): 47–65.

Der Matossian, Bedross. "The Armenian Commercial Houses and Merchant Networks in the 19th Century Ottoman Empire." *Turcica* 39 (2007): 147–74.

Der Matossian, Bedross. "The Taboo within the Taboo: The Fate of 'Armenian Capital' at the End of the Ottoman Empire." *European Journal of Turkish Studies* [online] (2011). https://doi.org/10.4000/ejts.4411

Der Matossian, Bedross. "Formation of Public Sphere(s) in the Aftermath of the 1908 Revolution among Armenians, Arabs, and Jews." In *"L'ivresse de la liberté" La Revolution de 1908 dans l'Empire Ottoman*, edited by François Georgeon, 189–219. Paris: Peeters, 2012.

Exertzoglou, Haris. "The Development of a Greek Ottoman Bourgeoisie: Investment Patterns in the Ottoman Empire, 1850–1914." In *Ottoman Greeks in the Age of Nationalism*, edited by Dimitri Gondicas and Charles Issawi, 89–115. Princeton: Darwin Press, 1999.

Geertse, Michel. "The International Garden: City Campaign: Transnational Negotiations on Town Planning Methods 1913–1926." *Journal of Urban History* 42, no. 4 (2016): 733–52.

Gözel-Durmaz, Oya. "The Distribution of the Armenian Abandoned Properties in an Ottoman Locality: Kayseri (1915–18)." *Middle Eastern Studies* 51, no. 5 (2015): 838–53.

Hartmann, Elke. "The 'Loyal Nation' and Its Deputies: The Armenians in the First Ottoman Parliament." In *The First Ottoman Experiment in Democracy*, edited by Christoph Herzog and Malek Sharif, 187–222. Würzburg: Ergon, 2010.

Kasaba, Reşat. "Izmir." *Review (Fernand Braudel Center)* 16, no. 4 (1993): 387–410.

Ketsemanian, Varak. "The Hunchakian Revolutionary Party and the Assassination Attempts Against Patriarch Khoren Ashekian and Maksudzade Simon Bey in 1894." *International Journal of Middle East Studies* 50, no. 4 (2018): 735–55.

Mermerian, Haroutiun K. *Turkahayots Hin Vajarakanutiwn yew Vajarakank: 1740–1890 [The Old Trade and Merchants of Turkish Armenians: 1740–1890]*. Istanbul: Sakayan, 1908.

Noradounghian, Gabriel. "Extraits des mémoires recueillis par Aram Andonian," translated from Armenian by Raymond H. Kévorkian. *Revue d'histoire contemporaine arménienne* 1 (1995): 199–245.

Saygı, Serhan Kemal. "İzmir'de II. Meşrutiyet Döneminde Ermeni Cemaati ve Meclis-i Mebusan'daki Temsilcileri [Armenian Community of Izmir and Their Representatives in the Parliament During the Second Constitutional Period]." *Tarih Okulu Dergisi [Journal of History School]* 8, no. 24 (2015): 621–47.

Stern, Robert A. M., David Fishman, and Jacob Tilove, eds. *Paradise Planned: The Garden Suburb and the Modern City*. New York: The Monacelli Press, 2013.

Toprak, Zafer. *Türkiye'de Milli İktisat, 1908–1918 [National Economy in Turkey, 1908–1918]*. İstanbul: Doğan Kitap, 2012.

Üngür, Erdem. "Kentsel Bir Altyapının Biyopolitikası: D-100 Karayolu [Biopolitics of an Urban Infrastructure: D-100 Highway]." PhD diss., Istanbul Technical University, 2017.

Yaren, Şehnaz, and Acar Şinasi. "Tarihten Bir Yaprak: Asır Öncesi Planlanan Bir Uydukent Projesi [A Page from History: A Satellite City That Was Planned a Century Ago]." *PLANLAMA: Journal of the Chamber of City Planners* 52 (2012): 76–78.

Yıldırım, Mustafa Necati. *Buralar Vaktiyle Çayırlıktı Usta: Bahçelievler [Master, These Lands Were Meadows Once: Bahçelievler]*. İstanbul: Heyamola Yayınları, 2010.

Contributors

Thanasis Betas is an independent historian of Greek social and economic history (20th century). His research interests concern labor and business history. His publications include "'In Order to Safeguard the Lives of Our Children and Families': Resistance and Protest of Women Workers in the Greek Tobacco Industry, 1945–1970" (2022); "Cairo, Athens, Salonica: Strikebreaking and the Anti-labour Practices of Employers and the State in the Early Twentieth Century Cigarette Industry" (2020); and "From the Tobacco Shop to the Cigarette Factory: Technological Changes, Gender and Surveillance in a Greek Cigarette Firm in the Early 20th Century" (2016).

Simos Bozikis studied economics at the University of Patras and history at the Ionian University. He is teaching at the Ionian University (Corfu) and is the author of *Greek Revolution and Public Economy: The Constitution of the Greek Nation State 1821–1832* (in Greek) (2020).

Maria Christina Chatziioannou is Research Director Emerita and former director of the Institute of Historical Research of the National Hellenic Research Foundation (Athens) (2019–2022). She has published on social and economic history (18th–20th centuries), merchant houses and entrepreneurs, social and economic networks, sovereign debt, retailing, and Italian Risorgimento. Some of her selected publications include "Greek Sovereign Debt and Loans in 19th-Century Public Discourse" (2019) and *On merchants' agency and capitalism in the Eastern Mediterranean 1774–1914* (2017).

Yaşar Tolga Cora is an associate professor in the Department of History at Boğaziçi University (Istanbul). He is a historian of social and economic history of the Armenian communities in the late Ottoman Empire. In 2022, he was awarded the Young Scientist Award (BAGEP) in the field of history by the Science Academy of Turkey. His publications include "The Market as a Means of Post-Violence Recovery: Armenians and Oriental Carpets in the Late Ottoman Empire (c.1890s–1910s)" (2021) and "'As Brave as Armenak Efendi': Ethnic Hierarchies and the Precarious Masculinity of an Ottoman Armenian Officer during the Great War" (2020).

Dimitris Dimitropoulos is Research Director at the Institute of Historical Research of the National Hellenic Research Foundation (Athens). His research interests focus on social and economic history, 17th–19th centuries, study of the settlements and the populations of the Greek lands under Ottoman rule, institutions and economy of the Aegean island societies 16th–19th centuries, and the Greek Revolution of 1821. Some of his selected publications include *Corsairs and Pirates in the Eastern Mediterranean, Fifteenth-Nineteenth Centuries* (2016, with G. Harlaftis and D. Starkey) and *Archive of Ali pasha* v. I-V [in Greek] (2007, 2009, 2018 with V. Panayotopoulos and P. Michailaris).

Antonis Hadjikyriacou is Assistant Professor of Ottoman and Turkish History at Panteion University (Athens). His research focuses on early modern Ottoman Cyprus from a Mediterranean vantage point, employing Critical GIS and Digital Humanities tools for the purposes of social, economic, and environmental history. His publications include *Peninsular Island: Cyprus and the Mediterranean during the Ottoman age of revolutions* [in Greek] (2023).

Alp Yücel Kaya is Professor of Economic History in the Department of Economics, Ege University (İzmir). He studied at the Middle East Technical University (Ankara) and at École des Hautes Études en Sciences Sociales (School of Advanced Studies in the Social Sciences, Paris). His research focuses on the conflictual world of property and labor relations in the Mediterranean from 18th to 21st centuries. He has recently edited *Coup-d'œil sur les conditions de la production de la richesse en Turquie, Articles publiés dans le Journal de Constantinople par Jon Jonesco (Ion Ionescu de la Brad) 1849–1857* (2022) and published "Bourgeois Revolution in Turkey (1908–1923)" (2023).

Phokion Kotzageorgis is Associate Professor of Ottoman History at the Aristotle University of Thessaloniki. His research interests are the social and economic history of the Ottoman Empire, urban history, demographic history, and the history of the Orthodox Church under the Ottomans. His recent publications include *Reconsidering Early Ottoman Palaeography and Diplomatics* (2022) and "Christians and Muslims in an Ottoman City: the Formation of the Society of Early Ottoman Thessaloniki" (2018).

Sophia Laiou is Associate Professor of Ottoman History at the Ionian University (Corfu). Her interests focus on the social and economic Ottoman history. Some of her recent publications include "The Ottoman State and the Black Sea Trade, End of the Eighteenth—Beginning of the Nineteenth century" (2018, with Edhem Eldem) and "Economic Networks in the Eastern Mediterranean: Kâtiboğlu Mehmed Efendi and his Christian Partner" (2019).

Dimitris Papastamatiou is Assistant Professor of Early Modern History at the Aristotle University of Thessaloniki. His research interests focus on the economic history of the Ottoman Empire. He is the author of *Wealth Distribution, Social Stratification and Material Culture in an Ottoman Metropolis*, 2017.

Yannis Spyropoulos is a researcher at the Institute for Mediterranean Studies—Foundation for Research & Technology Hellas (IMS-FORTH) in Rethymno, Greece, and the PI of the ERC project "JANET" (Janissaries in Ottoman Port-Cities: Muslim Financial and Political Networks in the Early Modern Mediterranean). His primary research interests revolve around the history of the early modern Ottoman Mediterranean. He is the editor of *Insights into Janissary Networks, 1700–1826* (2022), with Aysel Yıldız and M. Mert Sunar, *Payitaht Yeniçerileri: Padişahın "Asi" Kulları, 1700–1826* (2022).

Dimitrios Stergiopoulos is a PhD candidate in history at the University of California (San Diego) and was part of the research project "A Value Chain Analysis of Tobacco in Greece (1949–1981)" in the Institute of Mediterranean Studies—Foundation for Research & Technology Hellas (IMS-FORTH) in Rethymno, Greece. His research interests focus on the economic and political roles of bankers and financiers in Athens and Istanbul in the second half of the 19th century.

Yücel Terzibaşoğlu is Associate Professor of Economic and Social History in the Department of History, Boğaziçi University (Istanbul). His research focuses on agrarian regimes, land and labor, and landed and urban property in the Balkans, Anatolia, and the Middle East. His publications include "Landed Estates, Rural Commons and Collective Agriculture in Ottoman Niş and Leskofçe in the Nineteenth Century" (2022) and "The Ottoman Agrarian Question and the Making of Property and Crime in Nineteenth Century in Ottoman Rural Societies and Economies" (2015).

Ertan Ünlü is Assistant Professor of Early Modern History in the Department of History, Faculty of Languages, History and Geography, Ankara University. His research focuses on the Ottoman social and economic history of the 18th century. His special interests are the moneychangers (sarrafs), biographies of Ottoman elites, and military history. He is the author of *18. Yüzyılın İkinci Yarısında Osmanlı'da Sarraflar ve İlişki Ağları* (2024).

Artemis Yagou (PhD) is a historian of design and technology and is currently Research Associate at the Deutsches Museum (Munich). Her main interests are Greek material culture, the cultural history of technology, horology, and construction toys. Her publications include *Products, Users, and Popular Luxury in Early Modern Greece* (2024); *Technology, Novelty, and Luxury* (2022); and *Fragile Innovation: Episodes in Greek Design History* (2011).

Index

Note: Page numbers in *italic* indicate a figure and page numbers in **bold** indicate a table on the corresponding page.

Abbuşoğlu İbrahim 69
Abdülhamid I 69
Abdülhamid II 212–13, 240, 242–3
Abdüllatif Suphi Pasha 179
Fatma, bint Abdurrahman Ağa 29
Abdurrahman, Halil Ağa bin 25
Adriatic 2, 147
Aegean islands 9, 123, **125**, 126, *127*, 147–8
Aegean, the 107, 110, 147–8, 150
Aegina 124, 146
Afendaki *see* Efendaki
Africa 162
African 223–4
Agrapha 37
Agrinio 166
Ağustos *see* Naoussa
Ahmed Ağa bin Abdullah 31
Ahmed Ağa bin El-Hacc Hasan 28
Ahmed Ağa bin El-Hacc İbrahim 31
Ahmed Ağa bin Yunus 30
Ahmed Bey bin Mehmed Bey 25, 29
Ahmed Reşid Efendi 27
Ahmed Salim Beyefendi 245
Albania 92
Aleppo 69
Alexandretta 225
Alexandria 161, 163, 225
Alexopoulos **52**, 53, 59
Ali Ağa 31
Ali Ağa ibn Mahmud 27
Ali Ağa 207
Ali Ağa Çiftliği 210
Ali Beşe bin Mehmed 29
Ali Cevat Bey 238
Ali Paşa Tepedelenli 8, 91–99
Alléon, Jacques 175
Al-Şeyh Mustafa Efendi bin Al-Şeyh İbrahim Efendi 28
Amasya 175
America 162
Amina bint Ağazade Mustafa Ağa 27
Amina Hanım bint El-Hacc Ahmed Efendi 27
Anagnostis **52**
Anatolia 2, 4, 6, 10, 42, 49, 107, 202–3, 205, 208, 211, 213, 222–3, 225
Ancona 145–6
Andros 148, 174
Anna, daughter of Yakoumi Paikos 38
Antonopoulos family 135n20
Antwerp 175
Araboğlu 207
Araboğulları 208
Arap Çiftliği 210
Arif Bey 209–10
Argentis family 135n20
Arnavutköy 69, 71
Armenians 11, 50–1, 64, 242, 245
Artin (sarraf) 63, 65–72
Asia 36, 144
Asia Minor 127, 144
Ataullah Ağa 207
Atçalı Kel Mehmed 209
Athens 11, 80, 146–8, 162, 166, 173–6
Austria 40, 162
Aydın 206, 208–9, 211, 240
Ayo Vasili 29
Aziz Paşa 245
Azof Sea 144, 148, 150

Baghdad 69
Bahadırlı 206
Bahçelievler district 249
Bakırköy *see* Makriköy
Balanos, Christodoulos 38–42
Balkans 6, 9, 22, 36, 38, 49, 132, 189, 191, 225
Balkapanı Hanı 114
Baltatzis-Alléon Bank 175
Baltatzis, Emmanouil 175
Baltatzis, Evangelos 175
Baltatzis, Theodoros 175
Baltazzi, Aristides 212
Baltazzi, Dimitri 211
Baltazzi family 10, 202–3, 205, 210–12
Baltazzi, Manolaki 210–12
Baltazzi, Spiridone 210
Baltazzi, Theodoraki 211–12
Baltazzi, Yorkaki 211
Baltimore (USA) 91
Balyozyans family 210
Baydaroğlu İlyas Anton 69
Bayraktar Mustafa Paşa 204
Bedros, *sarraf* 63, 65–71
Beirut 225
Bekir Ağa 70
Berdiansk 175
Bergama 207–8
Beşe Yorgi or Christopoulo **52**
Beşiktaş 66, 70, 175
Beşir Ağa 63, 65–8, 70–1
Beyazid 243
Beyhan Sultan 69
Black Sea 2, 48–50, 53, 76, 123, 148, 175, 225
Bosnalı Halil Ağa ibn El-Hacc Ahmed 25
Bosporus 50–1, 66, 71
Botasis A. 135n20
Botasis G. 135n20
Boudouris family 135n20
British Empire 9, 143–4, 146, 148, 151, 222; *see also* Great Britain
Burgaz 71
Burgas 175
Burhaniye 42
Bursa 225
Burunören 207, 209
Büyükdere 66, 70–1
Büyük Yeni Han 66, 68

Cairo 9, 158
Callegari firm 77
Camondo family 175
Camondo, Abraham Behor 175
Camondo, Abraham Salomon 175
Camondo, Nissim 175
Camondo, Rafael 175
Çanakkale 223–4
Candia *see* Kandiye
Carathanassis firm 162
Carathanassis, Stamatis 162
Casali firm 77
Çatalservi 70
Çavuşoğlu 209
Çavuşzade Ahmed Reşid Efendi 27
Chalkidiki *see* Halkidiki
Chios 53, 65–6, 71, 108, 124, 127, 143, 147–8, 174
Chiots 148–50
Christinis family 135n20
Cihanzade Hüseyin Bey 69
Cevad Beyefendi 245
China 162
Cira Antoni **52**
Constantinople 2, 91–7, 127, 146–7; *see also* Istanbul
Corfu 91, 124, 126, 146, 166
Cortesi family 150
Costanza 148
Cousinery family 210
Crete 8, 107–9, 111–13, 114–15, 124, 127–30
Çuhacı Han 54
Cyprus 10, 124, 128–9, 218–29
Cypriots 222

Damianos, Nikolaos 175
Danube 69, 71, 176
Defterdâr Efendi **108**
Deligiannis family 135n20
Deligiannis, Kanellos *80*
Deligiannis, Theodoros 167
Denizli 207
Denmark 40–1, 162
Derviş Ali Efendi *see* Odabaşızade Derviş Ali Efendi
Derviş Ali Tarakçızâde **108**, 110
Danubian Principalities 93
Dikili 210
Dimitraki 38
Dimitraki, son of 65, 68–9
Dimitraki, son of Tzalik **52**, 54, 59n44
Dimitraki Moralı 42, **52**
Dimitrakis from Morea *see* Dimitraki Moralı
Dimitri of Chios *see* Dimitri Skanavi from Chios
Dimitri, Ralli **52**, 53, 59n40

Dimitri, Skanavi(s) from Chios 63, 65–6, 69
Dimitri, Skina 51–3
Dimitri son of Apostolo papa 51–**2**, 55, 58n28
Dimitri, son in law of **52**
Dilaver Kadın 192
Dolmabahçe Palace 175
Douma **52**
Drakeia (Greece) 161
Drosinis, Georgios 173
Durasallı çiftlik 206–7
Durmuşlu çiftlik 194

Ebubekir Ağa 207
Ebubekir Bey 70
Edremelde, çiftlik 192
Edremit *see* Burhaniye
Efendaki 109–10
Efrenciyan see Europeans
Eğin 65–6
Egypt 2, 31, 36, 49, 65, 67–8, 71, 107, 158–65, 167, 222
El-Hacc Abdülbaki Ağa ibn Mustafa Ağa 32
El-Hacc Ali Ağa ibn Hüseyin Ağa 30
El-Hacc Mehmed Ağa 31
El-Hacc Mehmed Ağa ibn Ömer 30
El-Hacc Mehmed bin Iskender 29
El-Hacc Mustafa bin Abdullah 29
El-Hacc Mehmed Emin Ağa bin El-Hacc Ebu Bekr 32
El-Hacc Mehmed Ağa ibn Ömer 30
El-Hacc Süleyman bin Abdullah 30
Emine Sultan 69
emin for the *beyt ül Mal-i Amme* 206
emin of *mukataa* of Bahadırlı 206
Emirgan 69
England *see* Great Britain
Epirus 78, 98, 124, 143, 145–7
Ermoupolis 124–7, 131
Ermoupolitans *127*, 135n20
Ermoupolitans-Syriots 124–6
Ertuğrul Bey 248
Ertuğrul, district 248
Esma Sultan 63, 65–6, 69, 71
Esseyid Abdulvahib Ağa ibn Abdülbaki 27
Esseyid Mustafa Ağa ibn Ali 30
Esseyyid Numan Ağa ibn Esseyyid Mehmed Efendi 31
Evrenos 191
Europe 1, 5, 7, 36–8, 40–3, 49–53, 55, 63, 76, 78–82, 143–4, 159, 176, 180, 222–3, 225, 242
Europeans 4, 38–40, 92

Famagusta 225
Fatma bint Abdurrahman Ağa 29
Fatma Hanım 192
Fener 51, 66–7, 70–1
Fenerkapısı 66, 70
Fikret Yüzatlı *see* Yüzatlı, Fikret
Fotilas family 135n20
France 3, 40, 56, 79, 109, 144, 158, 177
Fuad Paşa 212

Galaca, çiftlik 192
Galanti 175
Galata 49–50, 53, 70–1, 173–5, 177, 179
Gaza 225
Gazi Hasan Paşa 66
Gelenbe 208
Gediz 206–8
Genoa 144
Germany 162
Gerussi family 149
Giannitsis family 135n20
Gikas family 135n20
Giridî Derviş Ali 119n40
Gionis family 135n20
Golden Horn 50, 66, 71, 174
Gölge, çiftlik 192
Great Britain 3, 6, 56, 79, 132, 144–5, 147, 150, 159, 162, 177
Greece 9, 37, 76, 78, 92, 145, 159–64, 167, 173–4, 176; *see also* Greek State
Greek Kingdom 174; *see also* Greece and Greek State
Greeks 5, 7, 9, 37, 40, 49–51, 56, 91, 146, 150–1, 206
Greek State 5, 9, 123–4, 126, **131**, 132, 145–6, 148, 163; *see also* Greece
Gülhane 205

Habsburg Empire 9, 147, 150
Hacian, Levon 246
Hacı Eyüp Ağa 209
Hacı Hüseyin Ağa 207–8
Hacı İsmail Paşa 67
Hacı Konstantin 65
Hacı Mehmed Ağa 207, 210
Hacı Mehmed Ağa, Müridzade *see* Müridzade Hacı Mehmed Ağa
Hacı Mustafa Ağa 206–8
Hacı Osman Ağa 207
Hacı Ömer Ağa 208–9
Haci Vasili **52**
Hacian Levon 246
Hadjialexandris family 135n20
Hadjianagyrou family 135n20

Hadjimikes family 135n20
Haifa 225
Halkidiki 7, 37, 39, 41
Halil Ağa bin Abdürrahman 25
Halil Hamid Paşa 66
Hamide Hanım 192–3
Harissis, George 41
Harutyun Amira 66
Hasan Ağa 210
Haseki Mustafa Ağa **108**, 110
Hasırcı, çiftlik 209
Hatice Hatun 69
Hatmanzades 69
Havyar Han 53
Herakleion *see* Candia
Holland 144; *see also* Netherlands
Hungary 162
Hüseyin Ağa *see* Hacı Hüseyin Ağa
Hüseyin Bey 69, 96–7
Hosrovyan Efendi, K. 245
Hüseyin Ağa bin El-Hacc Hasan Ağa 28
Hüseyin Ağa bin El-Hacc Mustafa 30
Hüseyin Ağa (Karaosmanoğlu) 208
Hüseyin Avni Paşa, Grand Vizier 240
Hydra 41, 124–5, 127, 131, 134n16, 135n20, 146
Hydriots 124–7, 135n20

İbrahim *see* Muradoğlu İbrahim
Indochina 162
Ioannina 78, 91–2, 94, 98, 146, 223
Ionian Islands 124, 127
Iraq 2
İsmail Beşe bin Halil 29
İsmail Beşe bin Mustafa 29
İsmail Paşa *see* Hacı İsmail Paşa
Isparta 208–9
Istanbul 2, 7, 9, 11, 42–3, 48–56, 63–71, 107–8, 110–15, 124, 173–9, 181, 190, 208, 211, 219, 222, 238–9, 242–5, 248–50
İştip 220
Italy 8, 77, 158
İzmaragda 69, 71
İstefan 66, 68
İvaz Paşazade Halil Ağa 206
Izmir 51, 71, 108, 111–12, 124, 148–9, 175, 206–7, 210–12, 225, 238–41, 245

Jaffa 225
Janissaries 8, 21, 107–15
Japan 162

Kaftantzioglou 37
Kairis, Antonis 107–8
Kalaris family 135n20
Kalarrytes 78
Kallergis, Antonios 163
Kandiye 107–14
Kanorta 69
Kara Hasan, village 31
Kara Mehmed Beşe bin Abdurrahman 29
Kara Müteselim *see* Hacı Mehmed Ağa
Karaköy 71
Karaosmanoğlu family 10, 202–10, 213
Kara Osman 206
Karaosman Ağa 69
Karathanassis, Manolis 9, 162
Karathanassis, Stamatis 9, 162
Kasab Hızır, district 211
Kasos 124, 127
Kassandria 27
Kavala 32
Kelemerye 30
Keresteci Han 67, 70
Kıylı, çiftlik 209
Kifork 69
Kireç, çiftlik 192, 194
Kirişzade Haseki Mustafa Ağa ibn El-Hacc Ahmed 31
Koçana 220
Koldere, çiftlik 209
Komiano **52**
Kopanitsas family 135n20
Koronios, Georges 179
Kostaki **52**
Kostaki Kotsinoğlu 59n37
Kostaki son of Dimitri 65
Kostakis son of Scarlatos 42, 45
Koundouriotis family 135n20
Koutarellis, Alkiviades 161
Koutarellis brothers 161
Koutarellis, Dimitrios 161
Koutarellis, Konstantinos 161
Küçük, çiftlik 196
Küçük Mehmet Ağa 209
Küçük Yeni Han 66, 71
Kulaksiz family 210
Kurdoğlu Beşe ibn Abdülbaki 31
Kürkçüler Han 67, 70
Kuruçeşme 66, 71
Kyriaki **52**
Kyriakou *see* Tzanoglou, Manolaki
Kyriakoú Manolakis 40; *see also* Tzanoglou, Manolakis

Lamartine 212
Lamia 166
Langa Yenikapısı 66
Langaza, çiftlik 194–6
Lapierre family 220
Laras, Loukis 147–8
Larisa 96
Larnaka 223, 225
Lazarou family 135n20
Levant 21, 123
Limassol 223
Liverpool 175
London 147–8, 150, 175–6, 181
Luka 65
Lukaki 51–**2**

Macedonia 146
Mahmud I 66
Mahmud II 8, 113
Mahmutpaşa 70
Makaronya, çiftlik 210
Makriköy 238, 243, 246
Maksudzade, Polin 242, 244
Maksudzade, Simon Bey 242–4
Maksudian family 248–9
Malevizi 110
Mamaklı 207
Mamounis family 135n20
Manastir 220
Manchester 175, 239
Manisa 206–7, 209
Marmara sea 50
Marseille 40, 147, 149, 175–6, 178, 181, 211
Mavromati **52**, 53
Mavroyani, Nikola 66
Mavros family 146–7
Mattei family 220
Mediterranean 1–3, 6, 9–11, 48, 76, 79, 107, 123, 126–7, 132, 144–5, 148, 150–1, 158–60, 163, 176, 190, 225–6
Mehmed Çavuş 206
Mehmed V Reşad 248
Mela Yorgi **52**
Melahat Hanım 248
Melas, Eleni 146
Melas family 144, 145–7, 153n13
Melas, George Leon 146
Melas, Ioannis Stavrou 146
Melas, Konstantinos G. 147
Melas, Michail G. 147
Melas, Vasilios G. 147
Melas-Vikelas family 9
Melek Mehmed Paşa 69
Menemen 207–8, 210
Menexes, Christos 37–42
Menteşe 207
Merambello 110
Mersin 225
Mesmer 31
Mexis Ch. 135n20
Mexis Th. 135n20
Middle East 2–3, 36
Mihaili, çiftlik 207
Mihail Silaver? **52**
Milaitis family 135n20
Milan 150
Misou, Stefanos 96
Mitafoğlu Derviş Ağa 111
Monarchidis family 135n20
Monofatsi 110
Morea 9
Moscow 146
Mudanya 71
Muhtar Paşa 98
Murad II 206
Muradoğlu İbrahim 111, 114
Müridzade Hacı Mehmed Ağa 42
Mustafa bin Ahmed 29
Mustafa Ağa bin Ali 31
Mustafa Reşid Paşa 212
Mütevelli çiftlik 209
Mytilene 124

Nafpaktos 98
Naminda 30
Naoussa 40, 98
Nazif Bey 238
Negris, Phokion 163
Netherlands 3, 162
Nimatullah bint Ahmed Ağa 29
Nikas A. – Xenou Th. 135n20
Nikolaki 52
Nikolaou family 135n20
Nikolis family 135n20
Nizhny Novgorod 59n44, 146
Noroudiakian, Gabriel 242
Notaras family 135n20
Nshan Andonyan 248
Numan Paşa 10, 190, 193, 196, 198, 199n3
Nüzhed Beyefendi 245

Odabaşızade Derviş Ali Efendi 111–15
Odessa 146, 149, 226
Orhaniye, district 248
Ömer Ağa bin Abdullah 31

Ömer beşe 29
Ömer Efendi ibn Mehmed 30
Orhan Sultan 248
Orlandos family 135n20
Orloff family 135n20
Oskoli **52**
Osman Ağa 69
Osman Ağa Kamaryalı **108**, 110
Osman Ağa Neracioğlu **108**
Osman son of İbrahim 14
Osman Sultan 248
Ottoman Empire 1–6, 8–11, 21, 36–7, 42, 48, 50, 63–5, 72, 76, 78–9, 82, 92, 97–8, 107, 115, 124, 126, 132, 143–9, 151–2, 158–63, 167, 173–9, 203, 205, 211–12, 244, 249

Paiko 37
Palestine 224
Panama 162
Papalexopoulos family 135n20
Papaslı, çiftlik 207
Paris 174
Paros 124
Patras 39, 149
Patmos 124
Pehlivanoğlus family 110
Pelion 161
Peloponnese 39, 123, 125–7, 129–31
Peloponnesians 12, 124–5, 135n20
Pesaro 8, 77–9, 81
Pesmazoglou, Ioannis 163–6
Peterocochino, Virginia M. 150
Petrokokkinos, Georges 176, 178
Phanar, district 174
Phanariots 50–2, 93
Piraeus 166
Pirlepe 220
Pisa 174
Poniropoulos family 135n20
Psara 41, 124–5, 127, 131
Psarians 124–7, 135n20

Rabia bint Hasan 25
Raif İsmail Paşa 67, 69
Ragusa 145
Rallis, Antonios 149–50
Ravne, çiftlik 192
Refik Mustafa Efendi bin Hasan Efendi, reisülküttab 27
Rhodes 148
Rogkoti 37
Rostov 150
Roussos family 135n20
Rukiya 30
Rumeli 96, 206, 209
Rüşdü Paşa, Grand Vizier 210
Russia 48, 53, 176
Russian Empire 9, 143–8, 150, 207–8
Russian 50, 63, 107, 144, 150, 176, 208

Sadık Bey 209–10
Sadullah Bey 192
Salonica *see* Thessaloniki
Salvagou, Despoina 148
Samos 9, 159, 162
Samsun 225
Sandal Bedesten 69, 71
Sardis *see* Sart
Sarica 41
Sart 210
Scaramangas (Skaramangas) family 9, 135n20, 144, 147–51
Scaramanga, Erato Emm. (born in 1828) 148
Scaramanga, Erato Emm. (born in 1836) 148
Scaramanga, Katerina Emm. 148
Scaramanga, Maria Emm. (born in 1822) 148
Scaramanga, Maria Emm. (born in 1829) 148
Scaramangas, Andreas Emm. 148
Scaramangas, Emmanuel Emm. 148
Scaramangas, Emmanuel Geo. 148–50
Scaramangas, Fragoulis Emm. 148
Scaramangas, Georgios Emm. 148
Scaramangas, Zannis Emm. 148, 150
Serres 38–9, 51
Sevastopoulos family 146
Şeyh Ahmed Efendi ibn Şeyh Hasan Efendi 25
Sıdkı Mustafa Efendi 66
Sidon 225
Silahdar Mehmed Paşa 67
Sinan Paşa, district 70
Sivriada 71
Skopje 220
Skourtis family 135n20
Smith, Adam 189
Smyrna *see* Izmir
Smyrniots 148
Sofia 98
Spain 158
Spandoni 37, 41
Spartalian, Agop 239–40
Spartalian family 238–40, 249

Spartalian, Stephan 11, 238–50
Spartalian, Takavor 240
Spartalian, Yervand 240
Spartalian, Zareh 240
'Speranza' marine vessel 107, **108**, 109, 111, 115
Spetses 41, **125**, 127, 131
Spetsiots 124–7, 135n20
Spyro son of Thanasis **52**
Stefanos family 135n20
Strati **52**
Süleyman Ağa 66–7
Süleyman Paşa 96
Sungurlar, çiftlik 194
Switzerland 79
Syngros, Andreas 9–10, 173–9, 181
Syngros, Georgios 174
Syngros (Tsingros), Domeniko or Kyriakos 174
Syngrou (Tsingrou), Mondini (Nikoleta), nee Nomikou 174
Syria 2, 222, 225
Syros *127*, 146–50, 174–5; *see also* Ermoupolis

Tabakopoulo **52**
Taganrog 148, 150
Takavor Sukasyan Efendi 245
Tarabya 66, 70–1
Tatar, çiftlik 209–10
Tatavla 50, 53
Tavaslizade 207
Tepelenë 98
Thessalonians 21–38, *see also* Thessalonicans, 36–47
Thessaloniki 6–7, 10, 21–7, 29–32, 36–7, 39–42, 51, 79, 190, 225
Thessaly 52, 95, 166
Theotokis, Georgios 162
Tire 209, 212
Tombazis family 135n20
Tona, çiftlik 192
Topkapı Palace 206, 222
Torbalı 212
Trabzon 225
Trieste 53, 91, 145, 148–9, 175
Trikoupis, Charilaos 173
Tripoli 225
Tsamados A. 135n20
Tsamados D. 135n20
Tsorbatzioglu Asterio **52**
Turgutlu 206, 208
Turkey 5, 42, 239, 248; *see also* Ottoman Empire
Turks 91
Tzanoglou *see* Tzanoglou, Manolakis
Tzanoglou, Manolakis 40–1, 43, 45n20

Ucu 31
United States of America (USA) 91, 159, 242

Valide Han 53, 70
Valsamakis family 135n20
Valtohori *see* Sarica
Vardar 30
Varna 175
Vasiliou, Eleni *see* Melas, Eleni
Vasiliou family 147
Vathy 162
Veli Paşa 95, 98
Venice 144–5
Veroia 146
Vezir Han 66–8, 70
Vidin 203
Vienna 175
Vikelas, Dimitrios 146–8, 173
Vikelas family 144–7
Vrasta 32
Voulgaris family 135n20

Walsh, Robert 99

Xenos E. 135n20

Yakoumi, Paikos 38
Yakub 63, 65–71, 74n22
Yakup Paşa 209
Yanko son of Zarifi **52**
Yayaköy 206
Yanni Kyriako **52**
Yeğen Ali *see* Yeğen Ali Paşa
Yeğen Ali Paşa 206
Yeni Han 67, 70–1
Yeni, çiftlik 206–7
Yeniköy 70
Yetim Ahmed Ağa 209
Yorgo **52**
Yorgos 37
Yorgi Samata **52**
Yusuf Bey 39
Yusuf Muhlis Paşa 39, 41
Yüzatlı, Fikret 249

Zafiroğlu 54
Zagliver, çiftlik 192–6
Zaimis, Alexandros 167

Zakynthos 175
Zarifis, Georgios 175
Zarifis-Zafeiropoulos company 178
Zeliha Hanım 192
Zekiye Hanım 193
Zeyneb Hanım 192
Zeytinburnu 243
Ziya Bey 238
Zografos, Christakis 175
Zübeyde Hanım 192

For Product Safety Concerns and Information please contact our EU
representative GPSR@taylorandfrancis.com
Taylor & Francis Verlag GmbH, Kaufingerstraße 24, 80331 München, Germany

www.ingramcontent.com/pod-product-compliance
Ingram Content Group UK Ltd.
Pitfield, Milton Keynes, MK11 3LW, UK
UKHW020149200926
475702UK00016B/2629

9781032816593